Michael H. Trenk

# Real Options in
# Capital Investment

# Real Options in Capital Investment

## Models, Strategies, and Applications

Edited by *Lenos Trigeorgis*

PRAEGER

Westport, Connecticut
London

**Library of Congress Cataloging-in-Publication Data**

Real options in capital investment : models, strategies, and
  applications / edited by Lenos Trigeorgis.
          p.    cm.
      Includes bibliographical references and index.
      ISBN 0–275–94616–9 (alk. paper)
          1.  Capital investments.  2.  Decision-making.  3.  Corporations—
  Finance.  4.  Corporations—Growth.  I.  Trigeorgis, Lenos.
  HG4028.C4R368  1995
  332.63—dc20        94–13735

British Library Cataloguing in Publication Data is available.

Library of Congress Catalog Card Number: 94–13735
ISBN: 0–275–94616–9

First published in 1995

Praeger Publishers, 88 Post Road West, Westport, CT 06881
An imprint of Greenwood Publishing Group, Inc.

Printed in the United States of America

The paper used in this book complies with the
Permanent Paper Standard issued by the National
Information Standards Organization (Z39.48–1984).

10  9  8  7  6

**Copyright Acknowledgments**

The editor and the publisher gratefully acknowledge permission to use the following:

Excerpts from "A Market Utility Approach to Investment Valuation," by Eero Kasanen
and Lenos Trigeorgis in the *European Journal of Operational Research*, Volume 74, no.
2. Copyright © 1994. Used by permission of Elsevier Science Publishers B.V.,
Amsterdam.

Excerpts from "Reversion, Timing Options, and Long-term Decision-Making," by D. G.
Laughton and H. D. Jacoby in *Financial Management*, Volume 22, no. 3. Copyright
1993. Used by permission of the Financial Management Association, Tampa, Florida.

Excerpts from "Real Options and Interactions with Financial Flexibility," by Lenos
Trigeorgis in *Financial Management*, Volume 22, no. 3. Copyright 1993. Used by
permission of the Financial Management Association, Tampa, Florida.

# Contents

**PART III: STRATEGY, INFRASTRUCTURE,**

**AND FOREIGN INVESTMENT OPTIONS**

**PART IV: MEAN REVERSION/ALTERNATIVE**

**FORMULATIONS IN NATURAL RESOURCES,**

**SHIPPING, AND START-UP VENTURES**

## PART V: OTHER APPLICATIONS: POLLUTION
## COMPLIANCE, LAND DEVELOPMENT, FLEXIBLE
## MANUFACTURING, AND FINANCIAL DEFAULT

# Tables and Figures

## TABLES

# FIGURES

# *Preface*

This edited book integrates various new contributions to the growing "real options" literature. Similar to options on financial securities, real options involve discretionary decisions or rights, with no obligations, to acquire or exchange an asset for a specified alternative price. The valuation of real options (such as to defer, expand, contract, abandon, switch, or otherwise alter a capital investment), by providing a means to properly account for managerial flexibility and strategic considerations, has revolutionized corporate investment decision making.

A corporation's value creation and competitive position are critically determined by resource allocation and the proper evaluation of investment alternatives. At the international level, American companies have been steadily losing their competitive position relative to their Japanese and German counterparts, despite their use of more "powerful" quantitative techniques such as discounted cash flow (DCF) analysis, in recent decades. Growing numbers of practicing managers and academics are becoming convinced that the standard approaches to corporate resource allocation have failed because they cannot properly capture managerial flexibility to adapt and revise later decisions in response to unexpected market developments. In a constantly changing and always uncertain world marketplace, managerial operating flexibility and strategic adaptability have become vital in order to successfully capitalize on favorable future investment opportunities and limit losses from adverse market developments.

The field of capital budgeting admittedly remained stagnant for several decades until recent developments in real options provided the tools and unlocked the possibilities to revolutionize the field. The insights and techniques derived from option pricing are capable of quantifying the elusive elements of managerial operating flexibility and strategic interactions, which have thus far been ignored or underestimated by conventional net present value (NPV) and other quantitative approaches.

Interest in these developments, on the part of academics and practitioners alike, is unusually high. The book can serve as supplementary material for the academic market in, for example, advanced finance courses in option pricing or capital budgeting, doctoral seminars, or the library. It may also be of interest to the professional market (e.g., corporate planners and finance executives) and academics from related areas (e.g., decision analysts or economists), as well as to international readers (academics, doctoral students, and professionals).

The book's contributions are divided into five parts, covering sections on real options and alternative valuation paradigms for capital investment analysis; on the analysis of general exchange or switching options and of interdependencies among multiple such options; on strategic acquisitions, infrastructure, and foreign investment options; on mean reversion/alternative formulations in natural resource investments, shipping, and start-up ventures; and on other applications, including pollution compliance, land development, flexible manufacturing, and financial default options.

An overview of the various book chapters and how they fit together is useful at this point. In the introductory chapter, "Real Options: An Overview," I review the basic real option valuation principles and provide a comprehensive overview of the evolution of the real options revolution, with its major building blocks and thematic developments, finally pointing out future research directions.

Part I of the book comparatively deals with real options as one of several alternative valuation paradigms. In chapter 2, "Methods for Evaluating Capital Investment Decisions under Uncertainty," Elizabeth Olmsted Teisberg discusses the relationship between the discounted cash flow (DCF), decision analysis, and real option valuation paradigms. She focuses on pointing out potential pitfalls of applying each method and discusses practical issues and problems of implementation.

Chapter 3, "Merging Finance Theory and Decision Analysis," by Eero Kasanen and Lenos Trigeorgis, follows naturally the earlier chapter by showing that decision analysis and option pricing converge if a market utility function is used. This chapter in effect provides a unified approach for valuing primary and derivative assets, whether traded or not.

In chapter 4, "The Strategic Capital Budgeting Process: A Review of Theories and Practice," Van Son Lai and Lenos Trigeorgis review the capital budgeting process from a practical strategic and organizational perspective (including its different phases and interactions among different decision-making levels), showing how capital budgeting is integrated with strategic planning.

Part II focuses on general exchange or switching options that may cover most known real options as special cases and discusses interdependencies among several real options. Nalin Kulatilaka, in chapter 5, "The Value of Flexibility: A General Model of Real Options," discusses the value of flexibility in the form of switching between different modes of production in a discrete-time, dynamic programming framework. His general framework subsumes as special cases the options to wait, abandon, temporarily shut down, replace, and so on, and his ideas can be easily extended to flexible manufacturing.

Peter Carr, in chapter 6, provides a unified framework for valuing American options to exchange between dividend-paying risky assets (which covers standard American call and put options). Carr's chapter, which in a way can be viewed as a continuous-time counterpart of the dynamic programming framework, subsumes various known solutions as special cases and provides an application to the optimal project timing option.

In chapter 7, "Operating Flexibilities in Capital Budgeting: Substitutability and Complementarity in Real Options," Kulatilaka investigates how the value of a project is affected by the simultaneous introduction of several operating options (e.g., to wait to invest, to abandon, and to temporarily shut down). He also studies the impact of adding new options on the critical boundaries at which existing options are optimally exercised.

Part III deals with strategy, infrastructure, and foreign investment options. The value of growth, divestiture, and other flexibility options associated with strategic acquisitions is the subject of chapter 8, by Kenneth W. Smith and Alexander J. Triantis. The authors use rather simple numerical examples to illustrate the value and impact of such often-ignored strategic options as those associated with the combined growth options of the acquiring and target firms, strategic diversification, and future options to divest parts of acquired companies at a later time.

In chapter 9, "Corporate Governance, Long-term Investment Orientation, and Real Options in Japan," Takato Hiraki views the Japanese bank-oriented system of corporate governance as providing the basic infrastructure that enables Japanese companies to jointly develop and exercise real options. The interests of interrelated stakeholders, including management, are pursued through implicit contracts that are arranged so as to reduce agency costs and expand low-cost real options. The real options framework is used to explain conceptually the Japanese orientation toward long-term investment.

Chapter 10, by Gregory K. Bell, investigates the effects of exchange rate volatility on the entry, exit, and capacity decisions of the multinational firm. The author shows that the effects of volatility generally depend on whether the project involves a fixed-capacity commitment or allows for a flexible or variable scale. The various impacts of volatility on the minimum exchange rate supporting (triggering) entry or exit, the minimum capacity scale for entry, and the hysteresis (inertia) effect are also explored.

Part IV deals with the effect of alternative processes or formulations on certain types of projects, such as the effect of mean reversion on natural resources or shipping investments or that of a jump process on start-up venture growth options. In chapter 11, David G. Laughton and Henry D. Jacoby point out that failure to account for reversion in output prices may introduce a bias against long-term commodity projects, relative to a random walk model. The chapter focuses on commodity projects of different durations, with consideration of both now-or-never alternatives and projects involving an option to wait under price reversion.

In chapter 12, Petter Bjerksund and Steinar Ekern point out various option applications in shipping, such as time-charter contracts, new buildings, and second-hand tonnage. The chapter implements contingent claims analysis to evaluation problems involving mean-reverting cash flows in shipping. Cash flows from an operating ship are characterized by the mean-reverting Ornstein-Uhlenbeck (O-U) process, and a number of generic, closed-form analytic solutions are obtained, including that for a European call option on an asset, such as a time-charter contract, whose value follows a mean-reverting O-U process.

In chapter 13, "Valuing Start-up Venture Growth Options," Ram Willner values start-up companies as growth options using option pricing based on an alternative "jump" formulation of the discovery nature of new ventures. His model parameters are technical rather than market-driven (e.g., the average frequency of new discoveries), which the author claims may be easier to estimate for nontraded assets such as start-up ventures. Actual applications with venture capitalists suggest that the model should be applied in several contingent stages, thereby valuing a new business venture as a compound option.

Part V presents various other options applications, such as in pollution compliance, land development, flexible manufacturing, and financial default. Michael E. Edleson and Forest L. Reinhardt, in chapter 14, "Investment in Pollution Compliance Options: The Case of Georgia Power," focus on an actual case study of a utility that must comply with preset pollution levels and may buy or sell pollution "allowances." Management has several alternatives: it can continue operating on high-sulfur coal (and buy allowances), it can install expensive "scrubbers" (and sell allowances), or it may switch to low-sulfur coal (initially selling allowances, but later buying them). The decision is made more interesting and complicated by the presence of hybrid alternatives and multiple real options.

Chapter 15, "Optimal Land Development," by Laura Quigg, values real estate land as a real option. The author points out that the holder of land holds an option to build one of many types of buildings at an optimally chosen future time. The chapter values analytically the option to wait to invest (develop the land) and simultaneously determines the optimal exercise schedules. This option value provides a rationale for the existence of vacant land in the midst of otherwise thriving real estate markets. The impact of uncertainty on development and abandonment decisions is also examined.

In chapter 16, "Multiproduct Manufacturing with Stochastic Input Prices and Output Yield Uncertainty," Bardia Kamrad and Ricardo Ernst develop a general stochastic optimal control model to value the flexibility embedded in multiproduct manufacturing agreements under input price and output yield uncertainties. Their model, which can be solved numerically via stochastic dynamic programming as well as by using a multinomial lattice representation of the evolution of input prices and output yield uncertainty, also derives optimal production policies.

The last chapter, "Default Risk in the Contingent Claims Model of Debt," by Ann Fremault Vila and Martha A. Schary, provides an illustration of the application of option pricing techniques on the liability side to value bondholder as well as stockholder default options. The authors show how the degree of leverage and institutional features of bankruptcy law can affect the optimal abandonment decision. This perspective serves as a reminder that both real and financial options can affect a corporation's combined investment and financing decisions.

As the editor of a book like this, I owe my primary debt to the many authors, whose collective ideas essentially make up the work's contribution. This book would not have existed without their creativity and determination. On behalf of the contributors I would also like to thank various reviewers whose judgment and comments helped determine the shape of this volume, although they must remain anonymous. I owe an additional intellectual debt to Stewart C. Myers, Scott P. Mason, and George M. Constantinides for their constant encouragement over the years. My research assistant, Stefanos Hailis, has my appreciation for his patience and capable assistance in converting the technical parts of the book into TEX. My family also deserves special appreciation for their patience and support, despite my frequent neglect of their needs, during the development of this work.

The contributing authors and I invite your ideas and comments on the following contributed articles. Indeed, it has been our hope that a collection of these new developments may help spark further interest and subsequent developments in the vital and growing area of real options.

# Real Options in Capital Investment

# Chapter 1

# Real Options: An Overview

## Lenos Trigeorgis

*This chapter provides an overview of the basic valuation principles, litera-*
*ture and applications in real options. An oil example is first used to intro-*
*duce the basic nature of various real options found in capital investments.*
*Simple numerical examples are then employed to present basic, practically*
*useful principles for valuing upside-potential options, such as to defer an*
*investment or expand production, as well as various downside-protection*
*options, such as to contract, temporarily shut down, abandon for salvage*
*value or switch use, and default during project construction. The compre-*
*hensive literature review traces the evolution of the real options revolution,*
*organized around thematic developments. Various applications and future*
*research directions are also discussed.*

## 1.1  INTRODUCTION

Many academics and practicing managers recognize that the net present
value (NPV) rule and other discounted cash flow (DCF) approaches to
capital budgeting are inadequate in that they cannot properly capture
management's flexibility to adapt and revise later decisions in response
to unexpected market developments. Traditional NPV makes implicit assumptions concerning an "expected scenario" of cash flows and presumes
management's passive commitment to a certain "operating strategy" (e.g.,
to initiate the project immediately and operate it continuously at base scale
until the end of a prespecified expected useful life).

However, in the actual marketplace, which is characterized by change,
uncertainty, and competitive interactions, the realization of cash flows will
probably differ from what management expected initially. As new information arrives and uncertainty about market conditions and future cash flows
is gradually resolved, management may have valuable flexibility to alter its
operating strategy in order to capitalize on favorable future opportunities

or mitigate losses. For example, it may be able to defer, expand, contract, abandon, or otherwise alter a project at different stages during its useful operating life.

Management's flexibility to adapt its future actions in response to altered future market conditions expands an investment opportunity's value by improving its upside potential while limiting downside losses relative to management's initial expectations under passive management. The resulting asymmetry caused by managerial adaptability calls for an *expanded* NPV rule reflecting both value components: the traditional (static or passive) NPV of direct cash flows and the option value of operating and strategic adaptability. This does not mean that traditional NPV should be scrapped, but rather it should be seen as a crucial and necessary input to an options-based *expanded* NPV analysis:

Expanded (strategic) NPV  =  passive NPV of expected cash flows +

value of options from active management

(1.1)

An options approach to capital budgeting has the potential to conceptualize and quantify the value of options from active management. This value is manifest as a collection of real (call or put) options embedded in capital investment opportunities, having as an underlying asset the gross project value of expected operating cash flows. Many of these real options occur naturally (e.g., to defer, contract, shut down, or abandon), while others may be planned and built in at some extra cost (e.g., to expand capacity or build growth options, to default when investment is staged sequentially, or to switch between alternative inputs or outputs). Table 1.1 describes briefly the most common categories of encountered real options and the type of industries in which they are important, and lists representative authors that have analyzed them.

This chapter presents practically useful principles for quantifying the value of various real options and provides a comprehensive overview of the existing real options literature and applications. It shows the basics of valuing both upside-potential operating options, such as to defer an investment or expand production, and various downside-protection options, such as to abandon for salvage value or switch use, or abandon during project construction. The literature review traces the evolution of the real options revolution and is organized around thematic developments covering the early criticisms, conceptual approaches, foundations and building blocks, risk-neutral valuation and risk adjustment, analytic contributions in valuing different options separately, option interactions, numerical techniques, competition and strategic options, and various applications.

The rest of the chapter is organized as follows. Section 1.2 uses an

## Table 1.1
## Common Real Options

| Category | Description | Important in: | Analyzed by: |
|---|---|---|---|
| Option to *Defer* | Management holds a lease on (or an option to buy) valuable land or resources. It can wait (x years) to see if output prices justify constructing a building or plant or developing a field. | All natural resource extraction industries; real estate development; farming; paper products. | McDonald & Siegel (86); Paddock, Siegel, & Smith (88); Tourinho (79); Titman (85); Ingersoll & Ross (92). |
| *Time to Build* Option (*Staged Investment*) | Staging investment as a series of outlays creates the option to abandon the enterprise in midstream if new information is unfavorable. Each stage can be viewed as an option on the value of subsequent stages and valued as a compound option. | All R&D-intensive industries, especially pharmaceuticals; long-development capital-intensive projects, e.g., large-scale construction or energy-generating plants; start-up ventures. | Majd & Pindyck (87); Carr (88); Trigeorgis (93). |
| Option to *Alter Operating Scale* (e.g., to *Expand*; to *Contract*; to *Shut Down and Restart*) | If market conditions are more favorable than expected, the firm can expand the scale of production or accelerate resource utilization. Conversely, if conditions are *less* favorable than expected, it can reduce the scale of operations. In extreme cases, production may temporarily halt and start up again. | Natural resource industries such as mine operations; facilities planning and construction in cyclical industries; fashion apparel; consumer goods; commercial real estate. | Trigeorgis & Mason (87); Pindyck (88); McDonald & Siegel (85); Brennan & Schwartz (85) |
| Option to *Abandon* | If market conditions decline severely, management can abandon current operations permanently and realize the resale value of capital equipment and other assets in second-hand markets. | Capital-intensive industries, such as airlines and railroads; financial services; new product introductions in uncertain markets. | Myers & Majd (90). |

## Table 1.1 (continued)

| Category | Description | Important in: | Analyzed by: |
|---|---|---|---|
| Option to *Switch* (e.g., *Outputs* or *Inputs*) | If prices or demand change, management can change the output mix of the facility (product flexibility). Alternatively, the same outputs can be produced using different types of inputs (*process* flexibility). | Output shifts: Any goods sought in small batches or subject to volatile demand, e.g., consumer electronics; toys; specialty paper; machine parts; autos. Input shifts: All feedstock-dependent facilities, e.g., oil; electric power; chemicals; crop switching; sourcing. | Margrabe (78); Kensinger (87); Kulatilaka (88); Kulatilaka & Trigeorgis (93). |
| *Growth* Options | An early investment (e.g., R&D, lease on undeveloped land or oil reserves, strategic acquisition, information network/infrastructure) is prerequisite or link in a chain of interrelated projects, opening up future growth opportunities (e.g., new-generation product or process, oil reserves, access to new market, strengthening of core capabilities). Like interproject compound options. | All infrastructure-based or strategic industries, especially high-tech, R&D, or industries with multiple product generations or applications (e.g., computers, pharmaceuticals); multinational operations; strategic acquisitions. | Myers (77); Brealey & Myers (91); Kester (84, 93); Trigeorgis (88); Pindyck (88); Chung & Char- oenwong (91). |
| Multiple *Interacting* Options | Real-life projects often involve a *collection* of various options, both upward-potential enhancing calls and downward-protection put options, present in combination. Their combined option value may differ from the sum of separate option values (i.e., they interact). They may also interact with financial flexibility options. | Real-life projects in most industries discussed above. | Trigeorgis (93); Brennan & Schwartz (85); Kulatilaka (94). |

example to motivate discussion of various real options, while section 1.3 presents basic practical principles for valuing several such options. Section 1.4 provides a comprehensive overview of the real options literature, and the last section discusses future research directions.

## 1.2 EXAMPLE: AN OIL EXTRACTION AND REFINERY OPERATION

To facilitate our discussion of the various real options that may be embedded in capital investments, consider first the following example. A large oil company has a one-year lease to start drilling on undeveloped land with potential oil reserves. Initiating the project may require certain exploration costs, to be followed by the construction of roads and other infrastructure outlays, $I_1$. This would be followed by outlays for the construction of a new processing facility, $I_2$. Extraction can begin only after construction is completed; in other words, cash flows are generated only during the "operating stage" following the last outlay. During construction, if market conditions deteriorate, management can choose to forgo any future planned outlays. Management may also choose to reduce the scale of operation by $c$ percent, saving a portion of the last outlay, $I_C$, if the market is weak. The processing plant can be designed up front such that if oil prices turn out to be higher than expected, the rate of production can be enhanced by $x$ percent with a follow-up outlay of $I_E$. At any time, management may salvage a portion of its investment by selling the plant and equipment for their salvage value or switching them to an alternative use value, $A$. An associated refinery plant—which may be designed to operate with alternative sources of energy inputs—can convert crude oil into a variety of refined products. This type of project presents the following collection of *real options*.

### 1.2.1 The Option to Defer Investment

The lease enables management to defer investment for up to one year and thus to benefit from the resolution of uncertainty about oil prices during this period. Management would invest $I_1$ (i.e., exercise its option to extract oil) *only if* oil prices increase sufficiently, while it would not commit to the project, and would save the planned outlays, if prices decline. Just before expiration of the lease, the value creation will be $max(V - I_1, 0)$. The option to defer is thus analogous to an American call option on the gross present value of the completed project's expected operating cash flows, $V$, with the exercise price being equal to the required outlay, $I_1$. Since early investment implies sacrificing the option to wait, this option value loss is like an additional investment opportunity cost, justifying investment only if the value of cash benefits, $V$, actually exceeds the initial outlay by a substantial premium. As noted in Table 1.1, the option to wait is particularly valuable in resource extraction industries, farming, paper products, and real estate development, due to high uncertainties and long investment horizons.

## 1.2.2   The Option to Default during Construction (or the Time-to-Build Option)

In most real-life projects, the required investment is not incurred as a single, up-front outlay. The actual staging of capital investment as a series of outlays over time creates valuable options to "default" at any given stage (e.g., after exploration if the reserves or oil prices turn out to be very low). Thus, each stage (e.g., building necessary infrastructure) can be viewed as an option on the value of subsequent stages by incurring the installment cost outlay (e.g., $I_1$) required to proceed to the next stage, and can therefore be valued similarly to the valuation of compound options. This option is valuable in all R and D–intensive industries, especially pharmaceuticals; in highly uncertain, long-development capital intensive industries, such as energy-generating plants or large-scale construction; and in venture capital.

## 1.2.3   The Option to Expand

If oil prices or other market conditions turn out to be more favorable than expected, management can actually accelerate the rate or expand the scale of production (by $x$ percent) by incurring a follow-up cost $(I_E)$. This is similar to a call option to acquire an additional part ($x$ percent) of the base-scale project, paying $I_E$ as the exercise price. The investment opportunity with the option to expand can be viewed as the base-scale project plus a call option on future investment, namely, $V + max(xV - I_E, 0)$. Given an initial design choice, management may deliberately favor a more expensive technology for the built-in flexibility to expand production if and when it becomes desirable. As will be discussed further, the option to expand may also be of strategic importance, especially if it enables a firm to capitalize on future growth opportunities. As noted, when it buys vacant undeveloped land or builds a small plant in a new geographic location (domestic or overseas) to position itself to take advantage of a developing large market, a firm essentially installs an expansion/growth option. This option, which will be exercised only if future market developments turn out to be favorable, can make a seemingly unprofitable (based on passive NPV) base-case investment worth undertaking.

### 1.2.4   The Option to Contract

If market conditions are weaker than originally expected, management can operate below capacity or even reduce the scale of operations (by $c$ percent), thereby saving part of the planned investment outlays $(I_C)$. This flexibility to mitigate loss is analogous to a put option on part ($c$ percent) of the base-scale project, with the exercise price equal to the potential cost savings $(I_C)$, giving $max(I_C - cV, 0)$. The option to contract, just like the option to expand, may be particularly valuable in the case of new product introductions in uncertain markets. The option to contract may also be important, for example, in choosing among technologies or plants with a different construction-to-maintenance cost mix, where it may be preferable to build a plant with lower initial construction costs and higher maintenance expenditures in order to acquire the flexibility to contract operations by cutting down on maintenance if market conditions turn out unfavorable.

### 1.2.5   The Option to Shut Down (and Restart) Operations

In real life, the plant does not have to automatically operate (i.e., extract oil) in each and every period. In fact, if oil prices are such that cash revenues are not sufficient to cover variable operating (e.g., maintenance) costs, it might be better not to operate temporarily (especially if the costs of switching between the operating and idle modes are relatively small). If prices rise sufficiently, operations can start again. Thus, operation in each year may be seen as a call option to acquire that year's cash revenues $(C)$ by paying the variable costs of operating $(I_V)$ as exercise price, namely, $max(C - I_V, 0)$. Options to alter the operating scale (i.e., expand, contract, or shut down) are typically found in natural resource industries, such as mine operations, facilities planning and construction in cyclical industries, fashion apparel, consumer goods, and commercial real estate.

### 1.2.6   The Option to Abandon for Salvage Value

If oil prices suffer a sustainable decline or the operation does poorly for some other reason, management does not have to continue incurring the fixed costs. Instead, it may have a valuable option to abandon the project permanently in exchange for its salvage value (i.e., the resale value of its capital equipment and other assets in second-hand markets). As noted, this option can be valued as an American put option on current project value $(V)$, with exercise price the salvage or best alternative use value $(A)$, entitling management to receive $V + max(A - V, 0)$ or $max(V, A)$. Naturally, more general-purpose capital assets have a higher salvage and option abandonment value than special-purpose assets. Valuable abandonment options are generally found in capital-intensive industries, such as in airlines and railroads, in financial services, as well as in new product introductions.

### 1.2.7 The Option to Switch Use (Inputs or Outputs)

Suppose the associated oil refinery operation can be designed to use alternative forms of energy inputs (e.g., fuel oil, gas, or electricity) to convert crude oil into a variety of output products (e.g., gasoline, lubricants, or polyester). This would provide valuable built-in flexibility to switch from the current input to the cheapest future input or from the current output to the most profitable future product mix, as the relative prices of the inputs or outputs fluctuate over time. In fact, the firm should be willing to pay a certain positive premium for such a flexible technology over a rigid alternative that confers no or less choice. Indeed, if the firm can in this way develop extra uses for its assets compared to its competitors, it may be at a significant advantage. Generally, *process* flexibility can be achieved not only via technology (e.g., by building a flexible facility that can switch among alternative energy *inputs*), but also by maintaining relationships with a variety of suppliers, changing the mix as their relative prices change. Subcontracting policies may allow further flexibility to contract the scale of future operations at a low cost in the case of unfavorable market developments. As noted, a multinational oil company may similarly locate production facilities in various countries in order to acquire the flexibility to shift production to the lowest-cost producing facilities, as the relative costs, other local market conditions, or exchange rates change over time. Process flexibility is valuable in feedstock-dependent facilities, such as oil, electric power, chemicals, and crop switching. *Product* flexibility, which enables the firm to switch among alternative *outputs*, is more valuable in industries such as automobiles, consumer electronics, toys, and pharmaceuticals, where product differentiation and diversity are important or product demand is volatile. In such cases, it may be worthwhile to install a more costly flexible capacity to acquire the ability to alter the product mix or production scale in response to changing market demands.

### 1.2.8 Corporate Growth Options

As noted, another version of the option to expand with considerable strategic importance involves *corporate growth options* that set the path of future opportunities. Suppose, in the previous example, that the proposed refinery facility is based on a new, technologically superior *process* for oil refinement that is being developed and tested internally on a pilot plant basis. Although in isolation the proposed facility may appear unattractive, it might become only the first in a series of similar facilities if the process is successfully developed and commercialized and may even lead to entirely new oil by-products. More generally, many early investments (e.g., R and D, a lease on undeveloped land or a tract with potential oil reserves, a strategic acquisition, or an information technology network) can be seen as prerequisites or links in a chain of interrelated projects. The value of these projects may derive not so much from their expected directly measurable cash flows as from their ability to unlock future growth opportunities (e.g., a new-generation product or process, oil reserves, access to a newly expanding market, or strengthening of the firm's core capabilities or strategic positioning). An opportunity to invest in a first-generation high-tech product, for example, is analogous to an option on options (an interproject compound option). Despite a negative NPV, the infrastructure, experience, and potential by-products generated during the development of the first-generation product may serve as springboards for developing lower-cost or improved-quality future generations of that product, or even for generating new applications into other areas. However, unless the firm makes the initial investment, subsequent generations or other applications will not even be feasible. The infrastructure and experience gained can be proprietary and can place the firm at a competitive advantage, which may even reinforce itself if the effects of a learning cost curve are present. Growth options are found in all infrastructure-based or strategic industries, and especially in high-technology, R and D, or industries with multiple-product generations or applications (e.g., semiconductors, computers, and pharmaceuticals); in multinational operations; and in strategic acquisitions.

In a more general context, the operating and strategic adaptability represented by real options can be achieved at various stages during the value chain, from switching the factor input mix among various suppliers and subcontracting practices to rapid product design (e.g., computer-aided design) and modularity in design, and to shifting production among various products rapidly and cost-efficiently in a flexible manufacturing system.

## 1.3 BASIC PRINCIPLES FOR REAL OPTION VALUATION

This section illustrates, through simple numerical examples, basic, practical principles for valuing several of the previously discussed real options. For expositional simplicity, I will subsequently ignore any dividend-like effects (see section 1.4.4 for appropriate adjustments). Consider, as in Trigeorgis and Mason (1987), valuing a generic investment opportunity (e.g., as in the example of the oil extraction project).[1] Specifically, suppose we are faced with an opportunity to invest $I_0 = \$104$ (million) in an oil project whose (gross) value in each period will either move up by 80 percent or down by 40 percent, depending on oil price fluctuations: a year later, the project will have an expected value (from subsequent cash flows) of $180 (million) if the oil price moves up ($C^+ = 180$) or $60 if it moves down ($C^- = 60$).[2] There is an equal probability ($q = .5$) that the price of oil will move up or down in any year. Let $S$ be the price of oil or, generally, of a *twin security* that is traded in the financial markets and has the same risk characteristics (i.e., is perfectly correlated) with the real project under consideration (such as the stock price of a similar, operating, unlevered oil company). Both the project and its twin security (or oil prices) have an expected return (or discount rate) of $k = 20$ percent, while the risk-free rate is $r = 8$ percent.

In what follows we assume throughout that the value of the project (i.e., the value, in millions of dollars, in each year, $t$, of its subsequent expected cash flows, appropriately discounted back to that year), $V_t$, and its twin security price (e.g., a twin oil stock price in $ per share, or simply the price of oil in $ per barrel), $S_t$, move through time as follows:

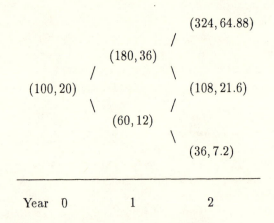

For example, the pair $(V_0, S_0)$ above represents a current gross project value of $100 million and a spot oil price of $20 a barrel (or a $20-a-share twin oil stock price). Under traditional (passive) NPV analysis, the current gross project value would be obtained by first discounting the project's end-of-period values (derived from subsequent cash flows), using the expected rate of return of the project's twin security (or, here, of oil prices) as the appropriate discount rate, namely, $V_0 = (.5 \times 180 + .5 \times 60)/1.20 = 100$. Note that this gross project value is, in this case, exactly proportional to the twin security price (or the spot oil price). After subtracting the current investment costs, $I_0 = 104$, the project's NPV is given by:

$$\text{NPV} = V_0 - I_0 = 100 - 104 = -4 \ (< 0). \tag{1.2}$$

In the absence of managerial flexibility or real options, traditional DCF analysis would have *rejected* this project based on its negative NPV. However, passive DCF is unable to properly capture the value of embedded options because of their discretionary asymmetric nature and their dependence on future events that are uncertain at the time of the initial decision. The fundamental problem, of course, lies in the valuation of investment opportunities whose claims are not symmetric or proportional and whose discount rates vary in a complex way over time.

Nevertheless, such real options can be properly valued using contingent claims analysis (CCA) within a backward, risk-neutral valuation process.[3] Essentially, the same solution can be obtained in the actual, risk-averse world as in a *risk-neutral* world in which the current value of any contingent claim could be obtained from its expected future values—with expectations taken over the *risk-neutral probabilities*, $p$, as imputed from the twin security's (or oil) prices—discounted at the *riskless interest rate*, $r$. In such a risk-neutral world, the current (beginning of the period) value of the project (or of the equityholders' claim), $E$, is given by:

$$E = [pE^+ + (1-p)E^-]/(1+r),$$
$$\text{with } p = [(1+r)S - S^-]/(S^+ - S^-). \tag{1.3}$$

The risk-neutral probability, $p$, can be estimated from the price dynamics of the twin security (or of oil prices):

$$p = [1.08 \times 20 - 12]/(36 - 12) = 0.4$$
$$\text{(as distinct from the actual probability, } q = 0.5),$$

and can then be used to determine "certainty-equivalent" values (or expected cash flows) that can be properly discounted at the risk-free interest rate. For example,

$$V_0 = [pC^+ + (1-p)C^-]/(1+r) = [.4 \times 180 + .6 \times 60]/1.08 = 100.^4 \tag{1.4}$$

In what follows, we assume that if any part of the required investment outlay (having a present value of $104 million) is not going to be spent immediately but rather in future installments, that amount will be placed in an escrow account earning the riskless interest rate.[5] We next illustrate how various kinds of both upside-potential options, such as to defer or expand, and downside-protection options, such as to abandon for salvage or default during construction, can enhance the value of the *opportunity* to invest (i.e., the value of equity or NPV) in the previously described generic project. Our focus here is on basic, practical principles for valuing one kind of operating option at a time.

### 1.3.1    The Option to Defer Investment

The company in our example has a one-year lease providing it with a pro-prietary right to defer undertaking the project (i.e., extracting the oil) for a year, thus benefiting from the resolution of uncertainty about oil prices over this period. Although undertaking the project *immediately* has a neg-ative NPV (of -4), the *opportunity* to invest afforded by the lease has a positive worth, since management will invest *only* if oil prices and project value rise sufficiently, while it has no obligation to invest under unfavorable developments. Since the option to wait is analogous to a call option on project value, $V$, with an exercise price equal to the required outlay next year, $I_1 = 112.32 \, (= 104 \times 1.08)$,

$$E^+ = max(V^+ - I_1, 0) = max(180 - 112.32, 0) = 67.68,$$
$$E^- = max(V^- - I_1, 0) = max(60 - 112.32, 0) = 0. \qquad (1.5)$$

The project's total value (i.e., the *expanded* NPV, which includes the value of the option to defer) from Equation (1.3) is:

$$E_0 = [pE^+ + (1-p)E^-]/(1+r) = [.4 \times 67.68 + .6 \times 0]/1.08 = 25.07. \quad (1.6)$$

From Equation (1.1), the value of the option to defer provided by the lease itself is given by:

*Option to defer* = expanded NPV − passive NPV = $25.07 - (-4) = 29.07$,
$$(1.7)$$

which, incidentally, is equal to almost one third of the project's gross value.[6]

### 1.3.2    The Option to Expand (Growth Option)

Once the project is undertaken, any necessary infrastructure has been com-pleted and the plant is operating, management may have the option to accelerate the rate or expand the scale of production by, say, 50 percent ($x = 0.50$) by incurring a follow-on investment outlay of $I_E = 40$, pro-vided oil prices and general market conditions turn out to be better than originally expected. Thus, in year 1, management can choose either to maintain the base-scale operation (i.e., receive project value, $V$, at no ex-tra cost) or expand by 50 percent the scale and project value by incur-ring the extra outlay. That is, the original investment opportunity is seen as the initial-scale project plus a call option on a future opportunity, or $E = V + max(xV - I_E, 0) = max[V, (1+x)V - I_E]$:

$$E^+ = max(V^+, 1.5V^+ - I_E) = max(180, 270 - 40) = 230 \text{ (expand)};$$
$$E^- = max(V^-, 1.5V^- - I_E) = max(60, 90 - 40) = 60 \text{ (base scale).}$$
$$(1.8)$$

The value of the investment opportunity (including the value of the option to expand if market conditions turn out to be better than expected) then becomes:

$$E_0 = [pE^+ + (1-p)E^-]/(1+r) - I_0 = [.4 \times \mathbf{230} + .6 \times 60]/1.08 - 104 = 14.5, \tag{1.9}$$

and thus, the value of the *option to expand* equals:

$$14.5 - (-4) = 18.5, \text{ or } 18.5\% \text{ of } V_0. \tag{1.10}$$

## 1.3.3   The Option to Contract

Analogous to the option to expand is the downside-protection option to contract the scale of a project's operation by forgoing planned future expenditures if the product is not as well received in the market as initially expected. Suppose that in the oil example, part of the investment cost, with a $104 present value necessary to initiate and maintain project scale, is to be spent next year. Specifically, $50 will have to be paid immediately as a start-up cost, and an investment of $58.32 (the future value of $54) is planned in one year. Of this amount, $18.32 will be necessary fixed costs, with the remaining $40 in variable costs to be divided among advertising ($33.32) and maintenance ($6.68) expenditures.

Suppose, also, that in one year, as an alternative to making the full $58.32 investment necessary to maintain the current scale of operations, management has the option to halve the scale and value of the project (i.e., $c = .5$) by making a lower, $25 outlay (i.e., saving $I_C = \$33.32$ by cutting down on the advertising expenses). If market conditions next year turn out unfavorably, management may exercise its option to contract the scale of the project's operation. That is, $E = (V - I_1) + max(I_C - .5V, 0)$, so that:

$$
\begin{aligned}
E^+ &= (180 - 58.32) + max(33.32 - 90, 0) = 121.68, \\
E^- &= (60 - 58.32) + max(0, 33.32 - 30) = 5 \text{ (halve)}.
\end{aligned} \tag{1.11}
$$

The investment opportunity, incorporating the option to contract, is then worth:

$$E_0 = [.4 \times 121.68 + .6 \times 5]/1.08 - 50 = -2.16, \tag{1.12}$$

so that the value of the *option to contract* equals:

$$-2.16 - (-4) = 1.84, \tag{1.13}$$

or about 2 percent of gross project value.

### 1.3.4   The Option to Temporarily Shut Down

Suppose now that part of the investment cost having a \$104 present value is to be spent later. Specifically, \$44 will have to be expended up front as a start-up cost, and an installment of \$64.80 (the future value of \$60 at the 8 percent riskless rate) is planned in one year. Of this amount, \$24.80 will be necessary fixed costs while the remaining \$40 is for discretionary variable expenditures for advertising and maintainance.

Suppose, further, that the project makes a 30 percent cash payout so that the cash revenues in a given year amount to 30 percent of the gross project value $(C = .3V)$. Next year, for example, the cash revenues would be $C^+ = .3 \times 180 = 54$ (with the balance representing expected cash revenues in subsequent years) if the oil market moves up, or $C^- = .3 \times 60 = 18$ if it moves down. In order to acquire these cash revenues, management would have to incur the \$40 in variable costs (as advertising and maintenance expenditures). Management has the option to obtain project value $V$ (net of fixed costs, $I_F$) minus variable costs $(I_V)$ or to shut down and receive project value minus that year's forgone cash revenue $(C)$, namely, $max(V - I_V, V - C) - I_F$. Alternatively, the option not to operate enables management to acquire project value (net of fixed costs) by paying the minimum of variable costs (if the project does well and management decides to operate) or cash revenues (that would be sacrificed if the project does poorly and it chooses not to operate), namely, $(V - I_F) - min(I_V, C)$. Thus,

$$
\begin{aligned}
E^+ &= V^+ - I_V = (180 - 24.8) - min(40, 54) = 155.2 - 40 = 115.2; \\
E^- &= V^- - C = (60 - 24.8) - min(40, 18) = 35.2 - 18 = 17.2. \quad (1.14)
\end{aligned}
$$

From the risk-neutral valuation relationship just described, the value of the investment opportunity (including the option to temporarily shut down next year) then is:

$$
\begin{aligned}
E_0 &= [pE^+ + (1 - p)E^-]/(1 + r) - I_0 = \\
&= [.4 \times 115.2 + .6 \times 17.2]/1.08 - 44 = 8.22, \quad (1.15)
\end{aligned}
$$

and the value of the option to shut down next year equals:

$$
8.22 - (-4) = 12.22, \quad (1.16)
$$

or 12 percent of current gross project value.

If the variable costs were equally divided between years 1 and 2, it can be easily shown that following a downmarket and temporary shutdown in year 1, operations would remain temporarily shut down in the second year if the market moves down again but would reopen in the event the market moves up. (This is distinct from permanent abandonment of the project, to be discussed later.)

## 1.3.5 Options to Abandon for Salvage Value or Switch Use

As a further downside protection, management has the option to abandon the oil extraction project at any time in exchange for its *salvage value* or value in its best alternative use, if oil prices suffer a sustainable decline. The associated oil refinery plant also can use alternative energy inputs and has the flexibility to convert crude oil into a variety of products. As market conditions change and the relative prices of inputs, outputs, or the plant resale value in a second-hand market fluctuate, equityholders may find it preferable to abandon the current project's use by switching to a cheaper input or a more profitable output, or simply selling the plant's assets to the second-hand market. Let the project's value in its best alternative use, $A$, (or the *salvage value* for which it can be exchanged) move over time as:

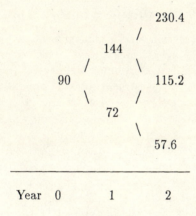

Note that the project's current salvage or alternative use value ($A_0 = 90$) is below the project's value in its present use ($V_0 = 100$)—otherwise management would have switched use immediately—and has the same expected rate of return (20%); it nevertheless has a smaller variance, so that if the market keeps moving up, it will not be optimal to abandon the project early for its salvage value, but if it moves down, management may find it desirable to switch use (e.g., in year 1 to exchange the present use value of $V_1 = 60$ for a higher alternative use value of $A_1 = 72$).[7] Thus, equityholders can choose the maximum of the project's value in its present use, $V$, or its value in the best alternative use, $A$, namely, $E = max(V, A)$:

$$E^+ = max(V^+, A^+) = max(180, 144) = 180 = V^+ \text{ (continue)};$$
$$E^- = max(V^-, A^-) = max(60, 72) = 72 = A^- \text{ (switch use)}. (1.17)$$

The value of the investment (including the option to abandon early or switch use) is then:

$$E_0 = [pE^+ + (1-p)E^-]/(1+r) - I_0$$
$$= [.4 \times 180 + .6 \times \mathbf{72}]/1.08 - 104 = +2.67, \qquad (1.18)$$

so that the project with the option to switch use is now desirable. The value of the option itself is:

$$\textit{Option to switch use} = 2.67 - (-4) = 6.67, \qquad (1.19)$$

or almost 7 percent of the project's gross value. This value is clearly dependent on the schedule of salvage or alternative use values.

### 1.3.6   The Option to Default (on Planned Staged Cost Installments) during Construction

Even during the construction phase, management may abandon a project to save any subsequent investment outlays if the coming required investment exceeds the value from continuing the project (including any future options). Suppose that the investment (of \$104 present value) necessary to implement the oil extraction project can be staged as a series of "installments": $I_0 = \$44$ out of the \$104 allocated amount will need to be paid out immediately (in year 0) as a start-up cost for infrastructure, with the \$60 balance placed in an escrow account (earning the risk-free rate) planned to be paid as a $I_1 = \$64.8$ follow-up outlay for constructing the processing plant in year 1. Next year management will then pay the investment cost "installment" as planned only in return for a higher project value from continuing; otherwise it will forgo the investment and receive nothing. Thus, the option to default when the investment is staged sequentially translates into $E = max(V - I_1, 0)$:

$$E^+ = max(V^+ - I_1, 0) = max(180 - 64.8, 0) = 115.2 \text{ (continue)};$$
$$E^- = max(V^- - I_1, 0) = max(60 - 64.8, 0) = 0 \text{ (default)}. \qquad (1.20)$$

The value of the investment opportunity (with the option to default) is given by:

$$E_0 = [pE^+ + (1-p)E^-]/(1+r) - I_0 = [.4 \times 115.2 + .6 \times 0]/1.08 - 44 = -1.33, \qquad (1.21)$$

and the *option to abandon by defaulting* during construction equals:

$$-1.33 - (-4) = 2.67, \qquad (1.22)$$

or about 3 percent of project value. Obviously, this value is dependent on the staged cost schedule.

Of course, for simplicity, these examples were based on a one-period, risk-neutral backward valuation procedure. However, this procedure can be easily extended to a discrete, multi-period setting with any number of stages. Starting from the terminal values, the process would move backward, calculating option values one step earlier (using the up and down values obtained in the preceding step), and so on. As the number of steps increases, the discrete-time solution naturally approaches its continuous Black-Scholes–type equivalent (with appropriate adjustments), when it exists. As discussed in detail later, the reader should also be cautioned that when several of the above-mentioned options are present simultaneously, they may interact such that their separate values are not additive.

## 1.4   AN OVERVIEW OF THE REAL OPTIONS LITERATURE

This section will attempt to describe stages in the development and evolution of the real options literature, while organizing the presentation around several broad themes. On the way, I will note how some of the new contributions presented in this edited volume fit within the broader literature development.

### 1.4.1   Symptoms, Diagnosis, and Traditional Medicine: Early Critics, the Underinvestment Problem, and Alternative Valuation Paradigms

The real options revolution arose in part as a response to the dissatisfaction of corporate practitioners, strategists, and some academics with traditional capital budgeting techniques. Well before the development of real options, corporate managers and strategists were grappling intuitively with the elusive elements of managerial operating flexibility and strategic interactions. Early critics (Dean, 1951, Hayes and Abernathy, 1980, Hayes and Garvin, 1982) recognized that standard discounted cash flow (DCF) criteria often undervalued investment opportunities, leading to myopic decisions, underinvestment, and eventual loss of competitive position. This occurred because financial analysts either ignored or did not properly value important strategic considerations. Decision scientists further maintained that the problem lay in the application of the wrong valuation techniques altogether and proposed instead the use of simulation and decision tree analysis (see Hertz, 1964, Magee, 1964) to capture the value of future operating flexibility associated with many projects. Proponents (e.g., Hodder and Riggs, 1985, Hodder, 1986) have argued that the problem rather arises from misuse of DCF techniques as commonly applied in practice. Myers (1987), while confirming that part of the problem results from various misapplications of the underlying theory, acknowledges that traditional DCF methods have inherent limitations when it comes to valuing investments with significant operating or strategic options (e.g., in capturing the sequential interdependence among investments over time) and has suggested that option pricing holds the best promise of valuing such investments. Later, Trigeorgis and Mason (1987) clarified the fact that option valuation can be seen operationally as a special, economically corrected version of decision tree analysis that is preferable for valuing a variety of corporate operating and strategic options. In the next chapter in this edited volume, Teisberg provides a practical comparative discussion of the DCF, decision analysis, and real option valuation paradigms. Baldwin and Clark (1992) have discussed the importance of organizational capabilities in strategic capital investment, while Baldwin and Trigeorgis (1993) proposed remedying the underinvestment problem and restoring competitiveness by developing specific adaptive capabilities to be viewed as an infrastructure for acquiring and managing real options.

## 1.4.2   A New Direction: Conceptual Real Options Approaches

Building on Myers's (1977) initial idea of thinking of discretionary investment opportunities as "growth options," Kester (1984) conceptually discussed strategic and competitive aspects of growth opportunities. Other general, conceptual real options frameworks are presented in Mason and Merton (1985), Trigeorgis and Mason (1987), Trigeorgis (1988), Brealey and Myers (1991), and Kulatilaka and Marcus (1988, 1992). Mason and Merton (1985), for example, provide a good discussion of many operating, as well as financing, options and integrate them in a project-financing framework for a hypothetical, large-scale energy project.

## 1.4.3   Generic Medicine: Foundations and Building Blocks

The quantitative origins of real options, of course, derive from the seminal work of Black and Scholes (1973) and Merton (1973) in pricing financial options. Cox, Ross, and Rubinstein's (1979) binomial approach enabled the development of a more simplified valuation of options in discrete time. Margrabe (1978) valued an option to exchange one risky asset for another, while Stulz (1982) analyzed options on the maximum (or minimum) of two risky assets and Johnson (1987) extended the analysis to several risky assets. These papers have the potential to help analyze the generic option to switch among alternative uses and related options (e.g., abandon for salvage value or switch among alternative inputs or outputs). Geske (1979) valued a compound option (i.e., an option to acquire another option), which in principle may be applied in valuing growth opportunities that become available only if earlier investments are undertaken. In chapter 6 of this volume, Carr combines these two building blocks to value sequential (compound) exchange options, involving an option to acquire a subsequent option to exchange the underlying asset for another risky alternative. In chapter 5, Kulatilaka describes an equivalent dynamic programming formulation for the option to switch among operating modes. This line of work has the potential, in principle, to value investments with a series of investment outlays that can be switched to alternative states of operation, and particularly to eventually help value strategic interproject dependencies.

## 1.4.4   Slightly Different Medicine: Risk-Neutral Valuation and Risk Adjustment

The actual valuation of options in practice has been greatly facilitated with Cox and Ross's (1976) recognition that an option can be replicated (or a "synthetic option" can be created) from an equivalent portfolio of traded securities. Being independent of risk attitudes or considerations of capital market equilibrium, such risk-neutral valuation enables present-value discounting, at the risk-free interest rate, of expected future payoffs (with actual probabilities replaced by risk-neutral ones), a fundamental characteristic of "arbitrage-free" price systems involving traded securities. Rubinstein (1976) further showed that standard option-pricing formulas can be alternatively derived under risk aversion, and that the existence of continuous trading opportunities enabling a riskless hedge or risk neutrality are not really necessary. Mason and Merton (1985) and, in chapter 3 of this volume, Kasanen and Trigeorgis maintain that real options may, in principle, be valued similarly to financial options even though they may not be traded, since in capital budgeting we are interested in determining what the project cash flows would be worth if they were traded in the market, in other words, their contribution to the market value of a publicly traded firm. The existence of a traded twin security (or dynamic portfolio) that has the same risk characteristics (i.e., is perfectly correlated) with the nontraded real asset in complete markets is sufficient for real option valuation. More generally, Constantinides (1978), Cox, Ingersoll, and Ross (1985, Lemma 4), and Harrisson and Kreps (1979), among others, have suggested that any contingent claim on an asset, whether traded or not, can be priced in a world with systematic risk by replacing its actual growth rate with a certainty-equivalent rate (by subtracting a risk premium that would be appropriate in market equilibrium) and then behaving as if the world were risk-neutral. This is analogous to discounting certainty-equivalent cash flows at the risk-free rate, rather than employing actually expected cash flows at a risk-adjusted rate. For traded assets in equilibrium or for those real assets that have no systematic risk (e.g., R and D and exploration or drilling for certain precious metals or natural resources), the certainty-equivalent or risk-neutral rate just equals the risk-free interest rate (minus any dividends). However, if the underlying asset is not traded, as may often be the case in capital-budgeting–associated options, its growth rate may actually fall below the equilibrium total expected return required of an equivalent-risk traded financial security, with the difference or "rate of return shortfall" necessitating a dividend-like adjustment in option valuation (see McDonald and Siegel, 1984, 1985). If the underlying asset is traded in futures markets, though, this dividend (or convenience-yield) type of return shortfall or rate of forgone earnings can be easily derived from the futures prices of contracts with different maturities (see Brennan and Schwartz, 1985a or 1985b). In other cases, however, estimating this return shortfall may require the use of a market equilibrium model (see McDonald and Siegel, 1985).

## 1.4.5   A Tablet for Each Case: Valuing Each Different Real Option Separately

A series of papers gave a boost to the real options literature by focusing on valuing quantitatively—in many cases, deriving analytic, closed-form solutions—one type after another of a variety of real options, although each option was typically analyzed in isolation. As summarized in Table 1.1, the option to defer or initiate investment has been examined by McDonald and Siegel (1986); by Paddock, Siegel, and Smith (1988) in valuing offshore petroleum leases; and by Tourinho (1979) in valuing reserves of natural resources. Ingersoll and Ross (1992) reconsidered the decision to wait in light of the beneficial impact of a potential future interest rate decline on project value. Majd and Pindyck (1987) valued the option to delay sequential construction for projects that take time to build when there is a maximum rate at which investment can proceed. Carr (1988) and Trigeorgis (1993a) also dealt with valuing sequential or staged (compound) investments. Trigeorgis and Mason (1987) and Pindyck (1988) examined options to alter (e.g., expand or contract) operating scale or capacity choice. The option to temporarily shut down and restart operations was analyzed by McDonald and Siegel (1985) and by Brennan and Schwartz (1985a). Myers and Majd (1990) analyzed the option to permanently abandon a project for its salvage value, seen as an American put option. Options to switch use (e.g., outputs or inputs) have been examined by, among others, Margrabe (1978), Kensinger (1987), Kulatilaka (1988), and Kulatilaka and Trigeorgis (1994). Baldwin and Ruback (1986) showed that future price uncertainty creates a valuable switching option that benefits short-lived projects. Future investment oportunities seen as corporate growth options are discussed in Myers (1977), Brealey and Myers (1991), Kester (1984, 1993), Trigeorgis and Mason (1987), Trigeorgis (1988), Pindyck (1988), and Chung and Charoenwong (1991).

## 1.4.6 The Tablets Interact: Multiple Options and Interdependencies

Despite its enormous theoretical contribution, the focus of the earlier literature on valuing individual real options (i.e., one type of option at a time) has nevertheless limited its practical value. Real-life projects are often more complex in that they involve a collection of multiple real options, whose values may interact. An early exception is Brennan and Schwartz (1985a), who determined the combined value of the options to shut down (and restart) a mine and also to abandon it for salvage. They recognize that partial irreversibility resulting from costs of switching the mine's operating state may create a hysteresis or inertia effect, making it optimal in the long term to remain in the same operating state even if short-term cash flow considerations seem to favor early switching. Although hysteresis is a form of interaction between early and later decisions, however, Brennan and Schwartz did not explicitly address the interactions among individual option values. Trigeorgis (1993a) focused on the nature of real option interactions, pointing out, for example, that the presence of subsequent options can increase the value of the effective underlying asset for earlier options, while the exercise of prior real options may alter (e.g., expand or contract) the underlying asset itself, and hence, the value of subsequent options on it. Thus, the combined value of a collection of real options may differ from the sum of separate option values. Using a numerical analysis method suitable for valuing complex multioption investments (Trigeorgis, 1991b), he presented the valuation of options to defer, abandon, contract or expand investment, and switch use in the context of a generic investment, first with each option in isolation and later in combination. He showed, for example, that the incremental value of an additional option, in the presence of other options, is generally less than its value in isolation and declines as more options become present. More generally, he identified situations in which option interactions can be small or large and negative as well as positive. In this volume, chapter 7, Kulatilaka examines the impact of interactions among three such options on their optimal exercise schedules. The recent recognition of real option interdependencies should subsequently enable a smoother transition from a theoretical stage to an application phase.

## 1.4.7   The Bitter Pill: Numerical Techniques

In the more complex real-life option situations, such as those involving multiple interacting real options, analytic solutions may not exist, and one may not even be always able to write down the set of partial differential equations describing the underlying stochastic processes. The ability to value such complex option situations has been enhanced, however, with various numerical analysis techniques, many of which take advantage of risk-neutral valuation. Generally, there are two types of numerical techniques for option valuation: (1) those that approximate the underlying stochastic processes directly, which are generally more intuitive; and (2) those approximating the resulting partial differential equations. The first category includes the Monte Carlo simulation used by Boyle (1977), as well as various lattice approaches such as Cox, Ross, and Rubinstein's (1979) standard binomial lattice method and Trigeorgis's (1991b) log-transformed binomial method; the latter methods are particularly well suited to valuing complex projects with multiple, embedded real options, a series of investment outlays, and dividend-like effects, as well as option interactions. Boyle (1988) showed how lattice frameworks can be extended to handle two-state variables, while Hull and White (1988) suggested a control variate technique to improve computational effeciency in cases where a similar derivative asset with an analytic solution is available. Examples of the second category include numerical integration and the implicit or explicit finite difference schemes used by Brennan (1979), Brennan and Schwartz (1978), and Majd and Pindyck (1987). Finally, a number of analytic approximations are also available: Geske and Johnson (1984) proposed an approach involving a compound-option analytic polynomial approximation, Barone-Adesi and Whaley (1987) used a quadratic approximation, and Johnson (1983) and others have used various problem-specific heuristic approximations. A comprehensive review of such numerical techniques is given in the articles by Geske and Shastri (1985) and Trigeorgis (1991b), as well as in a book by Hull (1989).

## 1.4.8 The General Environment: Competition and Strategic Options

An important area that deserves more attention, and where real options have the potential to make a significant difference, is that of competition and strategy. Sustainable competitive advantages resulting from patents, proprietary technologies, ownership of valuable natural resources, managerial capital, reputation or brand name, scale, and market power empower companies with valuable options to grow through future profitable investments and to more effectively respond to unexpected adversity or opportunities in a changing technological, competitive, or general business environment. A number of economists addressed several competitive and strategic aspects of capital investment early on. For example, Roberts and Weitzman (1981) found that in sequential decision making, it may be worthwhile to undertake investments with negative NPV when early investment can provide information about future project benefits, especially when their uncertainty is great. Baldwin (1982) found that optimal sequential investment for firms with market power that are facing irreversible decisions may require a positive premium over NPV to compensate for the loss in value of future opportunities that results from undertaking an investment. Pindyck (1988) analyzed options to choose capacity under product price uncertainty when investment is, again, irreversible. Dixit (1989a) considered firm entry and exit decisions under uncertainty, showing that in the presence of sunk or costly switching costs, it may not be optimal in the long term to reverse a decision, even when prices appear attractive in the short term. In chapter 10 of this volume, Bell combines Dixit's entry and exit decisions with Pindyck's capacity options for the multinational firm under volatile exchange rates. Kogut and Kulatilaka (1994) analyzed the international plant location option in the presence of mean-reverting exchange rate volatility, while Kulatilaka and Marks (1988) examined the strategic bargaining value of flexibility in the firm's negotiations with input suppliers.

From a more explicit real options perspective, a number of authors (e.g.,Myers, 1987; Kester, 1984, 1993; Trigeorgis and Mason, 1987; Trigeorgis, 1988; Brealey and Myers, 1991; and Trigeorgis and Kasanen, 1991) have initially dealt with competitive and strategic options rather conceptually. For example, Kester (1984) developed qualitatively various competitive and strategic aspects of interproject growth options, while Kester (1993) proposed a planned sequential, rather than parallel, implementation of a collection of interrelated consumer products when learning results from early product introductions (e.g., about available shelf space needed for similar subsequent products) and when competitive advantage is eroding. Trigeorgis and Kasanen (1991) also examined sequential project interdependencies and synergies as part of an ongoing strategic planning and control process.

Kasanen (1993) also dealt with the strategic problem of the interaction between current investments and future opportunities, using a spawning matrix structure to determine the optimal mix of strategic and operating projects. Trigeorgis (1991a) used quantitative option-pricing techniques to examine early investment that may preempt anticipated competitive entry, and to value the option to defer investment when it is impacted by random competitive entry (Trigeorgis, 1990b). Ang and Dukas (1991) incorporated both competitive and asymmetric information, arguing that the time pattern of discounted cash flows also matters, due to the possibility of premature project termination as a result of random competitive entry. Further departing from the common assumption of perfect competition, Kulatilaka and Perotti (1992) and Smit and Trigeorgis (1993) examined how the investment decisions of a firm influence the production decisions of competitors and the equilibrium market price when early investment generates a competitive advantage. A simpler game-theoretic treatment of competitive reactions under different market structures in a real options framework was given in Smit and Ankum (1993). Supplementing options analysis with game theoretic tools capable of incorporating strategic competitive counteractions promises to be an important and challenging direction for future research.

## 1.4.9   A Cure for All Kinds of Cases:
## A Variety of Applications

Besides theoretical developments, real options applications are currently also receiving increased attention. Real options valuation is being applied in a variety of contexts, such as in natural resource investments, land development, leasing, flexible manufacturing, government subsidies and regulation, R and D, new ventures and acquisitions, foreign investment and strategy, and elsewhere. Early applications naturally arose in the area of *natural resource investments* due to the availability of traded resource or commodity prices, high volatilities, and long durations, resulting in higher and better option value estimates. Brennan and Schwartz (1985a, 1985b) first utilized the convenience yield derived from futures and spot prices of a commodity to value the options to shut down or abandon a mine. Paddock, Siegel, and Smith (1988) valued options embedded in undeveloped oil reserves and provided the first empirical evidence that option values are better than actual DCF-based bids in valuing offshore oil leases. Trigeorgis (1990a) valued an actual minerals project considered by a major multinational company involving options to cancel during construction, expand production, and abandon for salvage. Bjerksund and Ekern (1990) valued a Norwegian oil field with options to defer and abandon. Kemna

(1993) described actual cases involving the timing of developing an off-shore oil field, valuing a growth option in a manufacturing venture, and making an abandonment decision about a refining production unit. Morck, Schwartz, and Stangeland (1989) valued forestry resources under stochastic inventories and prices. Stensland and Tjostheim (1990) also discussed some applications of dynamic programming to natural resource exploration. In this volume (chapter 11), Laughton and Jacoby study biases in the valuation of certain commodity projects of different duration characterized by a mean-reverting price process rather than the standard random walk assumption.

In the area of *land development*, Titman (1985), Williams (1991b), Capozza and Sick (1992), and Quigg, in chapter 15 in this volume, have shown that the value of vacant urban land should reflect not only its value based on its best immediate use (e.g., from constructing a building now), but also its option value should development be delayed and the land be converted into its best alternative use in the future. Quigg points out that it may pay to hold land vacant for its option value even in the presence of currently thriving real estate markets, and Quigg (1993) reported empirical results indicating that option-based land valuations are better approximations of market prices. In a different context, McLaughlin and Taggart (1992) viewed the opportunity cost of using excess capacity as the change in the value of the firm's options caused by diverting capacity to an alternative use. In *leasing*, Copeland and Weston (1982); Lee, Martin, and Senchack (1982); McConnel and Schallheim (1983); and Trigeorgis (1992) have valued various operating options embedded in leasing contracts.

In the area of *flexible manufacturing*, the flexibility provided by flexible manufacturing systems, flexible production technology, and other machinery having multiple uses has been analyzed from an options perspective by Kulatilaka (1988, 1993), Triantis and Hodder (1990), Aggarwal (1991), and Kulatilaka and Trigeorgis (1994), among others. For example, Kulatilaka (1993) valued the flexibility of an actual dual-fuel industrial steam boiler over a rigid alternative. In this volume (chapter 16), Kamrad and Ernst value the flexibility embedded in multiproduct manufacturing agreements under both input price and output yield uncertainties. Baldwin and Clark (1993) studied the flexibility created by modularity in design used to connect components of a larger system through standard interfaces.

In the area of *government subsidies and regulation*, Mason and Baldwin (1988) valued government subsidies to large-scale energy projects as put options, while Teisberg (1994) provided an option valuation analysis of investment choices by a regulated firm. In *research and development*, Kolbe, Morris, and Teisberg (1991) discussed option elements embedded in R and D projects. Option elements involved in the staging of *start-up ventures* are discussed in Sahlman (1988) and Trigeorgis (1993b). In this volume (chapter 13), Willner suggests a jump-process formulation of the discovery process for start-up ventures seen as multistage growth options. Strategic *acquisitions* of other companies also often involve a number of growth, divestiture, and other flexibility options, as discussed in chapter 8 in this volume by Smith and Triantis. (Other applications of options in the strategy area were mentioned earlier in this discussion.)

On the empirical side, Kester (1984) estimated that the value of a firm's growth options is more than half the market value of equity for many firms, and as much as 70 to 80 percent for more volatile industries. Similarly, Pindyck (1988) also suggested that growth options represent more than half of a firm's value if demand volatility exceeds 0.2. In *foreign investment*, Baldwin (1987) discussed various location, timing, and staging options that are present when firms scan the global marketplace. Bell, in chapter 10 of this volume, and Kogut and Kulatilaka (1994), among others, have examined entry, capacity, and switching options for firms with multinational operations under exchange rate volatility. In chapter 9, Hiraki suggests that in Japan, the bank-oriented corporate governance system serves as the basic infrastructure that enables Japanese companies to jointly develop corporate real options. Various other option applications are found in areas ranging from valuing mean-reverting cash flows in shipping, studied by Bjerksund and Ekern in chapter 12 of this volume, to *global warming* (e.g., Hendricks, 1991) and *environmental pollution compliance* options, analyzed by Edleson and Reinhardt in chapter 14 of this volume. The potential for future applications itself seems like a growth option.

Other comprehensive treatments of real options can be found in the articles by Mason and Merton (1985) and Trigeorgis and Mason (1987), a monograph by Sick (1989), an economics review article by Pindyck (1991), and a forthcoming *MIT Press* book by this author (Trigeorgis, 1995). The spring 1987 issue of the *Midland Corporate Finance Journal* (vol. 5, no. 1), a 1991 special issue of *Managerial Finance* (vol. 17, nos. 2/3), and part of the autumn 1993 special issue of *Financial Management* (vol. 22, no. 3) are also devoted to real options and capital budgeting.

## 1.5   CURRENT AND FUTURE RESEARCH DIRECTIONS

The contributed articles in this edited volume are indicative of an active literature that is currently evolving in several new directions: clarifying the relation of real options with alternative valuation paradigms (chapters 2–4); developing more general models and modeling interdependencies (chapters 5–7); conceptualizing strategic, infrastructure, and foreign investment options (chapters 8–10); examining mean reversion/alternative formulations (chapters 11–13); and extending applications to many diverse areas (chapters 14–17).

Other research directions deserving more attention in the future include the following:

1. Analyzing more actual case applications and tackling real-life implementation issues and problems.

2. Applying real options to the valuation of flexibility in other related areas, such as in competitive bidding, information technology or other platform investments, energy and R and D problems, international finance options, and so on.

3. Using real options to explain empirical phenomena that are amenable to observation or statistical testing, such as examining empirically whether managements of firms that are targets for acquisition may sometimes turn down tender offers in part due to the option to wait in anticipation of receiving better offers in the future.

4. Doing more field, survey, or empirical studies to test the conformity of theoretical real option valuation and its implications with management's intuition and experience, as well as with actual price data when available.

5. Focusing more on investments (such as in R and D, pilot or market tests, or excavations) that can *generate* information and learning (e.g., about the project's prospects) by extending/adjusting option pricing and risk-neutral valuation with Bayesian analysis or alternative (e.g., jump) processes.

6. Exploring in more depth endogenous competitive counteractions and a variety of competitive/market structure and strategic issues using a combination of game-theoretic industrial organization methods and option valuation tools.

7. Modeling more accurately the various strategic and growth options.

8. Extending real options in an agency context, recognizing that the potential (theoretical) value of real options may not be realized in practice if managers, in pursuing their own agenda (e.g., expansion or growth, rather than firm value maximization), misuse their discretion and do not follow the optimal exercise policies implicit in option valuation. This raises the need for the firm to design proper corrective incentive contracts (taking also into account asymmetric information).

9. Recognizing better that real options may interact, not only among themselves, but with financial flexibility options as well, and understanding the resulting implications for the combined, interdependent corporate investment and financing decisions.

Option valuation, indeed, has the potential, not only to help integrate capital budgeting with strategic planning, but also to eventually offer a consistent, unified treatment of the whole of corporate finance (involving both real and financial decisions).

## ACKNOWLEDGMENTS

Part of this overview chapter builds on material also used in the early part of Trigeorgis (1993b). I would like to thank *Financial Management* for permission to use this material. Part of Table 1.1 is also adapted from Baldwin and Trigeorgis (1993).

## NOTES

1. Trigeorgis and Mason (1987) used a similar example to show how options-based valuation can be seen operationally as a special, though economically corrected, version of decision tree analysis (DTA) that recognizes open-market opportunities to trade and borrow.

2. All project values are subsequently assumed to be in millions of dollars (with the word millions subsequently dropped).

3. As noted, the basic idea is that management can replicate the payoff to equity by purchasing a specified number of shares of the twin security and financing the purchase in part by borrowing a specific amount at the riskless interest rate, $r$. This ability to construct a *synthetic* claim or an equivalent/replicating portfolio (from the twin security and riskless bonds), based on no-arbitrage equilibrium principles, enables the solution for the current value of the equity claim to be independent of the actual probabilities (in this case, 0.5) or investors' risk attitudes (the twin security's expected rate of return or discount rate, $k = 0.20$).

4. This confirms that $V_0 = 100$, as obtained earlier using traditional DCF with the actual probability ($q = 0.5$) and the risk-adjusted discount rate ($k = 0.20$).

5. This assumption is intended to make the discussion more realistic and invariant to the cost structure makeup and is not at all crucial to the analysis.

6. This example confirms that CCA is *operationally* identical to decision tree analysis (DTA), with the key difference being that the probabilities are transformed to allow the use of a risk-free discount rate. Note, however, that the DCF/DTA value of waiting may differ from that given by CCA. The DCF/DTA approach in this case will overestimate the value of the option if it discounts at the constant 20 percent rate required of securities that are comparable in risk to the *naked* (passive) project:

$$E_0 = [qE^+ + (1 - q)E^-]/(1 + k) = [.5 \times 67.68 + .5 \times 0]/1.20 = 28.20.$$

Again, the error in the traditional DTA approach arises from the use of a single (or constant) risk-adjusted discount rate. Asymmetric claims on an asset do not have the same amount of risk (and hence, expected rate of return) as the underlying asset itself. CCA corrects for this error by transforming the probabilities.

7. I assume here for simplicity that the project's value in its current use and in its best alternative use (or salvage value) are perfectly positively correlated. Of course, the option to switch use would be even more valuable with a lower correlation between $V$ and $A$.

# PART I

## REAL OPTIONS AND ALTERNATIVE VALUATION PARADIGMS

# Chapter 2

# Methods for Evaluating Capital Investment Decisions under Uncertainty

## Elizabeth Olmsted Teisberg

*The literature on evaluating strategic decisions includes three methodologies that consider future uncertainty as well as managerial flexibility to respond to uncertain future developments: dynamic discounted cash flow analysis, decision analysis, and option valuation. However, there is little comparison of these approaches, and virtually no guidance for practitioners on the potential pitfalls in applying each technique. This chapter addresses two important practical concerns: (1) how should managers choose the type of analysis they use as a decision-aid, and (2) are there situations in which one approach is more appropriate, or clearly misleading? The chapter also presents some general insights from dynamic analysis of capital investment decisions.*

## 2.1  INTRODUCTION

Almost all firms recognize that they face major uncertainties about the future, yet most firms' strategic investment decisions are primarily based on a single projection of future events. Although managers do recognize that the failure to include a consideration of uncertainty can lead to costly errors, the difficulty of such planning leads many to ignore the potential costs and hope that serious problems will not arise.

Suppose a company is considering a strategic decision, such as building a large new plant or embarking on a large research project. Major projects such as these require significant commitments of both capital and managerial attention. The reward from the project depends not only on its technical success, but also on the market conditions and industry structure at the time of completion. Uncertain future developments and the firm's response to these developments can turn such projects into either resounding successes or abysmal failures. However, managers are often baffled by the question of how to include uncertain future outcomes and potential future strategic responses in a prospective analysis of a capital investment project.

The literature on project evaluation and capital budgeting proposes several answers to this question. Future uncertainty and the flexibility of managers to respond to future developments are considered in three methodologies: dynamic discounted cash flow analysis, decision analysis, and real option valuation (or "contingent claims analysis"). In principle, all three can be accomplished with the same, relatively simple, analytical technique of "folding back a tree" (i.e., solving a problem with backward recursion). However, the values and probabilities used in each type of analysis differ, and hence the results may differ when different techniques are used.

Proponents of each technique argue that when used correctly, their technique results in a correct valuation of the project or strategic decision under consideration (e.g., Hodder and Riggs, 1985; Hodder, Matheson, and Miller, 1977; and McDonald and Siegel, 1986). This may be true, given the assumptions of the models. It may also be true that if completely equivalent assumptions are used in each type of analysis, they will all give the same answer.[1] The problem is that the practice of each technique requires a number of assumptions and approximations, not all of which may be obvious. In practice, these assumptions and approximations differ among the various techniques, as well as among different practitioners of the same technique, so that different analyses produce different answers. Although this observation is not surprising, it does raise two important practical concerns: (1) how should managers choose the type of analysis they use as a decision aid, and (2) are there situations in which one approach is more appropriate, or, conversely, clearly misleading? The purpose of this chapter is to address these practical concerns.

The rest of the chapter is organized as follows. Section 2.2 gives a brief review of each methodology. Sections 2.3 and 2.4 discuss the practical implementation of each approach, pointing out potential pitfalls for each and indicating situations in which a given approach should be used or avoided. Section 2.5 reviews some general insights from dynamic analysis, drawing on all three techniques, and section 2.6 provides concluding comments.

## 2.2   METHODOLOGY REVIEWS

This section provides a brief overview of each of the three methodologies under consideration. The purpose of these overviews is to clarify what is meant by the terms, *dynamic discounted cash flow analysis, decision analysis,* and *real option valuation* rather than to provide a tutorial on each technique. The existing literature includes good introductions to each method (e.g., Hodder and Riggs, 1985; Howard, 1968; and Pindyck, 1991); however, it provides little comparison of techniques or discussion of practical considerations for choosing among them.

## 2.2.1   Dynamic Discounted Cash Flow Analysis

Discounted cash flow (DCF) analysis, and in particular, net present value (NPV) analysis, has been widely used as a criterion for evaluating projects. However, it is by now also widely recognized that the usual form of DCF analysis overlooks important strategic concerns about future uncertainty and flexibility to respond to situations that differ from those that were expected. Fortunately, the usual static approach of projecting expected cash flows and discounting them at the opportunity cost of capital is not the end of the story with respect to the DCF approach.

A *dynamic* version of discounted cash flow analysis begins by considering uncertain cash flows more carefully. Instead of assuming a predetermined decision path and a single (expected) scenario of future cash flows, the dynamic version requires the analyst to lay out all important future uncertainties and the possible future contingent decisions by using a decision tree or a dynamic program. By solving this tree or dynamic program, the analyst correctly takes into account the possibility of many future states of the world and incorporates in the analysis the best possible set of decisions (given the information supplied in the model) at each time and in each state. The outcome values and probabilities used in this analysis reflect the information available to the company at the present time, and future cash flow estimates are derived from data about similar projects. The chance of each outcome occurring is characterized either by using the subjective probability assessments of the person responsible for the decision or using statistical data from similar projects. In practice, probability estimates often are based on data from similar projects when they are available, and on subjective estimates when such data do not exist.

Like the static DCF method, this analysis uses the opportunity cost of capital as the (risk-adjusted) discount rate to determine the project's expected net present value. Estimates of the discount rate are typically based on market data about projects with similar risk profiles and, ideally, with identical risks. However, it is by now well understood that there is no single risk-adjusted discount rate that is appropriate for all cash flows to and from a project. Some critics even argue that there is no correct risk-adjusted discount rate because discounting should reflect only time preference.[2] However, even if one accepts the use of risk-adjusted discount rates, it is obvious that risks may vary for different components of cash flow (e.g., costs may have different risks than revenues), in different states of the world (i.e., given different descriptions of future events), or in different stages of a project's life. Thus, a correct application of dynamic DCF may require the use of a number of discount rates within the project analysis. The practical implications of multiple discount rates are discussed in the next section.

## 2.2.2   Decision Analysis

Decision analysis also requires a careful structuring of important uncertainties and possible future decisions. Furthermore, it uses the technique of folding back a decision tree to incorporate correctly the possibilities of many future states of the world and the best possible state-dependent decisions at each time (given the assumptions of the model).

Decision analysis, however, differs from a dynamic DCF analysis in that discounting is used only to reflect time preference and hence is done, appropriately, at the risk-free rate. Adjustments for risk aversion appear in the characterization of the utility function of the decision maker.[3] This type of analysis calculates the *expected utility* of the project or decision, which is the expected present value at the risk-free rate if the decision maker happens to be risk-neutral (i.e., if the utility function is linear).[4]

Values and probabilities again are based on the information about the project that is available to the decision maker at the time of the analysis. The likelihood of different future outcomes is represented by the decision maker's subjective probability beliefs. In practice, decision analysts usually put less emphasis on the information contained in market prices and focus instead on how the decision maker values the project (i.e., on his or her expected utility of the project, which may or may not be entirely based on how he or she believes the market value of the firm will be affected), rather than directly on how the project may affect the market value of the firm.

The expected utility and market values may differ for a number of reasons. First, the decision maker may value risk differently than does the market (i.e., he or she may assign a higher or lower cost to bearing risk than the cost that is reflected in market prices). Second, the decision maker may be concerned with project-specific risks that are diversifiable for investors but not for the firm's employees. In this case, the expected utility of the project may be less than the market value because the consequences of bad outcomes may be more severe for the firm's employees than they would be for investors, who can hedge through diversification. Third, the decision maker may have different information from what is reflected in market prices. He or she may have "inside" information that is yet not public, may not be aware of all of the relevant news and data that underlie market prices, may interpret the news and data differently from the market, or may simply not take into account all relevant market information.

## 2.2.3 Real Option Valuation

Option valuation determines the value of a project or investment opportunity from the values of other market-traded assets. The best-known option pricing formula is that of Black and Scholes (1973), which is the solution to a stochastic calculus problem. Subsequently, Cox, Ross, and Rubinstein (1979) developed a binomial option pricing method that relies on the same economic principles of arbitrage pricing but requires only basic algebra.[5] With this simplified approach, the mechanics for calculating the value of an option reduce to folding back a decision tree, as done for either a dynamic DCF analysis or a decision analysis. Trigeorgis and Mason (1987) demonstrated that option valuation need be no more complicated than dynamic discounted cash flow analysis, providing a simple example showing how similar the techniques are in terms of the mechanics of finding the solution.[6]

The difference among these techniques again revolves around how one chooses relevant values and represents uncertainty. Option pricing focuses on market value and uses the standard deviation of the rate of return on an *underlying* (or *twin*) *asset*. The underlying asset is an asset with the same risks as the project (or asset) that the firm would own if the option were "exercised," that is, if the investment were made and the project completed. For example, if the project involves the construction of a new plant, the underlying asset is an identical, completed, and operating plant. Similarly, if the project is the development of an oil field, the underlying asset is an otherwise identical but already developed oil field.

If a market-traded underlying asset is readily identifiable, the option pricing characterization of value is simpler than the DCF or decision analysis processes of specifying possible cash flows for the completed project. Otherwise, the market value of the underlying asset can be estimated using the same process of specifying possible cash flows for the completed project.

Unlike the previous two approaches, the actual probabilities of the possible future values do not need to be estimated for the option valuation approach. Furthermore, the option-pricing approach uses risk-free rather than risk-adjusted discount rates. Uncertainty is characterized by the range of possible future values for the underlying asset. The possible future values can be used as inputs to a simple equation to derive appropriate weights, which are used in place of the actual probabilities when the tree is folded back. These weights, which are sometimes referred to as *risk-adjusted probabilities*, are not truly probabilities; instead, they are the weights that are required so that the value of the option will leave no opportunities for risk-less arbitrage. They correspond to probabilities that would prevail in a risk-neutral world.

Note, however, that although no probabilities and no measures of risk aversion are used directly, the market value of the risk of the completed project is included through the market value of the underlying asset. Since the value of an option is a function of the value of its underlying asset, the market price of that asset reflects the risk of owning it. In essence, the use of the underlying asset value is a convenient trick for using existing information about how the market prices a particular risk profile, and hence for avoiding the need to estimate probabilities, risk-adjusted discount rates, or utility functions.

## 2.3   PRACTICAL IMPLEMENTATION

### 2.3.1   Dynamic Discounted Cash Flow Analysis

The dynamic version of discounted cash flow analysis offers a significant improvement over static DCF in that the dynamic analysis incorporates a consideration of future uncertainty and of decisions that managers can make in the future to manage risk and increase the value of a project or strategy. However, this approach also adds a significant complication in discounting cash flows.

Discounted cash flow analysis (whether static or dynamic) requires that each cash flow be discounted at the appropriate opportunity cost of capital, estimated as the rate of return on a traded asset with identical (or highly correlated) risk characteristics. The complication is that the appropriate cost of capital is not fixed; it depends on the risk of the cash flows and on whether that risk is correlated with other market risks. For example, if the costs of a project are contractually specified, they may be relatively certain, whereas the revenues from the same project could be highly volatile depending on the date the product goes to market and the economic conditions prevailing at that time. In this case, even in a static DCF analysis, the cash outflows should be discounted at a lower rate than the cash inflows. Furthermore, the risks may vary over time, with different possible states of the world, or across the various components of the cash flow stream.

Practical questions, therefore, arise as to how much effort to put into estimating each discount rate and how many different rates are enough to do a good analysis. Unfortunately, there is no simple answer to these questions. What is clear is that an analysis based on a single risk-adjusted discount rate may be misleading. If the results prove highly sensitive to the choice of discount rate, the analysis should be redone using a different method or with more careful attention to the risks of different components of the cash flows, the changes in these risks over time, and the differences in risk under different possible future conditions.

## 2.3.2 Decision Analysis

Decision analysis is not designed to focus on the *market* value of a project or strategy. It is designed to calculate the value of a project or decision to an individual decision maker, taking into account the information at his or her disposal, his or her (subjective) assessments of future uncertainty, and reflecting his or her utility function (including a measure of the decision maker's risk aversion). Thus, the value calculated in decision analysis may differ from the project's market value. In practice, decision analysis often fails to make use of information reflected in market prices and therefore may not be a good measure of the value of a project to a company's shareholders.

This, of course, does *not* mean that decision analysis is inappropriate for use in business decisions. It does mean, however, that when market information exists and is accessible, the effect of a project on the company's market value (or share price) may be better estimated with a different technique.[7] It also means that in situations where there is no market information or where the market information is not accessible or relevant, decision analysis may be a more appropriate analytic decision aid.

For example, suppose we want to evaluate the research and development of a new product that no other firms currently make or have announced plans to make. In such a case, there simply may be no market information about the product's value. Another example is the value of providing a new benefit to employees, such as flexible work hours. In this case, there probably is information embedded in the value of other firms' stocks (or in this company's stock price history) about the market value of possible productivity increases or improved morale. However, it may be virtually impossible to isolate the effect of the new benefit from other components of corporate market value. In each of these examples, the firm is faced with no accessible market data, either because there is no similar project in the market or because the value of the project cannot be separated out. In such circumstances, decision analysis offers a reasonable way to value the project or decision, including future uncertainty and possible future actions.

## 2.3.3 Real Option Valuation

Real option valuation, or *contingent claims analysis* (CCA) is the newest of the three approaches and perhaps the least well understood by practitioners. The emerging literature on real options may leave the nonspecialist reader with several misconceptions. First, part of the literature presents theory that makes the approach appear more complicated than it need be in practice.[8] Second, some authors appear to claim that option valuation is clearly superior to the earlier methodologies because it avoids the complexities of using risk-adjusted discount rates and of using utility functions to estimate market values. The option methodology does avoid these difficulties, but it presents other potential problems that practitioners should recognize. The following discussion explains how these problems arise and when they might be more or less serious than the problems with dynamic DCF or decision analysis.

The first problem concerns a determination of the value of the *underlying asset.* In principle, option pricing models determine the market value of an opportunity by calculating the value of an equivalent portfolio of assets (i.e., a portfolio of assets that has the same payoffs as the option in all states of the world). The basic argument is that to prevent riskless arbitrage opportunities, the portfolio and the opportunity must have the same current market price. Thus, the analysis requires the identification of an underlying asset (also called the *twin asset*) that has the same risks the opportunity in question will have *when the investment has been completed.* Since the value of the underlying asset is the gross value of the cash flows from the completed project, it may be very different from the net value of the opportunity to invest in the project, especially if the project has high or highly uncertain costs, requires a lead time during which conditions may change, or involves multiple stages of development. If the value of a completed project is observable, better understood, or easier to model than the value of the (potentially complex) opportunity to invest in the project, the option valuation technique can simplify the analysis significantly. Frequently, however, the market value of the underlying asset is not observable, so attention must be paid to how this value can be estimated.

If the underlying asset value is not directly observable, it can sometimes be estimated by identifying a portfolio of assets that constitutes a twin asset. For example, one might estimate the value of a plant that makes "widgets" by subtracting the value of a firm that makes only "gadgets" from the value of a firm that makes both "widgets" and "gadgets". However, even when it is clear that publicly traded firms have projects that are very similar to the one in question, it is not always easy to isolate the value of a single project that is part of a firm with many assets. This difficulty is similar to trying to estimate the risk premium (or risk-adjusted discount rate) associated with a given type of investment when no firm makes only that type of investment.

When it is difficult to isolate the value of the underlying asset in market prices, it may be reasonable to use estimates of the revenues of the completed project to estimate market value (see Teisberg Associates and Applied Decision Analyses, Inc., 1990). This approach is similar to the process of estimating cash flows for dynamic discounted cash flow analysis or decision analysis. However, with those two approaches, one would model the cash flows from *both* the investment process and the completed project. With the option approach, in contrast, one models the cash flows from the completed project to estimate the value of the underlying asset, and then uses that estimated asset value as an input to the option valuation.

The implication for practitioners is that the value of the underlying asset is a critical input to an option value analysis in that it reflects both the expected value and the risk of the completed project's cash flows. Thus, when the underlying asset is observable or can be accurately estimated, the option approach provides a way to estimate more directly the market value of an investment opportunity while avoiding the problems associated with risk adjustment or measuring risk aversion. However, when the value of the underlying asset cannot be estimated accurately, there may be insufficient market information for a credible options analysis.

A more subtle issue with real option valuation is the proper representation of dividend-like payouts (or forgone earnings). While many option-pricing models do consider this issue (e.g., Majd and Pindyck, 1987; McDonald and Siegel, 1986; Paddock, Siegel, and Smith, 1988; Teisberg, 1993, 1994; Teisberg and Teisberg, 1991), others neglect forgone earnings, instead implicitly (or explicitly) assuming that the value of the underlying asset increases at its cost of capital.[9] Although this is a reasonable assumption for valuing a financial call or put option on a firm that does not pay dividends, it can lead to misleading results in the context of "real" options on investment opportunities. For example, one of the well-known results of financial option-pricing theory is that it is never optimal to exercise a call option on a non-dividend-paying stock before its expiration. In the context of real investment opportunities, this could be interpreted as implying that investment should never be undertaken until the last possible chance to invest. Thus, if the opportunity is never likely to suddenly disappear, investment is never the right decision.

Clearly, a real option analysis without dividend-like adjustments is lacking in some potentially important considerations. "Dividends" in a real option context can be anything that may make the expected rate of change in the underlying asset less than the market cost of capital or that may make delay costly. Such "dividends" or forgone earnings can be caused by many factors, including competitive entry into the market, preemption in the introduction of a new product (Trigeorgis, 1986, 1991a), lost sales during a delay (Majd and Pindyck, 1987; Paddock, Siegel, and Smith, 1988), seasonal price trends (Teisberg and Teisberg, 1991), or regulatory disallowances and profit restrictions (Teisberg, 1993, 1994; Teisberg Associates and Applied Decision Analyses, Inc., 1990). Thus, the rate of forgone earnings is a second critical input to an option-pricing analysis. In some cases, such as expected sales losses during a start-up delay, the rate of forgone earnings may be relatively easy to estimate. In other cases, such as in competitive entry, the timing or magnitude of forgone earnings may be more difficult to estimate.

The rate of forgone earnings is the difference between the market cost of capital for the underlying asset (or the equilibrium return on a twin traded security) and the expected rate of value appreciation for the completed project. Theoretically, option analysis requires only this difference as an input. The estimation of this difference, however, often requires calculating both the cost of capital and the expected rate of appreciation for the completed project. Thus, in practice, a variation of the DCF problem of estimating costs of capital can reemerge. This variation of the problem may be less severe because only the costs of capital for the cash flows from the *completed* project need be estimated, rather than for all the cash flows, including the various investment phases.

Although most analyses to date assume that the rate of forgone earnings is constant, in some cases the rate of forgone earnings depends on time (Teisberg and Teisberg, 1991) or on the value of the underlying asset (Teisberg, 1993, 1994; Teisberg Associates and Applied Decision Analyses, Inc., 1990). For example, competitive entry or regulatory profit restrictions may be more likely to apply when the value of a completed project is high and the industry is profitable. The need to estimate the rate of forgone earnings is analogous to the dynamic DCF problem of estimating multiple discount rates and to the issue arising in both dynamic DCF and decision analysis of estimating state-dependent probabilities since any dynamic analysis requires a careful consideration of how the parameters may change in different future states of the world.

One of the distinguishing appealing features of the option valuation approach is the fact that the list of inputs is rather short. Instead of requiring estimates of cash flows and probabilities in many possible future states and at various times, option pricing requires only six basic input parameters. In addition to the current value of the underlying asset and the rate of forgone earnings, the inputs include the variance of the rate of return on the underlying asset, the cost of pursuing the opportunity under consideration (i.e., the cost of the investment), the riskless interest rate, and the time remaining until the opportunity disappears (if there is an expiration time). Considerations in the choice of each of these additional inputs are similar to, or easier than, the considerations one faces in a dynamic DCF or decision analysis.

Of these, a most crucial input is the variance of the rate of return on the underlying asset, which represents the amount of uncertainty about the future value of the underlying asset. One can either estimate the variance of return or simply specify the range of values that the underlying asset may have at future dates. Of course, this range or variance need not remain constant. On the contrary, it is rather straightforward to include different amounts of uncertainty at different times or in different future states of the world. For example, Majd and Pindyck (1987) recognized that if learning by doing is an important aspect of the project, then the variance of the rate of return should decrease as the project progresses.

The cost of the project is usually assumed to be known. McDonald and Siegel (1986) included uncertain costs for a single-stage project. Teisberg (1988) discussed approaches for including uncertain future costs in a model of a multistage investment that cannot be completed instantaneously. However, if cost uncertainty is an important factor, the simplest option-pricing approaches may not be applicable, or will at least need some modification.

The riskless interest rate is also typically assumed to be constant over time (or known at all times) in real option pricing, as it is in dynamic DCF and decision analysis. In general, a higher riskless interest rate is known to raise the value of an option, but most results are not highly sensitive to this parameter within a reasonable range. Option-pricing models with random interest rates have been developed, particularly for banking applications such as the valuation of loans with ceilings or floors on the interest rate.[10]

The final input variable is the time at which the opportunity under consideration disappears. For many projects there is no such explicit time. In some cases, this allows for a simpler solution, such as the perpetuity case discussed in McDonald and Siegel (1986). In other cases, the problem of no clear expiration can be bypassed by assuming that there is such a final time but that it is far in the future (as in Teisberg Associates and Applied Decision Analyses, Inc., 1990). If the final time is set far enough in the future, it will present no problems in practice, just as similar assumptions are not problematic in dynamic DCF or decision analysis. There are also some real options that do disappear at set times. For example, a patent provides exclusive rights and opportunities to its owner until it expires while oil leases provide rights to explore for oil for a specified amount of time. Moreover, firms may sign agreements (with other firms or with governments) that provide rights to build or develop a project within a specified time frame. However, without some explicit agreement, a real option usually lacks a definite expiration date.

## 2.4 CHOOSING AMONG METHODS

There is no dominant choice among these methods for all cases. Dynamic DCF relies on risk-adjusted discount rates which may vary over time, with different possible states of the world, and with different components of the cash flows. There is no clear or precise way to know when enough discount rates have been included in the analysis, but one should be uncomfortable with any recommendation that is highly sensitive to discount rate assumptions. Decision analysis calculates expected utility rather than market value and is not designed to estimate the effect of a project or decision on the firm's market value or share price. However, one would presume that the value to shareholders is a primary influence on the utility of a responsible manager. Option valuation estimates the equilibrium market value of a project or decision, but it requires a good estimate of the current market value of a project that is complete, as well as a measure of forgone earnings. If these inputs cannot be observed or estimated reasonably, the option valuation approach becomes less relevant.

In some situations the choice of method may be clear. Decision analysis is a good choice if estimating the market value of the project is not the intent of the analysis. Option valuation is a good choice if the analysis is intended to estimate the market value of the project or decision and if the underlying asset value and forgone earnings can be estimated accurately. Dynamic discounted cash flow analysis is a good alternative if forgone earnings cannot be estimated in a meaningful way but market valuation remains the goal and risk remains relatively constant.

There are other situations in which one of the approaches is clearly inappropriate. For example, the option valuation approach becomes less appropriate if the underlying asset is not valued in the market and cannot be estimated with confidence. For example, a research and development project can be modeled as an option on the product of the research, but if that product is not yet made and is not under development by any other market-traded firm, there may be no market data to determine the value of the underlying asset. A simple rule of thumb is to ask whether it is possible to invest in the results of this type of project by investing in other market-traded firms or assets. If the answer is yes, there may be market data on the underlying asset value (although it may not be easy to isolate), while if the answer is no, option pricing may be inappropriate. Similarly, decision analysis is inappropriate if market valuation is critical or if the relevant decision maker cannot be identified. Decision analysis estimates the expected utility of a project, so the appropriate utility function must be well defined.

All three approaches offer the benefits of a fully dynamic analysis; they include the effects of uncertainty and possible future decisions on the current decision and on the project valuation. Thus, any of them can be used to estimate the value of future decision flexibility, such as the ability to accelerate, delay, or cancel the project or to switch inputs or outputs (as in flexible manufacturing systems). Any of these approaches also makes it possible to calculate the value of gathering additional information before investing, or to calculate the value of investing at low levels to learn more about the project. Furthermore, each of the approaches enables a consideration of possible future actions or strategies of competitors, which cannot be considered in static analyses.

In general, dynamic analyses provide a framework for a more careful consideration of future uncertainty. Thus, the process of performing a dynamic analysis tends to broaden one's view of future possibilities and sharpen the logic of one's thinking about various strategic alternatives. The process itself can be more important than the particular analytical results. From this perspective, to the extent that option valuation enables the analyst to avoid estimating cash flows and their risks, it may shorten a valuable process of learning about the implications of various future scenarios.[11]

## 2.5    INSIGHTS FROM DYNAMIC ANALYSIS

Strategic investment decisions often require an allocation of resources that is irreversible (or costly to reverse). Flexibility to change the course, pace, or use of the project in the future may be valuable to the firm if the future unfolds in an unexpected way. For example, if a new plant designed to make "widgets" can also be used to make "gadgets," the firm can reduce the risk of exposure to bad conditions in the "widget" industry. Similarly, there may be value in having dual-fired boilers to reduce exposure to fuel price risk. There also can be value in being able to accelerate, delay, or abandon a project if industry conditions develop differently than expected.

The value of flexibility and the effect of future flexibility on current decisions can be significant. McDonald and Siegel (1986) provided examples in which uncertainty accounts for 5 to 100 percent of the value of an option to invest. Majd and Pindyck (1987) showed investment decision thresholds that differ from a "naive net present value analysis" by more than a factor of 20 when the future is very uncertain. Trigeorgis and Mason (1987) presented a simple example in which the value of flexibility is one-third of the project value. In general, the value of flexibility depends on the *chance* that it will become optimal to change the initial strategy and the additional *value* of the new strategy when it is used. Flexibility has more value when future uncertainty is high, when the cost of altering the project or strategy is low, when variable costs or future expenses are high relative to fixed costs, when the pattern of required investments is very uneven, or when the riskless interest rate is high. In a dynamic analysis these characteristics can all raise the value of the opportunity to invest.

The nature of future uncertainty, as well as the amount of uncertainty, can significantly affect strategic investment choices. On one hand, if uncertainty is resolved or reduced by investment, it may be optimal to invest even when the net present value (without flexibility) is negative. Thus, dynamic analyses tend to suggest more aggressive strategies for research projects or projects that involve learning by doing. On the other hand, if uncertainty is not reduced by investment, it may be optimal to delay investment in spite of a positive net present value (without flexibility). Thus, dynamic analyses tend to suggest less aggressive investment in projects such as capacity expansion or new plant additions unless there are costs to delay, such as outlays that are increasing faster than the rate of inflation, lost sales prior to project completion, or threats of competitive entry, preemption, or brand establishment.

In addition, dynamic analyses indicate that a longer window of opportunity to invest adds value to a project and that a longer investment lead time can reduce a project's value. Moreover, the value of a longer window of opportunity and the cost of a longer lead time can be estimated quantitatively with these techniques. This not only helps in valuing strategic investment opportunities but also can aid in the negotiation of contracts and lease terms.

## 2.6   CONCLUSION

Overall, the use of any of the dynamic approaches discussed here will enable a decision maker to include more strategic considerations in the analysis of a project than would a static analysis, which neglects uncertainty and possible responses to an uncertain future. These dynamic approaches also make possible a consideration of the interactions among decisions and events over time and among projects that are interdependent.

Of course, the practical value of using any type of analysis hinges on how the analysis is performed. Critics of traditional discounted cash flow analysis argue that DCF fails to consider future uncertainty and strategic responses to future events. However, it is the *practice* of the method that neglects these considerations; in principle, discounted cash flow analysis can be dynamic and can incorporate uncertainty, although this requires additional work—and thought. Similarly, the other dynamic techniques require careful structuring and choice of inputs. It is important that the shortcomings of standard DCF analysis not simply be replaced with the poor practice of other techniques.

Each approach requires some inputs that are difficult to estimate. With dynamic discounted cash flow analysis, the most difficult inputs to estimate are the probabilities of future cash flows and the proper risk-adjusted discount rates. With decision analysis, the most difficult inputs are the probabilities of future cash flows and the characterization of an appropriate utility function. With option valuation, difficulty can be encountered in estimating the underlying asset value and the rate of forgone earnings.

In each case, these potential difficulties arise in the characterization and valuation of risk. Whether this valuation is explicit (as in dynamic DCF and decision analysis) or implicit (as in option pricing), no analysis completely avoids the problem. Therefore, the choice among techniques must depend on the context and should be driven by a consideration of which method can best be used to characterize and value the risks of the strategic decision in question.

## NOTES

1. See Kolbe, Morris, and Olmsted (1987) for a comparison of decision analysis and discounted cash flow analysis that indicates that differences in results are usually due to implicit or explicit assumptions and approximations. See also chapter 3, by Kasanen and Trigeorgis, in this volume.

2. See Howard, Matheson, and Miller (1977).

3. The decision maker's utility function represents both time and risk preference. However, a cómmon approximation in practice is to take the present value of cash flows (at the riskless rate or rate of time preference) for different possible outcomes and then calculate the expected utility of these present values. For further discussion of this approximation, see Pollard (1969).

4. Utility need not be measured in dollars. Instead, the expected utility can be valued by the decision maker's certain equivalent, which represents the amount of cash today that will provide the same expected utility as the uncertain future cash flows.

5. The simplification derives from the assumption that at each instant of time uncertainty can be characterized by only two possible outcomes. Since one can make the time periods extremely short, this simplification is not very restrictive.

6. The reader should be cautioned about differences in the terminology used. For example, Trigeorgis and Mason (1987) refer to what I call dynamic DCF analysis as "decision tree analysis," while I distinguish between decision analysis (based on utility theory and axioms of choice) and a dynamic or "tree" version of DCF, as discussed by Hodder and Riggs (1985).

7. Kasanen and Trigeorgis, in chapter 3 of this volume, argue that decision analysis may still be used provided the market's utility function is used rather than that of a subjective decision maker. However, some decision analysts might object to the idea that the market has a "utility function."

8. When DCF and decision analysis are formulated with continuous rather than discrete mathematics, they also appear more complicated.

9. I have also seen several real option valuations neglecting dividend effects in

unpublished analyses used by firms. Practitioners should be cautioned that the neglect of dividend effects can dramatically change the managerial implications of the analysis.

10. For a discussion of these models, see Ritchken (1987).

11. Conversely, the argument that option valuation is a weaker approach when the market value of the underlying asset and the rate of forgone earnings must be estimated from an analysis of cash flows may be spurious; one learns more about the investment opportunity in the process of doing the cash flow analysis.

# Chapter 3

# Merging Finance Theory and Decision Analysis

## Eero Kasanen and Lenos Trigeorgis

*This chapter examines the sources of discrepancy between finance and decision theory when valuing the same investment lottery. It then presents a unified approach for determining the market value of any generic lottery, based on the notion of a market utility function that merges finance's market perspective with decision theoretic methodology. The proposed approach reconciles the two paradigms, and can be used to value both primary assets and contingent claims. Although market-based, it does not rely on the ability to trade, replicate or otherwise justify risk-neutral valuation in pricing options. Numerical simulation results are presented for a variety of plausible market utility functions "calibrated" from observed stock market data and then utilized to consistently price stock options.*

## 3.1  INTRODUCTION

The concepts, methodologies, and numerical valuation results frequently differ when the same risky investment (or "lottery") is valued using financial rather than decision theoretic analysis. From a theoretical point of view, many scholars may find it disturbing that there are two competing frameworks that address similar questions (with seemingly different apparatuses) but resulting in different answers. From a practical point of view, managers would appreciate it if various scholars could come up with consistent answers when starting from the same basic assumptions and information.

This chapter examines the sources of such discrepancy and proceeds to present a unified valuation framework integrating the paradigms of finance theory and decision analysis. The underlying premise is that if the two approaches are asked to adopt the same (i.e., the market's) perspective and use the same information (i.e., the relevant market information rather than subjective estimates), they should arrive at the same answer when valuing the same investment lottery. One key part of our inquiry is to determine the value to the firm of a nontraded asset, such as a real option. To this end, we rely on the concept of a market utility function to characterize the capital market's presumed consistent attitude toward risky investment lotteries. We assume that the capital market can be viewed as a composite decision maker having a utility function over its end wealth that can be used in estimating the market value of any investment lottery, including options. We thus propose observing capital market behavior (i.e., examining the prices of risky assets and other market data) to infer the nature of the market utility function and then using it to determine the market price of other risky assets.

Our results demonstrate that several reasonable utility functions from the linear risk tolerance (LRT) class that appeared in the literature (negative exponential, quadratic, generalized logarithmic, and the constant proportional risk aversion family) can potentially be used to characterize the risk behavior of the market within certain (risk aversion) parameter ranges. If the market has a consistent risk structure (as can be described by one of the above-mentioned utility families) in its behavior toward valuing various investment lotteries, then a particular market utility function can be specified, using market data to determine its risk aversion parameter. This particular "calibrated" market utility function can then be used to determine the market value of any type of investment lottery, be it a financial or real asset, a primary or derivative security, and traded or not.

Our numerical simulation results illustrate that a reasonable market utility function can be used to value options often with better than 0.1 percent accuracy, as compared to the value derived from standard (binomial) risk-neutral option pricing. Interestingly enough, the standard replication argument that enables risk-neutral valuation of options is not needed. In standard option pricing where option values are determined relative to the underlying asset price, since an investor's utility function does not affect option prices, we typically assume for convenience that investors are risk neutral (implying linear utility) and adjust the probabilities for the investment lottery accordingly, so that there is consistency in that the true underlying stock price is the value obtained in such a risk-neutral world. An alternate approach would be to adopt another assumption about preferences (e.g., a power utility function) and then to adjust the probabilities in such a way that the stock is again consistently priced. In some sense, our approach can be thought of as a variation of this procedure. We select a one-parameter market utility function (from the LRT class), and instead of adjusting probabilities to ensure consistency, we use the aggregate risk aversion coefficient ($m$) as the free parameter. This parameter is selected so as to ensure consistency with the value of the market, which in turn provides consistency with the underlying stock price.

In this respect, whether traded or not, options are treated here like any other generic investment lottery whose cash flows are valued by the market in the same way. Thus, instead of treating decision analysis and finance as different disciplines, and rather than using two valuation techniques within finance for valuing different types of securities (i.e., the Capital Asset Pricing Model for primary securities and option pricing for contingent claims), the proposed market utility approach provides a unified valuation framework for any type of investment lottery, whether traded or not. It thus marries finance theory with decision analysis applied to investment decision making under a single valuation paradigm by forcing the latter to adopt a market perspective.

The rest of the chapter is organized as follows. Section 3.2 examines the similarities and differences between finance theory and decision theory. Section 3.3 explains the concept of a market utility and discusses possible candidate utility families. Section 3.4, after recasting the decision problem from the market perspective and providing a translation of input information between the two disciplines so as to place them on an equal footing, proceeds to present the proposed market utility valuation model as applied to a generic investment lottery. Section 3.5 describes the procedure for testing the model in the case of valuing stock options. Comparative numerical simulation results testing several reasonable market utility functions are also presented, using standard option pricing as a benchmark. A summary and concluding remarks are provided in section 3.6.

## 3.2  FINANCE THEORY AND DECISION ANALYSIS: A COMPARISON

Finance theory and decision analysis are two approaches concerned with the same problem of how to make optimal investment decisions, but looking at the problem from a different perspective and often using a different set of assumptions and input data. This section reviews the similarities and differences between these two approaches as they are traditionally applied, in order to better understand the circumstances under which they may give the same or, on the other hand, significantly divergent answers to the same investment problem.[1] The underlying premise of this chapter is that if the two approaches adopt the same (i.e., the stockholders' or the market's) perspective, they should arrive at the same value when looking at the same problem with the same data.

Finance theory and decision analysis are similar in many respects. They are both concerned with the valuation of risky investments or lotteries. In particular, both attempt to determine the present (certain) value of a future uncertain lottery or stream of cash flows. To this end, they both project the possible future cash flows over time, depending on future developments and subsequent decisions.[2] They also agree that certain (or certainty-equivalent) cash flows should be discounted at the risk-free interest rate to reflect the time value of money.

The major difference between the two approaches concerns from whose perspective value is to be determined, which may then lead to differences in accounting for risk. In this respect, decision theory can accommodate the perspective of any decision maker (often the corporate manager, but possibly stockholders, employees, society, etc.). The risk attitude of the particular decision maker is thus quantified through his or her subjective utility function, and choices are made by selecting the investment alternative providing the highest expected utility based on certain axioms of consistent, rational behavior (see von Neumann and Morgenstern, 1947).

Finance theory, on the other hand, is more focused in that it only adopts the perspective of the stockholders or investors in the market (i.e., it is based on market equilibrium). The impact of an investment decision is not measured in terms of its subjective worth to an arbitrary decision maker, such as the manager or society at large, but rather in terms of its value to the market or its contribution to stockholder or investor wealth. Thus, the market value of a lottery is the same to all investors. What matters is the risk attitude of the *market*, which is seen as the only relevant decision maker. In finance, this market risk attitude is typically captured by adding a "market risk premium" to the risk-free interest rate when calculating the risk-adjusted rate used to discount the expected future cash flows. The risk premium reflects the market's attitude toward the risk inherent in those cash flows and must equal the extra return expected in the market by similar investments of comparable risk. Recognizing that stockholders and investors in the market have opportunities to trade and borrow that enable them to eliminate firm- or project-specific risks by diversifying their portfolios, finance academics and practitioners frequently determine an investment's market risk premium from the Capital Asset Pricing Model (CAPM), which posits a direct relationship between the risk premium and the investment's non-diversifiable or market risk, as measured by its beta ($\beta$). Of course, if one looks at the same cash flows from a different perspective (e.g., the manager's or the employees' viewpoint), the same project- or firm-specific risks (e.g., technical risks in R and D) may no longer be fully diversifiable, leading to a divergence between decision theory's subjective value estimates and finance theory's market-based valuation.[3]

Let us illustrate the basic similarities and fundamental differences between decision analysis and finance theory by examining how they would approach the same single-period generic investment lottery. The term lottery is used here to describe a generic investment opportunity offering the right to a future uncertain cash payoff. In this sense, all risky projects, stocks, bonds, financial or real options, whether traded or not, are seen as generic lotteries. The basic problem is to determine the current value of such a lottery.

Consider the following generic investment lottery offering a cash payoff, $L^+$, with probability $p$, or $L^-$ with complementary probability, next period:

$$L \quad \begin{array}{c} p \quad L^+ \\ \diagup \\ \diagdown \\ 1-p \quad L^- \end{array} \qquad (\star)$$

To determine the current value, $L$, of this lottery, one has to address questions such as the following:

1. Who is the decision maker? Specifically, are we interested in the subjective reservation price of an individual decision maker or in the equilibrium market price?

2. What are the characteristics of the decision maker (e.g., wealth, risk attitudes, access to lending and borrowing opportunities, ability to diversify, etc.)?

3. What are the characteristics of the investment lottery itself (e.g., spread of possible outcomes, correlation with the market, tradeability, etc.)?

4. What are the characteristics of the market (e.g., are similar lotteries traded; are prices of traded lotteries set by large, well-diversified investors; are risk-free lending and borrowing available, etc.)?

A stylized decision theoretic approach to this problem may proceed as follows. First, we would determine the utility function, $u(\ )$, capturing the basic risk attitudes of a specified decision maker (e.g., a corporate manager).[4] Given the characteristics of this generic lottery $(\star)$, the certainty equivalent value of the uncertain lottery payoff one year from now, $L_1$, can then be determined as follows:

$$L_1 = u^{-1}[pu(L^+) + (1-p)u(L^-)]. \qquad (3.1)$$

Once the inherent lottery uncertainty has been accounted for through the utility function, the future certainty equivalent can then be discounted at the risk-free interest rate, $r$, to obtain the current lottery value, $L$, namely,

$$L = u^{-1}[pu(L^+) + (1-p)u(L^-)]/(1+r). \tag{3.2}$$

Alternatively, this may be expressed as:

$$u[L(1+r)] = pu(L^+) + (1-p)u(L^-). \tag{3.2'}$$

That is, the current lottery value, $L$, must be such that the utility of the incremental wealth from the sale of the lottery (invested at the risk-free rate) one year from now should equal the expected utility of the uncertain lottery payoffs at that time.

More generally, however, the analysis of incremental wealth resulting from the lottery itself is not sufficient to fully capture the risk attitudes of the decision maker, as they may also depend on his or her other current wealth (or initial endowment), $W$. Suppose the outside wealth of the decision maker next period will be $W_1$ (this may be just $W[1+r]$, or it may itself be another uncertain lottery). Then, if the utility function is defined over total end wealth, the break-even price of the lottery (making the decision maker indifferent between choosing to either sell or keep the lottery), $L_u$, can be obtained from:[5]

$$u[W_1 + L_u(1+r)] = pu(W_1 + L^+) + (1-p)u(W_1 + L^-). \tag{3.3}$$

Decision theory would thus provide an estimate of the subjective reservation value derived from the lottery, given the level of outside wealth of the specified decision maker and the risk-free interest rate. The proper application of decision analysis thus takes into account the situation of the particular decision maker, in addition to the characteristics of the specific lottery. Risk preferences and outside assets do enter the valuation through the mind of the decision maker and affect his or her assessment of value. The risk-free rate is, of course, obtained from the capital markets. Risk is thus accounted for through the specific decision maker's subjective utility function, while the time dimension is captured through the risk-free discount rate.

We next present a stylized version of the standard financial discounted cash flow approach to the same lottery. The present value of the lottery, $L$, is typically determined by discounting the expected value of its end-of-period cash payoffs, $E(L)$, at a risk-adjusted rate ($k$):

$$L = E(L)/(1+k) = [pL^+ + (1-p)L^-]/(1+k). \tag{3.4}$$

The key task in finance, then, often centers on estimating the proper discount rate, $k$. Assuming that investors have opportunities to diversify and that they would therefore pay a premium only for nondiversifiable or market risk, finance academics and practitioners would typically obtain the discount rate from the Capital Asset Pricing Model (CAPM):

$$k = r + \beta(E(R_M) - r), \tag{3.5}$$

where $r$ is the risk-free interest rate (also used in the decision theoretic approach), $E(R_M)$ is the expected market rate of return, and $\beta$ is the lottery's systematic risk capturing the covariance of the lottery return, $R_L$, with the market return, $R_M$, obtained from $\beta = Cov(R_L, R_M)/Var(R_M)$.

Note that an individual decision maker's risk preferences or other wealth do not affect the lottery value from a finance viewpoint. Finance theory is interested only in the lottery's market value, namely, the price at which one could, as opposed to would want to, sell or buy the lottery in the market. According to "the law of one price," if there is a developed market for the lottery, it will have a well-defined market price, irrespective of whether the owner of the lottery has a higher or lower subjective reservation value.[6]

A basic underlying premise in financial theory is that capital markets already price all types of lotteries for well-diversified investors, and so the real task is to identify equivalent pairs (or "twin lotteries") to enable pricing of the lottery at hand. By contrast, decision analysis typically views each lottery and decision maker as being in a unique situation and focuses on maximizing personal utility, ignoring other potentially relevant information that is available in the market.

The same differences in perspective may lead the two approaches to somewhat different valuations in the case of multiperiod sequential decisions or contingent claims as well. However, it is worth noting that although decision theory relies on the same valuation methodology (based on decision tree analysis), finance, in practice, has to set aside its standard discounted cash flow (DCF) paradigm, which typically relies on the CAPM for estimating the discount rate, since the appropriate discount rate changes in a complex way (i.e., it does not remain constant) in the case of such discretionary asymmetric claims. Instead, finance turns to a different paradigm, based on option pricing or contingent claims analysis (CCA), to properly value such asymmetric claims or contingent investments.

In fact, option pricing can be seen as a special (risk-neutral) version of decision analysis that recognizes market opportunities to trade and borrow (see Trigeorgis and Mason, 1987). That is, it is a version of decision analysis that has adopted the market perspective, allowing determination of expected values using risk-neutral probabilities and discounting at the risk-free rate. Could a more general version of decision analysis with different risk structures, other than risk-neutrality, provide the same answers as option pricing or CAPM if armed with the market perspective?

Our answer is, in principle, certainly. If managers are supposed to act in the best interests of stockholders and the question of interest involves the *market* value of an investment or lottery, both finance and decision theory must adopt the market perspective, and their answers, using the same input information, must converge. Moreover, this must be the relevant question for any investment made by a public company, whether the investment is traded or not, and whether it is a primary or a derivative asset. The fundamental question of interest to finance is "how much would the asset be worth if it were to become part of the asset pool of the firm whose stock is traded, or, what is its value to the market?" The same question may even be of relevance to privately held firms if they might consider becoming public sometime in the future.

In what follows we attempt to merge the above two approaches under a unified valuation framework (which encompasses CAPM and option pricing) by adopting finance's market perspective while using classical decision theoretic methodology. To this end, we rely on the concept of a market utility function to characterize the capital market's attitude toward risky investments or lotteries.

## 3.3   THE CONCEPT OF MARKET UTILITY

Being interested in the *market* value of an investment lottery, let us follow the decision theoretic methodology but think of the "decision maker" as being the entire capital market, therefore taking all relevant market information into consideration. (In this case, the decision maker's other wealth would be the total market wealth, i.e., $W = M$). If the market is rational and consistent in its decision-making behavior toward investment lotteries, we could then estimate a market utility function that would enable us to calculate the market's reservation price for any lottery (i.e., its market price). This argument is based on the following *market utility hypothesis*:

> The aggregation of investors in the market ("the market") has an
> inherent, consistent risk attitude toward any investment lottery that
> can be characterized by a "market utility function." The market price
> of any investment lottery can be determined as if the capital markets
> apply the market utility function over total market wealth (including
> the lottery).[7]

Although the size of the market (relative to that of the lottery) is not traditionally included in financial valuation models, it can not be ruled out *a priori* that the size of a firm relative to the market might affect the market price, even if the firm's riskiness remains unchanged. Note also that although the functional form of the market utility function may be stable, its particular parameter values may vary with time, the business cycle, and similar factors.[8]

It remains, of course, an empirical question as to which family of utility functions is the best proxy for the market utility. Some plausible candidates that have been used in the literature include the quadratic (see Mossin, 1973, for its use especially in connection with CAPM; Rubinstein, 1974; Dybvig and Ingersoll, 1982); the negative exponential (see Raiffa, 1970; Pratt, Raiffa, and Schlaifer, 1965; Rubinstein, 1974); the generalized logarithmic utility (see Hakansson, 1970; Rubinstein, 1976a; Kraus and Litzenberg, 1975); and the constant relative or proportional risk aversion (CPRA) family, which includes the power functions (see Rubinstein, 1976b; Samuelson and Merton, 1969; Hansen and Singleton, 1983).

All the above candidate utility functions that we test represent the most commonly analyzed families that are part of the widely used linear risk tolerance (LRT) class of utility functions (see Ingersoll, 1987). This class of utility functions is able to capture most qualitatively varying, realistic risk attitudes, and it produces portfolio separation in which investors' portfolio choices over risky securities are independent of their individual wealth positions (see Cass and Stiglitz, 1970). With homogeneous investor expectations, it gives a two-fund separation whereby all investors hold combinations of two basic portfolios.

The *quadratic* utility function has been widely used in the academic literature and is the basis for commonly justifying the CAPM economy. Although firmly linked to CAPM theory, it has some problematic features since utility may decline after a certain wealth level and since it implies increasing absolute and relative risk aversion, which seems counterintuitive (see Huang and Litzenberg, 1988; or Copeland and Weston, 1988). However, it allows aggregation under homogeneous beliefs (see Mossin, 1973). The *negative exponential* utility exemplifies constant absolute risk aversion. The *power* utility function family exhibits constant proportional risk aversion and decreasing absolute risk aversion (while the marginal utility of wealth is positive and decreasing with wealth). These properties are intuitively plausible at the individual investor level, as well as being consistent with empirical findings by Friend and Blume (1975). The linear utility can, of course, be seen as a special case capturing risk neutrality (underlying standard option valuation). The *generalized logarithmic* utility (see Rubinstein, 1976a) exhibits decreasing absolute risk aversion and tolerates heterogeneity along with constant, increasing, or decreasing proportional risk aversion. (The simple logarithmic utility captures only constant proportional risk aversion.)

For this class of utility functions (under homogeneity conditions regarding beliefs and tastes), an aggregate or group utility function is shown to exist even in incomplete markets (see Rubinstein, 1974) and, therefore, we can price investment lotteries as if there were such a market utility function. In section 3.5, we present numerical simulation results using these functions as possible proxies for the market utility function, with standard risk-neutral option pricing used as a reference case. The structure of the market utility model is presented next, after ensuring that finance and decision analysis are placed on an equal footing by using the market's perspective and information set.

## 3.4   RECASTING THE DECISION PROBLEM FROM THE MARKET PERSPECTIVE (OR PLACING FINANCE AND DECISION ANALYSIS ON AN EQUAL FOOTING)

If decision theory were to adopt the market perspective by viewing the market as being *the* relevant decision maker and to use all relevant market information (including the size of market wealth), then the link between the cash payoffs of the given generic investment lottery, $L$, and the market wealth lottery, $M$, should be modeled explicitly. In finance, this link is typically captured through the beta or covariance of the lottery with the market return. Thus, instead of having two separate lotteries (with corresponding probabilities $p$ and $q$ for the lottery and market state payoffs),

$$
\begin{array}{cc}
& p \quad L^{+} \\
& \quad / \\
L & \\
& \quad \backslash \\
& 1-p \quad L^{-}
\end{array}
\qquad
\begin{array}{cc}
& q \quad M^{+} \\
& \quad / \\
M & \\
& \quad \backslash \\
& 1-q \quad M^{-}
\end{array}
$$

we must now directly capture their interdependencies through a combined conditional lottery.

### 3.4.1   A Conditional Generic Investment Lottery

Consider the following contingent lottery ($\star\star$) with built-in interactions with the market wealth movement:[9]

$$
M,L \;
\begin{array}{l}
\quad\; q \;\nearrow\; M^+ \;
\begin{array}{l}
p_1 \;\nearrow\; L^+ \\[4pt]
1-p_1 \;\searrow\; L^-
\end{array} \\[20pt]
1-q \;\searrow\; M^- \;
\begin{array}{l}
p_2 \;\nearrow\; L^+ \\[4pt]
1-p_2 \;\searrow\; L^-
\end{array}
\end{array}
\qquad (\star\star)
$$

Note that, in general, the probabilities of low or high lottery payoffs (e.g., $p_1, p_2$) are conditional on the market movements, in other words, on whether the market moves up, $M^+$, or down, $M^-$.

Of course, certain conditions of consistency between the contingent and the initial lottery must be satisfied. In particular, in terms of probabilities,

$$qp_1 + (1-q)p_2 = p. \qquad (3.6)$$

## 3.4.2   Translating between Decision Theoretic and Financial Input Variables

To ensure that decision theory and finance are placed on an equal footing, in that not only do they both adopt the same (i.e, the market) perspective, but they also both use the same information set, this section provides an explicit transformation between the set of variables and concepts used in CAPM-based finance theory and those used in decision analysis. The following basic definitional relationships will be useful in the process of translating from the decision-theoretic lottery inputs $(p, L^+, L^-, r; q, M, M^+, M^-, p_1, p_2)$ to the standard CAPM-based financial inputs ($E[L]$, as well as $r, \beta$, and $E[R_M]$ needed to obtain the risk-adjusted discount rate, $k$).

The expected rate of return of the generic lottery and the expected market return are, respectively:

$$
\begin{aligned}
E(R_L) &= p(L^+/L - 1) + (1-p)(L^-/L - 1) &\qquad (3.7)\\
E(R_M) &= q(M^+/M - 1) + (1-q)(M^-/M - 1).
\end{aligned}
$$

The variances of the returns for the two lotteries are given by:

$$
Var(R_L) = p(L^+/L - 1 - E(R_L))^2 + (1-p)(L^-/L - 1 - E(R_L))^2
$$

$$Var(R_M) = q(M^+/M - 1 - E(R_M))^2 + (1 - q)(M^-/M - 1 - E(R_M))^2$$
$$(3.8)$$

The systematic risk (beta) of the lottery, given the parameters of the conditional lottery $(\star\star)$, is given by:

$$
\begin{aligned}
\beta &= Cov(R_L, R_M)/Var(R_M) = (1/L)Cov(L, R_M)/Var(R_M) \qquad (3.9) \\
&= (1/L)[qp_1(M^+/M - 1 - E(R_M))(L^+ - E(L)) \\
&\quad + q(1 - p_1)(M^+/M - 1 - E(R_M))(L^- - E(L)) \\
&\quad + (1 - q)p_2(M^-/M - 1 - E(R_M))(L^+ - E(L)) \\
&\quad + (1 - q)(1 - p_2)(M^-/M - 1 - E(R_M))(L^- - E(L))]/Var(R_M),
\end{aligned}
$$

where $E(L) = pL^+ + (1 - p)L^-$.

We have not yet made any assumptions regarding the utility function or the probability distribution of the uncertain payoffs. Given the task of finding the market value of the basic lottery, $L$, we know under both paradigms the basic facts of the lottery, $p, L^+, L^-$; the current market wealth, $M$; and the risk-free rate, $r$. In the decision-theoretic approach, we are also given the parameters of the conditional lottery $(\star\star)$, namely, $q, M^+, M^-, p_1, p_2$. From this, one can obtain the basic parameters needed in the standard CAPM-based finance valuation scheme, namely, $E(L), \beta, E(R_M)$.

Regarding the opposite translation, suppose instead that we are given (or we can estimate) the standard CAPM-based financial inputs, such as $E(R_M), Var(R_M)$, and $\beta$ of the lottery. We would now like to transform these input variables in a way that is usable in the decision-theoretic framework. First, we need to determine the parameters of the market lottery $(q, M^+, M^-)$. Because there are three parameters in the market lottery but only the mean and variance of the distribution of the market return are given, we actually have a wide choice for the set of parameters $q, M^+$, and $M^-$. For modeling convenience, or if a particular distribution (such as lognormal) is more appropriate, we can impose other suitable functional conditions. For example, a convenient symmetric condition is the geometric relationship (suitable for the lognormal distribution),

$$M^+ = gM; \qquad\qquad M^- = (1/g)M. \qquad (3.10)$$

Given the standard financial inputs, $E(R_M)$ and $Var(R_M)$, and observing the market value, $M$, we can derive the values of $q$ and $g$ (needed to obtain $M^+, M^-$) from the basic relations (3.7) and (3.8). The resulting set of equations can be solved numerically. We can thus "calibrate" the geometric market lottery so that it is consistent with the required mean and variance of the distribution of the market rate of return.

Having determined the parameters of the market lottery, we next need to obtain the missing parameters for the conditional lottery ($\star\star$), $p_1$ and $p_2$. Recall that so far, we know $p$, $L^+$, and $L^-$ (from the original lottery); we can observe or estimate $M, \beta, E(R_M)$, and $Var(R_M)$ (from the market); and we can derive $q, g, M^+$, and $M^-$ (from the previous equations). Treating these parameters as given (constants) and $L$ as variable, it can readily be verified from Equation (3.9) for beta and the consistency condition in Equation (3.6) for the probabilities that $p_1$ and $p_2$ are linear functions of $L$. To see this, solving Equation (3.6) for $p_1$ gives:

$$p_1 = A + Bp_2, \tag{3.11}$$

where $A = p/q$, and $B = (q-1)/q$. From Equation (3.9) we can then obtain:

$$\beta = (Cp_1 + Dp_2 + E)/L, \tag{3.12}$$

where the coefficients $C, D$, and $E$ are given by:

$$
\begin{aligned}
C &= q(g - 1 - E(R_M))(L^+ - L^-)/Var(R_M), \\
D &= (1 - q)((1/g) - 1 - E(R_M))(L^+ - L^-)/Var(R_M), \\
E &= [qg + (1 - q)/g - 1 - E(R_M)](L^- - E(L))/Var(R_M).
\end{aligned}
$$

Substituting Equation (3.11) into (3.12) and solving for $p_2$, we obtain:

$$p_2 = FL + G, \tag{3.13}$$

with the coefficients $F$ and $G$ given by:

$$F = \beta/(BC + D); \quad G = -(AC + E)/(BC + D).$$

Finally, substituting $p_2$ from Equation (3.13) back into (3.11) above, yields:

$$p_1 = HL + I, \tag{3.14}$$

where $H = BF$, and $I = A + BG$.

We have thus obtained all the input data for the conditional lottery—$q, g(M^+, M^-), p_1$, and $p_2$—that is required for the market utility-based decision-theoretic valuation, given the standard inputs used in the finance-theoretic framework. Given an appropriate market utility function, we can then derive the price of a given lottery, whether traded or not, using the contingent lottery and pricing equation developed in the next section.

### 3.4.3 A Market Utility-Based Valuation

Once the market is seen as the relevant decision maker, we can then apply its utility function over its end wealth (including the lottery) to determine the price it would pay for that lottery. The market's price, $L_u$, would be the value inducing indifference between its expected utility over end market wealth next year *with* the lottery versus *without* the lottery, but after receiving the sale price, which can be invested at the riskless rate. The pricing equation thus becomes:

$$Eu(M + L) = Eu(M + L_u(1 + r)), \qquad (3.15)$$

which in the case of the above conditional lottery ($\star\star$), becomes:[10]

$$\begin{aligned}
&q(p_1 u(M^+ + L^+) + (1 - p_1)u(M^+ + L^-)) \\
&+ (1 - q)(p_2 u(M^- + L^+) + (1 - p_2)u(M^- + L^-)) \\
&= qu(M^+ + L_u(1 + r)) + (1 - q)u(M^- + L_u(1 + r)).
\end{aligned} \qquad (3.15')$$

Furthermore, if the market is indifferent between keeping its current wealth with certainty (growing at the risk-free rate) or receiving the uncertain market lottery, we can then also impose the following market lottery consistency condition:[11]

$$u(M(1 + r)) = qu(M^+) + (1 - q)u(M^-). \qquad (3.16)$$

This condition may be used to simplify the right-hand side of the pricing Equation (3.15), and it is also used later in estimating the parameter of the market utility function.

### 3.4.4   An Approximate Analytic (Practical) Valuation

As an approximation, the pricing equation may be reduced to a more compact analytic expression. For example, if the lottery (e.g., the value of the firm) is very small compared to the market lottery (i.e., the value of all assets in the market), then the changes in the market utility due to the lottery value changes can be closely estimated using first-order Taylor series expansion around the relevant market wealth.

For instance, using first-order Taylor series approximation (involving the first derivative of the market utility function around the market wealth, $u'[M]$), it can be seen that the price equation, (3.15), becomes

$$E(u(M) + Lu'(M)) = E(u(M) + L_u(1 + r)u'(M)), \qquad (3.17)$$

which, after some rearrangement, results in the compact expression:

$$L_u = \frac{E(L) + \frac{Cov(L, u'(M))}{Eu'(M)}}{(1 + r)}. \qquad (3.18)$$

Note the close resemblance between this pricing equation and the certainty-equivalent version of the CAPM relationship, where the first derivative of the market utility function around the market wealth, $u'(M)$, is here used instead of the market return, $R_M$. This expression permits a closed-form approximation of the lottery's current market value if the market utility function has a compact expression for its first derivative.

## 3.5 TESTING MARKET UTILITY FUNCTIONS FOR VALUING OPTIONS

The underlying premise of our approach to investment valuation has been that we can derive a market utility function from observed capital market behavior (i.e., by examining the prices of risky assets, changes in market wealth, and other market data) and then use it to consistently price any other primary or derivative asset, whether traded or not. This is fundamentally an empirical issue. A priori, we do not really know if the capital market actually behaves as if it has an aggregate utility function or what the shape of an appropriate market utility function might be.

The case of pricing options on company stock provides perhaps the best benchmark for testing the market utility valuation approach. In finance, options are treated as contingent claims or derivative securities that can be accurately priced by constructing an equivalent replicating portfolio from traded securities. The ability to continuously trade and replicate the option, which enables risk-neutral valuation, is considered crucial to standard option pricing.

Under the market utility valuation framework, an option is treated as just another generic investment lottery that can be valued using the same market utility function. No assumptions concerning the ability to trade or replicate the option, or to justify risk-neutral valuation, are needed under this framework.[12] The *market* value of an option to a public company should be the same, as long as it would provide the same cash flows in any state of nature, whether the option is traded or not and whether it is a financial or real option.[13] The cash flows to the public firm should be precisely the same, as should be their contribution to the market value of the firm (as would eventually be reflected in its stock price).

The testing procedure for determining the market utility function to be used in pricing an option would be similar to that for any other lottery. The specific form of the market utility function is estimated from the market lottery, while ensuring that the value obtained by applying the market utility to the underlying stock lottery is consistent with the observed underlying stock price. Then, the option price is calculated by applying this market utility function to the combined option-market lottery. More specifically, the test procedure follows these steps:

1. Assume the market's attitude toward any risky lottery can be described, in turn, by a single-parameter market utility function, $u(x; m)$, belonging to one of the linear risk tolerance (LRT) class of utility functions discussed earlier, namely,

   (a) the quadratic function, $x - mx^2$;

   (b) the negative exponential, $-e^{-x/m}$;

   (c) the generalized logarithmic, $ln(x + m)$; or

   (d) the power functions, $x^m$ and $-x^{-m}$ (members of the CPRA family).

2. Estimate the market utility parameter, $m$. Specifically, find the particular function from the presumed family that is consistent with the market lottery in that it satisfies the condition of market lottery consistency given in Equation (3.16). That is, given the information regarding the market lottery (i.e., $M, M^+, M^-, q$, and $r$), determine the parameter value, $m$, such that the above-mentioned market consistency condition holds. This specifies a particular function out of the presumed market utility family that can be used to price any lottery in that risk economy.

3. Check the consistency of the conditional market-stock lottery (and of the parameter, $p_2$) by ensuring that the value derived from the market utility pricing equation, (3.15), is consistent with the observed stock price. This consistency condition should hold in equilibrium if the market has the assumed risk structure.[14]

4. Determine the option payoffs at the end of the combined market-option lottery, from those of the underlying market-stock lottery $(M, M^+, M^-, q, r, S, S^+, S^-, p_1, p_2)$. (Although the payoffs are different, the probabilities will remain the same.) Then use the market utility function in Equation (3.15) to obtain the price of the option, $L_u$.

5. Repeat with another utility function, each time performing sensitivity analysis by changing the various parameters of the market, stock, and option lotteries. Finally, compare the option value obtained from the market utility valuation approach, $L_u$, with the option price, $L_o$, obtained from standard binomial, risk- neutral option pricing (see Trigeorgis and Mason, 1987; or Stapleton and Subrahmanyam, 1984) according to:

$$L_o = (p'L^+ + (1 - p')L^-)/(1 + r), \tag{3.19}$$

with the risk-neutral probability $p'$ calculated from:

$$p' = \frac{(1+r)S - S^-}{S^+ - S^-}. \tag{3.20}$$

## Table 3.1
## Numerical Results of Comparative Option Valuations Using Various Market Utility Functions

*Standard risk-neutral option pricing value (benchmark): 17.38*

| Market utility u(x; m) | m | utility price | % diff. |
|---|---|---|---|
| x - mx² | 0.200x10⁻⁶ | 17.31 | -0.400 |
| 1 - exp(-mx) | 0.686x10⁻⁶ | 17.41 | +0.201 |
| ln(x + m) | 425,204 | 16.78 | -3.466 |
| -xᵐ | 0.106 | 17.53 | +0.869 |
| xᵐ | 0.293 | 17.44 | +0.358 |

*Base-case assumptions*:
Market wealth state values, $M = 1m$; $M^+ = 1.2m$; $M^- = .833m$;
Stock state prices, $S^+ = 150$; $S^- = 66.67$;
Probabilities, $q = 0.7$; $p_1 = 0.8$; $p_2 = 0.3$;
Call option parameters: $S = 110$; $EX = 120$; $t = 1$; $r = 0.08$.

*Note:* % differences are calculated relative to the call option price determined from standard (binomial) risk-neutral option pricing as a benchmark.

Table 3.1 presents comparative numerical simulation results using the above market utility functions to value stock options, using standard (binomial) risk-neutral option pricing as a benchmark. In general, within a range of parameter values, any of the above-mentioned LRT class candidate utility functions, given consistent parameters on the underlying asset,

## Table 3.2
## Option Valuation Sensitivity Analysis Using the CPRA Market Utility Function, $u(x; m) = x^m$

| Parameter | m | option pricing | utility pricing | % diff. |
|---|---|---|---|---|
| **Market wealth, M (million)** | | | | |
| .01 | 0.293 | 17.38 | 17.38 | +0.030 |
| .1 | 0.293 | 17.38 | 17.38 | +0.015 |
| 1 | 0.293 | 17.38 | 17.44 | +0.357 |
| 10 | 0.293 | 17.38 | 17.02 | -2.074 |
| **Probability, $p_1$** | | | | |
| 0.5 | 0.293 | 17.38 | 17.44 | +0.358 |
| 0.8 | 0.293 | 17.38 | 17.44 | +0.358 |
| 0.9 | 0.293 | 17.38 | 17.44 | +0.358 |
| **Stock skewness, $S^+$ (same $S^-$)** | | | | |
| 130 | 0.293 | 22.87 | 22.94 | +0.321 |
| 150 | 0.293 | 17.38 | 17.44 | +0.357 |
| 160 | 0.293 | 15.52 | 15.53 | +0.073 |
| **Exercise price, EX** | | | | |
| 60 | 0.293 | 54.44 | 54.50 | +0.100 |
| 90 | 0.293 | 34.75 | 34.89 | +0.399 |
| 110 | 0.293 | 23.17 | 23.18 | +0.034 |
| 120 | 0.293 | 17.38 | 17.44 | +0.358 |
| **Risk-free interest rate, r** | | | | |
| 0.078 | 0.16 | 17.34 | 17.10 | -1.368 |
| 0.080 | 0.29 | 17.38 | 17.44 | +0.358 |
| 0.084 | 0.57 | 17.46 | 17.44 | -0.088 |
| 0.088 | 0.85 | 17.54 | 17.58 | -0.248 |

*Base case assumptions*:
Market wealth state values, M = 1m; $M^+$ = 1.2m; $M^-$ = .833m;
Stock state prices, $S^+$ = 150; $S^-$ = 66.67;
Probabilities, q = 0.7; $p_1$ = 0.8; $p_2$ = 0.3;
Call option parameters: S = 110; EX = 120; t = 1; r = 0.08.

*Note:* % differences are calculated relative to the standard (binomial) risk-neutral option pricing (which has a base-case value of 17.38, with base-case $m = 0.293$).

could price the options very accurately, often within 0.1 percent from standard option pricing.[15] The negative exponential, the quadratic, and the power functions performed quite well, with the logarithmic utility function resulting in the largest deviation.

Sensitivity analysis results in the case of the (CPRA) power utility function relative to standard option pricing are shown in Table 3.2. The results appear robust with respect to beta ($p_1$) and stock skewness, but are somewhat sensitive to the option's exercise price (EX) relative to the (given) underlying stock price and to the riskless interest rate. The above sensitivity analysis of the intuitively appealing power utility function did not reveal any disturbing anomalies. The results for other utility functions are similar. In general, these option valuation results verify that if the aggregate market utility function is calibrated to be consistent with the market and the stock lotteries, it will also work reliably with derivative securities.

The overall results confirm that the idea of first estimating the aggregate market utility function from the market lottery consistent with market data and then using it to price other assets seems promising. The various candidate market utility functions from the LRT class, when calibrated with the market and stock lotteries, produced quite accurate and consistent option prices as compared to standard risk-neutral valuation. These simulation results did not altogether remove any of the above-mentioned LRT candidate utility functions, as the valuations were basically consistent and close to each other. These results can provide some reassurance to those interested in empirically estimating an aggregate market utility function.

## 3.6 SUMMARY AND CONCLUSION

This chapter was an attempt to merge the paradigms of finance theory and decision analysis as applied to investment valuation. The two approaches generally differ in focus (e.g., what value or value to whom) and information used, which may result in different answers. We saw that the real issue is not whether finance-theoretic valuation (e.g., utilizing expected returns and betas) is better or worse than decision-theoretic valuation (utilizing a decision maker's utilities), but rather whether we should be interested in determining the subjective reservation price of some decision maker or the market price. Of course, if one is interested in some subjective value to the corporation's top management, then traditional decision analysis (using subjective probability estimates and corporate utilities) would be appropriate generally, and this subjective value would be given by the corporate break-even (selling or buying) reservation price, which generally depends on initial wealth. Finance, however, is typically interested in the market (rather than a subjective or private) value of an asset to a publically traded company. Even if the asset is not traded, as in the case of many real options, its undertaking would eventually increase the market value of the company; thus, any public company should be interested in the *market* value of an investment, rather than in some subjective value to the company's top management.

Rather than making assumptions about individual investor preferences and their aggregation, this chapter has turned the problem around by treating the capital market as a composite decision maker. Taking the concept of a market utility to its logical conclusion and utilizing standard utility-based decision theory, we developed a market utility approach for determining the market value of any generic investment lottery, including options. This market utility approach not only constitutes a unified and consistent approach to valuing both primary and derivative assets, it also provides a link of reconciliation between market-based financial valuation and subjective, decision-theoretic valuation. The numerical results suggest that a number of plausible LRT utility functions, as estimated from market data, can potentially be used in a consistent manner in option valuation. The consistency of the market utility valuation lends new support to the rationality of market pricing. This unified approach also challenges the need to apply different valuation paradigms for different types of assets (e.g., CAPM for primary assets and option pricing for derivative assets), and it does not rely on the ability to trade, replicate or otherwise justify risk-neutral valuation in pricing either financial or real options.

## ACKNOWLEDGMENTS

Parts of this chapter draw from E. Kasanen and L. Trigeorgis (1994), with the permission of the *European Journal of Operational Research*.

## NOTES

1. For another discussion on the similarities and differences between finance theory and decision analysis, see Teisberg (chapter 2 in this volume) and the Electric Power Research Institute report (1987).

2. Typically, decision analysis is more explicit in doing so through decision trees, while finance, in the final analysis, usually compresses the possible cash flow scenarios into a single estimate of their expected value.

3. Note that in the CAPM, only the market or systematic risk is relevant, while for option pricing, the total risk is important. Both concepts of risk may

be relevant in a unified valuation framework.

4. The utility function may be estimated by simulating other basic lotteries that cover the relevant range of cash payoffs. The underlying assumption here is that such a utility function is relatively stable and can therefore be used to price other, similar lotteries.

5. This is, in fact, the selling price of the lottery. Similarly, following Raiffa (1970, pp. 89–90), the subjective value to the decision maker from buying the same lottery, $L_b$, can be determined from equating the utility of his or her end wealth (if the decision maker does not buy) with the expected utility of the resulting end wealth if the lottery is bought, net of the price paid, namely,

$$u(W_1) = pu[W_1 + L^+ - L_b(1 + r)] + (1 - p)u[W_1 + L^- - L_b(1 + r)].$$

The selling and buying prices may differ slightly, since in the selling case the decision maker's wealth is assumed to include the lottery whereas in the buying case it does not. Our numerical simulation results at the end of the chapter are based on selling prices. However, buying prices were found in each case to be very close to the corresponding selling prices, and are therefore left out since they would not add any further insight to the issues under study.

6. To an individual, it may make sense in certain cases to consider both market and personal value. For example, in selling a house with the intent to buy a new one, the individual should analyze both his or her own preferences (subjective value) and the market conditions (market prices). However, to a publicly held firm, only the market value of a lottery should be relevant.

7. Other authors have made assumptions of a similar nature. For example, Rubinstein (1976b) assumed that conditions for weak aggregation are met such that security prices are determined as though all investors had the same characteristics as a representative ("average") investor with a CPRA utility function. Our hypothesis differs in that it attributes a characteristic utility function to the whole market (aggregation of investors) rather than to any individual or average investor (who may have a different utility function). Thus, we make no assumption about individual investment behavior.

8. The same holds true with other valuation models. For example, in CAPM the functional form is assumed to be constant but parameter values may fluctuate.

9. This is simply the discrete decision tree analogue of the continuous financial input structure.

10. It is worth noting that the conditional probabilities $p_1$ and $p_2$, are, through their dependence on $\beta$, interlocked with the lottery value, $L$. Thus, the decision-theoretic valuation equation, (3.15), which follows can actually become a convo-

luted implicit equation.

11. This assumes that the market has the same consistent risk attitude toward the market lottery as toward any other lottery.

12. Rubinstein (1976b) and Samuelson and Merton (1969) have also shown that the standard option-pricing formulas can be derived in discrete time under risk aversion (e.g., assuming the average investor has a CPRA utility function) and that the existence of continuous trading opportunities enabling a riskless hedge or risk neutrality are not really necessary.

13. If the underlying asset earns a below-equilibrium return because it is not traded, as in the case of many real options, there would exist a rate of return shortfall on the underlying asset that could be treated analogously to a dividend payout in option pricing (see McDonald and Siegel, 1984). In our generalized framework, the future prices of such a nontraded asset lottery ($L^+$ and $L^-$) would be lower, as a result of the dividend shortfall, than the corresponding prices of a similar-risk, traded financial asset. Nevertheless, the same valuation framework would be applied, resulting in the same market value as with any other lottery that would provide the same future cash flows in each state.

14. Note that the probabilities $p_1$ and $p_2$ are the actual probabilities of the stock lottery in this risk economy. As in standard (binomial) option pricing, we are given the current price and distributional dynamics of the underlying stock (i.e., $S$, $S^+$, and $S^-$). However, instead of calculating an equivalent (transformed) risk-neutral probability, $p'$, we apply the actual probabilities $p_1$ and $p_2$, but ensure their consistency with the observed stock price and the given risk structure.

15. The results start to deviate when the size of the option lottery becomes large compared to the size of the total market.

# Chapter 4

# The Strategic Capital Budgeting Process: A Review of Theories and Practice

## Van Son Lai and Lenos Trigeorgis

*The resource allocation process constitutes the main vehicle for a company's strategic thrust, and eventually determines its long-run competitive position. Strategic decision making in organizations is naturally driven by "bounded rationality," involving interactions among various stakeholders. A firm's resource allocation choices should reflect both the "bottom-up" process of capital budgeting and the "top-down" process of strategic planning in a complementary and interactive fashion. We describe the basic structure of the strategic resource allocation process, and illustrate the interaction among the different levels of organizational decision making. The potential of real options to better reflect strategic investment choices is also discussed.*

## 4.1   INTRODUCTION

Strategic decisions are products of corporate planning and top management deliberations that give shape and direction to an organization (Ansoff, 1965; Hofer and Schendel, 1978). Traditional areas that are the subject of strategic decision making (SDM) include organizational change, product/market posture, research and development, mergers, and restructuring and corporate control, as well as traditional capital investment.

Capital budgeting (CB), the process by which firms allocate resources among long-term assets, provides the major vehicle for the realization of strategic vision. Many major CB decisions may prove vital to a firm's future success or ultimate failure, especially if they are not easily reversible and commit the firm to a certain long-term path. On the other hand, other infrastructure and future-building investments may allow management valuable operating and strategic flexibility to rapidly and effectively adapt to changing market conditions.

How, then, can top management effectively influence resource allocation, and hence, the strategic direction of the organization? The strategic planning and capital budgeting processes typically serve as invaluable tools in helping corporate management align short- and long-term objectives. For most major decisions in many organizations, the decentralized, project-by-project mechanical approach to resource allocation has been replaced by strategic considerations. In practice, in most firms, business-level strategies are used to focus on important strategic investment choices while ruling out other investments that do not fit corporate strategy, often regardless of their cash-flow profitability. Projects with negative NPV of expected cash flows (e.g., R and D) may often be pursued, while other positive-NPV opportunities may be discarded on the basis of "strategic fit."

Substantial strides were made in the second half of this century in both the theory and the practice of capital budgeting, as discussed in various finance textbooks (e.g., Brealey and Myers, 1991; Levy and Sarnat, 1990; Clark, Hindelang, and Pritchard, 1984). Various surveys indicate an increasingly widespread use of discounted cash flow (DCF) techniques, especially in medium- and large-sized firms.[1] However, these techniques typically focus on narrowly defined problems. Several authors (Myers, 1984; Gold, 1976; Hastie, 1974; Pinches, 1982) have argued that the current emphasis of CB is misplaced because it fails to focus on the most important strategic issues. Further, little attention has been devoted to the overall strategic question of how effectively CB interfaces with the actual resource allocation process employed in organizations. Most of the focus has been on "technical" questions related to the selection or risk adjustment process. Many executives have contributed to the problem by attempting to implement CB techniques without adequately considering the firm's strategic objectives, information systems, formal or informal organizational processes, and control, evaluation, and reward structures (Gordon and Pinches, 1984).

This chapter focuses on the interaction between the processes of strategic planning (SP) and capital budgeting (CB). It attempts to move away from the stylized structure of standard CB models (e.g., involving an immediate single-project decision by a decision maker loyal to a single constituency). The chapter reviews and synthesizes three distinct streams of managerial literature: organizational decision making, strategic planning, and capital budgeting. The literature is abundant on the financial aspects of capital budgeting on a project-by-project basis, less so on the strategic decision-making process, and scant on their interdependent relationship. We present an explicative framework to better understand the linkages between the strategic decision-making and the capital budgeting processes.

The chapter has several goals. First, we attempt to link strategic planning and decision-making models with capital budgeting. We show next that SP and CB are decision-making processes with the same basic structure. Finally, we describe the potential of real options in addressing strategic aspects of capital budgeting.

The rest of the chapter is organized as follows. Section 4.2 provides a review of the process of strategic decision making (SDM), while section 4.3 examines capital budgeting within an organizational setting. Section 4.4 explores the interrelated nature of strategic planning (SP) and capital budgeting (CB) within a strategic CB system that supports the firm's strategic direction, and then discusses the relevance of CB to SP at the corporate, business, program, and project levels. Before concluding, we reexamine various approaches to strategic CB (section 4.5), pointing out the need to integrate SP and CB within a unified framework that helps management distinguish the "forest" from the "trees," while recognizing the value of creating and managing portfolios of real options.

## 4.2   THE STRATEGIC DECISION MAKING PROCESS

This section reviews briefly the generic strategic decision making (SDM) process, which can be seen to consist of three basic steps: (1) problem formulation and objective setting, (2) identification and generation of alternative solutions, and (3) analysis and selection of a feasible alternative. Although complex and dynamic, the SDM process has an identifiable basic structure driven by behavioral forces.

Several authors have argued that there generally exist several distinct levels or phases for any decision-making process (see Bower, 1970; or Mintzberg, Raisinghani, and Theoret, 1976). Anthony (1965) and Gorry and Morton (1971) referred to three distinct levels of decision making: operating, administrative, and strategic. Operating decisions, which are usually made by lower-level managers, involve minor resource commitments that are short-run in nature, repetitive, and of a highly routine or structured form. Strategic decisions, which are largely unstructured and nonroutine due to their uniqueness, require senior management attention and major organizational resource commitments that are more long-run in nature. Between these two bounds lie administrative decisions that typically involve middle-level managers, have a medium duration, and require moderate resource commitments. Mintzberg, Raisinghani, and Theoret (1976) pointed out that even strategic decision processes without a rigid sequential progression between phases have some basic underlying structure.

Several approaches to strategy formulation and the design of a strategic-planning system have been suggested in the literature (e.g., Ansoff, 1965; Hofer and Schendel, 1978; Vancil and Lorange, 1975). Step-by-step procedures are usually included in any framework designed to formulate a corporate strategy. These steps typically include identification of the firm's mission, establishment of goals and objectives consistent with that mission, and specification of appropriate product/market strategies (i.e., resource allocation decisions) once the firm has scanned its environment to determine the opportunities that best match its particular capabilities. Normative models of strategy formulation have limited applicability and usefulness, however, unless management is able to adapt them effectively to the organization's particular decision-making process. Accordingly, some portion of the literature examines the role of behavioral factors in organizational decision making (Ackerman, 1970; Bower, 1970; Carter, 1971). This perspective focuses on the dynamics of the interactions among various individuals and organizational subunits as they endeavor to influence strategic decisions.

## 4.3   THE CAPITAL BUDGETING PROCESS

In this section, we examine the capital budgeting (CB) process as part of overall organizational decision making. That is, CB is seen as a process and structure similar to the SDM process (discussed previously.) As such, the CB process also entails several phases that are permeated with organizational influences and expectations and is not merely the mechanical selection procedure presented in most finance textbooks.

As a process, capital budgeting consists of identifying relevant investment opportunities, classifying them according to some sensible scheme used in the company, collecting needed data and information (estimating cash flows and accessing risk) for viable alternatives, weighing each project's benefits and affinity to strategic objectives against its risks and constraints, and assessing the sensitivity of different assumptions and parameters to various economic scenarios.

The three levels of decision making described earlier apply to CB as a decision-making process as well. Operating CB decisions include expenditures on such items as minor office equipment and maintainance expenditures. Administrative CB deals with expenditures for replacing standard manufacturing equipment and minor adjustments in operating production scale. Strategic CB decisions may involve decisions concerning the acquisition or divestiture of a firm division, moving into a completely new product line, or building a plant in a new geographic market. In this chapter we focus on major nonroutine or strategic CB decisions.

That CB is, in fact, a decision-making process with its own distinct phases is supported by several field studies (e.g., Ackerman, 1970; Bower, 1970; Fremgen, 1973; King, 1974; Mintzberg, Raisinghani, and Theoret, 1976). While many phases could be identified, four major stages typically prevail, namely: identification, development, selection, and control. These phases typically occur sequentially, although they often interact. Further, the decision process may be likened to an open system, which is subject to exogenous factors with feedback and (error) control loops; this is the cybernetics paradigm.

Project definition and cash flow (CF) estimation are normally considered a difficult aspect of the CB process, while project implementation and control are also notably nontrivial. Indeed, the technical financial analysis and project selection stage, which typically receives the most attention in the literature, is in many cases the least problematic aspect of the process.

In the organizational literature dealing with the process of how decisions are actually made in organizations, the principal issues of concern are related to:

- The multiple goal structure of organizations and satisficing rather than value-maximizing (Simon, 1960);

- The internal politics of strategic decision making (Fahey, 1981);

- The executive bargaining and negotiation process, along with the role of coalitions (Cyert and March, 1963); and

- The reward and punishment systems (Ackerman, 1970).

These concerns have also been examined in several studies in relation to capital budgeting. The findings suggest a much more complicated decision process prevailing in the real world than the one typically described in finance textbooks. In his seminal study of the resource allocation process, for example, Bower (1970) argued that the set of problems corporations typically refer to as CB are, in fact, strategic management problems and that the personal stakes of managers cannot be ignored. Carter (1971) further noted that firms make their actual CB decisions on the basis of various criteria and threshold levels consistent with Simon's (1960) bounded rationality.[2]

Although the finance literature has promoted discounted cash flow (DCF) techniques for the selection of capital projects based on the assumption of firm value maximization, in practice, multiple goals accommodating several constituencies are often reported (e.g., Donaldson and Lorsch, 1983). The finance literature's concentration on refining evaluation techniques has also received its share of criticism, for example, by Hastie (1974): "I am continually amazed at the academic community's preoccupation with refining capital expenditure analysis rather than with improving investment decisions. Investment decision making could be improved significantly if the emphasis were placed on asking the appropriate strategic questions rather than on increasing the sophistication of measurement techniques" (p. 36).

## 4.4 THE LINKAGE OF CAPITAL BUDGETING AND STRATEGIC PLANNING

Given the exhibited isomorphism between the strategic decision-making process and capital budgeting, it is useful to examine how the two processes can be linked interactively. We first examine the influence of strategic planning (SP) on the capital budgeting (CB) process, and later review the contribution of CB to SP at the corporate, business, program, and project levels.

### 4.4.1 The Influence of Strategic Planning on Capital Budgeting

This section aims to provide insight into the strategic CB allocation problem by reviewing the procedures used by firms in practice. It has been argued that unless CB evolves to provide some direct tools for the development and evaluation of strategic objectives and opportunities, it will only be relevant once the firm's strategic objectives have been determined through employing some other criteria as a surrogate to long-run firm value maximization (Ansoff, 1965; Pinches, 1982; Myers, 1984). Indeed, DCF and other such CB techniques are limited in practice to the evaluation of operating projects or tactical paths to operationalize a firm's given set of strategic goals. Most discussions on CB treat it as distinct from the SP process. This portrayal of the two processes as separate from each other is misleading, however, especially when strategic commitments and options are involved. In most firms in practice, major capital expenditures are closely related to the firm's strategic positioning.

Based on interviews with multidivision firms, Rosenblatt (1980) classified the CB process that is followed in practice as either bottom-up or interactive (i.e., operating in both directions). Typically, projects are initiated at the division level and tactical information is generated at lower levels of the organization. Capital allocation, guidelines on target profitability, decisions regarding the desired mix of major income sources, and the magnitude of the division budgets are generally determined at the corporate level. In large firms, an intermediate level may often exist between divisions and headquarters. A formal system is often used to facilitate the interaction between the three hierarchical levels (corporate, divisional, and functional). Vancil and Lorange (1975) proposed a framework that orders planning activities in terms of three cycles of identifying and narrowing a firm's strategic options at the three organizational levels. Cycle 1 consists of the firm's objectives setting, Cycle 2 concerns the evaluation of broad programs or general strategies for a product line or business, and Cycle 3 concerns the evaluation of individual investment projects. Many projects may be part of the same program, and generally it is difficult to separate the evaluation of an individual project from the evaluation of the broader program of which it is a part.

Camillus (1984) further developed a "normative" CB system consisting of eight phases. Such a CB system is adapted and summarized in Table 4.1. Phases 1 to 3 (communication, triggering, and screening) are normally considered the domain of SP, while phases 4 to 8 (definition, evaluation, transmission, decision, and monitoring/post-audit) constitute the conventional capital budgeting system (CCBS).

In practice, the allocation of funds to a division by corporate headquarters typically depends on a set of strategic factors, internal and external opportunities, the effectiveness of the current mix of corporate resources, the division's share of corporate profits, the record of past performance, the growth potential and profitability of the products/markets in which the firm operates, and similar factors. In large, diversified companies, the headquarters focus more closely on the strategic and control aspects of the process. Being responsible for the control of overall capital expenditures by independent strategic business units (SBUs) or affiliates, corporate headquarters are likely to often view the CB process as part of the annual corporate budgeting process.

## 4.4.2  The Relevance of Capital Budgeting to Strategic Planning

This section examines the degree of adequacy of traditional financial concepts and techniques in making strategic decisions. Clearly, in a multilevel organizational system, there is often the need to apply an overall direction at the strategic level. Conventional methods for project evaluation (such as NPV, internal rate of return, and payback) are often applied in practice as a set of checks, once top managerial decisions have been made. Traditionally, CB techniques have been used by corporations in deciding which investments to choose from within a *given* menu of investment opportunities. Among others, Aggarwal (1980) has asserted that "DCF techniques

**Table 4.1**
**A "Normative" Capital Budgeting System**

| CB PHASE | PROCESS |
|---|---|
| 1. Communication | . <u>Corporation to division</u><br>- Corporate mission, strategy, policies, assumptions and resources availability<br>- Divisional charters<br>. <u>Division to function</u><br>- Divisional charters, strategy, policies, and assumptions<br>. Plenary meeting recommended |
| 2. Triggering | . <u>Corporate level</u><br>- IDEA system<br>- Involvement in SWOT analysis<br>- Portfolio planning models (BCG, GE, PARE, etc.)<br>. <u>Divisional level</u><br>- Management Information System (MIS)<br>- IDEA system<br>- SWOT analysis |
| 3. Screening | . Implicit in IDEA system & SWOT analysis<br>. Shortcomings responded to by involvement in SWOT analysis |
| 4. Definition | . Conventional Capital Budgeting System (CCBS) |
| 5. Evaluation | . CCBS |
| 6. Transmission | . CCBS |
| 7. Decision | . CCBS |
| 8. Monitoring/Post audit | . CCBS |

Notes:  IDEA: Channels other than the usual hierarchy for submitting ideas
SWOT: Strengths, Weaknesses, Opportunities and Threats
BCG: Boston Consulting Group
GE: General Electric
PARE: Potential and Resilience Evaluation (Derkinderen and Crum (1979)).

[a] Adapted from Camillus (1984).

are useful mainly for making *tactical* capital allocations rather than making strategic choices" (p. 33). Indeed, financial theory has yet to be utilized effectively in selecting strategic menus because CB techniques (with the notable exception of real options) have not been adequately developed in ways that make them directly applicable to the development of corporate strategy. Among other critics, Ansoff (1965) challenged traditional CB theory as follows: "The capital investment theory must be broadened to monitor the business environment and to search for new product-market entries under conditions of partial ignorance. It must be amended to deal with multiple conflicting objectives. It must be supplemented to identify unique product market opportunities and joint effects [synergy]" (p. 18).

One such framework (developed by Gordon and Pinches, 1984) views CB as a subset of strategic planning. Accordingly, the CB techniques must be "compatible" and consistent with the firm's strategic planning. As discussed in section 4.2, in large companies there are typically various decision subsystems. Each of these managerial levels may have a different focus (see Hofer and Schendel, 1978), as shown below:

| Managerial Level | Corporate | Business | Function |
|---|---|---|---|
| Allocation problem | Portfolio | Life cycle | Functional integration & balance |

We examine next in more detail the applicability of CB techniques to SP at the corporate, business, program, and individual project levels.

*Corporate Level.* Top management responsibilities involve the dual tasks of resource generation and resource allocation. These decisions at the corporate level are critical for a firm's long-term competitive position. Strategic planning (SP) helps management identify the businesses in which the firm has a competitive advantage and those it should sell or abandon. As Myers (1987) pointed out, SP can be viewed as CB on a larger scale. Unfortunately, according to Hofer and Schendel (1978):

> Traditional, project-oriented CB techniques are of limited use to top level managers in performing [the above] tasks, because these managers have neither the time nor the capacity to understand and usefully compare all the projects that would rise to the corporate level, nor do capital budgeting techniques by themselves have the capacity to consider the larger strategic context in which these business portfolio decisions must be made. (p. 70)

Due to the difficulty of applying standard DCF techniques to select strategic options, corporate management has often resorted to simple SP tools. One such tool has been the Boston Consulting Group's (BCG) growth matrix which focuses on the trade-off between the short-term need for funds or profitability (e.g., return on assets) and long-term growth. A product portfolio approach can be practically useful in the resource allocation process within a multiproduct, multimarket company aiming at long-term profitable growth while reducing the need for external financing. The importance of "integrating" the company's major strategic investment decisions and "balancing" its business unit portfolio has already been stressed in portfolio planning (Day, 1977). The relative simplicity of the BCG growth matrix, however, has been seen by practitioners as an advantage relative to alternative portfolio planning approaches (e.g., the General Electric or Arthur D. Little matrices). Alberts and McTaggart (1984) have developed a relatively more sophisticated, value-based profitability approach, under which the company is not guided in its capital allocation decisions simply by the potential for growth but rather by the potential for *profitable* growth.

*Business Level.* The overall investment strategy pursued at the corporate level would, subsequently, naturally determine the firm's competitive position at the business level, such as the selection of the products and markets in which the firm would compete. Some considerations relevant to this decision include product maturity spreads (life-cycle theory), synergy, geographic positioning, and distinctive competence (Johnson and Scholes, 1984). The financing aspects of the business strategy are also important, as discussed in Donaldson (1985) and Ellsworth (1983).

In applying CB techniques to determine an appropriate business strategy, one again confronts the problem of the relevant time horizon. CB theory suggests as a relevant time span the entire life of the investment based on the cash flow (CF) projection. If this standard were applied at the business level, the relevant time horizon would be extended until such time as the division or group went out of business (see Logue, 1980). In most cases, however, forecasting cash flows for such a long and uncertain period is impractical. In practice, the time horizon used in business strategy formulation ranges from the early stage of a business life cycle to the flex point of that cycle, when the business reaches its maturity stage. The business strategy—which is a metainvestment decision—thus ties the company to a sequence of investments consisting of broad programs and individual projects. The business strategy may encompass a time period longer than the constituent programs and projects, however, and can provide a framework against which particular programs and projects can be evaluated.

Since DCF techniques often cannot be employed satisfactorily in practice at the business level, the choice of a business strategy is usually conditioned by the probability of the company reaching a good degree of control of the business up to the stage at which the business matures. The probability of gaining a good market position, of course, depends mainly on alignment (a) between the business strategy and external market needs and conditions and (b) between the business strategy and the internal organizational processes, culture, and structure.

*Program Level.* As noted, whole programs and individual projects are hierarchically dependent on the business strategy. This means that many investment programs or projects must, in practice, pass a consistency (or affinity) test with regard to the SBU mission. Of course, since a whole set of investment program alternatives may potentially fit the chosen business strategy, a set of yardsticks is usually needed to differentiate the relative attractiveness of the various program alternatives. Finance theory suggests the use of some cumulative summary of the combined NPV (DCF) for the evaluation of such programs. However, in practice, detailed data are often not available for making reasonable projections at the program level and potential synergies and other interdependencies among individual projects within a given program may violate value additivity.

Other alternatives have naturally been suggested in the literature for the evaluation of broad business programs. A method called "constraint analysis" (Lorange, 1982), for example, relies on factors of business attractiveness versus company strengths for the selection of programs. Consistent with finance theory, regarding the forecast of the cash-flow schedule, Rappaport (1979) suggested that the forecast horizon should continue as long as the expected rate of return on incremental investment exceeds the cost of capital. (An estimate of the residual value would, of course, need to be incorporated.)

*Project Level.* It is at the individual project level that traditional CB techniques play a more relevant role, especially in the case of relatively small, independent, irreversible, and mutually exclusive projects. Basically, standard DCF techniques enable the comparison of investment alternatives that are homogeneous from a strategic point of view but differ in the timing, magnitude, and riskiness of the cash flows. Of course, if the investment scale is large relative to the size of the company, even a single project decision can have a strong impact on the firm's strategic profile and may, eventually, modify it. In such cases, projects may need to be analyzed as a portfolio, with consideration given to the covariances between projects and other interactions. Cross-sectional interdependencies among related projects and intertemporal links may seriously invalidate the principle of additivity underlying DCF techniques. Interactions among key variables (e.g., market share, investment life, salvage value, etc.) may also pose further complications (see Gold, 1976; Truitt, 1984).

Wissema (1984) suggested an approach to deal with such project eval-

uation issues. Given the definition of the company's strategy, he developed
a weighing procedure to assess strategic/synergistic investment criteria, including the degree of synergy of a proposed project with the rest of the
company and its affinity to the corporate strategy.

On the basis of this discussion, the relevance and applicability of DCF
techniques to strategic capital budgeting analysis is summarized in Table
4.2. The table shows the relevance (degree of applicability) as well as issues and problems one typically confronts when applying DCF techniques
at the various organizational levels (i.e., corporate, business, program, and
project). The notations "somewhat difficult" (SD), "very difficult" (VD),
and "impractical" (IMP) are used to indicate the degree of difficulty in
applying DCF techniques, corresponding to conditions of risk, uncertainty,
and ignorance, respectively. With respect to the issues of cash-flow estimation, risk-adjusted cost of capital, relevant time horizon, and interdependencies (both cross-sectional and intertemporal), DCF techniques are
generally found to be only somewhat difficult to apply at the individual
project level, very difficult to apply at the program and business levels,
and almost impractical at the corporate level.

## 4.5   APPROACHES TO STRATEGIC CAPITAL
##         BUDGETING

In this section, we review and discuss the merits of three basic approaches
to strategic capital budgeting. The first, which is typical of the business
strategy literature, is "soft" (qualitative) and more an "art than a science,"
incorporating broad management objectives and issues. The second, which
is characteristic of the traditional financial literature, is "harder" (quantitative) and relies on DCF and asset pricing theories, while broadly ignoring
behavioral issues. The third, which has its roots in option-pricing theory,
shows great potential in dealing with operating flexibility and strategic
adaptability in investment decision making.

### 4.5.1   Business Strategy Approach

According to Donaldson (1984), an integrating framework for strategic investment choices must explicitly recognize that the creation and preservation of corporate (not stockholder) wealth is the primary concern of business enterprises. Behind a process of multiple goal reconciliation lies a set
of superordinate organizational objectives. Usually implicit rather than
explicit, these objectives involve financial self-sufficiency as well as organizational and managerial survival. A legitimate structure to encompass

**Table 4.2**
**Summary of Applicability of DCF Techniques in Strategic Analysis**

| Issue — Managerial level | Cash flow estimation | | | Risk-adjusted cost of capital | | | Time horizon (Life cycle) | | | Interdependencies | | | | | |
|---|---|---|---|---|---|---|---|---|---|---|---|---|---|---|---|
| | | | | | | | | | | Cross-sectional | | | Inter-temporal | | |
| | SD | VD | IMP | SD | VD | IMP | SD | VD | IMP | SD | VD | IMP | SD | VD | IMP |
| CORPORATE | | | X | | | X | | X | X 1) | | | X | | | X |
| BUSINESS | | X 2) | | | X | | | X 3) | | | X | | | X | |
| PROGRAM | | X | | | X 3) | | X | | | | X | | | X | |
| PROJECT | X | | | X | | | X | | | X | | | X | | |

SD = somewhat difficult; VD = very difficult; IMP = impractical

1) industry; 2) residual value; 3) product life cycle

managerial responsiveness to a range of constituencies (customer, capital, and organization) still awaits to challenge financial theorists.

According to this framework, to be effective, managers must attend to *multiple constituencies* that parallel multiple organizational goals. Corporate and divisional goals often conflict: whereas corporate financial goals are primarily related to capital markets, most divisions are also concerned with sales growth, market share, and other product or market factors. Divisions often tend to go through something similar to a product life-cycle, with corresponding shifts in their financial requirements. Although perhaps more descriptive of actual managerial practice, however, this approach still lacks concrete tools for quantifying the relevant trade-offs and decisions.

### 4.5.2  Traditional Financial (DCF) Approach

As noted, traditional DCF analysis based on value maximization under passive management is most readily applicable on an incremental, project-by-project basis. However, if a firm actively pursues a particular strategy (e.g., market share dominance), particularly when it is evolving in response to changing market conditions, the adopted strategy may not be congruent with the underlying premise of these techniques (Myers, 1987; Pinches, 1982). According to Donaldson (1984), despite its theoretical appeal, DCF analysis may be seen as a partial discipline in the actual resource allocation process as it does not readily provide an intregrating framework for the long-term distribution of discretionary strategic resources among competing product lines. Along similar lines, Ansoff (1965) and Myers (1987) have pointed out that traditional CB techniques are unable to properly forecast the value of projects not yet in hand. Further, traditional CB techniques are difficult to use in situations involving multiple objectives, substantial project interdependencies (e.g., synergies), or other unique qualitative attributes.

Donaldson (1984) pointed out that the assumptions underlying the DCF techniques and the business strategy approach are both logical and internally consistent, but "one works from without while the other works from within." Myers (1987) attributed various misuses of finance theory, such as ranking based on IRR, inconsistent treatment of inflation, unrealistically high discount rates used in risk adjustment, and biases in assumptions, as major causes of disenchantment in using DCF techniques for strategic purposes. As noted, the application of DCF techniques encounters four major estimation problems: (1) the risk-adjusted discount rate, (2) the project's expected cash flow over the relevant time horizon, (3) the project's impact on the firm's other asset cash flows (cross-sectional links among projects), and (4) the project's impact on future investment opportunities (i.e., time series links across projects). According to Myers, the last problem is the most serious.

Von Bauer (1981) attempted to relate the portfolio strategy matrix approach to capital budgeting using CAPM concepts by stressing the risk-return tradeoff in the strategic planning process. Roll and Ross's (1984) arbitrage pricing theory (APT) approach may similarly be applied to the strategic portfolio problem in CB within a multiindex framework. However, the greatest promise to integrate the different perspectives to resource allocation in a quantifiable manner is held by real options techniques.

### 4.5.3 Real Options Approach

As noted, a major problem in applying DCF techniques to strategic analysis results from interdependencies among current and (uncertain or contingent) future decisions that make the risk-adjusted discount rate nondeterministic. An example is the interdependency among future investment (or growth) opportunities and today's capital commitments. Oftentimes, firms invest to enter a new market not so much because the immediate investment has a positive NPV, but rather because it positions the firm advantageously in the market and creates options for valuable follow-up opportunities. This is an example of a multistage decision that potentially involves options to expand, abandon, or alter the project at a future date. Strategic investments may thus create future assets as a by-product of the initial investment decision that cannot be adequately captured by conventional DCF analysis.

The developing apparatus of real options or contingent claims analysis (CCA) enables a formal analysis of these sequential types of discretionary investment decisions. In the simplest case, the opportunity to invest in a project is analogous to a call option to acquire a claim to the cash-flow value of a completed and operating project by paying a specified cost as the exercise price. Similarly, the first stage of a two-stage growth opportunity could be likened to an option on an option (i.e., a compound option). Of course, the application of financial option-pricing techniques to real assets is not always exact. For example, standard financial options have a specified maturity, whereas strategic investments typically involve unknown expiration dates. Similarly, standard financial options have fixed exercise prices, whereas the cost of exercising strategic options may be variable or uncertain. Moreover, many real projects may not be traded, offering a below-equilibrium rate of return or return shortfall analogous to a dividend payout (see McDonald and Siegel, 1984). There may also be competitive interactions and other complications.

Despite these challenges, a growing stream of literature using CCA in capital budgeting has emerged in recent years, highlighting the fact that standard DCF techniques often undervalue projects involving real operating options and other strategic interactions. Myers (1987), Kester (1984),

Mason and Merton (1985),McDonald and Siegel (1985, 1986), Brennan and Schwartz (1985a), and Trigeorgis and Mason (1987), among others, have promoted option-based valuation to capture the managerial operating flexibility and several strategic considerations embedded in capital investments. This real options literature has been growing, increasingly addressing relatively more complex problems, while currently it is turning more toward applications. These advances in real options have the potential to bring a new, integrative perspective to strategic capital budgeting.

Those employing strategic investment planning should definitely try to take advantage of real option valuation tools. An options-based strategic capital budgeting approach may be able to properly quantify not only managerial operating flexibility, but also synergies, intertemporal dependencies (growth options), and many other strategic aspects of project valuation (see Trigeorgis and Kasanen, 1991). Once investment opportunities are properly seen as collections of real options, strategic planning can more readily be viewed as involving the explicit recognition, creation, and management (optimal exercise) of the portfolio of real options associated with a firm's collection of current and future investment opportunities.

An options approach is thus better able to deal with capital investment as an ongoing *process* requiring active managerial involvement. As market conditions change, new investment opportunities may be created while old plans may have to be revised or even abandoned. As part of the strategic capital budgeting *process*, management should be constantly looking for opportunities to exercise the built-in real options or create new ones. If major changes occur in the marketplace or important options are exercised or created that may alter the remaining alternatives, the initial strategy may naturally need to be adjusted. A set of conditional control targets would also be useful to lower-level managers, contingent on the exercise of such major options. Of course, not only should the corporate strategy be flexible enough to evolve over time, but, naturally, the associated control targets should be readjusted as well.

## 4.6   CONCLUSIONS

Strategic capital budgeting was seen as the process by which top management makes decisions to commit large amounts of scarce financial resources to achieve strategic objectives. In the traditional financial literature (with the exception of the literature on real options), little attention has been devoted to strategic considerations in the asset planning and allocation process. The conventional formulation of the resource allocation problem has been framed in terms of individual projects within existing organizational units. However, these approaches do not always provide top management with the ability to make sound trade-offs consistent with the firm's overall corporate strategy. As a result, they tend to nourish the political/behavioral aspects of the budgeting process, which often becomes an exercise in power. Perhaps market share constraints, coalition formation, and other multiobjective constituencies' expectations observed in practice can be seen as insurance premiums, slack, or idiosyncracies in an attempt to account for biases resulting from the use of conventional capital budgeting techniques.

It may indeed be useful to view CB in terms of planning, allocation, and control phases that cast strategic planning concerns within an effective allocative structure and process. It is ultimately the firm's long-run strategy that fundamentally determines the allocation of major capital resources. Corporate strategy must, therefore, be clearly communicated to the various levels in the organization so that projects can receive a more complete examination of their potential strategic ramifications. Naturally, the capital expenditure analysis should not merely focus on figures and computations, but should also clearly communicate the basic assumptions and address the relevant strategic questions.

In many organizations, most major decisions on capital expenditures are formally reserved for top management. In practice, however, many decisions may actually be determined further down in the organization. Top management may have limited effective control over project-by-project decisions because of a lack or asymmetry of information. This underscores the need for a balanced decentralization of CB decision making, while top management can still maintain broad control via budgeting, planning, and control of the overall operation of the various divisions or groups.

In closing, strategic CB must, and can, reconcile the "top-down" and "bottom-up" processes of strategic planning and standard CB in a complementary and interactive way. Capital budgeting should not be treated as a mechanistic staff function of accept-or-reject, but rather should be harmoniously integrated with strategic planning. Top management should actively and continually be involved in shaping the desired investment strategy. In an uncertain business environment, the strategic plan is not simply a prespecified set of decisions taken up-front, but a direction and a process that must be modified when conditions change. As part of the strategic capital budgeting *process*, management should constantly look for timely opportunities to exercise existing investment options or create new ones. Further work needs to be done toward the proper integration of traditional CB within the company's overall resource allocation process, not only by highlighting relevant strategic considerations but also by expanding our evaluation methods to better suit strategic analysis. Real options techniques (as illustrated by the chapters in this volume) hold the promise to lead us toward that integration, as they can, and should, be properly interwoven with corporate strategic planning.

## ACKNOWLEDGMENTS

Lai thanks his colleagues at Laval for their advice and support and acknowledges financial support from the Social Sciences and Humanities Research Council of Canada. An earlier version of the chapter benefited from presentation at the 1992 Southern Finance Association meetings.

## NOTES

1. See, for example, Fremgen (1973), Kim and Farragher (1981), Klammer and Walker (1984), Rosenblatt (1980), and Scapens and Sale (1981).

2. Carter (1971) found the following: (1) subordinates may add bias to an objective appraisal depending on a number of factors, including uncertainty and superior-subordinate knowledge and perceptions; (2) the greater the uncertainty, the more criteria will be used for decision making; and (3) "new" projects will be submitted only when the organization's goals appear increasingly hard to achieve with projects similar to existing ones.

# PART II

---

# GENERAL EXCHANGE OR SWITCHING OPTIONS AND OPTION INTERDEPENDENCIES

# Chapter 5

# The Value of Flexibility: A General Model of Real Options

**Nalin Kulatilaka**

*This chapter develops a general dynamic programming framework to value projects that contain real options. The approach allows for a richer array of stochastic dynamics, including mean-reverting processes with state-dependent shortfalls from equilibrium drift rates. It is shown that many of the previously studied real options—such as waiting-to-invest, time-to-build, abandonment, and shutdown options—can be interpreted as special cases of this general model of flexibility.*

## 5.1 INTRODUCTION

Academics and managers have long been dissatisfied with the inability of conventional capital budgeting techniques, such as discounted cash flow (DCF) methods, to capture the strategic impact of projects.[1] In particular, DCF methods ignore the operating flexibility that gives management the option to revise decisions while a project is underway. Examples include decisions to shut down, to abandon, to expand, or to change the technology.[2]

In recent years the finance literature has addressed these criticisms by modifying conventional capital budgeting methods to include the impact of operating flexibilities. It is now well known that when investment is irreversible and future market conditions are uncertain, an investment decision must not be based solely on the usual net present value (NPV) rule. For example, an investment expenditure implicitly calls for sacrifice of the option to wait-to-invest (i.e., to invest instead at a time in the future), so that we must treat this lost option value as part of the investment cost.

McDonald and Siegel (1986) showed that even with moderate amounts of uncertainty, the value of the option to wait-to-invest can be significant, which suggests that an investment rule ignoring the option value can be grossly in error. Similar adjustments are necessary when there are options to abandon (McDonald and Siegel, 1986; Myers and Majd, 1990); options to temporarily shut down (McDonald and Siegel, 1985; Brennan and Schwartz, 1985a); options depending on the sequential nature of investment (Majd and Pindyck, 1987; Trigeorgis, 1993a); and options to choose capacity (Pindyck, 1988).[3]

This chapter generalizes the valuation of projects with embedded options. These options may arise naturally, as when managers exercise investment timing, abandonment, or temporary shutdown options, or they may be intentionally introduced, as when projects are designed with the capability to switch among alternative inputs or outputs.

In order to value future cash flows that depend on a stochastic state variable, $\theta$, and that can be modified by future operating decisions, we must first obtain the conditional cash flows under the different $\theta$ realizations and then derive the appropriate discount rates to reflect the risk levels in these cash flows. The first step is messy, but feasible. The second step, however, is rendered infeasible because the riskiness of the cash flows is affected by the operating decisions, while the decisions themselves are determined by the realizations of the random variable, $\theta$.

Contingent claims analysis (CCA) provides a solution to this problem by eliminating the need to deduce risk-adjusted discount rates. When $\theta$ is the price of a traded security, arbitrage arguments alone can be used to form a riskless hedge to value these cash flows in a risk-neutral world. The intuition behind this result relies on the fact that for traded securities, the drift rate of the price must equal its equilibrium rate of return. Therefore, by replacing the actual drift term by the risk-free rate, the risk in $\theta$ is priced within a market equilibrium model. That is, we can let $\theta$ grow at the risk-free interest rate and derive the cash flows under the various realizations of $\theta$, taking into account the impact of future operating decisions. The resulting cash flows can then be appropriately discounted at the risk-free rate, $r$.

In the valuation of real assets, however, the relevant stochastic state variable is unlikely to be the price of a traded security. In such cases, the drift rate need not necessarily be equal to the required equilibrium rate. There may, in fact, be a "shortfall" from the equilibrium return (see McDonald and Siegel, 1984). Here, the risk-neutrality argument can be extended by drawing an analogy to a traded security with a payout that is equal to the shortfall of the actual from the equilibrium rate of return, $\delta$. In order to value the asset or its derivatives in a risk-neutral world, the risk-neutral drift rate must be set equal to the risk-free rate less $\delta$. Hence, it is important to note that, unlike financial option pricing which is based entirely on arbitrage arguments, real option valuation may also require the use of equilibrium models to obtain this shortfall in the growth rate.

The traditional CCA approach to such derivative asset valuation is to solve the partial differential equation(s) governing the behavior of the derivative asset value subject to the associated boundary conditions. These equations typically yield closed-form solutions only for infinite-time problems under restrictive assumptions about the underlying stochastic process. In other cases, the equations must be solved numerically.

In this chapter we present an explicit dynamic programming formulation by approximating the continuous state-space with a discretization that is similar to that used in finite difference solution methods for partial differential equations. The primary advantages to our formulation are (a) the various operating options and the optimum operating rules become transparent and (b) a wide variety of stochastic processes and cash-flow dependencies can be included. A side benefit is that this discretization can provide an intuitive correspondence to important institutional aspects, such as costly recontracting and sluggish price adjustments.

The rest of the chapter is organized as follows. In the next section we introduce the stochastic dynamic programming procedure. For pedagogical simplicity, we first focus on the interaction between cash flows and operating decisions in an economy with risk-neutral agents. The model allows for project valuation and option exercise decisions to be jointly determined. We then suggest ways to incorporate risk aversion. Section 5.3 surveys the literature on real options to illustrate how ubiquitous such real options are, how critical they are to project valuation, and how our general model of flexibility can incorporate many such real options as special cases of the flexibility option. Section 5.4 concludes with some brief remarks about potential applications.

## 5.2   A GENERAL MODEL OF FLEXIBILITY

### 5.2.1   Characterizing Exogenous Uncertainty

The value of real options lies in the enhanced ability of the firm to cope with exogenous uncertainty. Hence, a first step in modeling the flexibility option is to characterize the sources and nature of this uncertainty. The exogenous uncertainty faced by the firm can generally be summarized by a stochastic variable, $\theta$, which follows a continuous-time diffusion process of the form:[4]

$$\frac{d\theta_t}{\theta_t} = \alpha(\theta_t, t)dt + \sigma(\theta_t, t)dZ_t, \tag{5.1}$$

where $dZ_t$ is a standard Wiener process, while $\alpha(\theta_t, t)$ and $\sigma(\theta_t, t)$ are, respectively, the instantaneous rate of return and the volatility of $\theta$.

The *risk-neutral* representation of this process will have the same volatility, $\sigma$, but the drift term will be modified to take account of the risk premium and any cash payouts. Hence, in a risk-neutral economy, $\theta$ will follow the process,

$$\frac{d\theta_t}{\theta_t} = \mu(\theta_t, t)dt + \sigma dZ_t, \tag{5.2}$$

where $\mu$ is the *risk-neutral* rate of return. Since $\theta$ is not necessarily the price of a traded security, and holding the underlying asset may generate benefits, $\mu$ does not have to equal the risk-free rate of interest. Equation (5.2) is the limiting case of the discrete-time stochastic process:

$$\frac{\Delta\theta_t}{\theta_t} = \mu\Delta t + \sigma\sqrt{\Delta t}\Delta Z_t, \tag{5.3}$$

where $\Delta Z_t$ are i.i.d. standard normal.

## 5.2.2   Technology Modes and the Value of the Project

In characterizing the operating technology, we use the concept of a "mode of operation." Modes may be "invest" versus "wait to invest," "use gas" versus "use oil," or "continue operations" versus "shut down" versus "abandon project." Each mode of the project will have an associated profit function. In general, there may be $M$ modes, indexed by $m$ and characterized by a profit function $\pi^m$, for $m \in (1, ..., M)$. These profit functions are defined for the duration of a single time period and have as their arguments the input and output prices and time.[5] The flow of profits in the interval $(t, t + \Delta t)$ depends on the value of $\theta_t$, and hence $\pi^m = \pi^m(\theta_t)$.

The cost of switching from mode $j$ to mode $k$ is denoted as $c_{jk}$. For example, if mode $j =$ "oil heat" and mode $k =$ "gas heat," $c_{jk}$ is the cost of converting from oil to gas. Continuing in a mode entails no switching costs: $c_{mm} = 0$ for all $m$.

The value of a *fixed-technology* project with a life of $T$ periods that is dedicated to mode $m$ can be expressed as:

$$V_m(\theta_0) = E_0\left[\sum_{t=0}^{T} \pi^m(\theta_t)\rho^t\right], \tag{5.4}$$

where $E_0[.]$ is the risk-neutral expectation operator conditional on information at time 0 (i.e., on the realization of $\theta_0$) and $\rho$ is the risk-free discount factor. Expected values can be obtained as probability weighted sums:

$$E_{t-1}\left[\pi(\theta^i)\right] = \sum_{j=1}^{S} \pi(\theta^j)p_{ij}, \tag{5.5}$$

where $p_{ij}$ is the risk-neutral probability of a transition between the discrete states $\theta_i$ and $\theta_j$ during the time interval $(t-1, t)$.

When the project is *flexible*—that is, the firm has an option to switch between various operating modes at specified switching costs—the value of the project may involve a series of nested options that arise from the ability to switch back and forth among operating modes. Given that the firm is operating in a particular mode, there may be a flow of income (or costs) that occurs at a rate that may depend not only on that mode, but also on the realization of $\theta$. The present value (using the risk-free interest rate, $r$) of net profit flows into the future *given optimal behavior* henceforth is denoted $F(\theta_t, m, t)$. Optimal behavior means that the firm always chooses the current mode to maximize the present value of current plus discounted expected future profits net of switching costs.

The value of the flexible project at the beginning of the last period of operation (at time $T$) depends on $\theta(T)$ and the mode of operation during the previous period, $m$.[6] If mode $j$ was used at time $T - \Delta t$ and $\theta_T = \theta^k$, then the project value function at $T$ can be written as:

$$F(\theta_{T-\Delta t} = \theta^k, m) = \max_{\ell} \left( \pi^\ell(\theta^k) - c_{m,\ell} \right), \tag{5.6}$$

where $c_{m,\ell}$ is the cost of switching from mode $m$ to mode $\ell$.[7]

In general, the dynamic programming equations at any time $t$ are based on the well known Bellman equation of dynamic programming and may be written in our notation as follows (where we assume that the firm arrives at time $t$ operating in mode $m$ and $\theta_t = \theta^k$):

$$F(\theta_t = \theta^k, m, t) = \max_{\ell} \left( [\pi(\theta^k, \ell, t) - c_{m,\ell}] + \rho E_t \left[ F(\theta_{t+\Delta t}, \ell) \right] \right), \tag{5.7}$$

for $\lambda, m = 1, ..., M$, $k = 1, ..., S$, and $t = 0, ..., T - 1$. The conditional risk-neutral expectations, $E_t[.]$, are taken over the possible realizations of $\theta$ and are weighted by the transition probabilities, $p_{ij}$ (as shown in section 5.2.4 below). These simultaneous dynamic programs must be solved numerically to obtain the value functions $F(\theta_t, m)$ for all $t$ and $m$. Furthermore, the critical values of $\theta$ at which the modes should be switched can be computed by equating the arguments within the max(.) in Equation (5.7).

The above equation shows that in each period, the firm must contemplate switching into a new mode (denoted by $\ell$). If it chooses mode $\ell$, it realizes profits of $\pi(\theta_t, \ell, t)$ but pays switching costs of $c_{m\ell}$ (which equals zero if $\ell = m$), and then arrives at the following period with value function $F(\theta_{t+1}, \ell, t+1)$. This value depends on the mode chosen for this period, $\ell$, as well as on the value of the state variable for next period, $\theta_{t+1}$. Because $\theta_{t+1}$ is still unknown at time $t$, we take expectations and discount. The firm in each period chooses the mode, $\ell$, that maximizes the value of the project.

If it were not for switching costs, the solution to this optimization problem would be simple: choose in each period the mode that maximizes $\pi(\theta_t, \ell, t)$ in that period. However, switching costs make a forward-looking analysis necessary. For example, a firm may decline to switch from oil to gas heat even when gas is marginally cheaper if either the cost of switching or the possibility of a reversal in the relative cost advantage (which would entail further switching costs) is high. The probability distribution of *future* oil-to-gas price ratios affects the *current* choice of technology. This "inertia" results in what is known as a *hysteresis band*. A hysteresis band is a range of values that the state variable may take for which mode switching is passed up, even when short-term cost conditions make switching appear profitable.

### 5.2.3   Solution Strategy

Equation (5.7) is a standard problem in dynamic programming that requires a backward solution technique.[8] At each date, we solve for *both* the value of the project and the optimal operating mode. We start at the terminal date, $T$. At this date, the project ends and $F(\theta_T, m, T) = S(\theta_T)$ for all $m$, where $S(\theta_T)$ is the salvage value of the project at $T$. Although the finite horizon may seem to be a restrictive assumption, $T$ can be made arbitrarily large.

One period earlier, at time $t = T - 1$, the optimal mode is the one that maximizes the right-hand side of Equation (5.7). This is an easy decision because $F(\theta_T, m, T) = S(\theta_T)$ for all $m$. Therefore, we simply choose the mode with the highest profit flow net of any switching costs. Hence, conditional on entering period $T - 1$ in mode $m$,

$$F(\theta_{T-1}, m, T-1) = \max_{\ell} \left( \pi(\theta_{T-1}, \ell, T-1) - c_{m\ell} + \rho E_{T-1}[S(\theta_T)] \right), \quad (5.8)$$

where $\ell, m = 1, ..., M$. Thus, we have a rule for both best mode choice and project value, which are conditional on the current mode entering period $T-1$ and the price at time $T-1$. Notice that we must solve for $M$ functions $F(\theta_{T-1}, m, T-1)$, one for each possible operating mode as we enter period $T - 1$.

At time $T - 2$, the problem is more difficult. Given that we arrive at $T - 2$ in a given mode $m$, we need to maximize the sum of profit flow net of switching costs, *plus* the present value of the expected project value at period's end, which now *does* depend on the mode chosen in this period. We therefore choose mode $\ell$ to maximize:

$$
\begin{aligned}
F(\theta_{T-2}, \ell, T-2) &= \max_{\ell} \left( \pi(\theta_{T-2}, \ell, T-2) - c_{m\ell} \right. \\
&\quad \left. + \rho E_{T-2}[F(\theta_{T-1}, \ell, T-1)] \right).
\end{aligned}
\quad (5.9)
$$

The first term in brackets is easy to calculate as a function of the current price, $\theta_{T-2}$. The second, expectational, term is more difficult. Note, however, that in the previous step we already solved for the function $F(\theta_{T-1}, \ell, T-1)$ for each possible mode choice. Hence, for each mode that we consider at time $T-2$, we take the expectation of this function over the possible values of $\theta_{T-1}$. This requires a specification of the evolution of $\theta_{T-1}$, given $\theta_{T-2}$. We defer this calculation to the next subsection. For now, we simply note that the expectation is calculated using standard tools of statistics.

At time $T-2$, we thus may choose the mode, $\ell$, that maximizes Equation (5.9), recognizing that mode choice affects both current profits and the value of the project brought forward into the next period. To do this we solve for the project values given each possible mode choice and then select the value-maximizing mode.

Now that we have solved $F(\theta_{T-2}, m, T-2)$ as a function of $\theta_{T-2}$ for each mode, we may step back another date to time $T-3$. At this date, we evaluate:

$$
\begin{aligned}
F(\theta_{T-3}, \ell, T-3) &= \max_{\ell} \left( \pi(\theta_{T-3}, \ell, T-3) - c_{m\ell} \right. \\
&\quad + \left. \rho E_{T-3}[F(\theta_{T-2}, \ell, T-2)] \right),
\end{aligned} \tag{5.10}
$$

using our knowledge of the $M$ value functions of $\theta_{T-2}$, namely, $F(\theta_{T-2}, m, T-2), m = 1, ..., M$. We again calculate the expected value of each function over the possible values of $\theta_{T-2}$ given the current value of $\theta_{T-3}$ and choose the mode (given $\theta_{T-3}$) that maximizes project value.

Clearly, we have established a recursive solution technique that enables us to work backward from time $T$ all the way to time 0. At each date $t$, given the value of $\theta_t$, we may choose the mode that maximizes the market value of the project carried forward.

## 5.2.4   Calculating Expectations[9]

Merton (1982) showed that as long as the state variable $\theta_t$ evolves continuously, we may act as though over short time intervals it had a normal distribution.[10] Therefore, we assume that $\Delta\theta_t$ over time period $\Delta t$ is normally distributed over the interval $\Delta t$, with a mean of $\mu\Delta t$ and a variance of $\sigma^2 \Delta t$. (We suppress the possible dependence of $\mu$ and $\sigma$ on $\theta_t$ and $t$ for notational simplicity. Later, we will show how $\mu$ must be determined to account for the necessary risk adjustments to project value.)

To discretize the range of possible values of $\theta_t$, we assume that $\theta_t$ may take one of $S$ possible values, $\theta^1, \theta^2, ..., \theta^S$. Given a value of $\theta_t^i$ at time $t$ in state $i$, the probability of $\theta_{t+1}^j$ in the next period being in state $j$ depends on the difference $j - i$. As the absolute value of $j - i$ increases, the probability falls in accordance with the normal distribution.

It is easy to show that, consistent with the discrete version of the normal distribution $\Phi(\mu, \sigma^2)$, a transition from state $i$ to state $j$ occurs with probability:

$$p_{ij} = \Phi\left[\frac{-\mu\Delta t + (j - i + \frac{1}{2})\Delta\theta}{\sigma\theta^i\sqrt{\Delta t}}\right] - \Phi\left[\frac{-\mu\Delta t + (j - i - \frac{1}{2})\Delta\theta}{\sigma\theta^i\sqrt{\Delta t}}\right], \quad (5.11)$$

where $\Phi[.]$ is the cumulative standard normal distribution, and the step size $\Delta\theta = \theta^{i+1} - \theta^i$, for all $i = 1, .., S$.

Special care must be taken with the end points $\theta^1$ and $\theta^S$. Lumping all exterior values to the boundary, we obtain the transition probabilities:

$$p_{iS} = 1 - \Phi\left[\frac{-\mu\Delta t + (S - i + \frac{1}{2})\Delta\theta}{\sigma\theta^i\sqrt{\Delta t}}\right] \qquad (5.12)$$

$$p_{Si} = \Phi\left[\frac{-\mu\Delta t + (1 - i + \frac{1}{2})\Delta\theta}{\sigma\theta^i\sqrt{\Delta t}}\right]. \qquad (5.13)$$

Using Equations (5.11), (5.12), and (5.13), it is easy to take the necessary expectations in Equation (5.7). Given the current value of $\theta_t$, we may then calculate the probability associated with any value of $\theta_{t+1}$. We can therefore use these probabilities to calculate the expected value of $F(\theta_{t+1}, m, t + 1)$ as we proceed along the backward iterative process.[11]

## 5.2.5   Risk-Adjustment Techniques

We have thus far showed how the operating decisions involved in managing real options can be made properly using tools of dynamic programming. We simplified these decisions by positing risk-neutral managers. We now examine a modification to the solution technique that can account for asset valuation in markets with risk-averse investors.

We rely on a result from Cox, Ingersoll, and Ross (1985, Lemma 4) that is akin to treating uncertainty through the use of certainty-equivalent cash flows rather than through risk-adjusted discount rates. Specifically, we continue to use the risk-free interest rate for purposes of discounting, but we replace the actual drift rate of the driving stochastic variable by a *certainty-equivalent drift rate*. This adjusted drift equals the actual drift on the variable minus the risk premium that would emerge in market equilibrium on an asset with the same risk features as the stochastic variable.

The intuition behind this result is that instead of discounting actually expected cash flows at risk-adjusted interest rates, we may use the risk-free interest rate and adjust for risk by appropriately reducing the *expected* cash flows used in the calculations. Cox, Ingersoll, and Ross showed that the correct cash-flow adjustment requires a reduction of the drift rate by the risk premium.

An alternative intuitive interpretation of this result is to imagine that we are valuing the project in an economy with risk-neutral agents. Such agents would, of course, use the risk-free rate to discount cash flows. However, all assets in this economy would be expected to earn only the risk-free rate of return, in other words, there would be no risk premiums. Thus, equilibrium drift rates on securities in this risk-neutral economy would be lower than they are in our actual economy by the risk premium. Cox and colleagues proved that asset values in this economy would be precisely equal to values in our economy.

*Case 1: Financial Assets.* If the state variable were the stock price of a firm paying no dividends (a particularly easy case), for example, the certainty-equivalent drift would be simply the risk-free rate since the stock's expected rate of capital gains should, in equilibrium, exceed the risk-free rate by just the fair risk premium.

Call $\mu$ the actual drift rate on the stock, $\xi$ the risk premium, and $r$ the risk-free rate. Then, for the non-dividend-paying stock,

$$\mu - \xi = r. \tag{5.14}$$

If instead, the stock were paying dividends, say at a continuous yield of $\delta$, then to provide a fair total rate of return to investors the stock would offer an expected capital gains yield of $g = \mu - \delta$, and the certainty-equivalent drift rate on the stock would be:

$$g - \xi = (\mu - \delta) - \xi = r - \delta. \tag{5.15}$$

Therefore, for traded financial securities, the certainty-equivalent drift will equal the risk-free rate minus the income yield on the security. This equals the total rate of return the risky asset offers its investors minus (a) the risk premium on the asset and (b) the income yield on the asset (i.e., $\delta$). However, since $\mu - \xi = r$ (by the definition of the risk premium), we need not know $\xi$ or even rely on a model of risk premiums to calculate value in this case. We simply replace the actual drift rate, $\mu$, with its certainty-equivalent equilibrium value, $r - \delta$, and pursue the dynamic program as previously described. Both of these values ($r$ and $\delta$) are easily observed.

*Case 2: Nonfinancial Assets.* In most real options applications, however, the relevant state variable will not be a security price. Instead, it typically will be the price of some input or output. When that price is for a natural resource on which futures contracts trade, it still is relatively easy to perform the risk adjustment.

For instance, to determine the equilibrium expected drift rate of copper, we compute the costs of storing copper (denoted as $s$), the benefits of storing copper (net convenience yield, $c$), the expected appreciation rate ($g$), and the fair total rate of return (given risk) on an investment in copper ($\mu$), and then impose the equilibrium condition that $\mu = g + c - s$, or $g = \mu + s - c$.

Next, reducing this equilibrium drift rate by the fair risk premium on copper results in a certainty equivalent drift of $g_{ce} = (\mu - \xi) + (s - c) = r - \delta$, where $\delta = c - s$ is the convenience yield net of storage cost. Thus, the net convenience yield of copper plays precisely the same role as the dividend yield for stocks. Both represent the component of total returns realized from sources other than expected capital gains.

Estimating the net convenience yield still may be difficult, but at least it is open to econometric attack (see Brennan and Schwartz, 1985a). Moreover, when assets are traded on futures markets, $\delta$ may be computed directly with minimal effort. The reason is that copper futures prices for delivery at different dates, 0 and $T$, should obey the parity relationship that:

$$F(T)/F(0) = e^{(r-\delta)T}. \qquad (5.16)$$

*Case 3: Goods Prices.* Many assets, whether financial or real, have the common property that they are stored, and therefore, the expected price appreciation relative to risk ought to be subject to equilibrium principles of risk versus return. The storage of an asset implies that agents believe that its expected price appreciation is sufficient to compensate for time value and risk, net of marginal convenience yield. In many cases, however, the driving state variable is an input or output price of some commodity that is not stored in equilibrium. The paths of these prices, therefore, are free to evolve without regard to their risk characteristics. In general, in these cases, $\delta$ will be both time and state dependent. In our example,

$$
\begin{aligned}
E(\Delta \theta_t) &= \mu(\theta_t, t)\Delta t \qquad (5.17)\\
\mathrm{Var}(\Delta \theta_t) &= \sigma^2(\theta_t, t)\Delta t.
\end{aligned}
$$

This specification states that in a small time interval, $\Delta t$, price is subject to both systematic trends and random disturbances. The random disturbances have mean $\mu$ and a standard deviation of $\sigma\sqrt{\Delta t}$. In this specification, drift (i.e., the expected rate of price change) has no relationship to risk. However, we can use our "$\delta$ strategy" based on the relationship in Equation 5.15 (that $g - \xi = r - \delta$), which implies that $\delta = (r + \xi) - \mu$, or:

$$\delta = [\text{Required return given risk}] - [\text{Actual drift from price dynamics}].$$
$$(5.18)$$

Here, however, there is no way to avoid the reliance on an equilibrium model of risk and return, such as the CAPM. Such a model is necessary to calculate the first term on the right-hand side of Equation (5.18).

Still, this approach offers considerable advantages over the conventional constant-discount-rate NPV methodology. As the state variable evolves and the project becomes more or less a "long shot," the appropriate discount rate also changes. Thus, while it might be reasonable to use an equilibrium model to estimate the discount rate appropriate to copper price risk, which might be reasonably stable, for example, it would not make sense to apply a fixed discount rate to most projects with embedded options that depend on the price of copper. For these projects, the risk level itself evolves over time. Even if the calculation of the discount rate for the asset in Equation (5.18) is not perfectly precise, it is likely to be much more precise than any attempt to calculate directly a discount rate for a project that is dependent in a nonlinear way on the underlying asset price.

## 5.3 EXAMPLES OF REAL OPTIONS

### 5.3.1 Waiting-to-Invest Option

McDonald and Siegel (1985) interpreted the investment timing problem in terms of options and showed that naive use of the NPV rule can lead an analyst astray by ignoring the value of the waiting-to-invest option that is "killed" when an investment is committed. In fact, the presence of the timing option requires that the analyst choose from a set of *mutually exclusive* investments; in this case, "invest today" or (possibly) "invest later." In the case of mutually exclusive investments, a positive NPV is not sufficient for project acceptance. Instead of taking every positive-NPV project, we must choose the NPV-maximizing alternative, recognizing that future decisions *and* discount rates will depend on the realizations of stochastic variables.

In order to apply our general model of flexibility to value the waiting-to-invest option, we define the initial mode of operation, before any investment decision has been made, as mode 1. The production mode is mode 2. The switching cost, $c_{12}$, is the initial investment cost, $I$. The profit flow in mode 1 is $\pi(\theta_t, 1, t) = 0$. Once investment is initiated by incurring the switching cost, the firm receives the stream of future net revenues, $\pi(\theta_t, 2, t)$, which have a present value of $F(\theta_t, 2, t)$. Because $F(\theta_t, 2, t)$ may fall below $I$ when the output price falls, the firm at time $t$ may optimally choose to wait to invest (i.e., remain in mode 1) even when $F(\theta_t, 2, t) > I$, i.e., NPV > 0. Once a project is initiated and the investment cost has been incurred, the firm may not return to the null mode. Hence, we set $c_{21} = \infty$.

## 5.3.2    The Time-to-Build Option

The waiting-to-invest option is, in fact, a fairly crude representation of much more complex timing options that firms regularly exercise. Rather than instantaneous lump-sum investments, as envisioned in the formulation of the waiting-to-invest option, most actual investments typically are spread out over time and offer opportunities for acceleration or delay. Majd and Pindyck (1987) studied this problem.

To illustrate the time-to-build option, consider the construction of a hydroelectric project. Not only is a large initial investment required, but the project also takes time to complete. For instance, it may involve damming a river to obtain needed water resources, developing the necessary infrastructure, building a distribution network, and so forth. As a consequence, the investment normally will be committed in installments. At any point prior to completion, if uncertainty is resolved in a way that is detrimental to the project's economic viability, it can be scrapped and future expenditures saved. Alternately, if uncertainty is resolved favorably, then it may be worthwhile to speed up the investment (at a higher cost) to accelerate the project's flow of profits.

Many large investment projects have the following characteristics leading to time-to-build option values:

- Investment decisions and associated cash outlays occur sequentially over time;

- There is a maximum rate at which outlays and construction can proceed, namely, it takes "time to build"; and

- The project yields no cash returns until it is completed.

Suppose that the maximum rate at which investments can be made each period is $\lambda$ and that a total investment of $M\lambda$ (i.e., $M$ investments of $\lambda$) is required to obtain an operational plant. An operational plant is worth $V(\theta_t, t)$. We define the mode as the number of investment units made so far. Then $\pi(\theta_t, m, t) = 0$ for $m < M$,

$$
c_{ij} = \begin{cases} \lambda & \text{for } j - i = 1 & \text{(unit investment)} \\[2mm] M\lambda & \text{for } j - i > 1 & \text{(maximum investment rate)} \\[2mm] \infty & \text{for } j < i & \text{(irreversibility)} \end{cases}
$$

and $F(\theta_t, m, t) = V(\theta_t, t)$ for $m = M$.

### 5.3.3 The Abandonment Option

Like the timing of investments, the timing of disinvestments can also be interpreted as real options. This abandonment timing problem was studied by McDonald and Siegel (1985), who showed how it arises from a re-interpretation of the variables of the waiting-to-invest problem. While the McDonald and Siegel analysis was limited to the infinite time case, Myers and Majd (1990) examined the abandonment timing problem in a finite time horizon.

As an example of the abandonment problem, consider a garment-manufacturing project that is found to have a negative NPV based on conventional cash-flow analysis. This naive analysis assumes that once the project has been initiated, it will be operated until the end of its economic life. The technology involved is unlikely to become obsolete in the near future and, furthermore, there exists an active market for used machines. Hence, if conditions turn out poorly, the firm may abandon the project prior to the end of its economic life, sell the machines in the second-hand market to retrieve the salvage value, and avoid future liabilities.[12] Such abandonment options are extremely common in many manufacturing projects where there are active secondary markets for the capital equipment.

The abandonment option may make the project attractive even if NPV based on expected cash flow is negative. The abandonment option limits the downside exposure of the project: the worst outcome is the project's salvage value. The firm retains all upside potential if market conditions improve. Hence, the project resembles a call option where the holder has limited liability but still profits from any positive market movements.

To examine the abandonment option within our framework, define the production state mode as 1 and call the abandonment state, mode 2. The producing firm is in mode 1, deriving profit flows of $\pi(\theta_t, 1, t)$. If the salvage value of the project is $S$, then $c_{12} = -S$. Because abandonment is an irreversible decision, we set $c_{21} = \infty$. The asymmetry (that $c_{21} \neq c_{12}$) makes the abandonment option nontrivial. Firms may optimally keep currently nonprofitable projects operating to keep alive the potential for future profits should market conditions improve. The optimal abandonment decision must trade off salvage value and current losses against the potential for future profits.

There are some important and obvious design implications of the abandonment option. In projects with alternative design configurations where some utilize specialized, user-specific capital while others utilize general, less specialized equipment, the latter designs may dominate when their higher abandonment option values are taken into consideration.

## 5.3.4  Shutdown Option

Instead of permanently abandoning a project, it may, in some instances, be feasible to temporarily shut down operations during lean periods. Mc-Donald and Siegel (1986) and Brennan and Schwartz (1985a) analyzed this problem of the temporary shutdown and start-up of projects in response to exogenously evolving stochastic economic conditions.

For example, consider the operation of a copper mine that has a high component of variable operating costs. When the mine is in operation and output prices fall unexpectedly, management has the option to temporarily shut down mining operations to avoid incurring operating losses. Once prices recover sufficiently, the mine can again be made operational. The operating decision of the mine must take into account several factors:

- The price of copper;

- The costs of production;

- Whether the mine is currently in operation or already shut down;

- Switching costs associated with shutting down and starting up the mine;

- The level of fixed costs when the mine is shut down; and

- The capacity of the mine and the amount of reserves in the ground, factors that, together with the rate of extraction, endogenize the economic life of the mine.

Similar options arise in certain manufacturing projects where operations can be curtailed or completely shut down during low-price periods. Once prices recover, production can resume. This option to temporarily shut down a plant has the effect of truncating the lower tail of the cash-flow distribution. Again, the operator of the mine has a claim similar to a call option on copper. If copper prices rise, the operator profits. If they fall, losses can be limited by the option not to engage in the transaction.

The following mode definitions make the shutdown problem a special case of our general flexibility option. Define mode 2 as the shutdown mode with profits $\pi(\theta_t, 2, t) = -FC$, where $FC$ is the per-period fixed cost when the plant is shut down. Starting up operations to enter production mode 1 entails a switching cost of $c_{21}$. The profits in mode 1 are $\pi(\theta_t, 1, t)$. Shutdown can be achieved at a cost $c_{12}$. If $c_{21} = c_{12} = 0$, then the firm would operate whenever $\pi(\theta_t, 1, t) > 0$. Costly transactions, however, require nontrivial timing decisions.

## 5.3.5 Growth Options

As Myers (1977) pointed out, a major source of value from infrastructure (platform) investments arises from their ability to enhance the upside potential of a project during good market conditions by making follow-on investments. Kulatilaka and Perotti (1993) studied such growth options under assumptions of both perfect and imperfect competition.[13]

Consider, for example, a consumer electronics firm that is contemplating implementing a penetration-marketing strategy by building a plant in Spain. Current market conditions do not warrant even a small-scale manufacturing facility in Europe (i.e., the facility has a negative NPV). However, if the product catches on in Europe, the firm can expand the Spanish operation and penetrate the very large market of the European Economic Community. Given today's information, however, the expansion merely raises expected losses by increasing the scale of operation. Hence, the plant will be rejected.

However, this analysis misses the fact that the expansion will be carried out only if market conditions turn out to be favorable. Having a presence in Europe in the form of the small Spanish operation gives the firm an option it would otherwise not have to grow and meet a large European demand should it materialize. This option need be exercised only if the initial product catches on. In this case, the larger plant will have a large, positive net present value. The negative net present value of the first Spanish plant must be weighed against the value of the growth option it generates, namely, the ability to undertake a positive-NPV investment if market conditions improve. In general, when current investments facilitate future investment opportunities, otherwise negative-NPV projects will become viable.

To fit our general model of flexibility, we characterize the firm before it undertakes the investment as being in mode 1 (waiting-to-invest). Once an additional investment outlay, $I$, is made (i.e., the cost of switching from mode 1 to mode 2, $c_{12} = I$, is incurred), the firm will be operating in mode 2.[14] The firm can expand its scale by a factor, $B$, by making an additional investment of $B(I)$.

Inclusion of growth options can be vital in the *design* stage of infrastructure projects. For instance, a highway project may be designed, at some cost, to accommodate future capacity requirements. A six-lane bridge may be built as part of a four-lane road system. This feature conveys an option to later convert the road system to six lanes. Otherwise, expansion may later be too expensive to pursue. Although the incremental investment cost may be wasted if the need for extra capacity never materializes, the value of the expansion option it creates may justify the cost *ex ante* if there is a sufficiently large probability of increased demand. Growth options are critical in the evaluation of investments in information technology.

## 5.3.6   Input Flexibility

Firms may pay for the capability to switch input technology to take advantage of changing relative prices. This capability represents a real option since it gives the firm the ability to choose *ex post* the low-cost technology. An example of a flexibility option is offered by a power plant that can be fired with either coal or oil. The plant operator chooses the lower-cost alternative. This operating option is purchased at a price, namely, the extra cost required to establish the switching capability. Kulatilaka (1993) modeled the valuation of a flexible-fuel industrial steam boiler using this model of flexibility by defining each fuel type as a mode of operation.

Another input flexibility option arises when firms locate factories in different countries. As exchange rates fluctuate, one or another plant becomes the low-cost producer and the management can choose *ex post* the lowest-cost input mix. Hence, the location option becomes in part an implicit exchange-rate option. Kogut and Kulatilaka (1994) modeled the international plant location problem in the presence of volatile real exchange rates as a flexibility option.

## 5.3.7   Output Flexibility

Some production plants are designed to produce a range of outputs. When management can shift the output mix in response to market prices, the firm holds implicit options on the relative prices of potential outputs. These options raise the value of the production facility, and can make it worthwhile to build a facility even if NPV for any given output appears negative. The output flexibility option means that only *one* output price must rise to make the plant viable. While it may be unlikely for the price of any given output to rise enough for project viability, it may be likely that at least one will do so.

An example of a project with substantial output flexibility is a petroleum refinery that can produce a diverse mix of outputs. Depending on the relative price of the outputs, the refinery can vary the output mix to capture the highest profits. Many agricultural examples (e.g., switching crops based on the relative price) also fit in this category.

In the case of choosing between two outputs, the relative price can be defined as the state variable $\theta$. Then the profit function of the numeraire output will be held constant, while that of the other output will be a function of $\theta$.

## 5.3.8   Option Interactions

In practice, a project can contain several concurrent real options. Brennan and Schwartz (1985a) described such a problem and valued a natural resource project whose commodity output price evolves stochastically and is determined in competitive markets. The impact of the presence of multiple real options is the focus in Trigeorgis (1993a) and in Kulatilaka in chapter 7 of this volume, where the latter uses the present formulation of the flexibility model.

## 5.4   CONCLUDING REMARKS

We have presented a general model of flexibility that contains various known real options as special cases. The model makes explicit the underlying dynamic program, and thus elucidates the decision process more clearly than standard contingent claims models. In addition, since the model is solved numerically, compared to the standard model it can handle more complex projects with multiple real options, nonlinear profit functions, and sources of uncertainty that contain state-dependent parameters.

Not surprisingly, this approach bears close resemblance to other numerical techniques used in option pricing. It is similar to a binomial formulation in that both use the risk-neutral representation of the stochastic process. The risk-adjustment techniques discussed here will also be applicable in a binomial setting where the $\delta$ adjustments will produce state-dependent, risk-neutral probabilities. As with finite-difference methods used in solving the option partial differential equation, both time and the state variable are treated in discrete steps.

This modeling technique could be valuable in modeling many real applications. For instance, Kogut and Kulatilaka (1994) analyzed the international plant location problem in the presence of mean-reverting real exchange rates, while Kulatilaka (1993) valued the flexibility of a dual-fuel industrial steam boiler when firms face volatile energy prices. In chapter 7 in this volume, this framework is used to study option interactions that are found in more complex problems containing multiple real options.

## ACKNOWLEDGMENTS

This chapter is an elaboration of a model first introduced in an MIT Energy Laboratory working paper. I thank Alan Marcus, Robert McDonald, Jim Paddock, Robert Pindyck, Dan Siegel, Martha Schary, Lenos Trigeorgis, and David Wood for comments on earlier drafts. Any remaining errors are my own.

## NOTES

1. See, for example, Hayes and Abernathy (1980) and Hayes and Garvin (1982).

2. These issues are raised by Myers, Kensinger, and Trigeorgis and Mason in a series of articles contained in the spring 1987 issue of the *Midland Corporate Finance Journal*.

3. An overview of applying contingent claims valuation models to real investment and production decisions is given in Mason and Merton (1985).

4. The assumption of perfect competition is common to the entire real options literature. In imperfectly competitive markets, however, the investment decisions of a firm will influence the production decisions of competitors and, hence, the market price (see Kulatilaka and Perotti, 1992). Flexibility is also of some strategic bargaining value to the firm in its negotiations with input suppliers because it can provide a credible threat to use an alternative production mode and switch away from the given input (see Kulatilaka and Marks, 1988).

5. In the continuous-time case, $\pi^i$ can be defined as the instantaneous-flow profit.

6. $\Delta t$ and the contract periods (or the times at which the options can be exercised) need not be identical. The contract times must, however, be in the set of values spanned by the time discretization.

7. When $c_{m,\ell} = 0$, the value is not state dependent. Then the problem with $M = 2$ becomes that of valuing a security whose payoff is the maximum (or minimum) of two assets (see Stulz, 1982).

8. Portions of this section also appear in Kulatilaka (1993).

9. A very similar derivation for a mean-reverting stochastic process appears in Kulatilaka (1993).

10. The mean and variance of that distribution, however, may change over time. Therefore, over longer time periods, the ratio $\theta_T/\theta_0$ may be quite unlike a normal distribution. For example, if we let the mean change in $\theta_t$ be proportional to the level of $\theta_t$ in each period, then $\theta_T/\theta_0$ will be lognormally distributed, even if the distribution of changes in each small time period is approximately normal.

11. Notice also that the discretization of the normal distribution must account for time units. If we posit a normal distribution with mean and variance of $\mu$ and $\sigma^2$ per year, for example, then for time period $\Delta t$, the parameters of the distribution will be $\mu \Delta t$ and $\sigma^2 \Delta t$.

12. Since garment making employs simple, nonspecific technology, there exists a good market for used industrial sewing machines. Although not made explicit here, this analysis can easily be modified to incorporate the correlation between

the used market value of the industrial sewing machines and the profitability of the garment industry. In other words, the scrap value may be stochastic and correlated to the market price of garments, $\theta$.

13. Learning effects, investments in goodwill and other "perishable" forms of capital make expansion options a key in many investments that involve new technology or new markets. Here we ignore the possibility that growth may impact the future market structure and thereby influence the trajectory of future prices.

14. The initial investment and the subsequent switching costs may also depend on time and $\theta$.

# Chapter 6

# The Valuation of American Exchange Options with Application to Real Options

Peter Carr

*An American exchange option gives its owner the right to exchange one risky asset for another at any time prior to expiration. A model for valuing these options is developed using the Geske-Johnson approach for valuing American put options. The formula is shown to generalize much previous work in option pricing. Application of the general valuation formula to the timing option in capital investment decisions is presented.*

## 6.1  INTRODUCTION

An American exchange option gives its owner the right to exchange one risky asset for another at any time up to, and including, its expiration. Margrabe (1978) valued a European exchange option that gives its owner the right to such an exchange only at expiration. Margrabe also proved that the exercise of an American exchange option will only occur at expiration when neither underlying asset pays dividends. However, when the asset to be received in the exchange pays sufficiently large dividends, there is a positive probability that an American exchange option will be exercised *prior* to expiration. This positive probability induces additional value for the American exchange option over its European counterpart.

The purpose of this chapter is to develop a general formula for valuing American exchange options. The formula generalizes the solution of Geske and Johnson (1984) for the value of an American put option. The generalization essentially involves redefining the exercise price as the price of a traded asset. If either asset involved in the exchange has constant value over time, then an exchange option reduces to an ordinary call or put option. Consequently, this general formula for American exchange options may be used to value standard call or put options as special cases. Furthermore, the timing option inherent in a capital investment decision can also be valued.

The chapter values American exchange options when both underlying assets pay dividends continuously. Any asset (e.g., a coupon bond) whose payoffs accrue over time may be considered to yield a continuous payout. Furthermore, an asset may behave as if it pays dividends if, for example, it furnishes a convenience yield or earns a below-equilibrium expected rate of return. Nontraded real assets may offer a below-equilibrium return and may involve flexibilities to switch operating modes or exchange one asset for another. As a result, the general valuation formula may be used to value real options. For analytical tractability, the dividends from the underlying assets are presumed to provide a constant yield. When the dividend yield on the asset to be received in the exchange is strictly positive, American exchange options may be exercised early.

The Geske-Johnson approach is used here to value an American exchange option because it possesses two advantages over other methods. First, the solution may be differentiated to afford comparative statics results. Second, a polynomial approximation to the exact formula is computationally more efficient than either finite-difference methods or the binomial method (see Geske and Shastri, 1985).

The chapter is organized as follows. The next section reviews some of the relevant option-pricing literature. The valuation formula for an American exchange option is derived in section 6.3. The following section then incorporates some previous results as special cases of the general solution. Applying the general valuation model to the timing option in investment theory and other real options is discussed in section 6.5. The final section concludes the chapter.

## 6.2   LITERATURE REVIEW

This chapter is concerned with valuing exchange options on dividend-paying assets that may rationally be exercised early. As an introduction, this section reviews previous work on valuing European exchange options and American puts. To focus the discussion, consider the European option to exchange asset $D$ for asset $V$ at time $T$. Asset $D$ is referred to as the *delivery asset*, and asset $V$ as the *optioned asset*. The payoff to this European option at $T$ is $max(0, V_T - D_T)$, where $V_T$ and $D_T$ are the underlying assets' terminal prices. Suppose that the underlying asset prices $V_t$ and $D_t$, prior to expiration, follow a geometric Brownian motion of the form:

$$\frac{dV_t}{V_t} = (\alpha_v - \delta_v)dt + \sigma_v dZ_t^v \qquad (6.1)$$

$$\frac{dD_t}{D_t} = (\alpha_d - \delta_d)dt + \sigma_d dZ_t^d$$

$$\text{cov}\left(\frac{dV_t}{V_t}, \frac{dD_t}{D_t}\right) = \sigma_{vd}dt, \quad t \in [0, T],$$

where $\alpha_v$ and $\alpha_d$ are the expected rates of return on the two assets, $\delta_v$ and $\delta_d$ are the corresponding dividend yields, $\sigma_v^2$ and $\sigma_d^2$ are the respective variance rates, and $dZ_t^v$ and $dZ_t^d$ are increments of standard Wiener processes at time $t$. The rates of price changes, $\frac{dV_t}{V_t}$ and $\frac{dD_t}{D_t}$, can be correlated, with the covariance rate given by $\sigma_{vd}$. The parameters $\delta_v$, $\delta_d$, $\sigma_v$, $\sigma_d$, and $\sigma_{vd}$ are assumed to be nonnegative constants, although they can be allowed to be deterministic functions of time.

McDonald and Siegel (1985) showed that, under certain assumptions, the value of a European exchange option on such dividend-paying assets is given by:

$$e(V, D, \tau) = Ve^{-\delta_v \tau}N_1(d_1(Pe^{-\delta \tau}, \sigma^2 \tau)) - De^{-\delta_d \tau}N_1(d_2(Pe^{-\delta \tau}, \sigma^2 \tau)),$$
$$(6.2)$$

where:

$N_1(d) \equiv \int_0^d \frac{e^{-z^2/2}}{\sqrt{2\pi}}dz$ is the standard normal distribution function,

$d_1(Pe^{-\delta \tau}, \sigma^2 \tau) \equiv \frac{\ln(Pe^{-\delta \tau}) + \sigma^2 \tau/2}{\sqrt{\sigma^2 \tau}}$,

$P \equiv \frac{V}{D}$ is the price ratio of $V$ to $D$,

$\delta \equiv \delta_v - \delta_d$ is the difference in the dividend yields,

$\sigma^2 \equiv \sigma_v^2 + \sigma_d^2 - 2\sigma_{vd}$ is the variance rate of $\frac{dP}{P}$, and

$d_2(Pe^{-\delta \tau}, \sigma^2 \tau) \equiv d_1(Pe^{-\delta \tau}, \sigma^2 \tau) - \sigma\sqrt{\tau}$.

(To simplify the notation, the second argument of $d_1$ and $d_2$ will be dropped whenever it can be inferred from the first argument.)

The underlying assets in the McDonald and Siegel model are not necessarily traded. Consequently, they develop their valuation formula using an equilibrium argument. When the underlying assets are traded, an arbitrage argument also leads to Equation (6.2). Black and Scholes (1973) also showed that their valuation formula can be alternatively derived using an equilibrium model or an arbitrage argument. In the Black-Scholes model, the expected rate of return on the underlying asset is irrelevant given the current asset price. Similarly, Equation (6.2) indicates that the expected rates of return, $\alpha_v$ and $\alpha_d$, are irrelevant given the current asset values, $V$ and $D$.

In contrast to the Black-Scholes formula, however, the risk-free rate of interest, $r$, is also absent from the formula.[1] The reason for this is that the exchange option value is linearly homogeneous in the asset prices $V$ and $D$ under the stochastic process (6.1).[2] Consequently, the weights that eliminate risk in the hedge portfolio also make it costless. A no-arbitrage equilibrium then implies that the hedge portfolio earns zero return, rather than the interest rate, $r$. Since the expected rates of return and the interest rate are irrelevant given the current asset prices, investors need not agree on the dynamics of these rates. However, agreement *is* presumed on the constant variance rate, $\sigma^2$, and on the constant dividend yields, $\delta_v$ and $\delta_d$.

If these dividend yields are set equal to zero, then Margrabe's (1978) formula for a European exchange option results. Under further parameter restrictions and the additional assumption of a constant (positive) riskless rate, $r$, formulas for European call and put options can be obtained. To value a call option, suppose that we "zero-out" the variance rate of the delivery asset ($\sigma_d^2 = 0$) so that, to avoid arbitrage, its expected rate of return must be the riskless rate ($\alpha_d = r$). Further, suppose that the delivery asset pays dividends at the riskless rate ($\delta_d = r$) so that its value is constant over time ($\frac{dD}{D} = 0$). A call option is thus a special type of an exchange option where the delivery asset, $D$, has a constant value over time. Under the assumed parameter restrictions $\delta_d = r$ and $\sigma_d^2 = 0$, Equation (6.2) reduces to Merton's (1973) formula for a European call option on a dividend-paying stock:

$$c(V, D, \tau) = V e^{-\delta_v \tau} N_1(d_1(Pe^{-\delta\tau})) - De^{-r\tau} N_1(d_2(Pe^{-\delta\tau})), \qquad (6.3)$$

where $V$ is the current price of the underlying asset, $D$ is the exercise price of the call option, $\delta = \delta_v - r$, and $\sigma = \sigma_v$. If the underlying asset pays no dividends ($\delta_v = 0$), then the standard Black-Scholes (1973) formula for a European call option emerges.

As is the case for a call, a put option is also a special kind of an exchange option. In contrast to a call, however, the delivery asset for a put option is risky, while the optioned asset, $V$, has a constant value over time. The value of asset $V$ will similarly be constant ($\frac{dV}{V} = 0$) if its variance rate vanishes ($\sigma_v^2 = 0$) and if it yields dividends at the riskless rate $r$ ($\delta_v = r$). Making these substitutions in Equation (6.2) yields the formula for a European put option on an asset paying continuous dividends:

$$p(V, D, \tau) = V e^{-r\tau} N_1(d_1(Pe^{-\delta\tau})) - De^{-\delta_d\tau} N_1(d_2(Pe^{-\delta\tau})), \qquad (6.4)$$

where $V$ is the exercise price of the put option, $D$ is the current price of the underlying asset, $\delta = r - \delta_d$, and $\sigma = \sigma_d$. If the underlying asset pays no dividends ($\delta_d = 0$), the Black-Scholes European put option formula arises if we make use of the following identities:

$$d_1(Pe^{-r\tau}) \;=\; d_1\left(\frac{Ve^{-r\tau}}{D}\right) = -d_2\left(\frac{D}{Ve^{-r\tau}}\right)$$

$$d_2(Pe^{-r\tau}) \;\; = \;\; d_2\left(\frac{Ve^{-r\tau}}{D}\right) = -d_1\left(\frac{D}{Ve^{-r\tau}}\right). \qquad (6.5)$$

Up to this point, the focus has been exclusively on European options. Unfortunately, the general equation, (6.2), does not hold for American exchange options. If an American exchange option is sufficiently in the money, it will pay to exercise early when asset $V$ has a positive dividend yield. For an American *put*, since this asset yields dividends at the riskless rate, $r$, there is always a positive probability of premature exercise.

Geske and Johnson (1984) accounted for this possibility of early exercise when they derived a valuation formula for American put options. Their approach is to view an American put option as the limit to a sequence of pseudo-American puts. A pseudo-American option can only be exercised at a finite number of discrete exercise points. As the number of possible exercise points grows, the value of a pseudo-American option approaches that of a true American one. Unfortunately, for a large number of exercise points, the valuation formula becomes cumbersome. The authors circumvent this problem by extrapolating from the values of puts with a small number of exercise points. The valuation formulas for these lower-order puts can be easily implemented.

The next section generalizes the Geske-Johnson approach to American exchange options on dividend-paying assets. The resulting solution incorporates many of the option pricing formulas which have appeared in the earlier literature. In particular, the formulas discussed in this section arise as special cases.

## 6.3   VALUATION OF THE AMERICAN EXCHANGE OPTION

This section derives the valuation formula for an American exchange option on dividend-paying assets. Let $t$ be the valuation date and $T$ the option expiration date. The first step involves dividing the option's time to maturity, $\tau \equiv T - t$, into $n$ equal intervals. Let $E_n(\tau)$ be the value of a pseudo-American exchange option with time to maturity $\tau$. The subscript $n$ indicates that the option can be exercised at any of the $n$ end points of each interval. Then $E_1(\tau)$ is just the value of a European exchange option, as given by Equation (6.2).

$E_2(\tau)$ is the value of an exchange option that may be exercised at $\frac{T}{2}$ or at $T$. This option will not be exercised at mid-life if the opportunity cost of exercise, namely, the value of the option from Equation (6.2), exceeds the cash proceeds of exercise, that is, if:

$$Ve^{-\delta_v\Delta t}N_1(d_1(Pe^{-\delta\Delta t})) - De^{-\delta_d\Delta t}N_1(d_2(Pe^{-\delta\Delta t})) > V - D, \quad (6.6)$$

where $\Delta t = \dfrac{\tau}{2}$.

Both $V$ and $D$ are random prices as of the valuation date, $t$. However, the exercise condition can be reexpressed in terms of a single random variable by taking the delivery asset as a numeraire. Dividing by the delivery asset price, $D$, and substituting the price ratio $P$ for $\frac{V}{D}$, yields:

$$Pe^{-\delta_v\Delta t}N_1(d_1(Pe^{-\delta\Delta t})) - e^{-\delta_d\Delta t}N_1(d_2(Pe^{-\delta\Delta t})) > P - 1. \quad (6.7)$$

Let $P^*$ be the unique value of the price ratio, $P$, which makes Equation (6.7) an equality. That is, the critical price ratio, $P^*$, is defined by:

$$P^*e^{-\delta_v\Delta t}N_1(d_1(P^*e^{-\delta\Delta t})) - e^{-\delta_d\Delta t}N_1(d_2(P^*e^{-\delta\Delta t})) = P^* - 1. \quad (6.8)$$

For values of the price ratio $P$ greater than the critical price ratio $P^*$, the option is exercised to yield proceeds of $V - D$ at the intermediate exercise date $\frac{T}{2}$. Otherwise, the option is held and would pay off $max(0, V - D)$ at the expiration date $T$. The risk-neutral valuation relationship of Cox and Ross (1976) may be used to value these contingent payoffs, as follows:

$$
\begin{aligned}
E_2(\tau) \;=\; & V\left[e^{-\delta_v\Delta t}N_1\left(d_1\left(\frac{Pe^{-\delta\Delta t}}{P^*}\right)\right)\right. \\
& \left. +\; e^{-\delta_v T}N_2\left(-d_1\left(\frac{Pe^{-\delta\Delta t}}{P^*}\right), d_1(Pe^{-\delta T}); -\sqrt{\frac{1}{2}}\right)\right] \\
& -\; D\left[e^{-\delta_d\Delta t}N_1\left(d_2\left(\frac{Pe^{-\delta\Delta t}}{P^*}\right)\right)\right. \\
& \left. +\; e^{-\delta_d T}N_2\left(-d_2\left(\frac{Pe^{-\delta\Delta t}}{P^*}\right), d_2(Pe^{-\delta T}); -\sqrt{\frac{1}{2}}\right)\right],
\end{aligned}
$$
$$(6.9)$$

where $N_2(x_1, x_2; \rho)$ is the standard bivariate normal distribution function evaluated at $x_1$ and $x_2$ with correlation coefficient $\rho$, given by:

$$N_2(x_1, x_2; \rho) \equiv \int_{-\infty}^{x_1}\int_{-\infty}^{x_2}\frac{\exp\left\{-\frac{1}{2(1-\rho^2)}[z_1^2 - 2\rho z_1 z_2 + z_2^2]\right\}}{2\pi\sqrt{1-\rho^2}}dz_2dz_1.$$

This functional form for $E_2(\cdot)$, in turn, can be used to determine the pseudo-American exchange option value, $E_3(\tau)$, an option that can be exercised at times $\frac{T}{3}$, $\frac{2T}{3}$, or at $T$. Whether the option is exercised early depends on whether the price ratio, $P$, reaches certain critical values at the intermediate dates $\frac{T}{3}$ and $\frac{2T}{3}$. The option will not be exercised at the first exercise point, $\frac{T}{3}$, if the opportunity cost of exercise, $E_2(\frac{2T}{3})$, exceeds the cash proceeds from exercise, $V - D$. Dividing again by the delivery asset price, $D$, leads to the defining equation for the first critical value, $P_1^*$:

$$
P_1^* \left[ e^{-\delta_v \Delta t} N_1 \left( d_1 \left( \frac{P_1^* e^{-\delta \Delta t}}{P^*} \right) \right) \right.
$$
$$
+ \left. e^{-\delta_v 2\Delta t} N_2 \left( -d_1 \left( \frac{P_1^* e^{-\delta \Delta t}}{P^*} \right), d_1(P_1^* e^{-\delta 2\Delta t}); -\sqrt{\frac{1}{2}} \right) \right]
$$
$$
- \left[ e^{-\delta_d \Delta t} N_1 \left( d_2 \left( \frac{P_1^* e^{-\delta \Delta t}}{P^*} \right) \right) \right.
$$
$$
+ \left. e^{-\delta_d 2\Delta t} N_2 \left( -d_2 \left( \frac{P_1^* e^{-\delta \Delta t}}{P^*} \right), d_2(P_1^* e^{-\delta 2\Delta t}); -\sqrt{\frac{1}{2}} \right) \right]
$$
$$
= P_1^* - 1, \text{ where } \Delta t = \frac{\tau}{3}. \tag{6.10}
$$

Assuming that the pseudo-American option survives its first exercise point, $\frac{T}{3}$, it will also not be exercised at the next exercise point, $\frac{2T}{3}$, if its value alive, $E_1(\frac{\tau}{3})$, exceeds its exercise value, $V - D$. Again, dividing by the delivery asset price, $D$, leads to the defining equation for the second critical value, $P_2^*$:

$$
P_2^* e^{-\delta_v \Delta t} N_1(d_1(P_2^* e^{-\delta \Delta t})) - e^{-\delta_d \Delta t} N_1(d_2(P_2^* e^{-\delta \Delta t})) = P_2^* - 1.
$$

Risk-neutral valuation can again be employed to write the valuation formula for the pseudo-American exchange option, $E_3(\tau)$, as:

$$
\begin{aligned}
E_3(\tau) &= V[e^{-\delta_v \Delta t} N_1(d_1(\tfrac{Pe^{-\delta \Delta t}}{P_1^*})) \\
&+ e^{-\delta_v 2\Delta t} N_2(-d_1(\tfrac{Pe^{-\delta \Delta t}}{P^*}), d_1(Pe^{-\delta 2\Delta t}); -\sqrt{\tfrac{1}{2}}) \\
&+ e^{-\delta_v \tau} N_3(-d_1(\tfrac{Pe^{-\delta \Delta t}}{P_1^*}), -d_1(\tfrac{Pe^{-\delta 2\Delta t}}{P_2^*}), d_1(Pe^{-\delta \tau}); \Omega_3)] \\
&- D[e^{-\delta_d \Delta t} N_1(d_2(\tfrac{Pe^{-\delta \Delta t}}{P_1^*})) \\
&+ e^{-\delta_d 2\Delta t} N_2(-d_2(\tfrac{Pe^{-\delta \Delta t}}{P^*}), d_2(Pe^{-\delta 2\Delta t}); -\sqrt{\tfrac{1}{2}}) \\
&+ e^{-\delta_d \tau} N_3(-d_2(\tfrac{Pe^{-\delta \Delta t}}{P_1^*}), -d_2(\tfrac{Pe^{-\delta 2\Delta t}}{P_2^*}), d_2(Pe^{-\delta \tau}); \Omega_3)],
\end{aligned}
$$
$$
\tag{6.11}
$$

where $\Delta t = \frac{\tau}{3}$, $N_3(x_1, x_2, x_3; \Omega_3)$ is the standard trivariate normal distribution function evaluated at $x_1$, $x_2$, and $x_3$ with a correlation matrix $\Omega_3$, given by:

$$
N_3(x_1, x_2, x_3; \Omega_3) \equiv
$$
$$
\int_\infty^{x_1} \int_\infty^{x_2} \int_\infty^{x_3} (2\pi)^{-3/2} |\Omega_3|^{-1/2} \exp\left\{ -\frac{1}{2} z' \Omega_3^{-1} z \right\} dz_1 dz_2 dz_3,
$$

with $z$ as the $3 \times 1$ vector,

$$\begin{bmatrix} z_1 \\ z_2 \\ z_3 \end{bmatrix},$$

and $\Omega_3$ as the $3 \times 3$ symmetric matrix:

$$\begin{bmatrix} \sqrt{\frac{1}{1}} & \sqrt{\frac{1}{2}} & \sqrt{\frac{1}{3}} \\ \sqrt{\frac{1}{2}} & \sqrt{\frac{2}{2}} & \sqrt{\frac{2}{3}} \\ \sqrt{\frac{1}{3}} & \sqrt{\frac{2}{3}} & \sqrt{\frac{3}{3}} \end{bmatrix}.$$

By induction, the value of the general pseudo-American exchange option, $E_n$, is:

$$E_n = Vw_1(\delta_v) - Dw_2(\delta_d) \tag{6.12}$$

where:

$$
\begin{aligned}
w_1(\delta_v) \equiv\ & e^{-\delta_v \Delta t} N_1\left(d_1\left(\frac{Pe^{-\delta \Delta t}}{P_1^*}\right)\right) \\
& + e^{-\delta_v 2\Delta t} N_2\left(-d_1\left(\frac{Pe^{-\delta \Delta t}}{P_1^*}\right), d_1\left(\frac{Pe^{-\delta 2\Delta t}}{P_2^*}\right); -\sqrt{\tfrac{1}{2}}\right) \\
& + e^{-\delta_v 3\Delta t} N_3\left(-d_1\left(\frac{Pe^{-\delta \Delta t}}{P_1^*}\right), -d_1\left(\frac{Pe^{-\delta 2\Delta t}}{P_2^*}\right), d_1\left(\frac{Pe^{-\delta 3\Delta t}}{P_3^*}\right); \Omega_3\right) \\
& + \cdots \\
& + e^{-\delta_v \tau} N_n\left(-d_1\left(\frac{Pe^{-\delta \Delta t}}{P_1^*}\right), \ldots, -d_1\left(\frac{Pe^{-\delta(n-1)\Delta t}}{P_{n-1}^*}\right), d_1(Pe^{-\delta \tau}); \Omega_n\right)
\end{aligned}
$$

and

$$
\begin{aligned}
w_2(\delta_d) \equiv\ & e^{-\delta_d \Delta t} N_1\left(d_2\left(\frac{Pe^{-\delta \Delta t}}{P_1^*}\right)\right) \\
& + e^{-\delta_d 2\Delta t} N_2\left(-d_2\left(\frac{Pe^{-\delta \Delta t}}{P_1^*}\right), d_2\left(\frac{Pe^{-\delta 2\Delta t}}{P_2^*}\right); -\sqrt{\tfrac{1}{2}}\right) \\
& + e^{-\delta_d 3\Delta t} N_3\left(-d_2\left(\frac{Pe^{-\delta \Delta t}}{P_1^*}\right), -d_2\left(\frac{Pe^{-\delta 2\Delta t}}{P_2^*}\right), d_2\left(\frac{Pe^{-\delta 3\Delta t}}{P_3^*}\right); \Omega_3\right) \\
& + \cdots \\
& + e^{-\delta_d \tau} N_n\left(-d_2\left(\frac{Pe^{-\delta \Delta t}}{P_1^*}\right), \ldots, -d_2\left(\frac{Pe^{-\delta(n-1)\Delta t}}{P_{n-1}^*}\right), d_2(Pe^{-\delta \tau}); \Omega_n\right),
\end{aligned}
$$

with $\Delta t = \frac{\tau}{n}$. $N_k$ is the standard $k$-variate normal distribution function with correlation matrix $\Omega_k$:

$$\int_{\infty}^{x_1} \int_{\infty}^{x_2} \cdots \int_{\infty}^{x_k} (2\pi)^{-k/2} |\Omega_k|^{-1/2} \exp\left\{-\frac{1}{2} z' \Omega_k^{-1} z\right\} dz_1 dz_2 \cdots dz_k,$$

with $z$ as the $k \times 1$ vector,

$$\begin{bmatrix} z_1 \\ z_2 \\ \vdots \\ z_k \end{bmatrix},$$

$\Omega_k$ as the $k \times k$ symmetric matrix whose $i - j$th element is

$$\sqrt{\frac{i}{j}} \quad \begin{matrix} i = 1 \dots j \\ j = 1 \dots k, \end{matrix}$$

and where $P_k^*$ is the critical value of $P$ at $k\Delta t$, $k = 1 \dots n - 1$.

Since the discrete exercise policy employed here is not strictly optimal, the pseudo-American exchange option value, $E_n$, is actually a lower bound on the true American exchange option value. However, arbitrary accuracy can be achieved for sufficiently large values of $n$. Unfortunately, the formula involves $n$-variate normal distribution functions that are not tabulated for large values of $n$. This problem can be solved by extrapolating for $E_n$ from its lower-order values. The three-point Richardson extrapolation, which achieves reasonable accuracy, is:[3]

$$E_n \approx \frac{1}{2}E_1 - 4E_2 + \frac{9}{2}E_3. \tag{6.13}$$

## 6.4  SPECIAL CASES

In this section, the parameters of the general valuation formula, Equation (6.12), are restricted to yield various known special cases. In particular, the valuation formulas for standard American put and call options are easily derived. The valuation formulas for the European options given in section 6.2 also arise as special cases. Throughout this section, the riskless rate is assumed to be (a positive) constant.

### 6.4.1  American Put Option

Recall that a put is an exchange option whose optioned asset's value is constant over time. As in section 6.2, constant value is achieved ($\frac{dV}{V} = 0$) by "zeroing-out" asset $V$'s variance rate ($\sigma_v^2 = 0$) and equating its dividend yield to the riskless rate ($\delta_v = r$). Making these substitutions yields the formula for an American put on a dividend-paying stock:

$$P_n = V w_1(r) - D w_2(\delta_d), \tag{6.14}$$

where $V$ is the exercise price of the put option, $D$ is the current price of the underlying asset, $\delta = r - \delta_d$, and $\sigma^2 = \sigma_d^2$. If the underlying asset for the American put pays no dividends ($\delta_d = 0$), then the Geske-Johnson formula for an American put arises.[4]

### 6.4.2 American Call Option

If the underlying asset for an American call pays a continuous dividend at a constant yield, then the option may rationally be exercised before maturity. To value such a call option with the general valuation formula (6.12), the delivery asset parameters are restricted to achieve constant value. In particular, by setting $\delta_d = r$ and $\sigma_d^2 = 0$, we obtain:

$$C_n = Vw_1(\delta_v) - Dw_2(r), \tag{6.15}$$

where $V$ is the current value of the underlying asset, $D$ is the exercise price of the call option, $\delta = \delta_v - r$, and $\sigma^2 = \sigma_v^2$.

As the dividend yield on the underlying asset becomes smaller, the critical price ratios required to trigger early exercise become larger. When this dividend vanishes ($\delta_v = 0$), no finite asset price will be sufficiently high to induce exercise at any time prior to maturity. As a result, $P_k^* = \infty, \forall k = 1 \ldots n-1$ in Equation (6.12), and the Black-Scholes formula is consequently obtained.

### 6.4.3 European Exchange Options

Recall that the early exercise of an exchange option occurs when the price ratio exceeds the critical price ratio, $P^*$. To value an exchange option that precludes exercise on any given date prior to maturity, the critical price ratio corresponding to that date can be set to infinity. As a result, a European exchange option can again be valued by setting $P_k^* = \infty, \forall k = 1 \ldots n - 1$ in Equation (6.12). The general formula then reduces to McDonald and Siegel's (1985) formula, shown in Equation (6.2), for a European exchange option on dividend-paying assets. Section 6.2 demonstrated that this formula, in turn, contains Margrabe's (1978) solution for an exchange option on non-dividend-paying assets, as well as the Merton (1973) and Black-Scholes (1973) option formulas.

## 6.5 APPLICATION TO REAL OPTIONS

In this section, the general valuation formula, Equation (6.12), is used to illustrate valuation of the timing option available to firms when making real investment decisions. McDonald and Siegel (1986) have valued a firm's option to invest (at time $t$) a random amount, $D_t$, to undertake a project whose current value to the firm is $V_t$. If $V_t$ and $D_t$ are not prices of traded assets, their expected growth rates may actually differ from the expected rate of return required for their risk in equilibrium in the financial markets. Let $\delta_v$ and $\delta_d$ be the assumed constant difference (return shortfall) between these expected rates. If the firm could invest only at a fixed time point, $T$, then the value of the option to invest would be given by Equation (6.2) for a European exchange option. Using an equilibrium argument, McDonald and Siegel valued this option when its life is either infinite or random.

The general valuation formula, Equation (6.12), can also be derived in an equilibrium model. The formula may then be used to value a timing option that expires within a fixed period of time. Concrete examples of this situation may occur when a firm has an option to buy land or to drill for oil within, say, six months. Alternatively, a patent, injunction, or a temporary competitive advantage may allow a firm to exploit a production opportunity for a limited period of time.

The option to abandon a project, having current value $D_t$, in exchange for its salvage (or best alternative use) value, $V_t$, has been studied in Myers and Majd (1990) and McDonald and Siegel (1986). This abandonment option is a mirror problem to that of the timing option and can be similarly valued with our general formula with a suitable reinterpretation of variables. Other real options, such as to switch inputs or outputs in production, can be valued similarly.

The major impediment to such real option applications appears to be the potential unobservability of the asset values, $V_t$ and $D_t$. In certain situations, these values can be backed out of a valuation model that employs observable prices as inputs. For example, Brennan and Schwartz (1985a) valued a mine when the ore is traded in the futures markets. Assuming that a geometric Brownian motion is a reasonable approximation for the dynamics of the mine's value, the American option to buy or sell the mine can be valued using the results of this chapter.

Alternatively, the effect of the unobservability of the asset values, $V_t$ and $D_t$, can be included in the valuation model. For example, one could assume that these quantities are observed with noise, the principal effect of which would be to induce suboptimal exercise. In particular, real options might be exercised when they are out-of-the-money, and deep in-the-money options may sometimes fail to be optimally exercised. These effects work to reduce option value relative to the case with perfect observability. The magnitude of mispricing would depend positively on the amount of noise (or the variance of the error term).

## 6.6 CONCLUSION

This chapter has developed a model for valuing American exchange options on dividend-paying assets. After a brief review of the literature, a general formula was developed which was shown to encompass many earlier results under suitable parameter restrictions. In particular, this general formula values both European and American calls and puts as special cases. The general valuation formula was also applied to valuing the timing option in investment theory.

The forgoing analysis may be extended to allow for imperfect capital markets, stochastic interest rates, and discrete dividends. Furthermore, the formula for the American exchange option can be used to value certain financial options, such as options in exchange offers or options embedded in convertible or commodity-linked bonds.

## ACKNOWLEDGMENTS

A slightly longer version of this chapter appeared as the second essay in my Ph.D. dissertation, "Essays on Exchange" (University of California at Los Angeles). I would like to thank the following individuals for their comments and support: Warren Bailey, Jim Brandon, Michael Brennan, Tom Copeland, Dan Galai, Bob Geske, Mark Grinblatt, David Hirshleifer, Craig Holden, Eduardo Schwartz, Erik Sirri, Sheridan Titman, Walt Torous, Brett Trueman, and the participants of the UCLA finance workshop. They are not responsible for any errors. Financial support was provided by a fellowship from the Social Sciences and Humanities Research Council of Canada, a John M. Olin scholarship, and an Allstate Dissertation Fellowship.

## NOTES

1. Merton (1973) also showed that the risk-free rate, $r$, need not appear in the Black-Scholes formula if the present value of the exercise price is replaced by the price of a zero-coupon bond paying the exercise price at expiration.

2. A function $f(x_1, x_2)$ is *linearly homogeneous* if $f(\lambda x_1, \lambda x_2) = \lambda f(x_1, x_2)$ for any $\lambda > 0$.

3. See the Appendix of Geske and Johnson (1984) for a derivation of this formula. The formulas for $E_1, E_2$, and $E_3$ are given by Equations (6.2), (6.9), and (6.11), respectively.

4. To express the formula in the Geske-Johnson (1984) notation, make the following substitutions in Equation (6.14): $X = V$, $S = D$, $\frac{S_t^*}{S} = \frac{V}{DP_t^*}$, and use the identities given by Equation (6.5) in section 6.2.

# Chapter 7

# Operating Flexibilities in Capital Budgeting: Substitutability and Complementarity in Real Options

## Nalin Kulatilaka

*This chapter uses a numerical example to illustrate the interdependencies between options to wait-to-invest, to temporarily shut down, and to expand the scale of a project (growth option). It is confirmed that the incremental value of an option may increase or decrease when added to projects that already contain other operating options. Waiting-to-invest is worth less in the presence of shutdown or growth options, implying "substitutability" between waiting-to-invest and the other two options. But shutdown becomes more valuable in the presence of the growth option, implying "complementarity" between them. We also examine the impact of adding new options on the critical boundaries at which existing options are exercised.*

## 7.1  INTRODUCTION

The presence of operating flexibilities that confer management an ability to revise decisions while the project is underway has been the focus of study in the growing literature on real options.[1] McDonald and Siegel (1986) showed that the value of the option to wait-to-invest can be large and that an investment criterion that ignores this option value can be very misleading. Similar operating flexibilities are associated with options to abandon (McDonald and Siegel, 1986; Myers and Majd, 1990); options to temporarily shut down (McDonald and Siegel, 1985; Brennan and Schwartz, 1985a); sequential options (Majd and Pindyck, 1987); and options to alter capacity (Pindyck, 1988).[2] Most of this literature has dealt with one option at a time.

While the impact of the presence of a single real option at a time is well understood, when many real options are present simultaneously the inter-actions between these options will affect not only the value of the project (and the contributions from each option), but also the critical boundaries at which exercise of the options becomes optimal. In some cases, the presence of one real option may complement the value of another, while in other cases the option values may be substitutes. The focus of this chapter is to investigate the effect of introducing real options on the valuation and the optimal operating rules for projects that already contain other real options.

In chapter 5 of this volume, I developed a model of flexibility whereby a project can be operated in one of several modes with costly switching between the modes, providing a set of nested compound options. Kulati-laka and Marcus (1988) extended this analysis by casting the problem in a discrete-time compound option framework to obtain analytical solutions in terms of cumulative multivariate normal distributions. An analytically more elegant and computationally more tractable formulation is developed in Mason and Merton (1985). They handled such multiple options in a continuous-time formulation where the boundary conditions can be used to solve for the option values and critical prices. Trigeorgis (1993a) drew analogies to financial call and put options to study real option interactions and show the value "non-additivity" of real options. He used a stylized ex-ample involving five different options and showed that while in some cases the interaction effects are small, they are quite significant in others. These results, however, are based on a restrictive set of assumptions regarding the stochastic dynamics of the exogenous uncertainty.

This chapter uses a general dynamic-programming framework that en-ables simultaneous evaluation of the effect of *many* such operating options. Each option can be seen as a special case of a more general "flexibility" option that allows the firm to choose from an entire menu of available tech-nology modes. In addition, I take account of the fact that the underlying stochastic variables are likely to be the prices of nontraded assets, in which case standard arbitrage arguments are inappropriate to value real options. Instead, relying on the Cox, Ingersol, and Ross (1985) extension of the risk-neutrality argument, I adjust for rate-of-return shortfalls in the prices of nontraded real assets. A numerical example is used to illustrate options to wait-to-invest, to temporarily shut down, and to expand a project, which shows how the value of each option and the critical exercise price boundaries are affected by the inclusion of other options.

The rest of the chapter is organized as follows. The next section presents the dynamic-programming formulation of flexibility, with careful attention paid to the assumptions underlying the exogeneity of uncertainty and the treatment of risk. In section 7.3, I show how the flexibility model can be specialized to value a project that offers options to wait-to-invest, to shut down temporarily, and to expand in scale, with numerical simulations illustrating these results. Section 7.4 concludes the discussion.

## 7.2  A MODEL OF FLEXIBILITY

### 7.2.1  Characterizing Exogenous Uncertainty

In this section we briefly summarize the model of flexibility that is more fully described in chapter 5 in this volume and in Kulatilaka (1993). Traditionally, models of real options treat the project value as the exogenous stochastic variable. The presence of real options, however, influences that project value. Suppose the value of the project *without* the options follows a lognormal stochastic process. Inclusion of an option to temporarily shutdown would truncate the distribution of future cash flows. The resulting project will then be a nonlinear transformation of the original one and, hence, will no longer follow the same process.[3] If, on the other hand, we characterize the project with the single option (shutdown) as following a lognormal process, the project including two options (shutdown and expansion) will no longer follow the same process. Hence, it is not possible to separately identify the effects attributable to the two options.

Here we assume that the price of a factor input or of an output, rather than project value, is the exogenous stochastic variable. For example, firms in many industries face uncertainty in competitively-determined energy prices, so the real options for an input-price–taking firm will not significantly affect the market price of that input.

Specifically, the exogenous uncertainty faced by the firm is generally characterized by a stochastic variable, $\theta$, which in a *risk-neutral* economy will follow the dynamics:

$$\frac{d\theta_t}{\theta_t} = \overline{\alpha}dt + \sigma dZ_t, \tag{7.1}$$

where $\overline{\alpha}$ is the *risk-neutral* rate of return, obtained as $r - \delta$ or as $\alpha - \xi\sigma$, where $\alpha$ is the actual drift rate and $\xi$ is the risk premium based on an equilibrium asset pricing model; $\sigma$ is the volatility of $\theta$, and $dZ_t$ is the increment of a standard Wiener process.[4] Equation (7.1) is the limiting case of the discrete-time stochastic process,

$$\Delta\theta_t = \overline{\alpha}\theta_t\Delta t + \sigma\theta_t\sqrt{\Delta t}\Delta Z_t. \tag{7.2}$$

It is easy to show how transition probabilities can be derived and used in forming risk-neutral expectations of future cash flows, even when they are influenced by real options in nonlinear ways (see Kulatilaka, 1993, or section 5.2.4 in chapter 5 of this volume).

We define the various operating modes of the project using profit functions. The operating modes may characterize different production processes as well as states that describe waiting-to-invest, shutting down, and abandoning the project. Suppose a project consists of $M$ modes with profit functions, $\pi^i, i = 1, ..., M$.

The value of a *fixed technology* project of life $T$ periods that is dedicated to mode $m$ can be expressed as:

$$V_m(\theta_0) = E_0 \left( \sum_{t=0}^{T} \pi^m(\theta_t)\rho^t \right), \tag{7.3}$$

where $E_0(.)$ is the risk-neutral expectation operator conditional on information at time 0 (i.e., on the realization of $\theta_0$), and $\rho$ is the risk-free discount factor. Expected values are obtained as probability weighted sums:

$$E_{t-1}\left[\pi(\theta^i)\right] = \sum_{j=1}^{S} \pi(\theta^j)p_{ij}, \tag{7.4}$$

where $p_{ij}$ is the risk-neutral probability of a transition between the discrete states $\theta_i$ and $\theta_j$ during the time interval $(t-1, t)$.

The value of a general *flexible* project (i.e., one that can switch among $M$ alternative modes) at the beginning of the last period of operation (at time $T$) depends on $\theta(T)$. In addition, since switching between modes involves costs, the mode of operation during the previous period will also influence the current value of the flexible project, $F$. If mode $j$ was used at time $T - \Delta t$ and $\theta_T = \theta^k$, then the project value function at $T$ can be written as:

$$F(\theta_{T-\Delta t} = \theta^k, m) = \max_{\ell} \left( \pi^\ell(\theta^k) - c_{m,\ell} \right), \tag{7.5}$$

where $c_{m,\ell}$ is the cost of switching from mode $m$ to mode $\ell$.[5]

In general, the dynamic-programming equations at any time $t$ can be written as:

$$F(\theta_t = \theta^k, m) = \max_{\ell} \left( \pi^\ell(\theta^k) - c_{m,\ell} \right) + \rho E_t \left[ F(\theta_{t+\Delta t}, \ell) \right], \tag{7.6}$$

for $i, j = 1, .., M, \ k = 1, ..., S, \ \text{and} \ t = 0, .., T - 1$.

# 7.3 AN ILLUSTRATIVE EXAMPLE

I illustrate the valuation of the flexibility option by applying it to a project that offers options to wait-to-invest, to shut down temporarily, and to expand the scale of the project (a growth option). In some instances firms can get exclusive licenses (e.g., through patents) whereby a positive-NPV investment can be postponed without losing it forever. These and other postponement decisions are included in the waiting-to-invest scenario. The temporary shutdown option is also a common feature in many projects. Of course, in many manufacturing projects that have large fixed costs or long-term input (e.g., labor) contracts, however, the costs of shutting down and starting up may be very costly. In other instances (e.g., mining projects) where the switching costs are relatively small, however, the shutdown option may be extremely valuable. Expansion options are equally prevalent. Typically, the option to expand takes advantage of the current operating status in a market. Learning effects, investments in goodwill and other "perishable" forms of capital make expansion options a key in many investments that involve new technology or markets.[6] In what follows, I will consider each option separately and investigate its impact on project value, on the value of other options, and on the critical values of $\theta$ at which the option should be exercised.[7]

## 7.3.1 Definition of Operating Modes

I characterize the firm before it undertakes the investment as being in mode 1 ("waiting-to-invest"). Once investment outlay $I$ is made (i.e., the cost of switching from mode 1 to mode 2, $c_{12} = I$, is incurred), the firm will be operating in mode 2.[8] While it is in operation, the firm has the ability to shut down temporarily (mode 3). It can also expand its scale by a factor, $B$, by making an additional investment of $(B-1)I$ (e.g., if the project increases its size to fivefold its current size, the incremental capacity required will cost a proportionate amount).[9] Shutting down the plant will incur certain costs $(c_{23})$, and while the firm remains shut down it continues to incur specified fixed costs, $\pi_{sd}$. From the shut-down mode, the firm can start up in the production mode (incurring a startup cost, $c_{32}$), but can not expand operations. In addition, the expanded project itself contains an option to temporarily shut down (mode 5) with associated shutdown and start-up switching costs, $c_{45}$ and $c_{54}$, respectively, and fixed shutdown costs $B\pi_{sd}$. The possible operating modes, associated profit flows, and switching costs are summarized in Table 7.1.

**Table 7.1**
**Description of Operating Modes, Profit Flows, and**
**Switching Costs**

| Mode | Description | Profit Flow |
|------|-------------|-------------|
| 1 | waiting-to-invest | 0 |
| 2 | production (initial scale) | $\pi(\theta)$ |
| 3 | shutdown (initial project) | $-\pi_{sd}$ |
| 4 | expanded scale | $B\pi(\theta)$ |
| 5 | shutdown (expanded project) | $-B\pi_{sd}$ |

| Switching Costs | | |
|---|---|---|
| $c_{12}$ | = | initial investment cost |
| $c_{23}$ | = | cost of shutting down the initial project |
| $c_{32}$ | = | cost of starting up the initial project |
| $c_{45}$ | = | cost of shutting down the expanded project |
| $c_{54}$ | = | cost of starting up the expanded project |

## 7.3.2  Numerical Example

In order to investigate potential interactions among the various operating options, I subsequently conduct numerical simulations. The price dynamics in the base case are modeled as a geometric Brownian motion so that the results can be compared against those of earlier papers. The risk-neutral drift rate then becomes $r - \delta$, where $\delta$ is the shortfall from the equilibrium rate of return and $r$ is the risk-free rate of interest.

If $\theta$ is the price of a traded asset, then $\delta$ will be the cash payout or the convenience yield net of storage costs.[10] In general, for nontraded assets $\delta$ can only be determined from an equilibrium asset pricing model as the difference between the required rate of return and the actual drift rate. In the base-case simulations, we use a geometric Brownian motion process where the shortfall, $\delta$, is set to zero, or, in other words, the risk-neutral drift rate, $\overline{\alpha} = r$.[11] In subsequent simulations I examine the sensitivity of project and option values to changes in $\delta$.

A particularly interesting case is when $\theta$ follows a mean-reverting process with $\overline{\alpha} = \lambda\left(\overline{\theta}/\theta_t - 1\right)$. Suppose the equilibrium risk premium for the underlying real asset is $\alpha$.[12] The required equilibrium drift rate will then be $r + \xi$, where $\xi$ is the market price of risk of $\theta$. Then mean reversion would generate a shortfall, $\delta(\theta, t)$, that is both state and time dependent. The risk-neutral drift rate, $\overline{\alpha}$, will then equal the actual drift rate less the risk premium:

$$r - \delta = r - ((r + \xi) - \overline{\alpha}) = \overline{\alpha} - \xi. \tag{7.7}$$

In all cases, the volatility of $\theta$ is assumed to be proportional to $\theta$, namely, $\sigma(\theta, t) = \sigma\theta$.[13] The base-case variance is 9 percent per annum (i.e., $\sigma = 30\%$), and the risk-free interest rate is set at 5 percent annually. The state-space is discretized over the range 0 to 2.0 for $\theta$. The project life of ten years is divided into 100 discrete time steps (i.e., $\Delta t = 0.1$ years), and the per-period profit function of the operating mode is set at $\pi(\theta) = -1.0 + \theta$. The initial investment level is chosen so that NPV at $\theta = 1$ equals zero. While the project remains temporarily shut down, the firm incurs a fixed cost of $\pi_{sd} = 0.10$ per period. These base-case parameters are summarized in Table 7.2.

**Table 7.2**
**Summary of Base Case Parameters**

| | |
|---|---|
| Price dynamics | $d\theta_t / \theta_t = \overline{\alpha} dt + \sigma dZ$ |
| Risk-neutral price dynamics | $d\theta / \theta = (r - \delta)dt + \sigma dZ$ |
| Shortfall from equilibrium growth | $\delta = 0$ |
| Risk-free interest rate | $r = 5\%$ |
| Volatility of $\theta$ | $\sigma = 30\%$ |
| Normal operating profit function | $\pi(\theta_t) = (-1.0 + \theta_t)\Delta t$ |
| Expansion scale | $B = 5$ |
| Shutdown cost | $\delta_{sd} = 0.1$ |
| Start-up cost | $\delta_{su} = 0.1$ |
| Initial investment | $I = 0$ |
| Life of project | 10 years |
| Discrete time steps | $T = 100$ |
| Discrete $\theta$ steps | $S = 100$ |

Table 7.3 presents the base-case NPVs (evaluated at $\theta_0 = 1$) under various project configurations. As the various timing options are included, the project value increases unambiguously. For instance, while the project has NPV = 0 when considered now-or-never, it is worth 0.51 when the initial investment is optimally timed (i.e., with the waiting-to-invest option included); 0.17 when production can be temporarily shut down to avoid losses; and 1.98 when recognizing the growth potential (i.e., incorporating the expansion option).

When two options are present simultaneously, of course, the project value is greater than the cases when each option is included in isolation. However, this joint value is less than the sum of the values of two sepa-

**Table 7.3**

**Base Case Project Values with Various Combinations of Options (Evaluated at $\theta_0 = 1$)**

| Naive NPV | 0 |
|---|---|
| Wait-to-invest option (WTI) | 0.51 |
| Shutdown option (SD) | 0.17 |
| Growth (expansion) option (GR) | 1.98 |
| WTI + SD | 0.52 |
| WTI + GR | 2.38 |
| SD + GR | 2.20 |
| WTI + SD + GR | 2.46 |

rate options. In other words, the joint project value satisfies the following bounds:

$$\max[NPV_A, NPV_B] \quad < \quad NPV_{A+B} \quad < \quad NPV_A + NPV_B$$
$$\max[0.51, 0.17] \quad < \quad 0.52 \quad < \quad 0.51 + 0.17$$
$$\max[1.98, 0.51] \quad < \quad 2.38 \quad < \quad 1.98 + 0.51$$
$$\max[1.98, 0.17] \quad < \quad 2.20 \quad > \quad 1.98 + 0.17.$$

This general failure of value additivity carries through when further options are included. The main focus in this chapter is to study the behavior of individual option values, when viewed in isolation and in the presence of other options. Tables 7.4, 7.5, and 7.6 report the *incremental* values of wait-to-invest (WTI), shutdown (SD), and growth (expansion) (GR) options alone and in the presence of other options for several volatility values under the geometric Brownian motion (base-case) and mean-reverting process assumptions.

In each case, the earlier results of value-additivity violations are corroborated. For example, consider the values of the waiting-to-invest option for $\sigma = 30\%$. The waiting-to-invest option is worth 0.51 when in isolation, 0.35 in the presence of a shutdown option, 0.40 in the presence of an expansion (growth) option, and 0.26 when both the shutdown and the growth options are present. These results make intuitive sense. By making the investment, the firm reduces its flexibility (to optimally time the investment later) so that in bad future states of the world, it would incur losses. By waiting, the firm can make a more informed decision and reduce potential losses. The presence of the option to temporarily shut down has the effect of truncating the downside of the distribution of future cash flows and, therefore, it reduces the value of the wait-to-invest option. We can, thus, interpret the options to wait and shut down as being substitute hedging strategies.

**Table 7.4**
**Incremental Value of the Waiting-to-Invest Option,**
**Alone and in the Presence of Other Options (Valued at $\theta = 1.0$)**

| $\sigma$ | Geometric Brownian Motion $\delta = 0, \alpha = \bar{\alpha}, r = 5\%$ | | | | Mean-reverting Process $\lambda = 25\%, \bar{\theta} = 1.0, r = 5\%$ | | | |
|---|---|---|---|---|---|---|---|---|
| | alone | with shutdown | with expansion | all | alone | with shutdown | with expansion | all |
| 10% | 0.14 | 0.14 | 0.10 | 0.10 | 0.23 | 0.23 | 0.19 | 0.19 |
| 20% | 0.32 | 0.27 | 0.25 | 0.21 | 0.50 | 0.42 | 0.41 | 0.33 |
| 30% | 0.51 | 0.35 | 0.40 | 0.26 | 0.77 | 0.47 | 0.65 | 0.36 |
| 40% | 0.67 | 0.38 | 0.55 | 0.28 | 0.98 | 0.45 | 0.82 | 0.33 |
| 50% | 0.81 | 0.36 | 0.66 | 0.26 | 1.12 | 0.39 | 0.94 | 0.28 |

**Table 7.5**
**Incremental Value of the Shutdown Option,**
**Alone and in the Presence of Other Options (Valued at $\theta = 1.0$)**

| $\sigma$ | Geometric Brownian Motion $\delta = 0, \alpha = \bar{\alpha}, r = 5\%$ | | Mean-reverting Process $\lambda = 25\%, \bar{\theta} = 1.0, r = 5\%$ | |
|---|---|---|---|---|
| | alone | with expansion | alone | with expansion |
| 10% | 0.00 | 0.00 | 0.00 | 0.00 |
| 20% | 0.05 | 0.06 | 0.09 | 0.09 |
| 30% | 0.17 | 0.22 | 0.32 | 0.37 |
| 40% | 0.34 | 0.47 | 0.59 | 0.75 |
| 50% | 0.54 | 0.80 | 0.85 | 1.19 |

In Table 7.5, the addition of the expansion option tends to increase the value of the shutdown option. The shutdown option allows the firm to limit losses by temporarily shutting down during loss-making periods, while preserving the upside potential by starting up when conditions improve. The presence of the expansion option enhances this upside potential and the value of the shutdown option. Similarly, the presence of the shutdown option helps the firm take advantage of the growth opportunity, as shown in Table 7.6. Thus, the shutdown and growth options act as complements to one another. The right-hand panels of Tables 7.4, 7.5, and 7.6 report similar results when the underlying source of uncertainty follows a mean-reverting process. While the general results are unaffected, the impact of further options can be attenuated by mean reversion.

**Table 7.6**
**Incremental Value of the Growth (Expansion) Option,**
**Alone and in the Presence of Other Options (Valued at $\theta = 1.0$)**

| | Geometric Brownian Motion $\delta = 0, \alpha = \overline{\alpha}, r = 5\%$ | | Mean-reverting Process $\lambda = 25\%, \overline{\theta} = 1.0, r = 5\%$ | |
|---|---|---|---|---|
| $\sigma$ | alone | with shutdown | alone | with shutdown |
| 10% | 0.51 | 0.51 | 0.90 | 0.90 |
| 20% | 1.23 | 1.24 | 1.98 | 1.98 |
| 30% | 1.98 | 2.03 | 3.05 | 3.10 |
| 40% | 2.65 | 2.78 | 3.90 | 4.06 |
| 50% | 3.20 | 3.46 | 4.46 | 4.80 |

We next turn to the effect of additional options on the optimal exercise values. Table 7.7 presents these threshold values for the waiting-to-invest and growth options for a variety of volatility parameter values. As expected, when more options are added (reading down a column) the critical thresholds are generally reduced. For example, at the base-case volatility of 30 percent, the waiting-to-invest option alone increases the investment threshold from 1.0 (under naive NPV) to 1.36. When the shutdown option is also present, the firm should be willing to invest earlier, at a lower price of 1.17. This general tendancy is observed over the entire range of parameter values.

## 7.4   CONCLUSION

We have presented a computationally feasible technique to investigate how the value of a project is affected by the simultaneous presence of several operating options. In contrast to most previous studies that consider operating options one at a time, we here treat them jointly. This process makes the interdependence between the operating options more explicit. Our numerical example including the options to wait-to-invest, to shut down temporarily, and to expand the scale of operations confirms that project value increases with the introduction of additional options. The incremental contribution to project value of each option, however, can be attenuated by *substitute* options (e.g., waiting-to-invest and shutdown) but enhanced by *complementary* options (e.g., shutdown and growth options).

**Table 7.7**

**Impact of Additional Options on the Threshold Value (Base Case: $\theta = 1$)**

Investment Threshold

| $\sigma$ | Geometric Brownian motion | | | | | Mean-reverting Process | | | | |
|---|---|---|---|---|---|---|---|---|---|---|
| | 10% | 20% | 30% | 40% | 50% | 10% | 20% | 30% | 40% | 50% |
| Naive NPV | 1.00 | 1.00 | 1.00 | 1.00 | 1.00 | 1.00 | 1.00 | 1.00 | 1.00 | 1.00 |
| WTI | 1.14 | 1.25 | 1.36 | 1.46 | 1.58 | 1.10 | 1.25 | 1.35 | 1.45 | 1.55 |
| WTI + GR | 1.12 | 1.14 | 1.17 | 1.22 | 1.25 | 1.10 | 1.20 | 1.20 | 1.20 | 1.25 |
| WTI + SD | 1.09 | 1.23 | 1.30 | 1.35 | 1.37 | 1.10 | 1.20 | 1.30 | 1.35 | 1.35 |
| WTI + GR + SD | 1.08 | 1.13 | 1.17 | 1.17 | 1.18 | 1.10 | 1.20 | 1.15 | 1.10 | 1.10 |

Expansion Threshold

| $\sigma$ | Geometric Brownian motion | | | | | Mean-reverting Process | | | | |
|---|---|---|---|---|---|---|---|---|---|---|
| | 10% | 20% | 30% | 40% | 50% | 10% | 20% | 30% | 40% | 50% |
| Conventional NPV | 1.00 | 1.00 | 1.00 | 1.00 | 1.00 | 1.00 | 1.00 | 1.00 | 1.00 | 1.00 |
| GR | 1.15 | 1.20 | 1.30 | 1.40 | 1.50 | 1.20 | 1.25 | 1.35 | 1.45 | 1.55 |
| GR + SD | 1.15 | 1.20 | 1.30 | 1.35 | 1.35 | 1.20 | 1.25 | 1.30 | 1.35 | 1.35 |

*Note:* WTI = waiting to invest, GR = growth (expansion) option, and SD = shutdown option.

# ACKNOWLEDGMENTS

This is a substantially revised version of a working paper, "Interdependencies between Operating Options," MIT Energy Laboratory, Working paper MIT-EL 88-005WP. I thank Alan Marcus, Robert McDonald, Lenos Trigeorgis, David Wood, and seminar participants at Boston University for useful discussions. All remaining errors are my own.

# NOTES

1. These flexibilities are discussed by Myers, Kensinger, and Trigeorgis and Mason in a series of articles in the spring 1987 issue of the *Midland Corporate Finance Journal*.

2. A general overview of contingent claims valuation in real investment decisions appears in Mason and Merton (1985).

3. Several previous papers handled this by assuming that the project including an option follows a sufficiently simple stochastic process. Although this can skirt the issue of exogeneity when we consider projects with a single operating option,

it is inadequate when there is more than one option involved.

4. See Kulatilaka (1993) for details on the risk adjustment.

5. When $c_{m,\ell} = 0$, the value is not state dependent. Then, the problem with $M = 2$ becomes that of valuing a security whose payoff is the maximum (or minimum) of two assets (Stulz, 1982).

6. Here, we again ignore the possibility that growth may impact the future market structure and, thereby, influence the trajectory of future prices. Kulatilaka and Perotti (1992) address this issue of growth options in imperfectly competitive markets.

7. Note that as project characteristics change with the inclusion of each option, the exogenous project value assumption made in previous studies does not permit this sort of comparison.

8. The initial investment and the subsequent switching costs may also depend on time and $\theta$.

9. For pedagogical simplicity, I am ignoring economies of scale in building the plant and in the production operations. Scale economies, heterogeneity in technology, learning effects, and any externalities can, however, be explicitly included within this framework.

10. This result follows immediately from the spot-futures parity condition.

11. This is equivalent to assuming that $\theta$ is the price of a traded security. I also performed simulations with other values of $\delta$ and were able to replicate results in McDonald and Siegel (1986).

12. Within a general asset pricing model (e.g., Cox, Ingersoll, and Ross, 1985), the risk premium is given as the market price of risk times the volatility of $\theta$.

13. In order to ensure a nonnegative $\theta$, it is sufficient to have $\sigma(\theta, t)$ be proportional to the square root of $\theta$.

# PART III

## STRATEGY, INFRASTRUCTURE, AND FOREIGN INVESTMENT OPTIONS

# Chapter 8

# The Value of Options in Strategic Acquisitions

## Kenneth W. Smith and Alexander J. Triantis

*Many of the strategic synergies in an acquisition are not immediately realized, but rather affect the combined growth options of the acquiring and target firms—through lowering their exercise price, increasing upside potential, or allowing for improved timing of exercise. In addition, an acquirer with flexible resources may significantly increase the value of its flexibility options by pursuing a strategic diversification policy. Divestiture options may also add significant value by substantially limiting the downside risk of acquisition programs. This chapter examines the valuation of such strategic options associated with acquisitions.*

## 8.1 INTRODUCTION

In recent years, corporations have been much maligned for destroying shareholder value through acquisitions. Porter's (1987) study of acquisitions concludes that only the lawyers, investment bankers, and original sellers have benefited from these transactions, while the acquiring firms' shareholders generally have not. Recent analyses of pre- and postacquisition cash flows suggest that, on average, acquisitions have failed to increase profitability through restructuring, transfering skills, or exploiting synergies, and thus takeover premiums do not seem to be justified.[1] Not surprisingly, critics argue that many acquisitions that reduce shareholder value are driven by motives consistent with increasing managerial welfare.[2] For example, firm growth and diversification often tend to increase the value of human capital more than shareholder value.

Managers have responded to the increased concern about postacquisition value by firming up acquisition criteria so that fewer mistakes are made.

For example, many companies have put in place criteria designed to limit the profit and loss (P&L) downside to acquisitions (e.g., threshold Return on Revenue or Return on Capital Employed criteria). Unfortunately, these criteria often fail to link realized returns and management's future discretionary actions to the recovery of the price paid for the acquisition. Use of conventional cash-flow valuation analyses to estimate the target enterprise's future cash flows and separately identify, schedule, and value future management actions to realize potential synergies and improve returns, place a higher standard on target selection and postacquisition management.

These approaches, however, may err on the conservative side. First, such criteria may discriminate against longer-term acquisition programs that, through a series of acquisitions over time, can significantly change an acquirer's competitive position (and even the structure of its industry) through the development of *growth options.* Cash flow analysis often fails to appropriately value alternative courses of action in such industry restructuring situations. For example, *not* pursuing an acquisition that would position the corporation in a key emerging market segment may have the effect of foreclosing important future strategic options. Moreover, allowing competitors to acquire their way into dominant positions in such segments could indeed threaten a company's current market position.

Second, firms with significant flexibility in organization, marketing, manufacturing, and financing may reap additional benefits from strategic acquisitions that involve diversification. Beyond specific actions to improve and integrate the new businesses, the resulting portfolio may open up strategic alternatives to efficiently utilize the firm's resources in the future. For example, a firm with flexible distribution channels may purchase another firm whose product demand is negatively correlated with its own and quickly adapt existing marketing and distribution, expanding its customer base to cushion the downside in periods of weak demand for its current products. An acquisition program that focuses on strategic, rather than financial, diversification will not only decrease the variance of the firm's future cash flows, but more importantly, it may significantly increase firm value by enhancing the value of the firm's *flexibility options.*

Third, conventional acquisition analysis does not always account for the option to divest parts (or all) of the acquired companies at a later date.[3] Future sale of these assets to companies that would value them at equal or close to their original purchase prices may substantially limit downside risk. For example, idle real estate may be sold off for an alternative use. While some divestitures may occur soon after an acquisition, an acquirer may instead hold on to its *divestiture options* and optimally plan the timing of their exercise.

In short, many acquisitions create valuable options. The acquirer will make decisions regarding discretionary investments, divestments, and resource allocation that depend on future conditions, analogous to financial options. Like financial options, strategic advantages associated with acquisitions introduce the ability to truncate downside risk while preserving upside potential, and thus can make a considerable contribution to shareholder value, which is not typically accounted for in a simple discounted cash flow value. Table 8.1 provides several examples of such growth, flexibility, and divestiture options as they arise in strategic acquisitions.

**Table 8.1**
**Examples of Options Embedded in Strategic Acquisitions**

Growth Options

- A computer firm purchases another software start-up company rather than developing its own competing software.

- An international airline acquires a U.S. airline to break into the U.S. market and increase traffic on existing or potential future routes.

- A large publishing firm buys a smaller niche periodical firm enabling launches into related specialized periodicals in the future.

Flexibility Options

- A firm in the aggregates business buys undeveloped quarry sites which have future potential for municipal waste disposal.

- A diversified retailer switches use of shopping mall leased space in response to varying market conditions for each business.

- A newsprint maker with virgin fiber mills acquires a mill capable of using recycled fiber.

Divestiture Options

- An acquirer can divest real estate with a more valuable alternative use.

- An acquiring airline can sell off selected routes or airport gates after purchasing another airline.

- An acquirer sells companies that have not met growth targets, thereby truncating downside risk.

The rest of the chapter examines valuation considerations for strategic options associated with acquisitions. Section 8.2 discusses the purchase and development of growth options through acquisitions. Section 8.3 analyzes flexibility options and discusses the significance of acquisitions which focus on strategic diversification. Section 8.4 examines the valuation of divestiture options. Section 8.5 provides concluding remarks.

## 8.2  DEVELOPING GROWTH OPTIONS THROUGH ACQUISITIONS

A firm's value is comprised of the value of assets in place and the value of growth options that may arise from the firm's superior technological position, significant market share, effective marketing and distribution channels, or other strategic advantages that facilitate further growth.[4] The use of the term *options* highlights the fact that the firm has some discretion over its future investments. Management can choose to commit capital in the future (analogous to paying the exercise price of a financial option) in order to capture the present value of subsequent cash flows associated with the project (analogous to the price of the underlying stock in the case of a stock option). Alternatively, it can decide not to pursue the investment if circumstances make the investment unattractive in the future. The growth option is valuable to the firm since it need not currently commit to undertaking the future investment, enabling the firm to truncate downside risks. Growth options are particularly valuable in high-tech or emerging industries ranging from computer hardware and software to biotechnology, new markets where there may be a very significant upside in future demand, but at the same time there is considerable technological risk and uncertainty.

Strategic acquisitions can serve as a vehicle to facilitate growth in a company. There are several ways in which growth may be enabled by acquisitions. First, a firm seeking to quickly enter into a new market niche may find it cheaper or more expedient to purchase such a growth option rather than develop it on its own. The firm may acquire a smaller "threshold company" that has developed an entrepreneurial concept and is now looking to grow but may not have the necessary manufacturing, distribution or other infrastructure or access to low-cost capital to achieve its goal. The acquirer that can best provide such a resource base will likely be able to purchase the target at a price lower than its value will be once it is integrated into the acquiring firm. Generally, a target firm may have several growth options that the acquiring firm lacks and considers especially valuable. Alternatively, an acquiring firm may have growth opportunities that it has trouble developing on its own, and thus may profit through acquisitions from the transfer of technological skills or access to distribution channels that allow marketing to new geographic locations or customer segments.

Frequently, acquisitions may involve a substantial interaction between growth options in the purchasing and acquired firms. For instance, both firms may share common opportunities for growth in a particular industry. A firm considering an acquisition may feel that joining its efforts with another firm and exploiting the resultant synergies may be valuable, especially if the move serves to strengthen its competitive position by decreasing costs or increasing the speed of developing growth opportunities.

To illustrate, consider the professional and trade periodicals industry, which is characterized by frequent new product introductions and acquisitions. Competitors such as Thomson, McGraw-Hill, and Reed International make numerous product acquisitions, most often in audience segments that they already serve. In making these acquisitions, the acquirer receives the future cash flows of acquired products and synergy values, plus three important options.

First, in combination with their own entries in the segment, these acquirers build up circulation lists and advertiser relationships overwhelmingly superior to any others in the industry, thereby enhancing the value of their options to invest in new magazine launches or other advertising products within their segment. These options may have lower exercise prices and yield larger profits, and can be exercised if and when market conditions are favorable.

Second, through such acquisitions, these firms may have enhanced the option value of acquiring other periodicals—either existing or future startups—because the operational synergies with a subsequent related periodical would be even higher than they would be with just the original slate alone. Thus, each acquisition has higher value within the broader context of the firm's long-run acquisition program.

Third, and not unrelated to the first two options, an acquirer can, through the purchase, eliminate the seller's option to grow into the market through new product launches or acquisitions. Without such acquisitions, the buyer and the seller each hold an option to reposition their products or to launch line extensions to capture a share of each other's market. Consequently, the status quo may not be a reliable base-case scenario. A firm must clearly recognize the cost of not reacting to changes in its competitive environment and may utilize acquisitions as a vehicle for the preservation of its competitive advantage.

To illustrate how one may go about valuing the growth option components involved in an acquisition, consider the following case. ABC Publishing is considering acquiring Tech Magazines for a price of $100 million. The present value (PV) of Tech's cash flows based on its current publications is estimated to be $90 million. ABC also estimates that through significant consolidations in operations, there would be a cost savings of $5 million. Based on these figures alone, the Tech purchase has a negative net preset value (NPV) of -$5 million and thus does not seem attractive.

The manager of ABC's technical publications division, however, points out that both he and Tech's managers have been independently considering launching a publication on laptop computers. The market for publications in this area seems promising, but is as yet untested. ABC's manager forecasts that his firm would optimally wait for two years before deciding whether to launch such a magazine. However, he also predicts that competition with Tech would result in both firms launching the new publication after only one year if it is profitable to pursue this market at all. Based on their current market power, ABC and Tech would split the new market equally.

The cash-flow estimates required to value the growth option are given below in Table 8.2, both for the case where ABC expands into the new market on its own, as well as for the situation where it first acquires Tech. Note that the PV of profits from the new publication if ABC acquires Tech is more than twice than if it proceeded on its own. This is due to a reduction in operating costs through economies of scale. Similarly, by joining forces with Tech, ABC can establish economies which reduce the fixed cost of launching the magazine.

Since we assume that the growth options in each case are European, we may use the Black-Scholes pricing formula to value these options.[5] (We assume that the present value of profits has a volatility of $\sigma = 50\%$.) The last row of Table 8.2 reports the estimated option values. The acquisition effectively increases ABC's growth option value by $9.85.(= 11.82 - 1.97) million, through purchasing Tech's growth option and developing both options jointly. Taking this growth option value into account, the NPV of the acquisition is in fact $4.85 million, as compared to the -$5 million valuation which ignored the growth option contribution of the acquisition.

## Table 8.2
**Growth Option Valuation (Millions of $) If ABC Proceeds to Expand Alone or If It First Acquires Tech**

|                                    | Proceed Alone | Acquire Tech |
|------------------------------------|---------------|--------------|
| Present value of profits ($S$)     | 10            | 25           |
| PV of launching cost ($Xe^{-rt}$)  | 10            | 15           |
| NPV ($S - Xe^{-rt}$)               | 0             | 10           |
| Option value                       | 1.97          | 11.82        |

The $9.85 million increase in growth option value comes from three sources. First, ABC purchases Tech's option to develop its half of the market. Second, there are economies of scale which are obtained from developing the larger-scale joint growth option, translating into lower costs for the launch and subsequent operation of the new publication. Note that while this synergy results in an effective increase of $10 million in the NPV shown in Table 8.2, these gains are only realized if ABC does in fact exercise its growth option. Finally, by avoiding a race with Tech to reach the market first, ABC may be able to wait longer (two years, rather than one) before deciding whether it should launch the new publication or not. This incremental value of waiting contributes $1.06 million (= 11.82 - 10.76), where $10.76 million is the Black-Scholes value of the combined growth option with a one-year horizon.

This simple example illustrates that the value of a firm's growth option may be enhanced through acquisitions by decreasing the exercise price, increasing the present value of future profits earned upon exercise, and allowing for greater flexibility in timing the exercise of the option. Acquisitions in industries that are consolidating because of scale economies or globalization can be viewed in a similar way. Each successful acquisition can enhance the value of the option to acquire further by enlarging the size and scope of synergies with possible future targets and by reducing the risk of being left out of an industry consolidation or being structurally disadvantaged in the future.

## 8.3   FLEXIBILITY OPTIONS AND STRATEGIC DIVERSIFICATION

Synergy gains achieved through acquisitions are often a result of the consolidation of resources. Reducing duplication in administration expenses, sharing marketing distribution channels, and utilizing excess plant capacity all provide incremental value to the purchasing firm. These synergy gains, which are often estimated under a static scenario assumption regarding the markets in which the combined business units operate, can be seen to have additional value if the effects of uncertainty are more carefully analyzed.

In particular, there may be important flexibility options that derive value from the presence of uncertainty *and* diversification opportunities for an acquiring firm. If the acquiring (or integrated) firm possesses significant flexibility in organization, manufacturing, distribution, or financing, then such flexible resources may be more fully exploited by diversifying across products or lines of business whose profitabilities are not highly positively correlated. The distinction between such strategic diversification and financial diversification must be emphasized. The latter is sometimes defended by claiming that it is a means of reducing business risk. Critics of such diversification-driven acquisition programs, however, point out that shareholders can usually diversify more efficiently on their own, and that it is the acquiring firm's managers, not its shareholders, who stand to gain the most from such reduction in risk.[6] Besides, there may be a substantial price paid by firms who fail to "stick to their knitting."

Consider the following illustration of how an acquirer pursuing strategic diversification can enhance the value of its flexibility options. Company A, an automobile manufacturer, has followed a strategy that stresses the importance of maintaining flexible resources, including distribution channels, labor force, and manufacturing facilities. For example, it has recently modernized its production facilities and equipped them with flexible tooling such that it is now capable of producing a wide variety of different vehicles. These facilities have the capacity to produce 100,000 cars per year. Based on this capacity, the firm has an annual fixed operating cost (FOC) of $80 million. Management forecasts demand over the next year to be either 95,000 or 75,000 cars, depending on whether the price of oil (currently at $20) will be $15 or $25 a barrel, respectively.[7] The profit per car (before the FOC is covered) is $1,000.

**Table 8.3**
**Projected Cash Flows and Present Values (Millions of $)**

|                          | A       | B        | C       | A+B       | A+C      |
|--------------------------|---------|----------|---------|-----------|----------|
| Price of oil ($/barrel)  | 15  25  | 15  25   | 15  25  | 15    25  | 15  25   |
| Profit before FOC        | 95  75  | 5  25    | 20  20  | 100  100  | 100  95  |
| FOC                      | 80  80  | 15  15   | 15  15  | 80    80  | 80  80   |
| Net profit               | 15  -5  | -10  10  | 5    5  | 20    20  | 20  15   |
| Present value            | 2.86    | 1.90     | 4.76    | 19.05     | 16.19    |

The management of Company A is concerned about the possibility of incurring a $5 million loss should the price of oil increase to $25 next year (see column A in Table 8.3). Since there is currently unused production capacity, management is considering alternatives to use this excess capacity. Since Company A does not currently have any additional new lines of its own to introduce over the next year, it is considering the purchase of one of two smaller automobile companies whose cars could be produced and sold using A's flexible resources. Company B sells only compact cars whose demand increases with the price of oil and is thus negatively correlated with that of Company A. Company C, on the other hand, specializes in vehicles whose demand is insensitive to the price of oil (and thus, uncorrelated with that of Company A). Both companies B and C have the same profit ($1,000) per car as Company A. Each has one manufacturing plant, with a capacity of 25,000 cars, and a FOC of $15,000. The cash flows for B and C are as shown in Table 8.3.

The last two columns in Table 8.3 show the combined cash flows of Company A should it acquire either Company B or Company C. If Company B is purchased, the combined demand for the two firms will be exactly 100,000, so A's resources are sufficient to manufacture and sell all the vehicles. Given that the fixed operating cost remains at $80 million, this would result in a $20 million profit, regardless of the price of oil.[8] If Company C is purchased instead, Company A can again choose to utilize only its own flexible resources, and can sell off C's facility. While some of C's demand can be covered by utilizing the excess capacity of A's facilities, if the price of oil decreases to $15, Company A would choose to operate at full capacity, forgoing the revenue from 15,000 of C's cars rather than keeping C's plant open at an FOC of $15,000. This would generate a combined profit (for A and C) of $20 million for next year if the price of oil declines, and $15 million if it rises.

In the last row of Table 8.3, the present values for the independent companies and for the integrated companies are shown. These values are obtained using a one-period binomial option-pricing model (see Cox, Ross, and Rubinstein, 1979; or Trigeorgis and Mason, 1987). For example, given that today's oil price is $20 and assuming that $1.00 invested today in a risk-free security returns $R = \$1.05$ in one year, based on a risk-neutral probability, $p = (R-d)/(u-d) = (1.05-.75)/(1.25-.75) = .6$, we can calculate the value of companies A and C combined as $(.6 \times 15 + .4 \times 20)/1.05 = \$16.19$ million. The present values of A and B are similarly calculated to be 2.86 and 1.90, respectively. The present values of C and A + B are easily seen to be 4.76 (= 5/1.05) and 19.05 (= 20/1.05), respectively.[9]

The values in Table 8.3 indicate that Company A is better off acquiring Company B than C, assuming that it would pay a fair current market price to purchase either B or C (namely, $1.90 million for B or $4.76 million for C). The incremental value from acquiring B is $14.29 (= 19.05 - 2.86 - 1.90) million, while that from acquiring C is only $8.57 (= 16.19 - 2.86 - 4.76) million. Company B is thus a better acquisition than C, even though C appears less risky and more valuable on its own. The critical difference between these purchases is that the correlation between the demands for A and B is -1, and thus, the two demands complement each other in such a way that A's capacity is always fully utilized and the demand for the cars of both A and B is completely satisfied. In addition, B's facility can be shut down resulting in considerable savings in production costs for the integrated firm.

This example illustrates that flexible production capacity can be very valuable, particularly when a firm is able to create a portfolio of products whose cash-flow streams are negatively correlated. The greater the uncertainty surrounding the demand for a firm's products, and the lower the correlation among these product demands, the more valuable will be the combined benefits of flexibility and diversification. While a typical diversification program reduces risk by narrowing the distribution of cash flows, strategic diversification can truncate the downside risk while preserving the upside potential.

The newsprint industry provides a case where firms have used acquisitions to enhance their flexibility option value. In particular, manufacturers in this industry have moved quickly to acquire recycled newsprint capacity. These manufacturers may use their sales organizations, distribution networks, and some of the same production resources to swing between recycled and virgin fiber based on market demand and pricing opportunities. A pure virgin fiber or pure recycled-based newsprint manufacturer could be equally profitable to the diversified producer if supply and demand conditions remained stable and in balance, but if market conditions change, companies with diversified production capabilities can more effectively exercise their valuable flexibility options.

In many industries, corporate real estate is considered one of the most valuable assets. This is often due, at least in part, to the fact that real estate may be one of the firm's most flexible assets. Acquisitions may introduce flexibility options by adding real estate that is flexible due to its location or zoning, or they may increase the value of the acquiring firm's existing assets by creating a diversified portfolio of businesses that is likely to exploit the flexibility of the real estate in the future.

As an illustrative example, consider the aggregates business, in which some sand and gravel operations have been converted into municipal waste disposal sites. These businesses serve different markets with entirely different products but share a valuable flexible asset, namely, real estate with certain special characteristics. A key criterion for site selection for either purpose is that the site should be sufficiently close to a major city to have favorable transportation economics, but far enough from local communities to offend as few people as possible. The operating skills are relatively simple and similar in both businesses. At some stage in the development of many aggregate resources, the property can be more valuable as a landfill site. This happens when the marginal value of further extraction falls below the value of filling in the hole with garbage. Major aggregates companies serving large urban centers are continually developing their asset bases by acquiring underdeveloped aggregates businesses and real estate. When they acquire sites that can later be used as landfill sites, they in fact acquire valuable options. In anticipation of the eventual conversion of some sites, they can invest in the protracted regulatory process and make the capital investments to convert the site, or they can exercise the option to sell the site at an appropriate time to a waste disposal company.

Another resource that is highly flexible is financial capital. Flexibility is particularly valuable in the presence of resource constraints. A firm that can easily raise additional capital on demand need not worry about integrating its various business units to ensure a balance of supply and demand for cash within the entire organization. However, most firms are, to some degree, capital rationed, if only by virtue of the costs associated with raising capital in financial markets. Of course, capital can be more or less expensive to raise depending on the prevailing circumstances in the firm's core business and in the financial markets. Thus, many acquisition programs emphasize the need to create a balanced portfolio of business units to enable cross-financing within the organization.

For example, acquisition programs can be designed to maintain a portfolio which is balanced on the basis of the stage of growth of each product or business unit. Pharmaceutical companies, for example, appear to strive for a balanced mix of marketable drugs, patents pending, and R and D activity. Uncertainties in each of these activities create currently unpredictable cash requirements at various stages of development in the future. Such future uncertainties make product diversification and the ability to cross-finance especially valuable.

## 8.4   ACQUISITION AND DIVESTITURE OPTIONS

Given the availability of appropriate financing arrangements, most firms have an option to acquire other firms or to purchase a portfolio of shares in other firms. The choice between these two alternatives centers on the relative benefits and costs of obtaining control of another business. To some firms, the option to acquire and control other firms is more valuable than it is to others because of more favorable strategic positioning. However, for all firms with valuable acquisition options, there are two important additional considerations.

The first concerns the timing of exercise of these acquisition options. Option pricing theory dictates that in certain circumstances it is worthwhile to hold on to an option even if it is "in-the-money." In the case of acquisitions in an environment characterized by an absence of competition, a firm may delay its decision to acquire while waiting for more resolution of uncertainty regarding market conditions and other economic factors such as interest rates. However, since competition for specific targets is often significant, firms in practice may not be able to wait indefinitely to acquire a target, but must instead react quickly at the right time.

The second important consideration in evaluating an acquisition has to do with the potential for partially undoing it through a divestiture option. Any acquisition investment is at least partially reversible since an investor may purchase an asset and later resell it (or parts of it). Of course, the success of such a strategy hinges on the timing of the buy and sell decisions to yield a profit, as well as on the transaction costs involved. An acquiring firm has the ability to divest an acquired business in the future—provided it does not irreversibly integrate the business with the rest of the firm—if the market price for the unit turns out to be higher than its actual value to the firm.

Often, firms acquire a business in order to realize synergy gains, but these gains may turn out to be fictitious. In such cases, divestment may effectively truncate the resulting poor returns on the acquisition investment. Clearly, the option to divest is an important consideration in risky consolidation plays. For example, during the 1980s, Maxwell Communication bought several commercial printing businesses in the United Kingdom and North America. It subsequently divested all of them (well before the death of the founder and subsequent demise of the empire). Whatever Maxwell's original strategy, and regardless of its effectiveness, the divestments clearly truncated the downside risk substantially.

An acquirer may, of course, purchase a firm with the original intent to later sell off some units but then hold the option to sell until an appropriate time to exercise the option. This may be when the business develops further or perhaps until industry consolidation progresses to the point that it becomes a seller's market. An example of the valuation and optimal timing of exercise of such a divestiture option is given below.

PJP is a large conglomerate considering the acquisition of another firm which has substantial holdings of real estate. If the acquisition goes through, PJP has plans to develop one particular piece of real estate for a distribution facility in two years' time. Based on its projected use, PJP has valued this piece at $20 million. Market conditions for the firm's business will of course cause the value of this real estate to the firm to fluctuate over the next two years. However, if the firm's business outlook turns sour and the distribution facility turns out to be unprofitable, the firm would be able to quickly sell off this centrally located land for at least $15 million. To account for this floor on downside risk in its valuation of the acquisition, PJP's management uses a simple two-year, binomial model. Management assumes that the value of the real estate to the firm will either appreciate by 50 percent or depreciate by 40 percent each year, as illustrated in the left tree of Figure 8.1.

The right-hand tree in Figure 8.1 illustrates the value of the land, taking into account that it can be sold at any time for $15 million. For example, in the worst-case scenario, at the end of two years the land could be sold for $15 million, mitigating the downside risk. The value in the downstate at

**Figure 8.1**
**Value of Real Estate (Millions of $)**

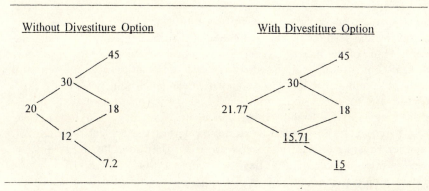

the end of the first year is calculated to be $15.71 (rather than $12) million from the discounted value of $18 and $15 million, given an annual risk-free rate of 5 percent and a risk-neutral probability of 0.5 ($p = (R-d)/(u-d) = (1.05 - .6)/(1.5 - .6) = .5$).

Note that even though the value of the real estate to PJP as a site for its distribution facility may be only $12 million at the end of the first year, it is still not optimal for the firm to sell it at that time for $15 million if it can sell it for that price at the end of the second year. The firm would prefer to retain the option to develop the land at the end of the second year if business conditions improve (with a conditional value of $18 million). The incremental value of waiting to divest in this case amounts to $0.71 million at the end of the first year. The divestiture option increases time-zero value to $21.77 million. Thus, the additional value to PJP of having a divestiture option is equal to $1.77 million ($21.77 - $20 million), representing the current value of the ability to limit its downside risk in future periods. In practice, of course, a resale price for an asset is not guaranteed as assumed in this simple example, requiring the use of more sophisticated option-pricing techniques.[10] The basic intuition behind the valuation and exercise of such acquisition and divestiture options, however, is still instructive.

## 8.5   IMPLICATIONS AND CONCLUSIONS

The practical necessity of introducing more stringent acceptance criteria for many acquisitions is well founded. However, it is crucially important that appropriate valuation techniques be employed to capture the various strategic considerations that could support many acquisitions. If the values of strategic options are underestimated, companies may miss valuable growth opportunities and risk losing their current competitive position.

Options valuation techniques can be very effective in capturing many strategic benefits from acquisitions. The key point is to recognize the discretionary future acquisition and divestiture decisions that must be exercised in an optimal fashion (with the benefit of waiting for additional information). Many of the strategic synergies in an acquisition are not immediately realized, but rather should be seen as growth options that are acquired (and perhaps, combined with the firm's own), developed, and potentially exercised in the future at some additional cost if they prove to be fruitful. A growth option established through an acquisition may be quite valuable even if it is not expected to be exercised within the typical time horizon used for considering capital expenditures. Furthermore, flexibility options may be valuable to firms that have or acquire flexible resources and pursue a strategic diversification policy. Although counterintuitive to many managers, such options are more valuable with increased uncertainty about product prices, demand, industry dynamics, and interest rates.

Capturing the precise benefits and costs of an acquisition program is, of course, case-specific. However, the nature of the major uncertainties faced by the firm in its market environment is certainly an important factor affecting valuation. In the long run, the options acquired, created, or developed, and the actions taken to optimally exercise these options, will determine the success of an acquisition program.

## ACKNOWLEDGMENTS

The authors are grateful to the editor, Lenos Trigeorgis, for detailed comments on an earlier draft.

## NOTES

1. For example, Ravenscraft and Scherer (1987) reported declines in profitability on conglomerization (pp. 75–122).

2. Morck, Schleifer, and Vishny (1990), and Amihud, Lev, and Travlos (1990) found that acquisitions are more likely to be value-decreasing when the acquiring firm's management stock ownership is low and, thus, agency problems may be prominent.

3. Porter (1987) reported the percentage of acquisitions divested for a sample of 33 large diversified U.S. companies during the period 1950–1986. He found that on average, corporations divested more than half their acquisitions in new

industries and 74 percent in the case of unrelated acquisitions. Ravenscraft and Scherer (1987) also presented detailed evidence on sell-offs (see pp. 123–191).

4. The concept of modeling investment opportunities as growth options was first introduced by Myers (1977). Keste (1984) explored this framework in greater detail, discussing the critical factors that affect the value of growth options. He also provided empirical evidence showing that growth options constitute a significant portion of firm value in many industries.

5. To use the Black-Scholes formula, we must assume that the present value of profits from the new magazine is lognormally distributed (see Black and Scholes, 1973).

6. See, for example, Levy and Sarnat (1970), who argued that individual shareholders may diversify more cheaply than would a firm, which may have to pay a premium to acquire a block of the target's shares.

7. For simplicity, we are ignoring cash flows out further than one year, and we are considering only two possible oil price scenarios in each year.

8. For simplicity, we assume that Company B's production facility can be closed down, at least temporarily, without incurring significant costs. In reality, there may be substantial costs associated with closing and reopening plants. In addition, while our simple binomial structure restricts the highest value of combined demand (in this case to 100,000 cars per year), if more oil price states were allowed the total demand could potentially exceed Company A's capacity. A more complex multiperiod model would be required to address these issues.

9. Note that these values are calculated without knowing the actual probability of the price of oil increasing and without employing the firm's hurdle rate for new investments (which would likely provide a downward-biased estimate of these values).

10. See, for example, Fischer (1978) or Margrabe (1978), both of whom valued an option with an uncertain exercise price.

# Chapter 9

# Corporate Governance, Long-term Investment Orientation, and Real Options in Japan

**Takato Hiraki**

*This chapter explains the Japanese long-term investment orientation that has resulted in fast growth and competitive advantage by viewing the Japanese bank-oriented corporate governance system through an options perspective. The main bank system and other related complementary systems involving implicit contracts serve as the basic infrastructure for the development of corporate real options enabling operating flexibility. The various interrelated corporate stakeholders, including the main bank, are jointly involved in the capital investment and real options development process, sharing the costs and resulting benefits. In this way, the value of real options in Japan is effectively embedded in the main bank-oriented system.*

## 9.1   INTRODUCTION

Project selection criteria used in capital budgeting, such as traditional net present value (NPV) and internal rate of return (IRR) rules, have recently been subjected to critical review by both practitioners and academics alike, primarily in the United States. The criticism has mainly focused on the fact that these discounted cash flow (DCF)-based selection rules often lead to short-term results and ignore projects' longer-term prospects. This short-sighted behavior presumably leads to slower growth, more unemployment, and reduced competitiveness of the U.S. economy, particularly in comparison to the Japanese economy (e.g., Porter, 1992).

A proposed solution to this *underinvestment* problem is the use of revised or expanded criteria applying a contingent claims framework to modify the NPV rule, as suggested by Mason and Merton (1985), Trigeorgis and Mason (1987), and Trigeorgis (1991), among others. In spite of its sound theoretical underpinnings, however, there is not much evidence yet that the U.S. manufacturing sector has accelerated the rate of capital investment, nor that the proposed expanded (real options–based) framework has gained popularity in use among manufacturing firms. This observation suggests that the existing U.S. corporate governance structure and the infrastructure of the U.S. economy may not support the use and full realization of the real options potential in the capital budgeting process of U.S. manufacturing firms.

This chapter describes how the Japanese financial system provides a more supportive environment in which real options can be more actively sought and incorporated into the corporate capital investment process. In contrast to their U.S. counterparts, Japanese firms have more successfully incorporated real options by uniquely tying them into the infrastructure of the Japanese economic system, especially the main bank system.

The chapter is organized as follows. Section 9.2 describes the main bank system in Japan and the structure of real options development by Japanese firms. Section 9.3 examines the process of real options cost sharing, which is rather unique to Japanese firms. Section 9.4 discusses future implications both for United States and Japanese firms and concludes.

## 9.2  THE MAIN BANK SYSTEM AND REAL OPTIONS DEVELOPMENT IN JAPAN

### 9.2.1   The Main Bank System in Japan

The financial system in an economy plays an important role in monitoring corporate management performance (Aoki, 1992a, 1992c). There are three stages in this monitoring process: *ex ante* monitoring, *interim* monitoring, and *ex post* monitoring of a project. In the Japanese financial system, these monitoring functions are basically delegated to the main bank or banks, whereas in the United States separated external agents and (internal) stakeholders *independently* (and more narrowly) monitor managerial performance, the capital investment process and related operating results over time. Depending on the degree of a firm's reliance on the bank source of funds and its operating performance, the relationship with the main bank varies considerably across the spectrum of Japanese manufacturing companies.

Given that the pecking order theory of capital structure is more descriptive of the Japanese practices than those in the United States, better-performing firms with sufficient internally generated funds would tend to be less subject to main bank monitoring and restrictive controls.[1] Main bank-based monitoring has more direct implications for worse-than-average performers due to their greater downside risk. Nevertheless, the main bank system is important for the best-performing manufacturing firms (characterized by low debt ratios) as well, and it is thus a necessary part of corporate governance structure for all Japanese companies.[2] The main bank system provides both basic insurance (which can be viewed as a put option) and monitoring functions. It is, in fact, the main bank system that supports and distinguishes the Japanese firms' ability to develop future real options. As a result, Japanese firms could afford to invest aggressively in infrastructure within the firm, for example, in flexible manufacturing systems (FMSs), on a continual and long-term basis during the last several decades. Consequently, Japanese firms' adaptability to environmental changes has become expanded and more effectively integrated.

The Japanese main bank-based monitoring system, coupled with c-shareholdings, lifetime employment, an incomplete market for managers and skilled workers, industrial group formation practices, a labor force, and a labor union-tied Employee Stockowner Option Plan (ESOP) system, has helped form a relatively unique and efficient corporate governance structure, as discussed in Aoki (1992b) and Kester (1992b). Basically, the mechanism of enhancing managerial flexibility is embedded within the corporate governance system itself. Virtually all corporate relations are governed by long-term stable and reciprocal business relations or "implicit" contracts that represent a major source of efficiency and competitiveness for Japanese firms (see Kester, 1992a, 1992b). In this way, potentially conflicting interests of various corporate stakeholder groups are coordinated and opportunistic behavior is overridden by the most important objective, long-term maximization of joint value. This explanation is consistent with the argument of reduced agency costs for Japanese firms, as suggested in Prowse (1990).

As part of these "implicit" contracts, the main bank is both allowed and expected to get involved with the firm's day-to-day management. Generally, a group of stakeholders with combined claims (e.g., being both creditors and shareholders at the same time) would delegate monitoring functions to the main bank.[3] The main bank would then practice both *ex ante* and *interim* monitoring and, when necessary, would interfere with management during the *ex post* monitoring process. Such *ex post* monitoring might include main bank's involvement with replacing existing management, committing financial resources for the firm's continued operation (i.e., reorganization) or costly voluntary liquidation. The main bank and other complementary systems are, therefore, essential components in the value creation process of capital investment. Once the basic investment infrastructure is thus in place, managers are better able to fully devote their attention and resources in developing and exercising real options.

## 9.2.2   Real Options Development by Japanese Firms

As noted by Jaikumar (1989), Japanese manufacturing firms have aggressively invested in flexible manufacturing systems (FMSs). The resulting operating flexibility is well treated within a real options framework. Other examples include the Total Quality Management (TQM) system viewed from a real options perspective by Baldwin and Trigeorgis (1993), and the kanban ("just-in-time") inventory and production control system originally developed by Toyota, as discussed by Monden (1981a, 1981b, 1981c). Many operating flexibilities derive from infrastructure investments in a core asset, system, or information and manufacturing technology. Such an infrastructure investment (whether tangible or intangible) is valuable since it increases contingency opportunities and the value of real options.[4] Basically, those firms equipped with such basic infrastructure are better able to increase potential gains or reduce losses through appropriate timely operational adjustments.

The contingent plans of such firms typically include various standard operating flexibility options. Table 9.1 reviews several operating option examples, such as (a) multiple-product flexibility, (b) input switch, (c) production scale adjustment, (d) deferral, (e) learning process, and (f) "just-in-time" flexibility. As shown in the table, some of these options are unique to Japanese firms, or are more widely recognized among Japanese firms than by U.S. firms. Further, financial (main bank) arrangements can be viewed not only as a set of real (e.g., put) options but, more important, as the infrastructure of infrastructure (Table 9.2). Table 9.3 describes infrastructure elements that substantially depend on financial arrangements. If a firm has such infrastructure (core investment) elements, then the spectrum and value of real options can increase significantly. The main bank system thus provides the broad infrastructure for the development of the within-the-firm infrastructures necessary for enhancing managerial flexibility or real options.

The main bank system can be generally extended to include industrial group and other (non-main bank) financial relations. As described in Table 9.2, additional insurance is provided through cross-shareholdings that can reduce product demand and material supply risk. There are also other systems complementary to the main bank system which are unique to individual sector markets and interactively contribute to real option value. For example, the lifetime employment system and incomplete (or low-mobility) labor market practices jointly support a job rotation system and various extensive and continual in-firm employee-training programs. These can enhance the value of operating flexibility by enabling quick and smooth

# Table 9.1
## Operating Options Valued by Japanese Firms

| Type or Source of Flexibility | Description |
|---|---|
| (a) Product line producing one or several kinds of products (output switch)# | As the demand for a product changes adversely, a new product is quickly introduced with manufacturing flexibility. The Japanese manufacturers in automobile and high-technology industries have focused on this flexibility due to sophisticated domestic consumers and high quality standards. This flexibility has, in turn, helped them become more competitive in foreign markets. |
| (b) Production facility allowing the use of alternative process or technology, depending on the price of inputs (input switch) | To produce the same product, process flexibility can contribute to maintaining low production costs and profitability when the cost of alternative product inputs fluctuates. A major production facility is designed and maintained so as to quickly adjust to these changes through the use of different technologies depending on the relative cost of the inputs. (Japanese manufacturers do not necessarily have a superior advantage in this type of flexibility as seen in the less competitive chemical industry.) |
| (c) Production scale adjustment (including shut down on a permanent basis)# | This flexibility makes it possible for a manufacturer to expand or contract the scale of operations by changing the utilization of production facilities or resources. Since Japanese manufacturers are more vertically integrated or related to suppliers and customers, this production scale adjustment for them is easier than for their U.S. competitors. (The scale expansion is supported by industrial group companies and financial institutions while the downward adjustment sometimes involves industry-wide coordination, for example through arranged mergers as seen in the |
| (d) Option to defer an investment decision# | A project with negative NPV may become profitable if it can be deferred over a certain time period. For example, output prices can increase or borrowing rates decrease unexpectedly. This flexibility is more beneficial to Japanese manufacturers because of their stable and reciprocal relations with contractors and financial institutions than to their U.S. competitors. (If the necessary funds are raised through an investment banking channel, this flexibility is more limited. In this sense, Japanese companies have some advantage over their U.S. competitors due to financing flexibility provided by closely related lending institutions.) |
| (e) Learning process* | The payoff provided through the learning process (or learning curve) is similar to that provided by a call option. The value of this flexibility is not usually incorporated into the passive NPV. The (uncertain) payoff from this option is truncated since the learning process is expressed by an upward sloped curve, especially under the unique Japanese (permanent) employment and job rotation and training systems. |
| (f) "Just-in-time" and other information-based production/ inventory controls* | Because of the famous Toyota's *kanban* system for production/inventory controls, the use of resources is more effectively prearranged. The payoff provided by this flexibility is similar to (c), though the scale adjustment here is based on a short interval like a day or even shorter. Japanese manufacturers on average have more advantage than their U.S. competitors regarding this type of flexibility. |

*Note;*
\* unique to the Japanese system or firms.
\# more widely seen among Japanese firms.

**Table 9.2**
**Financial Arrangements Viewed as Options**

| Type or Source of Flexibility | Description |
| --- | --- |
| (a) Rescue loans by a main bank (conditional insurance)* | This is an "implicit" put option provided by a main bank. Since the exercise price is set at a very low project value, this option by itself does not contribute additional value immediately. This insurance service is provided in exchange for corporate control and monitoring rights, including intervention by the main bank in the case of financial distress. This arrangement creates the basic infrastructure required for the development of real options by Japanese manufacturers. |
| (b) In-group purchasing and other commitments* | Through cross-shareholding practices, Japanese manufacturers are more vertically integrated and better able to cope with very severe horizontal and international competition. Interrelated companies hold put options in each other in terms of "implicit" agreements on purchases and sales, which are arranged at the project-planning stage. |

*Note*:
* unique to the Japanese system or firms.
# more widely seen among Japanese firms.

adjustments to new product market and technological developments.

As noted, the main bank's role is an integral part of the entire system. In exchange for providing an insurance function, the main bank almost exclusively retains monitoring responsibilities, especially in *ex post* monitoring.[5] *Interim* monitoring is more related to the exercising and (re-)building of real options. During this *interim* monitoring process the main bank usually allows a great deal of discretion to the firm's management while maintaining careful monitoring, without strict control.

## 9.3  JAPANESE INVESTMENT DECISIONS AND THE COST SHARING OF REAL OPTIONS

As noted, the single overriding managerial objective under the Japanese corporate governance system is to maximize the long-run wealth of the interrelated corporate stakeholders as a whole. This overall objective allows for transfering of wealth across agents (broadly defined stakeholders, including employees) over time. Managerial performance is generally evaluated both in terms of profitability and market share (growth) performance over a period of time. While in *ex ante* monitoring it is up to the firm to conduct the capital budgeting function, the analysis usually assumes undertaking the best technology available to realize maximum flexibility in the future.

**Table 9.3**
**Infrastructure Investments and Other Arrangements**

| Type or Source of Flexibility | Description |
|---|---|
| (a) Investment in infrastructure# | Infrastructure investments consist of both tangible and intangible core assets on which individual operating flexibility options are based. Flexible manufacturing systems (FMS), coupled with computer-based information systems, are evidential. On the other hand, Total Quality Management (TQM) supports production management as software or know-how required in order to meet customer demand. In addition to accumulated technology through R&D, some aspects of Japanese management provide the intangible infrastructure required for certain real options. For example, the Japanese labor force is well trained and specializes in more than one area of operation. |
| (b) Layoffs of unskilled workers, bonus cut, and various cost-cutting programs* | In Japan, there usually exist regular (lifetime) employees and part-time workers. Regular employees are generally treated better, but they are subject to bonus cuts and are expected to be cooperative in various cost-cutting programs implemented during less profitable periods. These unique systems to Japanese companies also provide the infrastructure in order to more effectively build and manage real options. |

*Note:*
* unique to the Japanese system or firms.
# more widely seen among Japanese firms.

During this *ex ante* evaluation process, management often relies on the payback criterion (in addition to some engineering cost analysis), although using a more generous standard or a longer cutoff which implicitly incorporates potential real options value. Most Japanese firms do not rely on the seemingly more scientific DCF techniques, although they do perceive some significant value in managing real options over time.[6] It is not yet very clear how capital investments are integrated into the overall strategic decision-making process and how managerial flexibility attained through major asset acquisitions is quantified by Japanese firms.

Of course, real options are not free. Under the Japanese corporate governance system, the cost of real options is implicitly expected to be paid and shared by the various stakeholders, in other words, by all involved in the cooperative, joint value-maximizing relationship over time. Since all corporate stakeholders are expected to share the costs and play an important role in enhancing the value of real options, they also expect to share in the rewards over time and in various (nondirect) forms. In this process, the main bank may charge compensatory deposits and trustee fees in subsequent bond issues to cover its risk taking over time.[7] The firm's major suppliers and customers may make a firm commitment in the project in exchange for favorable trading terms and/or managerial and operational support, particularly after the project turns out to be profitable. A similar "implicit" arrangement is also possible with the firm's employees and union.

Subsequent benefits to the cooperative stakeholders, who can be seen as joint option writers, do not usually take a direct monetary form, but rather an indirect tied-in sales or trades form. There typically exists an implicit mutual understanding that the benefits from real options development would be jointly shared by the firm and all its stakeholders.[8] This "implicit" agreement among all stakeholders makes it possible for the firm to expand or enhance its contingency plans more flexibly through appropriate capital investments.

Part of the resulting real options value naturally belongs to the firm's management, since most operational flexibility is inherent in the investment project itself. However, part of this value is jointly created by the firm and its various stakeholders. Thus, this value is expected to be shared by the firm and its stakeholders in a cooperative manner. Under the implicit contract system, however, the firm is usually not required to compensate stakeholders up front or when the project is not profitable. This implicit real options cost-benefit–sharing practice appears to be very efficient and is probably a source of the much criticized "unfair advantage" attributed to the Japanese corporate governance system.

The Japanese system is flexible enough to allow paying (often in installments over time) the cost of real options and sharing the benefits later, when much of the uncertainty is resolved. Such an arrangement enables all sides to gain *ex post* in the longer term. The firm compensates its stakeholders when it can best afford to do so. This practice is, of course, only possible with long-term reciprocal relations among the various stakeholder groups. In fact, the management of Japanese firms is expected to be able to coordinate conflicting interests among the firm's various stakeholders from a longer-term viewpoint. This view is based on an understanding that building valuable real options depends on the creation of an efficient within-the-firm infrastructure of reliable long-term relations with the various internal and external stakeholders.

## 9.4   IMPLICATIONS AND CONCLUSIONS

The delegation of a monitoring role to the main bank in Japan is based on a consensus of almost all stakeholders. As part of this understanding, the main bank is responsible for monitoring and correcting poor management. This can take the form of *ex post* interference, management replacement, merger arrangement, or voluntary liquidation by the main bank.[9] It is generally believed that most Japanese city banks are fully qualified as a responsible main bank in terms of project evaluation and sovereign behavior. Serious doubts have been raised recently, however, due to a series of seemingly unethical behaviors engaged in by some of the largest banks in Japan.

Although the current main bank system has in general been viewed as a major contributing factor to Japanese industrial competitiveness, the system has not always been free of problems. This has become more evident during the recent prolonged recession, which has affected almost all lending institutions. Both the monitoring and insurance functions of the main banks have recently become less effective than in the past.[10] Once a main bank loses credibility with a related firm and its stakeholders, the firm's infrastructure for generating additional value through real options can be severely damaged. If this occurs frequently throughout the whole economy, the entire system may become in danger of collapsing. In that event, a significant portion of the value related to operating and managerial flexibility could be lost very quickly, and the presumed competitive advantage of Japanese corporations could be lost to the United States and other foreign competitors. U.S. companies might then have a good chance to surpass the Japanese in terms of basic infrastructure for real options development if they adopt a real options perspective.

There is another threat to the main bank system in Japan. During the stock market bubble-formation period covering several years through 1990, many Japanese manufacturing firms have eased main bank relationships, choosing to issue new equity and equity-linked debt, and accumulate free cash flows (Jensen, 1986). Most of these free cash flows have not been invested for infrastructure enhancement, but instead have been used to buy other firms' stock. This development further threatens the once very efficient main bank system in Japan. It is not certain whether the main bank-oriented and investment-led growth of the Japanese industrial sector can be continued after the 1990s.

In conclusion, a real options perspective on the Japanese corporate governance structure provides several important implications. First, the main bank system and related complementary structures may have been the hidden source of efficiency, competitiveness, and growth in the Japanese manufacturing sector. Second, investment-led growth, propelled by real options, requires a longer-term perspective when the investment project is evaluated *ex ante*. Third, the investment horizon may become shorter as the extent of main bank reliance of Japanese manufacturers decreases, as can be seen from recent trends. Finally, the main bank-oriented corporate governance system in Japan may become in danger of collapsing if the governance structure of the monitoring agent (i.e., the main bank) collapses due to loss of credibility.

It generally appears that the financial system adopted in each economy has uniquely evolved to achieve different macroeconomic goals. Thus, simply importing the Japanese governance system may be inappropriate for many U.S. firms. U.S. policymakers should instead search for other alternatives to facilitate investing in the infrastructure of manufacturing firms. In the meantime, Japanese firms may have to search for other sources for further efficiency than the traditional main bank system as the degree of market orientation in the economy increases.

## NOTES

1. Internally generated after-tax earnings (or cash flows) come first, followed by (long-term) borrowing from banks and securities issues (equity, equity-linked bonds, and straight bonds). Reflecting favorable market conditions, equity or equity-linked issues have sometimes had higher priority than bank loans. Japanese firms preferred equity-linked bonds and equity to straight bonds during the 1980s.

2. For example, Toyota Motor Co., which is without any substantial borrowing needs most of the time, has maintained a main bank relationship with Tokai Bank.

3. The role given to the main bank is uniquely compared with the market for corporate control in the United States (Aoki, 1992a, 1992c). The main bank involvement in *ex post* monitoring reduces the cost of financial distress for the Japanese firms, as pointed out in Hoshi, Kashyap, and Scharfstein (1990).

4. Investment in such a core asset inherently generates future growth options since enhanced productivity, product quality and efficient operational controls can be a source for tomorrow's growth (e.g., see Kester, 1984). In this discussion, these growth options are distinguished from ordinary (strategically managed) real options.

5. Of course, actual main bank interference automatically means a shift in the monitoring stage from *interim* to *ex post*.

6. Japanese firms typically use very restrictive payback standards for incremental investments. For example, a three-year payback for product model changes is not unusual for durable consumer goods.

7. The compensatory deposit practices—which have been restricted or prohibited recently—cause the effective rate of corporate borrowing to be substantially higher than the nominal or stated rate. The main bank almost exclusively assumes a trustee position for corporate bond issues, earning fees whose domestic rates are very high (often 10 times as high as those in the U.S. market).

8. Most stakeholders, by and large, have an ownership position due to the cross-shareholding arrangements.

9. In the case of voluntary liquidation, for example, the main bank is expected to take care of the distressed firm's employees as a part of its implicit responsibility.

10. A good example of a monitoring failure is the Sumitomo Bank–Itoman Co. relationship, which became corrupt around 1990.

# Chapter 10

# Volatile Exchange Rates and the Multinational Firm: Entry, Exit, and Capacity Options

## Gregory K. Bell

*This chapter examines the effects of volatile exchange rates on the entry, exit, and capacity decisions of an exporting monopolist. The effects of volatility are seen to depend on whether the project is of fixed scale or of variable scale. For fixed-scale projects, volatile exchange rates raise the exchange rate required to trigger entry into a foreign market and lower the exchange rate required to trigger exit, thus increasing hysteresis (inertia) in the firm's entry and exit behavior. For variable-scale projects, volatility may increase the optimal capacity at entry and reduce the degree of hysteresis. In this case, the decline in the exchange rate that triggers exit is offset by a decline in the exchange rate that triggers entry for capacities of a certain minimum scale or greater.*

## 10.1 INTRODUCTION

The entry, exit, and capacity decisions of multinationals all represent real options. The volatility of the underlying exchange rate affects the value of these options and consequently the market structure of international competition (see Baldwin, 1988; Baldwin and Krugman, 1989). I examine the impact of volatile exchange rates on the hysteresis and scale of irreversible investments committed to foreign markets.[1]

Managers must be aware of the implications of real options and volatile exchange rates in order to appropriately assess foreign market opportunities and the threat of foreign competition. Firms may perceive opportunities to enter foreign markets as the result of product development, the dismantling of trade barriers, or shifts in foreign tastes and demand. These opportunities represent real options in the firm's investment portfolio.

The option to enter a foreign market is similar to a call option where the exercise price is the cost of the investment required to enter the market. The cost of the investment depends on the capacity the firm chooses to commit to the foreign market. Similarly, the option to exit is analogous to a put option; the firm gives up the value of its asset position in the foreign market in return for a salvage or best-alternative-use value.[2]

Investments to enter a foreign market are often sunk in the form of firm-, market-, or industry-specific production or distribution capacity, brand equity, learning economies, and so on. The irreversible nature of these investments generates a hysteresis or inertia in a firm's entry and exit behavior. Options are never optimally exercised unless they are *in-the-money*. The option to enter is not exercised unless expected operating profits are at least sufficient to provide the required rate of return on *committed* capital. The option to exit or abandon is not in-the-money until operating profits are insufficient to provide the required rate of return on the *recoverable* or *salvageable* capital. The difference between the cost of committed capital and the realizable value of recoverable capital generates the potential for hysteresis.

The insights of option pricing can be very useful to managers. For example, a standard result of option pricing theory is that an option's value increases with a (mean-preserving) increase in volatility. In the case of an export market opportunity, the volatility of the exchange rate is naturally critical. The more volatile the exchange rate, the more valuable the option to enter the market would be, and hence the expected operating profits must be higher to warrant exercising the option. Similarly, given a firm already operating in the foreign market, the more volatile the exchange rate the more valuable the option to exit, and therefore expected operating profits must be lower to warrant exercising the abandonment option. Higher exchange rate volatility thus raises the expected operating profits required for entry into the foreign market and lowers the expected operating profits required for exit. The gap between the expected profits that trigger entry and exit induces a hysteresis in the firm's investment behavior. An increase in volatility widens the gap, increasing hysteresis. Hysteresis may thus be viewed as a result of the interaction between the sequentially exercised options to enter and exit the market.

Dixit (1989a) modeled the entry and exit decisions of a risk-neutral firm in a market characterized by an exogenous and volatile product price. He showed that an increase in volatility raises the product price that triggers the firm's entry and lowers the product price that triggers the firm's exit, therefore hysteresis increases with volatility. Dixit proved this for fixed-scale investments.[3] I extend Dixit's analysis by superimposing the capacity choice problem as well.

For most multinationals, foreign market entry is not a binary choice variable. The decision concerns not only whether to invest or to wait, but also how much capacity to build. Consider the problem of capacity choice faced by a multinational with a profitable export opportunity.[4] Each unit of capacity can be viewed as representing an option to operate (see Pindyck, 1988). To exercise the option, the firm pays an exercise price equal to the marginal cost of production and receives a return equal to the marginal revenue. The operating option's value increases with an increase in exchange rate volatility. The option's cost is the price of installing a unit of capacity, here assumed to be nonstochastic and invariant to changes in the exchange rate. Since an increase in volatility increases the option's value without affecting its cost, more options to operate are acquired and hence more capacity is built than would otherwise be the case. This *excess capacity* is constructed to enable the firm to expand production and take advantage of a potentially profitable future appreciation in the foreign currency.

The cost of adjusting capacity is central to the decision of entry scale. Pindyck (1988) presented a model of optimal capacity choice under product price uncertainty that allows for downward-sloping demand and price-setting behavior. If the costs of adding capacity are minimal, then greater product price volatility leads to smaller initial investments in capacity. If, however, the costs of adding capacity later are relatively high, then greater volatility leads to larger initial investments in capacity.[5] I extend Pindyck's model to incorporate exit options and an analysis of hysteresis when the source of uncertainty is exchange rates, rather than product price.

The remainder of this chapter is organized as follows. Section 10.2 sets out the base case, which describes the entry, exit, and capacity decisions of an exporting monopolist operating under a regime of certain exchange rates. I consider the issues for both fixed- and variable-scale projects. Section 10.3 extends the analysis to a regime of volatile exchange rates. Section 10.4 compares the degree of hysteresis and the optimal capacity between the two regimes. Section 10.5 concludes with some issues for further investigation.

## 10.2 CERTAIN EXCHANGE RATE REGIME

A monopolist based at home considers constructing a facility to produce "widgets" for export to the foreign market.[6] Instantaneous construction is permitted only once at a constant cost of $k$ per unit of infinitely-lived capacity.[7] The firm's discount rate is $\rho$. The salvage value of installed capacity is $l$ per unit; the higher the $k/l$ ratio, the more sunk or irreversible is the investment. One unit of capacity is required to produce one unit of output per period. Variable production costs are assumed to be zero;

therefore a firm active in the market produces at capacity. The inverse demand curve in the foreign market is $P(Q)$, the marginal revenue is $\theta(Q) \equiv P(Q) + QP'(Q)$.[8] The exchange rate, $R$, is the only parameter in the model that can be stochastic.[9] $R$ is the Home Currency price of Foreign Currency, $R \equiv HC/FC$. The $HC$ revenue from the sale of $Q$ units in the foreign market is, thus, $RP(Q)Q$. For numerical examples I assume linear demand, $P(Q) = a - bQ$, and parameter values: $a = 1$, $b = 0.1$, $k = 10$, and $\rho = 0.05$.

## 10.2.1   Entry with Variable Scale

For the base case, assume that the exchange rate is expected to be constant. To determine optimal capacity, $\bar{K}$, for a variable-scale project, the monopolist solves the following standard problem:

$$\max_k \; K(RP(K) - \rho k). \tag{10.1}$$

The firm thus builds optimal capacity as a function of the exchange rate:

$$\bar{K}(R) = \frac{\rho k - RP(\bar{K})}{RP'(\bar{K})}. \tag{10.2}$$

Note that $\bar{K}'(R) > 0$. An appreciated $HC$ reduces $HC$ revenues relative to costs and lowers optimal capacity. A depreciated $HC$ raises $HC$ revenues relative to costs and increases optimal capacity.

For a variable-scale project, the entry trigger under certainty, $\bar{R}_H(K)$, is the exchange rate at which a plant of size $K$ is optimally built. $\bar{R}_H(K)$ equates marginal revenue in $FC$ to the per-period cost of capacity in $HC$:

$$\bar{R}_H(K) = \frac{\rho k}{\theta(K)}. \tag{10.3}$$

## 10.2.2   Entry with Fixed Scale

$\bar{R}^o(K)$ is the breakeven exchange rate for constructing a plant of fixed capacity, $K$. Where production technology or other constraints impose a fixed scale on the project, the monopolist can profitably build and operate a plant of size $K$ at any exchange rate greater than $\bar{R}^o(K)$. The minimum exchange rate at which the firm would choose to construct a fixed-scale facility of capacity $K$ equates the average revenue in $FC$ to the per-period cost of capacity in $HC$:

$$\bar{R}^o(K) = \frac{\rho k}{P(K)}. \tag{10.4}$$

## 10.2.3 Exit

If the monopolist were already operating in the market with a plant of size $K$ and the $HC$ were to unexpectedly and permanently appreciate, the monopolist would remain in the market unless the exchange rate were to drop below the exit trigger, $\bar{R}_L(K)$. At exchange rates below $\bar{R}_L(K)$, the $HC$ has appreciated such that production does not yield revenues sufficient to provide the required return on the recoverable capital, $\rho l K$. $\bar{R}_L(K)$ equates the product price in $FC$ to the avoidable costs in $HC$:

$$\bar{R}_L(K) = \frac{\rho l}{P(K)}. \qquad (10.5)$$

## 10.2.4 Hysteresis

The difference between the exchange rates that trigger entry and exit is related to hysteresis. A measure of hysteresis is the percentage difference between these exchange rates. For fixed-scale projects, assuming investment is undertaken as soon as it is profitable, that is at $\bar{R}^o(K)$, the measure of hysteresis is:

$$\bar{H}_F = \frac{\bar{R}^o(K) - \bar{R}_L(K)}{\bar{R}^o(K)} = 1 - \frac{l}{k}. \qquad (10.6)$$

This measure of hysteresis is thus independent of scale and is only a function of the degree to which investment in the market is sunk and irreversible. The more irreversible the investment, the greater the hysteresis. If $l = 0$, such that investment in capacity is completely sunk (i.e., the option to abandon is worthless), an active firm will never leave the market and hysteresis will be 100 percent. If $l = k$, such that investment in capacity is completely reversible, there will be no hysteresis; any appreciation of the $HC$ will drive an active firm from the foreign market.

For projects where scale is a choice variable, the measure of hysteresis is:

$$\bar{H}_V = \frac{\bar{R}_H(K) - \bar{R}_L(K)}{\bar{R}_H(K)} = 1 - \frac{l}{k} \frac{\theta(K)}{P(K)}. \qquad (10.7)$$

Hysteresis is now a function of both irreversibility and market power, where market power is measured as the ratio of price to marginal revenue. The greater the firm's market power, the greater the hysteresis.

Figure 10.1 plots hysteresis as a function of capacity, $K$, for investments that are 10, 50, or 100 percent reversible. Hysteresis is most significant for the most irreversible technology (i.e., for $l/k = 0.1$). For fixed-scale investments undertaken at $\bar{R}^o(K)$, hysteresis is independent of scale. For variable-scale investments, hysteresis increases with capacity, starting at the fixed-scale level and approaching 100 percent as $K$ approaches 5. When

**Figure 10.1**
**Hysteresis as a Function of Capacity in a Certain Exchange Rate Regime**

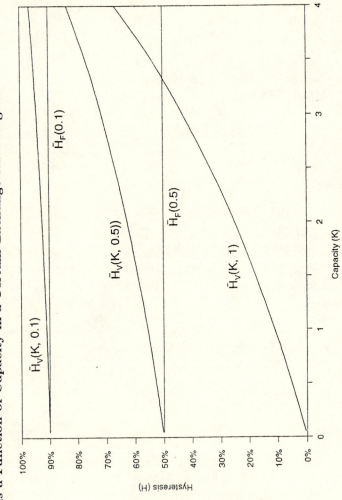

*Note:* The figure compares hysteresis for fixed- and variable-scale projects in a regime of certain exchange rates. For fixed-scale projects, hysteresis is a function of the irreversibility of the investment, $\bar{H}_F(l/k)$. For variable-scale projects, hysteresis is a function of capacity and irreversibility, $\bar{H}_V(K; l/k)$.

scale is a choice variable, hysteresis can be significant even for completely reversible investments; the $HC$ must appreciate by 25 percent before a firm that optimally entered with a completely reversible capacity of 2 units will choose to exit.

## 10.3 VOLATILE EXCHANGE RATES

This section introduces uncertainty by considering a volatile exchange rate regime. Assume that $R$ evolves exogenously over time as a geometric Brownian motion of the form:[10]

$$\frac{dR}{R} = \sigma dz. \tag{10.8}$$

The percentage change in $R$ is thus assumed to follow an Ito process with zero drift and a constant instantaneous variance, $\sigma^2$. The variable $dz$ is the increment of a Wiener process equal to $\omega(t)dt^{1/2}$, where $\omega(t)$ is a serially uncorrelated standard normal random variable.[11]

The decision to enter the foreign market depends on the exchange rate at the time the opportunity to invest arises. This opportunity may arise as the result of the firm's research and development, the dismantling of international trade barriers, or the readiness of management to pursue international markets. Once the opportunity arises, the firm must choose whether to wait or to invest. If the firm owns an option on a fixed-scale project of size $K$, this decision is similar to the one analyzed in Dixit (1989a): invest if the exchange rate exceeds the entry trigger, $R \geq \tilde{R}^o(K, \sigma)$; otherwise, wait until the $HC$ depreciates to $\tilde{R}^o(K, \sigma)$. If the firm owns an option on a variable-scale project, however, it maximizes value by choosing an entry strategy, $(\tilde{K}; \tilde{R})$, that optimizes across both the capacity installed and the exchange rate at the time of entry.

### 10.3.1 Entry and Exit with Variable Scale

For a firm owning an entry option on a variable-scale project, the basic decision is either to wait, or to invest and build the optimal capacity given the exchange rate, $\tilde{K}(R, \sigma)$. If the firm waits, it incurs the opportunity cost of forgone profits. If the firm invests, it incurs the expected cost of regret. The cost of regret arises from the potential for suboptimal capacity. If the $HC$ appreciates, the firm will have too much capacity; if the $HC$ subsequently depreciates, the firm will have too little. This cost of regret is a decreasing function of $R$ since $K'(R) > 0$ and marginal revenue is a decreasing function of quantity, $\theta'(K) < 0$. The opportunity cost of forgone profits, however, is an increasing function of $R$. If $R$ is such that the firm optimally chooses to wait, then the firm will invest at $R^\star(\sigma) > R$, when the cost of regret is offset by the opportunity cost of forgone profits. At $R^\star(\sigma)$ the firm invests in a plant of minimum scale, $K^\star(\sigma)$. If the profit opportunity arises when $R \geq R^\star(\sigma)$, then the optimal strategy is to immediately invest the optimal capacity, $K(R,\sigma) \geq K^\star(\sigma)$.

To examine the effect of volatility on the firm's entry, exit, and capacity decisions, consider the situation presented in the base case.[12] The monopolist owns an option to enter the foreign market.[13] Let $G(K^\star; R)$ represent the value of the option to invest in minimum scale, $K^\star(\sigma)$, when the exchange rate is $R \leq R^\star(\sigma)$.[14] For the monopolist to willingly hold this option, it must earn the required rate of return.[15] Since the only component of the return is the expected capital gain from holding the option:

$$E[dG(K^\star; R)/dt] = \rho G(K^\star; R). \tag{10.9}$$

By Ito's Lemma,

$$dG(K^\star; R) = \sigma R G_R(K^\star; R)dz + \frac{1}{2}\sigma^2 R^2 G_{RR}(K^\star; R)dt. \tag{10.10}$$

Taking expectations yields:

$$\frac{1}{2}\sigma^2 R^2 G_{RR}(K^\star; R) = \rho G(K^\star; R). \tag{10.11}$$

The solution for $G(K^\star; R)$ is:

$$G(K^\star; R) = A(K^\star)R^{1-\beta} + D(K^\star)R^\beta \qquad \text{for } R \leq R^\star(\sigma), \tag{10.12}$$

where $A(K^\star)$ and $D(K^\star)$ are constants and $\beta$ is given by:

$$\beta = \frac{1 + (1 + \frac{8\rho}{\sigma^2})^{1/2}}{2} > 1, \tag{10.13}$$

with $\dfrac{\partial \beta}{\partial \sigma} < 0$, $\lim\limits_{\sigma \to 0} \beta = \infty$, and $\lim\limits_{\sigma \to \infty} \beta = 1$.

The value of a firm already active in the foreign market includes the value of the option to exit in addition to the value of ongoing operations. If the $HC$ appreciates sufficiently, the firm will choose to exit the foreign market. Upon exiting, the firm receives salvage value, $l$, per unit of capacity. The firm is not otherwise allowed to adjust its capacity level once it has entered the market. When the firm exits, it sells 100 percent of its capacity and is not permitted to reenter the market in the future.[16]

Let $J(K; R)$ be the value of a firm active in the foreign market. The firm's required rate of return is composed of two parts, the expected capital gain on the option to exit and the operating profits. The instantaneous expected return is, therefore:

$$E[dJ(K; R)/dt] + KRP(K) = \rho J(K; R). \tag{10.14}$$

Using Ito's Lemma and taking expectations yields:

$$\frac{1}{2}\sigma^2 R^2 J_{RR}(K;R) + KRP(K) = \rho J(K;R). \tag{10.15}$$

The solution for $J(K;R)$ is:

$$J(K;R) = S(K)R^{1-\beta} + T(K)R^\beta + \frac{KP(K)R}{\rho} \quad \text{for } R \geq \tilde{R}_L(K). \tag{10.16}$$

The last term in Equation (10.16) is the value of an active firm if there is no salvage value to capacity. If $l = 0$, an active firm will never exit the foreign market because the marginal cost of production is also 0. The first two terms in Equation (10.16), therefore, represent the value of the option to exit.

Equations (10.12) and (10.16) completely describe the value of the firm's position, either in or out of the foreign market, at all exchange rate values, $R$. There are seven variables to be determined, namely, the four constants, $A(K^\star), D(K^\star), S(K)$, and $T(K)$; the schedules of exchange rates that trigger entry and exit at various capacities, $\tilde{R}_H(K)$ and $\tilde{R}_L(K)$; and the minimum scale trigger point, $(K^\star; R^\star)$.

Seven boundary conditions determine these seven unknowns:

a. $G(K^\star; 0) = 0$;

b. $G(K^\star; R^\star) = J(K^\star; R^\star) - kK^\star(\sigma)$;

c. $G_R(K^\star; R^\star) = J_R(K^\star; R^\star)$;

d. $k = J_K(K;R)$ at time of entry;

e. $lK = J(K; \tilde{R}_L)$;

f. $0 = J_R(K; \tilde{R}_L)$;

g. $\lim_{R \to \infty} J(K;R) = KRP(K)/\rho$.

Condition (a) states that if the $FC$ becomes worthless, so does the option to invest in the foreign market. Condition (b) is the value-matching condition: at the trigger point, the option to enter the foreign market must be worth as much as the capacity in place less the cost of entry. Condition (c) is the smooth-pasting condition which ensures that the option to invest at minimum scale is exercised at the lowest exchange rate at which the option is worth more dead than alive.[17] Condition (d) is the standard requirement at entry to build until the marginal cost of an additional unit of capacity is equal to the marginal benefit.

Conditions (e) and (f) are the value-matching and smooth-pasting conditions for the exit option, similar to conditions (b) and (c) for the entry option. Together, the two conditions ensure that there is no change in the value of the firm upon the transition from operations to exit at the optimal exit point, $\tilde{R}_L(K)$, and that changes in firm value as $R$ approaches $\tilde{R}_L(K)$ are smooth and continuous. Condition (g) requires that the value of the option to exit approaches zero as $R$ becomes very large; the probability that $R$ will fall sufficiently far to encourage the firm to exercise its option to exit becomes very small as $R$ increases asymptotically.

Conditions (a) and (g) yield $A(K^\star) = T(K) = 0$. This leaves the following system of equations to be solved:

$$G(K^\star; R) = D(K^\star)R^\beta;$$

$$(10.17)$$

$$J(K; R) = S(K)R^{1-\beta} + \frac{KP(K)R}{\rho}.$$

The solution is as follows (all values are nonnegative):

$$D(K^\star) = \frac{K^\star(\sigma)(R^\star)^{-\beta}}{(2\beta - 1)\rho}[\beta P(K^\star)R^\star(\sigma) - (\beta - 1)\rho k];$$

$$S(K) = \frac{lK\tilde{R}_L(K)^{\beta-1}}{\beta};$$

$$(10.18)$$

$$K^\star(\sigma) = \frac{-P(K^\star)}{\beta P'(K^\star)};$$

$$\tilde{R}_L(K) = \frac{(\beta - 1)l\rho}{\beta P(K)}.$$

For the firm owning an option on a variable-scale project, condition (d) can be solved numerically for the entry schedule, $\tilde{K}(R, \sigma)$ for $R \geq R^\star(\sigma)$, and by substituting for the value of $K^\star(\sigma)$, one can solve numerically for $R^\star(\sigma)$.

Note that $\partial K^\star(\sigma)/\partial \beta < 0$ and, since $\partial \beta/\partial \sigma < 0$, $K^{\star\prime}(\sigma) > 0$. A mean-preserving increase in the exchange rate volatility thus raises the value of the option to invest. The entry trigger equates the value of the option to invest with the value of the assets in place less the cost of exercising the option. To increase the value of the assets in place, operating profits must increase. To increase profits, the $HC$ must depreciate, raising the exchange rate, $R$. As $R$ increases, however, so too does the project's optimal scale.

Consequently, the minimum scale of entry increases as the exchange rate volatility increases.

Consider now the case where the opportunity to invest in the foreign market arises when $R \geq R^\star(\sigma)$ and the firm immediately enters with optimal scale, $\tilde{K}(R,\sigma) \geq K^\star(\sigma)$. When the firm enters the foreign market, it acquires an option to exit, valued at $S(K)R^{1-\beta}$. The value of the option to exit increases with an increase in the salvage value of capacity, $\partial S(K)/\partial l > 0$. The expected cost of regret, incurred at entry, is lower when there is an opportunity to exit and recover some portion of the initial investment. Since the cost of regret is lower, the profits of entry need not be as large to trigger investment and, accordingly, $\partial \tilde{R}_H(K;\sigma)/\partial l < 0$. Of course, the value of the option to exit also increases with an increase in the volatility of the exchange rate since a more volatile exchange rate raises the probability that the option to exit will be exercised. Since the option to exit is worth more if volatility is higher and the option to exit is acquired upon entry, lower profits upon entry can be tolerated, so that $\partial \tilde{R}_H(K;\sigma)/\partial \sigma < 0$.

In a sense, then, the option value of capacity induces firms operating in a regime of volatile exchange rates to invest *earlier* than firms operating in a regime of certain exchange rates. Similarly sized plants are built at lower exchange rates since for $R \geq R^\star(\sigma), \tilde{K}(R,\sigma) > \tilde{K}(R)$. The incidence of entry, however, is *postponed* under conditions of uncertainty and the *postponement* increases with an increase in volatility. The firm operating under volatile exchange rates does not build plants with capacity less than minimum scale, $K^\star(\sigma)$, even though such plants might be profitable in a regime of certainty.

## 10.3.2 Entry with Fixed Scale

The problem for a fixed-scale project is treated similarly, except that condition (d) governing optimal scale is not used and there is no issue of minimum scale. The minimum exchange rate that supports entry for a fixed-scale project, $R^o(K)$, can be found numerically by substituting for $D(K)$ and $S(K)$ from the solution in Equation (10.18) and then solving either condition (b) or (c). A recursive solution for the minimum entry trigger is:

$$\tilde{R}^o(K) = \frac{\beta}{\beta - 1}\bar{R}^o(K) - \frac{(2\beta - 1)S(K)\tilde{R}^o(K)^{1-\beta}\rho}{(\beta - 1)KP(K)}. \tag{10.19}$$

The first term in the above expression is the minimum entry trigger for $l = 0$; the second term captures the effect of the option to exit. As in the case of the variable-scale project, the presence of this option lowers the minimum exchange rate required for entry, $\partial \tilde{R}^o(K)/\partial l < 0$. As opposed to volatility's effect on the variable-scale project, however, an increase in exchange rate volatility raises, rather than lowers, the minimum entry trigger for a fixed-scale project. For any given salvage value, an increase in volatility raises the cost of regret incurred at entry. Since capacity is fixed, the only way to raise the profits of entry is to raise the exchange rate that supports entry; accordingly, $\partial \tilde{R}^o(K)/\partial \sigma > 0$.

### 10.3.3 Exit

Irrespective of the project type, the exit trigger under uncertainty is lower than the exit trigger under certainty since $\tilde{R}_L(K) = \bar{R}_L(K)((\beta - 1)/\beta)$, and the difference between the two increases with volatility. In an uncertain environment, exit incurs an expected cost of regret related to the probability that the exchange rate will depreciate in the future and continuing operations will yield profits for a firm that chooses to remain active in the market. As the $HC$ appreciates and $R$ falls, however, the cost of regret declines while the opportunity cost of forgone returns on recoverable capital increases. At some value of $R < \bar{R}_L(K)$, the cost of regret equals the opportunity cost of forgone returns and the firm exits. $\tilde{R}_L(K)$ is lower for higher values of $\sigma$, which increases the cost of regret, $\partial \tilde{R}_L(K)/\partial \sigma < 0$, and $\tilde{R}_L(K)$ is higher for higher values of $l$, which increases the opportunity cost of forgone returns, $\partial \tilde{R}_L(K)/\partial l > 0$.

## 10.4  HYSTERESIS

The effect of exchange rate volatility on hysteresis depends on the type of project. Regarding the exchange rate that triggers exit, volatility leads to a lower exit trigger for both fixed- and variable-scale projects. Regarding the exchange rate that triggers entry, however, volatility leads to a higher entry trigger for fixed-scale projects but a lower entry trigger for variable-scale projects. As a consequence, volatility unambiguously increases hysteresis for fixed-scale projects, confirming the result obtained in Dixit (1989a). The effect of volatility on hysteresis for variable-scale projects, however, is ambiguous.

We again measure hysteresis as the percentage difference between the exchange rates that trigger entry and exit. Unfortunately, an analytic solution for the degree of hysteresis does not exist for firms operating in a regime of volatile exchange rates. Nevertheless, it can be shown that the factors that influence the degree of hysteresis for fixed- and variable-scale projects are the same under a regime of volatile exchange rates as under a regime of certainty. For fixed-scale projects, hysteresis, $H_F$, is a function of volatility and irreversibility, but is independent of scale. The more volatile the exchange rate and the more irreversible the investment, the greater is hysteresis.

For variable-scale projects, hysteresis, $\tilde{H}_V$, is a function of capacity, as well as volatility and irreversibility. The effect of irreversibility is again straightforward: the more irreversible the investment, the greater the hysteresis. The effects of capacity and volatility, however, are difficult to separate. For a given level of volatility, greater capacity raises both the entry and exit triggers. For a given capacity, on the other hand, greater volatility lowers both the entry and exit triggers.

The effects of capacity and volatility on hysteresis are illustrated in Figure 10.2. The figure graphs hysteresis as a function of capacity, for fixed- and variable-scale projects, under conditions of both certain exchange rates ($\sigma = 0$) and of volatile exchange rates ($\sigma = 0.1$ and $\sigma = 0.2$). The investments are assumed to be 50 percent sunk. The minimum capacity for variable-scale projects, $K^\star(\sigma)$, marks the intersection of $\tilde{H}_F(\sigma)$ and $\tilde{H}_V(K;\sigma)$. For both types of projects, an increase in volatility increases hysteresis. For variable-scale projects, an increase in capacity increases hysteresis for a given level of exchange rate volatility. For projects of fixed scale, hysteresis is constant (independent of capacity).

Figure 10.2 confirms that hysteresis under volatile exchange rates exceeds hysteresis under certainty, irrespective of the project type. It is also apparent from Figure 10.2 that the difference in hysteresis between the two exchange rate regimes depends fundamentally on the project type. For fixed-scale projects, the difference in hysteresis increases with volatility. For variable-scale projects, however, the difference in hysteresis decreases as capacity increases.

Figures 10.3 and 10.4 plot the difference in hysteresis between volatile and certain exchange rate regimes for fixed- and variable-scale projects, respectively. Investments are considered to be 10, 50, or 100 percent reversible. For fixed-scale projects, Figure 10.3 illustrates the incremental effect of exchange rate volatility on hysteresis. Note the significantly greater impact of volatility on hysteresis for the more reversible investments. To trigger exit under volatile exchange rates, given $\sigma = 0.4$, an investment that is 10 percent reversible ($l/k = 0.1$) requires only an additional 9 percent appreciation of the $HC$. Under similar circumstances, to trigger exit of an investment that is completely reversible ($l/k = 1$) requires an 85 percent appreciation in the $HC$.

To illustrate the difference in hysteresis between volatile and certain exchange rate regimes for variable-scale projects, Figure 10.4 assumes that the optimal capacity upon entry is equal to a minimum scale, $K = K^\star(\sigma)$.

Note that the difference in hysteresis for any combination of volatility and irreversibility is significantly lower for variable-scale projects in Figure 10.4 than for fixed-scale projects in Figure 10.3. For instance, given $\sigma = 0.1$

## Figure 10.2
## Hysteresis as a Function of Capacity in Certain and Volatile Exchange Rate Regimes

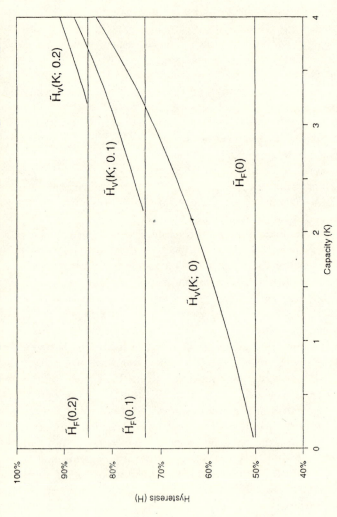

*Note:* The figure plots hysteresis for fixed- and variable-scale projects under certain and volatile exchange rate regimes. Investments are assumed to be 50 percent reversible. Hysteresis for fixed-scale projects depends only on volatility, $\bar{H}_F(\sigma)$. Hysteresis for variable-scale projects depends on capacity and volatility, $\bar{H}_V(K; \sigma)$.

**Figure 10.3**
**Difference in Hysteresis between Volatile and Certain Exchange Rate Regimes—Fixed-Scale Project**

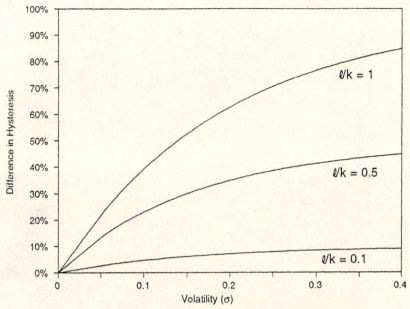

*Note:* The figure graphs the difference in hysteresis at different degrees of irreversibility (e.g., $l/k = 0.1$ implies project is 10 percent reversible).

and an investment that is 50 percent reversible ($l/k = 0.5$), the fixed-scale project requires an additional 23 percent appreciation of the $HC$ to trigger exit in a volatile exchange rate regime, whereas the variable-scale project requires only an additional 10 percent appreciation. Furthermore, the effect of uncertainty on the difference in hysteresis for minimum-scale projects is not monotonic. The difference in hysteresis initially increases and then decreases as uncertainty and minimum-scale increase. Since the difference in hysteresis must decrease with an increase in scale, the decline in the difference as volatility and scale increase in tandem is attributed to the negative effect of increasing minimum scale assumed in Figure 10.4.

To isolate the effect of volatility for variable-scale projects, I assume a constant scale and plot the difference in hysteresis. Figure 10.5 plots the difference in hysteresis, $\tilde{H}_V(K; l/k) - \tilde{H}_V(K; l/k)$, for a variable-scale project of size $K = 4$ and investments that are 10, 50, or 100 percent reversible.[18] Figure 10.5 indicates that the incremental effect of uncertainty on hysteresis is monotonic and increasing for variable-scale projects as it is

**Figure 10.4**
**Difference in Hysteresis between Volatile and Certain Exchange Rate Regimes—Variable-Scale Project**

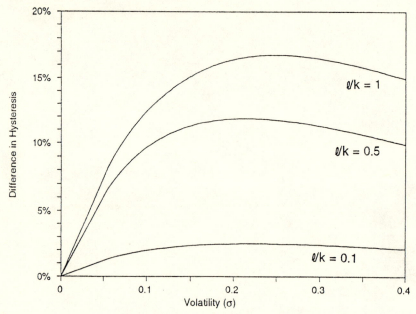

*Note:* The figure graphs the difference in hysteresis at different degrees of irreversibility (e.g., $l/k = 0.1$ implies project is 10 percent reversible).

for projects of fixed scale, but the magnitude of the effect is considerably less than for fixed-scale projects (such as those shown in Figure 10.3).

## 10.5  CONCLUSIONS

This chapter investigates the effects of exchange rate volatility on the entry, exit, and capacity decisions of an exporting monopolist. I find that the effects of volatility generally depend on whether the project is fixed- or variable-scale. For fixed-scale projects, volatility raises the minimum exchange rate that supports entry into the foreign market and lowers the exchange rate that triggers exit. Consequently, hysteresis is more significant under expectations of volatile exchange rates than under expectations of certainty. For variable-scale projects, volatility raises the minimum scale of entry and the minimum exchange rate supporting entry. Given that entry is optimal, however, volatility also increases the capacity invested at each level of the exchange rate. As a result, although volatility still increases hy-

**Figure 10.5**
**Difference in Hysteresis between Volatile and Certain Exchange Rate Regimes under Constant Scale—Variable-Scale Project**

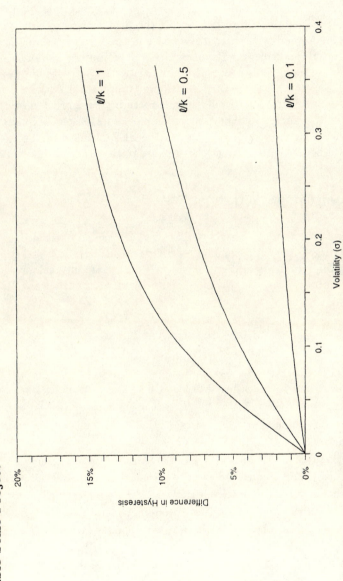

*Note:* The figure graphs the difference in hysteresis for a variable-scale project of capacity 4 units given investments at various degrees of irreversibility: $\tilde{H}_V(4, \sigma, l/k) - \tilde{H}_V(4, l/k)$.

steresis, the effect is significantly reduced since the decline in the exit trigger is partially offset by a decline in the entry trigger for capacities of minimum scale or greater.

This work can be extended to consider technology choice, capacity adjustment, and competition. For example, the assumption of infinite costs of capacity adjustment is restrictive. If the firm makes its entry decision anticipating an ability to increase capacity in the future, one might expect smaller initial investments in capacity. There is also the issue of competition in a global oligopoly. As noted, competition at home would appear to have little effect on the results. Assuming Cournot behavior, the impact of symmetric competitors would be manifest in the market power terms present in the analysis. The issue of competitors based in different exchange rates is more complex, however, because changes in the exchange rate would benefit one party at the expense of the other.

## ACKNOWLEDGMENTS

I thank Jose Campa, Elizabeth Teisberg, Michael Whinston, Lenos Trigeorgis (the editor), and seminar participants at Harvard University for many useful comments and suggestions. I also gratefully acknowledge financial support from the Division of Research at the Harvard Business School.

## NOTES

1. Hysteresis is the persistent effect of a temporary change in a variable. In this chapter, hysteresis refers to the persistent effect on market structure of a temporary fluctuation in exchange rates that induces a foreign competitor to enter a domestic market.

2. See Pindyck (1991) for a survey of the literature on real options.

3. Campa (1991) studied the effect of exchange rate volatility on foreign direct investment in the U.S. wholesale trade industry in the 1980s. He found some support for Dixit's (1989b) hypothesis regarding volatility and entry behavior, namely, that higher volatility in the relevant bilateral exchange rate leads to lower incidence of foreign entry.

4. Kogut and Kulatilaka (1994) also considered this issue from the standpoint of a multinational firm investing in a global production network.

5. See Caballero (1991) for more on the role of capacity adjustment costs and the sign of the investment-uncertainty relationship.

6. The "widgets" need not be uniquely designed for the foreign market. It is sufficient that additional capacity be required at home in order to supply the export market. The analysis requires that the home country have a monopoly on the supply of widgets, but it is invariant to the firm's status as a monopolist or Cournot oligopolist.

7. Majd and Pindyck (1987) and Teisberg (1988) analyzed some of the issues regarding construction lags and investment rates under uncertainty.

8. As customary, the expressions $Y'(X)$ and $Y''(X)$ are defined as the first and second derivatives of the function $Y$ with respect to the variable $X$.

9. This is a partial equilibrium analysis. Baldwin and Krugman (1989) and Krugman (1988) developed models with feedback to the exchange rate.

10. Numerous studies of exchange rate variability have found it difficult to reject the null hypothesis that the real exchange rate follows a random walk. See Frankel and Meese (1987).

11. The stochastic process for $R$ can be amended to include jumps or mean reversion.

12. Much of the analysis follows Dixit (1989a).

13. The option is assumed to be infinitely lived. There is no time limit on the investment opportunity, such as there might be if the option were due to a patent that would expire or an innovation that could be copied.

14. The monopolist actually owns a portfolio of options, one for each level of $K$. Since $R$ is a continuous process, however, for $R < R^\star(\sigma)$ only the option to invest $K^\star(\sigma)$ will ever be exercised.

15. Pindyck (1991) discussed the issues regarding an appropriate rate of return. If spanning holds, such that there is a portfolio of traded assets whose price is perfectly correlated with the value of the firm's investment opportunity, then the return on the portfolio of assets anchors the required return on the investment opportunity. If spanning does not hold, however, then there is no *correct* rate of return on the investment opportunity and valuation is subject to an arbitrary choice of the discount rate.

16. Dixit (1989a) allowed the firm an option to reenter after exit.

17. The intuition behind the smooth-pasting condition is developed in Dixit (1992).

18. To be relevant, the constant scale must be greater than the minimum scale, $K^\star(\sigma)$. The minimum scale for $\sigma = 0.36$ is approximately 4 units.

# PART IV

---

# MEAN REVERSION / ALTERNATIVE FORMULATIONS IN NATURAL RESOURCES, SHIPPING, AND START – UP VENTURES

# Chapter 11

# The Effects of Reversion on Commodity Projects of Different Length

## David G. Laughton and Henry D. Jacoby

*Failure to account for possible reversion in output prices may bias invest-
ment choices against longer-run commodity projects. For now-or-never
choices, reversion lowers uncertainty in long-term revenues and the appropriate level of risk discounting, introducing a bias when ignored. If there
is operating flexibility (e.g., a timing option), the effects are more complex,
involving influences also from the variance and the future central tendency
of the cash flows. These effects can counteract each other, and the bias
can run either way depending on the project. Neglect of reversion generally
biases against longer-lived projects, although timing options of longer duration can be overvalued. The results suggest a reevaluation of standard DCF
procedures and options analyses based on random-walk models.*

## 11.1  INTRODUCTION

Standard methods of discounted cash flow (DCF) analysis have been criticized for introducing a bias against long-term investments (e.g., see Hayes
and Garvin, 1982; MacCallum, 1987). It is easy to think of reasons why
this complaint may be valid. Most DCF applications ignore the value from
the real options that accompany investment projects, and it is likely that
longer-lived projects tend to embody more options than short-lived ones.
Where this is true, the result is a tendency to undervalue longer-term investments (Myers, 1987). Organizations may also apply premiums in discount
rates to compensate for suspected overoptimism in cash flow estimates. To
the extent that long-term cash flows tend to be positive and the overopti-

mism is not exponentially growing with the term of the cash flows being estimated, this practice will also introduce a bias against the long term.

In this chapter, we use modern asset pricing methods to consider a third possible source of such bias. Let us suppose that a key time-series variable, on which the cash flows have a positive dependence, has a tendency to revert to a long-term equilibrium in the face of short-term shocks. Ignoring the effects of this reversion can influence the analysis of the risk characteristics of project alternatives of different length and bias their relative valuation. We show this effect in situations where the reverting variable is the output price, as may be the case for certain commodity-production projects. Both now-or-never investment decisions and investment timing options are considered.

Output price reversion has a straightforward effect on now-or-never decisions if there are no operating options. The stronger the reversion, the less is the uncertainty in long-term revenues when compared to short-term ones. With less uncertainty, the risk discounting for long-term revenues should be reduced in relation to that for short-term revenues. This is the first of several influences of reversion on project value, and we refer to it as the "risk-discounting" effect. Because of this effect, the neglect or underestimation of reversion introduces a bias against project alternatives with larger long-term revenues, even if the valuation is done properly in other respects. Moreover, the use of a single discount rate to value project alternatives with different operating lives may introduce a bias against long-term opportunities.

If options are embedded in the project alternatives, however, the effects of output price reversion are more complex. Because of the risk-discounting effect, reversion tends to increase the value of any claim to cash flows that increase with long-term prices (including call options), and to decrease the value of claims to cash flows that decrease with prices (including put options). Lower uncertainty also tends to depress directly the value of long-term options of *any* type. We call this the "variance" effect, and it reinforces the risk-discounting effect for put options, while it mitigates, if not overwhelms, it for call options.

Finally, the reversion of future term structures for central tendencies of the price can have direct effects on asset values. These may be called "future-reversion" effects. They exist for American options for which the timing of the exercise is optional, and may also exist for options with payoffs generated by cash flows that would occur over a period of time. The impact of these future-reversion effects can depend on whether or not the option is currently in the money, and whether the reversion is to price levels where the option would be in-the-money in the future.

Because of potential interaction among these effects, which may counteract each other, the bias from ignoring reversion might be in favor of or against the long term depending on the situation. In the investment timing examples we study, the bias remains against the project with a longer duration, even if the strength of the bias is reduced somewhat (compared to a now-or-never decision) by the introduction of the timing option. On the other hand, for a given operating project, timing options of longer duration can be relatively *overvalued* if reversion is neglected.

In section 11.2, we summarize the price and valuation models used in the analysis, with more details delegated to the Appendix. To maintain consistency with the evaluation framework we have found useful in other work (Jacoby and Laughton, 1992), we assume the price process has a lognormal structure. This condition allows a nonstochastic discounting framework to be applied to the valuation of the related output price claims. To facilitate the valuation of the initial timing option, we use price models that result in a simple, one-dimensional state space indexed by the contemporaneous price. Section 11.3 uses sample commodity projects to illustrate how reversion can affect the evaluation of now-or-never decisions and options on projects of different operating length. The results suggest a number of areas for further investigation, which are discussed in section 11.4.

## 11.2   THE VALUATION PROCEDURE

The situations that we examine satisfy three conditions. First, the investing organization is a price-taker in the output market, so that the price is an underlying exogenous variable. Second, uncertainty in future output prices is the only uncertainty underlying the decisions to be made, and it results in positive risk discounting in the valuation of claims to any fixed future output. These first two conditions are imposed so that we may focus on a simple model. Third, the structure of the potential production opportunity (i.e., the profile of production and sales, and project costs) is independent of when the project is undertaken. This last condition is imposed for expositional clarity. It ensures that the effects of reversion in the examples are not confounded with effects arising from any time dependency of the project cash flows themselves.

The model of output prices is formulated in the expectation of those prices. Given the expectation at the beginning of period $s$ for the price at time $t$, denoted $E_s(P_t)$, the change over time in that expectation is of the form:

$$dE_s(P_t) = E_s(P_t)\ \sigma\ exp[-\gamma(t - s)]dz_s, \qquad (11.1)$$

where $dz_s$ is a normal random variable with zero expectation and variance $ds$. The term $\sigma$ is the short-term volatility in the expectation of price, assumed constant for all times $s$. The degree of reversion is captured by the volatility decay parameter $\gamma$.[1]

With no reversion ($\gamma = 0$), a shock at time $s$ has the same proportional influence on expectations for a price in the far future as for one near at hand. If $\gamma > 0$, then the influence of new information arriving at $s$ "decays" as one looks farther into the future. To facilitate interpretation of the results, the degree of reversion is discussed in terms of the half-life of the effect of new information, $H \equiv \ln(2)/\gamma$. In the calculations below, reversion is studied by comparing $H = \infty$ (no reversion) with $H = 3$ years (reversion).

The phenomenon of reversion reflects the fact that, in many parts of the economy, a current development is less and less relevant to the state of the economy the farther out into the future one looks. In effect, information becomes stale-dated. This can be expected to happen in markets for commodities (e.g., hydrocarbons, many metals) that are influenced by long-term forces of supply and demand which limit the length of time that an exceptionally "low" or "high" price can be sustained. After a short-term shock, the price tends to revert to some "normal" long-term equilibrium path, perhaps determined by the long-run marginal cost or, in the case of a cartelized commodity like oil, the long-run profit-maximizing price sought by cartel managers.[2] The greater this reversion tendency, the greater is the decay in the effect of new information on future prices.

For the following comparative-statics analyses of alternative assumptions about reversion, we presume that managers think about uncertainty and riskiness within the time span of the principal revenue flows of typical new investments. For example, a manager who is familiar with projects that produce most of their output within a 10-year horizon after startup will tend to think about price conditions over this period. We summarize this medium-term view by the conditions in the center of the productive life, 5 years into the future. In the calculations below we thus presume that managers focus on a medium-term "reference time" of 5 years, which we denote $t_{ref} = 5$, and under alternative models of reversion hold constant the probability distribution and the risk discounting of the price at that time.[3]

To achieve the desired probability distribution, different degrees of reversion are accompanied by adjustments to the short-term volatility, $\sigma$. For example, if $\sigma = 0.10$ in annual terms in the absence of reversion, then for $t_{ref} = 5$ years and $H = 3$ years the corresponding short-term volatility is 0.16. The procedure for making these adjustments is presented in the Appendix.

Figure 11.1 shows the term structure of the current price distributions under these two models if the current term structure of price medians is flat at \$20 (shown by the central dotted line).[4] The other lines show 0.9 and 0.1 fractiles. The effect of the change from a model with no reversion ($H = \infty$) shown by the dashed lines, to a model with reversion ($H < \infty$) shown by the solid lines, is to pull in the distant tails of the probability distribution

**Figure 11.1**
**Current Output Price Distributions**

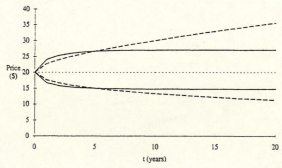

*Note:* Median or 0.5 fractile (dotted line) at \$20. Also, 0.9 and 0.1 fractiles with no reversion (dashed lines), and with reversion at a half-life of $H = 3$ years (solid lines).

of output price, and to fatten the fractiles for $t < t_{ref}$. The "knowledge" of the long-term distribution embodied in the reversion process keeps the price closer to the current term structure of medians and causes the total amount of uncertainty to approach a constant in the long term.

The behavior of this model can be further illustrated by showing these same fractiles conditioned on some realized price in the future. Figure 11.2 shows the result with reversion ($H = 3$ years) if the realized price in year 5 is \$26.66. The median drifts downward over the period $t > 5$ years, reverting toward the original median of \$20. With no reversion ($H = \infty$), the fractiles in Figure 11.2 would originate at the same point, but would have the shape of Figure 11.1 with a term structure of medians constant at \$26.66.

The underlying assets of the derivative asset valuation are a set of output price claims, discussed in the Appendix. The expected rate of return at time $s$ for a claim maturing at time $t$ is modeled as:

$$\mu_{s,t} = r + \phi\sigma \, exp[-\gamma(t - s)], \qquad (11.2)$$

where $r$ is the risk-free interest rate and $\phi$ is the price of risk for the output price uncertainty. The risk-free rate is 3 percent per year. The annualized price of risk for the no-reversion model is set to 0.40. In the comparative-statics exploration of reversion, we also preserve the current risk discounting of the price claim maturing at $t_{ref}$, by an adjustment in $\phi$. As shown in the Appendix, for $t_{ref} = 5$ years and $H = 3$ years, annualized, the price of risk is 0.42.

The price expectations $E_0(P_t)$ and the expected rates of return $\mu_{s,t}$ yield

**Figure 11.2**

**Reversion in Future Output Price Distributions if the Realized Price in Year 5 Is \$26.66**

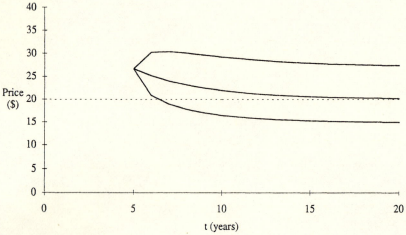

*Note:* Current median or 0.5 fractile (dotted line) at \$20, future 0.9, 0.5, and 0.1 fractiles (solid lines) with reversion at $H = 3$ years.

a set of price claim values, and the forward prices implicit in these values represent the term structure of price expectations with respect to their risk-adjusted measure (see Cox, Ingersoll, and Ross, 1985). This risk-adjusted measure then forms the basis of the derivative asset valuation procedure, detailed in the Appendix.

## 11.3   PROJECT COMPARISONS WITH AND WITHOUT REVERSION

We now consider the errors that are introduced to project evaluation if reversion is not properly incorporated into the now-or-never evaluation of a mutually exclusive pair of projects of different length, or of timing decisions in undertaking the projects. The project alternatives compared have operating lives of $L = 10$ years and $L = 20$ years. Two examples are considered. In order to highlight the interaction between reversion and duration, Example 1 is constructed so that both projects have the same value at any given level of the output price (and zero value at the current price) when assessed on a now-or-never basis without reversion ($H = \infty$). For Example 2 we then present a more realistic set of projects with cash-flow patterns more typical of actual project alternatives of differing operating duration.

Both examples, though simplified for exposition, could be characteristic of investments in commodity-production products.

### 11.3.1 Example 1: Interaction between Reversion and Operating Duration

In this first example, the construction of project alternatives is as follows. For each project, there is an initial capital expenditure of $100 million (m), taken to be known with certainty, and a constant stream of known annual operating costs having a present value of $100m at the time the project is begun. Whenever initiated, therefore, the cost of each project is $200m. At a 3 percent annual risk-free rate, these assumptions are consistent with an annual operating cost of $6.75m for the 20-year project, and $11.75m for the 10-year project.[5]

Under a price model without reversion, the value of a claim to the project revenue stream is proportional to the output price at the time of initiation. This condition holds because the value at any time of a claim to a future price is proportional to the current price at that time, and the revenue stream for each project is equivalent to a portfolio of such claims. The level of annual production for each project is chosen by applying Equation (11.2), so that the present value of revenue is $200m, yielding a zero NPV for undertaking either project. We assume a term structure of price medians that is flat at $20 per unit, with the result that there are 0.923m units of annual production for the 20-year project and 1.405m units for the 10-year project.

If there is no reversion, the projects have the same value at initiation if undertaken in any future state. But this equality of value in future states does not hold under a model *with* reversion. The costs have the same value, but the median of future prices in any state is proportional not to the contemporaneous price but to a term-dependent power of that price (see Figure 11.2), with the term structure of those powers decaying from 1 to 0 as the term is increased from 0 to $\infty$. This complicated structure for the conditional price medians influences the valuation of the price claims and makes the value of the revenue stream at project start a complicated function of the output price in the initiation state.

*Now-or-Never Projects.* The comparison on a now-or-never basis is shown in Table 11.1. To achieve the correct valuation, the analysis must account properly for the difference in project operating life and for the degree of reversion in the output prices. Failure to do so will introduce a bias into the comparison between the long-lived and the short-lived project. The table shows the correct valuation and the result of two such errors:

Table 11.1
**Bias in the Now-or-Never Valuation for the Set of Projects in Example 1 ($ Millions)**

|                          | Reversion (H = 3 years) | | No Reversion (H = ∞) | |
| ------------------------ | -------- | -------- | -------- | -------- |
| Project Duration         | 10 years | 20 years | 10 years | 20 years |
| Value                    | 3.6      | 24.1     | 0.0      | 0.0      |
| Discount rate, Project   | 0.093    | 0.070    | 0.101    | 0.100    |
| Discount rate, Revenue   | 0.063    | 0.053    | 0.067    | 0.067    |
| Value (10 year rate)     | 3.6      | 4.8      | 0.0      | -1.0     |

applying the same discount rate to both projects, and ignoring reversion altogether in the valuation. The left panel of the table (first line) shows the true valuation of the two projects with reversion ($H = 3$ years). The present value of the 10-year project is $3.6m, which is less than the value of $24.1m for the longer alternative. While either project is better than nothing, the long-term alternative is preferred to the short-term one.

An appropriate discount rate for each project may be defined (*ex post*) as the single constant annual discount rate that, if used in discounting the cash flows of the median price scenario, yields the correct value of the project. The discount rates thus defined are presented on the second line. The annual discount rate for the 10-year project is 0.093. The discount rate of the 20-year project is lower, at 0.070. There are two reasons for this difference. First, reversion in the prices tends to lower the volatility of revenue in the out years and thus reduce the risk-discounting in the overall revenue stream. This effect can be seen in the pattern of discount rates for the revenue stream for each project: 0.063 for the shorter project versus 0.053 for the longer one. Second, the unit costs are higher for the shorter project ($8.36 versus $7.31), increasing the operating leverage and thus raising the discount rate.[6]

To illustrate the first error, consider what happens if the proper difference in discounting is not taken into account and the longer project is discounted at the same rate as the shorter project. This result is shown on the last line of the table. The value of the longer project would then be $4.8m, or $19.3m less than its true value. Faulty analysis in this case still suggests that the longterm project should be chosen over the short-term project (or over doing nothing), but if the long-term alternative had higher start-up costs of $5m the analysis would suggest that the short-term project be selected and that undertaking the long-term project is worthless.

In this example, bias is also introduced even if there is no reversion, but the magnitude of the bias is less. Without reversion ($H = 0$), the three alternatives (doing nothing or undertaking either project) all have zero value by construction. However, the use of a short-term discount rate would bias the value of the long-term project down to -\$1.0m, as shown in the right panel of Table 11.1.

To illustrate the second possible error, note that the neglect of reversion would introduce bias against the long-term project in an otherwise correct valuation of this set of projects. If reversion is present ($H = 3$ years), the 20-year project (\$24.1m) is preferred to the shorter-lived project (\$3.62m). If reversion is not taken into account ($H = \infty$), the choice is (by construction in this example) one of indifference.

*Project Timing Options.* Next, we consider the relative value of commodity development leases conveying the right to begin development in any year up to a maturity (or relinquishment) time $T$. The lease expiration is allowed to vary from 0 (now-or-never evaluation) to 10 years. The start options are valued using an approach described in Laughton and Jacoby (1991). The first step in the analysis is to calculate the value of the project in each possible starting state. Because both the cash-flow model and the underlying output price model are stationary with respect to the starting time, this value is independent of the starting time.[7] But, as we noted above, it does depend on the output price at the starting time, or "starting price." Figure 11.3 presents the value function for each of the two projects at the time it is initiated as a function of the starting price, for price models with and without reversion.

By construction, the two projects have the same value function under the price model with no reversion, so the graph for $L = 10$ years, $H = \infty$ coincides with that for $L = 20$ years, $H = \infty$. With reversion, however, the value functions differ. First, for each project the dependence of the value function on the starting price weakens with reversion, and the effect is greater for the long-term project. Second, the starting price at which each project has a "now-or-never" value of zero (i.e., the starting-price intercept of the value function) is lower with reversion. Again, the difference is greater for the long-term project.

The differences in the sensitivity of project value to starting price are the result of counterbalancing forces mentioned earlier. One is the future reversion effect. Without reversion, shocks to the price have permanent effects, and higher or lower prices are likely to be maintained. With reversion, the term structure of price distributions will tend in the long term toward the original distribution, as shown in Figure 11.2. This tendency decreases the dependence of statistics of the conditional price measure (such

**Figure 11.3**
**Now-or-Never Project Value versus Starting Price**

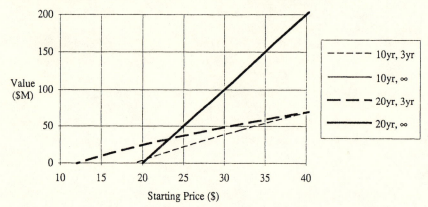

*Note:* Project length $L = 10$ or $20$ years, with reversion ($H = 3$ years) and no reversion ($H = \infty$).

as the value function) on the conditioning price. The longer the term and the higher the degree of reversion, the greater is this effect, decreasing the dependence of the value function on the starting price.

Risk-discounting effects also play a role in changing the slopes of the functions. Greater risk discounting of short-term revenues under the reversion model also tends to decrease the dependence of value on starting price by decreasing project value at all starting prices. This influence is stronger for the shorter-term project, which tends to make the slope for the short-term project less steep than for the long-lived one. Similarly, decreased risk discounting for longer-term revenues *increases* the starting-price dependence of the value functions under the reversion model by increasing the value for all starting prices. However, it does so more for the longer project than the shorter one, which tends to make the short-term project less sensitive than the long-term one. In this example, the dominant force is the future-reversion effect, leading to the shifts in the value functions shown in Figure 11.2.

The differences in the starting-price intercept of the value function shown in Figure 11.3 also result from a combination of effects. At prices below the current $20, the revenues are more valuable under reversion, both because reversion decreases risk discounting in the valuation of the revenues and because, in states defined by price levels below the current price, reversion increases the term structure of the conditional price medians. The risk-discounting effect occurs also in those future states where the price is at the current (and long-term median) level, and it is sufficiently large

**Figure 11.4**
**Timing Option on a Five-Year Commodity-Production Lease—**
**Critical Starting Price versus Starting Time**

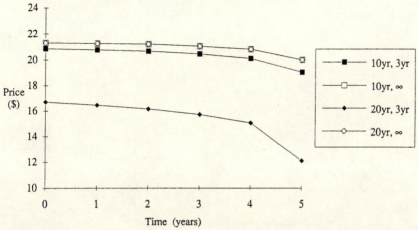

*Note:* Project length $L = 10$ or $20$ years, with reversion ($H = 3$ years) and no reversion ($H = \infty$).

that with reversion both projects are in the money, although more so for the long-term project ($3.6m for the 10-year project and $24.1m for the 20-year one, as shown in Figure 11.3 and Table 11.1). Recall that, without reversion, both projects are *at the money* (i.e., NPV = 0).

In the second step of the procedure, the value function of each project is used as an input to a Black-Scholes-Merton formulation of the American option for project start.[8] The result of this calculation is the value and the critical starting-price exercise boundary, $P_S^*$, at each possible starting time $s$ for this timing option.[9] Figure 11.4 shows this boundary for each project under each price model, given an option of length $T = 5$ years. At year 5, the option offers only a now-or-never choice, and the project is started at prices where its "now" value is positive. Thus, for each project, the critical starting price, $P_S^*$, at $s = T = 5$ years is the starting-price intercept of the value function in Figure 11.3.

For the years before $s = T = 5$ years, the price must be higher than the now-or-never break-even price to justify starting instead of waiting, because the option to wait has value. The value of the option to wait is greater, and the critical starting price is higher, the longer the option has to run. Note that because without reversion, there is a greater chance of still higher prices when the contemporaneous price is above its original median, the wait option is worth more in any future high-price state and a higher

**Figure 11.5**
**Timing Option on a Five-Year Commodity-Production Lease—**
**Option Value versus Maturity Time for Example 1**

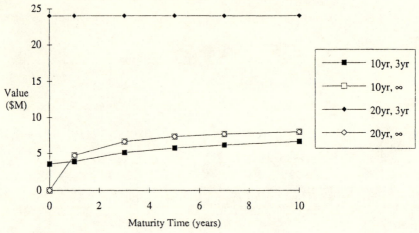

*Note:* Project length $L = 10$ or $20$ years, with reversion ($H = 3$ years) and no
reversion ($H = \infty$).

price is required to justify starting either project. This effect is larger for
the longer-term project.

Figure 11.5 shows the value of options on each project under the two
price models for option lengths ranging from $T = 0$ (now-or-never) to a
maximum of $T = 10$ years. (The result for $T = 0$ is the same as that shown
for "now" projects in Table 11.1, if that value is positive or zero.) As one
would expect, the option value is a non-decreasing function of the option
length, $T$, regardless of the project or price model.

Again, it is assumed that the proper specification of price reversion is
$H = 3$ years. Note first that, for all option lengths from $T = 0$ to $T = 10$
years, the 20-year project would be started immediately and the option
to undertake it is more valuable than the option on the 10-year project,
although by decreasing amounts for longer options. However, without reversion, an option on the long-term project has, by construction, the same
value as an equivalent option on the short-lived one. Therefore, the neglect
of reversion in an otherwise correct valuation will result in a bias against
the project with a long operating duration if there is management flexibility
about when to start the project, just as was the case with a now-or-never
decision. Although the option to wait reduces the bias introduced by a
misspecification of the degree of reversion, the option value is not large
enough to overcome the much greater difference in now-or-never values for

the longer project.

For either project, neglecting reversion would provide a relative bias in *favor* of longer-term timing options. For the 10-year project, the decreased slope of the value function under reversion makes the major difference. For the 20-year project, the options are so far in the money under reversion that the option to wait has no incremental value for any option length.

## 11.3.2   Example 2: A More Realistic Project Structure

In the second pair of projects, the 10-year project is the same as in the first example. The 20-year project has the same constant annual operating costs and·production during its lifetime as the 10-year project. Now, however, the capital cost of the longer project is 50 percent greater than that of the short-term one, at $150m.[10]

*Now-or-Never Projects with No Operating Options.* The results of the now-or-never analysis are shown in Table 11.2. The value of the 10-year project is $3.6m, as before. The value of the longer alternative is $17.0m, which means once again that a proper evaluation would suggest that the longer-term alternative be taken.

**Table 11.2**
**Bias in the Now-or-Never Valuation for the Set of Projects in Example 2 ($ Millions)**

|  | Reversion (H = 3 years) | | No Reversion (H = ∞) | |
| --- | --- | --- | --- | --- |
| Project Duration | 10 years | 20 years | 10 years | 20 years |
| Value | 3.6 | 17.1 | 0.0 | -19.0 |
| Discount rate, Project | 0.093 | 0.075 | 0.101 | 0.110 |
| Discount rate, Revenue | 0.063 | 0.053 | 0.067 | 0.067 |
| Value (10 year rate) | 3.6 | -3.8 | 0.0 | -11.0 |

The discount rates again reflect the lower risk in the longer-term revenues. The annual discount rate for the 10-year project is 0.093 as before, which exceeds the 20-year rate of 0.075. Therefore, the longer-term project would again be undervalued if its cash-flows were discounted with the shorter-term discount rate. Because of this bias, the faulty analysis in this case would incorrectly suggest that the shorter project is preferred, and that the longer project has a negative "value" of -$3.8m.

In this situation, however, the bias would not occur if there were no reversion. As the right-hand side of Table 11.2 shows, without reversion ($H = \infty$) the short-term project is preferred to the long-term one, and the use of a short-term discount rate actually would bias the value of the long-term project upwards, from -$19.7m to -$11.8m.[11] In this case, therefore, price reversion is an essential ingredient in generating bias against the long-term arising from constant discounting.

Finally, the neglect of reversion would again introduce bias in an otherwise correct valuation of this pair of projects, as shown in the top line of the table. With reversion, the longer project is preferred. If reversion is ignored, the analysis suggests that the short-term project is better, and that the long-term project has negative value on a now-or-never basis.

*The Timing of Project Start.* For Example 2, the form of the value function is similar to that shown in Figure 11.3. For the same reasons as in the first example, the "reversion" functions are less steep than the "no reversion" functions, and the intercepts of the functions shift as well. The main difference from the first example is that, without reversion, the value function of the 20-year project is no longer identical to that of the 10-year project, but rather is steeper and has a higher price intercept. Similarly, the critical starting price has a shape similar to that in Figure 11.4, except that for the 20-year project it is higher under both price models than in the first example.

The value of the timing option as a function of maturity, $T$, is shown in Figure 11.6 for each project under both price models. As before, the options range from $T = 0$ (now-or-never) to a maximum option length of $T = 10$ years, and the results for $T = 0$ are the same as those shown for the "now" project in Table 11.2 or zero, whichever is greater. As before, the option value is a non-decreasing function of the option length whatever the project or price model. The timing options for this 20-year project have lower value than in Example 1, although the pattern and conclusions are essentially the same.

Again, the neglect of reversion in an otherwise correct valuation will result in a bias against the long-term project if management can choose when to start it, just as with a now-or-never decision. Although the option to wait reduces the effect of the bias introduced by a misspecification of the degree of reversion, the effect on value of adding the start option does not overcome the much greater now-or-never value of the longer project.

For either project, neglecting reversion would provide a bias in favor of longer-term options. This happens for two reasons. First, without reversion the projects are at (or out of) the money (where the wait option is relatively more valuable) instead of being in the money, as in the case with reversion. Second, the neglect of reversion results in an overestimate of the

**Figure 11.6**
**Timing Option on a Five-Year Commodity-Production Lease—**
**Option Value versus Maturity Time for Example 2**

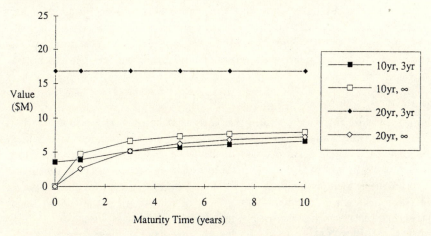

*Note:* Project Length $L = 10$ or 20 years, with reversion ($H = 3$ years) and no reversion ($H = \infty$).

effects of different price levels on the value of an initiated project.

## 11.4   CONCLUSIONS AND EXTENSIONS

Reversion in cash flows can have a significant impact on the relative evaluation of project alternatives, particularly if there is a substantial difference in project lives, or if alternatives with the same operating life have different distributions of cash flows between the near and the long term. We have classified the effects of such reversion for situations in which the cash flows increase with a variable that reverts, and we have shown examples of these effects when the reverting variable is the output price.

We identify three mechanisms by which reversion can affect value. First, by decreasing long-term uncertainty, reversion decreases the amount of risk discounting that is appropriate for long-term cash flows that need to be corrected for risk, increasing their value (the risk-discounting effect). Second, by decreasing long-term uncertainty, it also tends to lower directly the value of options (the variance effect). Finally, future reversion of the term structure of the cash-flow determinants can have direct effects on value (future reversion effects).

The analysis of projects with different operating lives shows that reversion may justify the use of lower effective discount rates in the valuation, on a now-or-never basis, of long-term as compared to short-term projects. Whenever output price shows reverting behavior, there may be a bias against projects with long operating durations if all alternatives are evaluated using the same discount rate. The results in the third line of Tables 11.1 and 11.2 give an idea of the correction that may be appropriate if reversion forces are strong (as our assumption of $H = 3$ years implies). Calculations of the type demonstrated here can be useful in estimating this correction for other degrees of reversion and other generic project structures.

In otherwise correct valuations that neglect reversion (e.g., by modeling the price as following a random walk), there may be bias for or against long-term alternatives, depending on the situation. A bias *against* the long term is typically caused by overdiscounting of long-term cash flows. A bias *in favor* of the long term occurs when such overdiscounting is dominated by an overestimate of the value of the options embedded in the investment alternative, which typically is caused by an overestimation of the variance of the long-term cash flows. The effects of reversion on the future term structure of the cash flows can thus result in different biases, depending on the cash-flow pattern. In our timing option examples, the neglect of reversion results in a bias against options for projects with long operating duration. However, for the same project with at least a moderate operating duration, neglecting price reversion may introduce a relative bias in favor of longer options.[12]

Given the importance of this phenomenon for practical calculations of the value of commodity-production projects, this research should be extended in several directions. First, random-walk models, which are the mainstay of the real options literature, do not account for reversion. Our results suggest that it may be useful to revisit earlier work (e.g., that by Brennan and Schwartz, 1985a; Pindyck, 1991; and Laughton and Jacoby, 1991). Second, a more complete study should be done of the effects on project values of the interaction of cash-flow reversion with different measures of asset duration, as well as with other aspects of asset structure such as the degree of operating leverage and the relative size of early sunk costs. The analysis needs to take account of the strength of reversion that is believed to hold for specific products like oil and other commodities. Further, it would be useful to explore the effects of reversion in the context of different types of operating flexibility, such as initial capacity and technology choices, and post-startup options, including capacity or technology changes, temporary shutdowns, and abandonment.

# APPENDIX

This Appendix describes the price model and the valuation method used in the analysis, and also presents the comparative statics for different reference times.

## A.1 The Price Process

The price model is formulated in terms of the evolution of the price expectations. The information needed to determine the revision of future expectations is assumed to be provided by the most recent unanticipated revision in the expectation of the current price. For any given period, $s$ to $s + ds$, the revision of expectations for all times at or after $s + ds$ is determined by a normal random variable, $dz_s$, having zero expectation and variance $ds$. This variable represents information coming from the output market during the period just after time $s$, in the form of the final movement in the expectation for the price at the end of that period. It is independent of the other $dzs$, because each $dz$ represents new information at a different time.

The revision of each price expectation is modeled to be proportional to the expectation of that price at the beginning of the period and to the normalized information for that period. Thus, given the expectation at the beginning of period $s$ for the price that will occur at time $t$, $E_s(P_t)$, the change over that period in the expectation of that price is :

$$dE_s(P_t) = E_s(P_t)\sigma_{s,t}dz_s, \tag{11.A1}$$

where the proportionality constant $\sigma_{s,t}$ is the volatility of the expectation of the price at time $t$ in the period beginning at time $s$.

Two restrictions are placed on the form of the volatility of $\sigma_{s,t}$ (see Jacoby and Laughton, 1991). First, $\sigma_{s,t}$ at any future time $s$ must be modeled as known with certainty at the time of the analysis, namely, it may not vary according to the state of the economy at the time $s$. This assumption allows the use of a simple nonstochastic discounting model in the valuation. Second, the decay in the volatility term structure is expressed by an exponential form,

$$\sigma_{s,t} = \sigma_s \, exp[-\gamma(t - s)], \tag{11.A2}$$

where $\gamma$ is the rate of decay. As noted, the amount of reversion may also be measured by the half-life $H$ of the decay process, where $H \equiv \ln(2)/\gamma$. In Laughton and Jacoby (1993) it was shown that a one-dimensional state space, indexed by the contemporaneous price, occurs only for price models from a slightly more general class of processes among those with multivariate lognormal probability measures.

For convenience, the short-term volatility, $\sigma_s$, is held constant for all $s$ and denoted $\sigma$, which yields the following form for the price model:

$$dE_s(P_t) = E_s(P_t)\sigma \, exp[-\gamma(t - s)]dz_s. \qquad (11.A3)$$

## A.2 The Valuation Procedure

The underlying assets of the derivative asset valuation are the set of output price claims. The current term structure of their values is calculated as:

$$V_0(P_t) = E_0(P_t) \, exp(- \int_0^t ds \, \mu_{s,t}), \qquad (11.A4)$$

where $V_0(P_t)$ is the current value of the claim maturing at time $t$. The expected rate of return at time $s$ for the claim maturing at time $t$, $\mu_{s,t}$, is taken to be the sum of the risk-free rate, $r$, assumed to be constant for convenience, and a risk premium that is proportional to the amount of volatility at time $s$ in the expectation of the price at time $t$, $\sigma_{s,t}$. The proportionality constant, which is called the price of risk and is denoted by $\phi$, is also held constant over time for ease in presentation. It is presumed to be positive, so that there is risk discounting in the valuation of the output price claims. Using the expression for $\sigma_{s,t}$ in Equation (11.A2), and with $\sigma_s$ modeled to be a constant, denoted $\sigma$, the expected return at time $s$ for a claim maturing at time $t$ is:

$$\mu_{s,t} = r + \phi\sigma \, exp(-\gamma(t - s)). \qquad (11.A5)$$

The structure of forward prices implicit in these price claim values is the term structure of expectations of the prices with respect to their risk-adjusted measure (Cox, Ingersoll, and Ross, 1985). In our lognormal price model, the risk-adjusted distribution is also lognormal and the covariances of the price logarithms with respect to the risk-adjusted distribution are the same as those with respect to the true distribution (Jacoby and Laughton, 1991). This measure may be labeled by the state at which it is defined, and each state is determined by its time, $s$, and the realized level of the price at that time, $P_s$, which we denote by $P$. We denote the risk-adjusted measure for the state $(s, P)$ by $dm_s(P_{\geq s} \mid P_s = P)$, and use it in the computation at time $s$ of the value of any asset with cash flows (denoted by the index $CF$ and occurring at time $t$) that are contingent only on the then future prices:

$$V_s(Asset \mid P_s = P) = \sum_{CF \in Asset} V_s(CF \mid P_s = P), \qquad (11.A6)$$

where

$$V_s(CF \mid P_s = P) = exp(-r(t_{CF} - s)) \int dm_s(P_{\geq s} \mid P_s = P) X_{CF}(P_{\geq s}),$$

(11.A7)

and where $X_{CF}$ indicates the functional dependence of the cash-flow amount for the cash flow $CF$ on the time series of the future prices. Value calculations can also be based on Black-Scholes-Merton boundary problems that correspond to the integrals in Equation (11.A4) (see Laughton and Jacoby, 1991).

## A.3 Comparative Statics with Finite Reference Times

For $H = \infty$ (no reversion), the current associated variance of the price at time $t_{ref}$ has the form $\sigma^2 t_{ref}$. We calculate the magnitude of the appropriate adjusted volatility for a finite half-life relative to the volatility for $H = \infty$, which in these examples is maintained at 0.1 in annual terms. Therefore, the $\sigma$ appropriate for a finite half-life is a function of this short-term volatility for $H = \infty$, as well as the reference time and the half-life, it is denoted $\sigma(t_{ref}, H, \sigma)$. The current associated variance of the price at $t_{ref}$, given a finite half-life $H$, is of the form:

$$\frac{\sigma^2(t_{ref}, H, \sigma)}{2\gamma}(1 - exp(-2\gamma t_{ref})),$$

(11.A8)

where $\gamma \equiv ln(2)/H$. Equating this to the variance for $H = \infty$, gives the following expression for the adjusted volatility:

$$\sigma(t_{ref}, H, \sigma) = \sigma \left[ \frac{2\gamma t_{ref}}{1 - exp(-2\gamma t_{ref})} \right]^{1/2}.$$

(11.A9)

For example, the adjusted volatility for $t_{ref} = 5$ years, $H = 3$ years and $\sigma = 0.1$ is $\sigma(5, 3, 0.1) = 0.16$.

Similarly, we want to preserve the current risk discounting of the price claim maturing at $t_{ref}$, which can be accomplished by an adjustment in the price of risk, $\phi$. It also becomes a function of $\sigma, H$ and $t_{ref}$, as well as the price of risk for $H = \infty$, which is set at 0.4 in annual terms for all of these examples. The risk discount factor with $H = \infty$ has the form $exp(-\phi\sigma t)$. If the adjusted price of risk is denoted $\phi(t_{ref}, H, \sigma, \phi)$, the risk discount factor for finite $H$ is:

$$exp \left[ -\frac{\phi(t_{ref}, H, \sigma, \phi)\sigma(t_{ref}, H, \sigma)}{\gamma}(1 - exp(-\gamma t_{ref})) \right].$$

(11.A10)

Combining Equations (11.A9) and (11.A10) gives the following expression for the adjusted price of risk:

$$\phi(t_{ref}, H, \sigma, \phi) = \phi \frac{\gamma t_{ref}}{1 - exp(-\gamma t_{ref})} \left[ \frac{2\gamma t_{ref}}{1 - exp(-2\gamma t_{ref})} \right]^{-1/2} . \quad (11.A11)$$

For $\phi = 0.4$, the adjusted price of risk is $\phi(5, 3, 0.1, 0.4) = 0.42$.

## ACKNOWLEDGMENTS

This research has been supported by the Natural Science and Engineering Research Council of Canada, Imperial Oil University Research Grants, Interprovincial Pipeline Co., Saskoil, Exxon Corp., the Social Science and Humanities Research Council of Canada; the Central Research Fund, a Nova Faculty Fellowship, the Muir Research Fund and the Institute for Financial Research of the University of Alberta; and by the MIT Center for Energy and Environmental Policy Research. Parts of this chapter draw from Laughton and Jacoby (1993).

## NOTES

1. There is a corresponding process in the price $P_t$ itself, which is the more customary form for this type of model when used in real options work (e.g., Pindyck, 1991; Brennan and Schwartz, 1985a). This was derived by Laughton and Jacoby (1993). A specification outlined by Treynor and Black (1976) in an early paper applying modern asset pricing concepts to project evaluation is similar to ours, as is one for the uncertainty in risk-free interest rates used in the valuation of derivative securities on treasury bonds (Turnbull and Milne, 1991).

2. Pindyck and Rubinfeld (1991, pp. 462–465) have found instances of this type of behavior. They reject no-reversion models for oil and copper prices on the basis of Dickey-Fuller unit root tests using more than 100 years of data.

3. This presumption about managerial behavior makes a bias against the long term more difficult to demonstrate than would the assumption of a very short-term reference time.

4. For other studies using this price model, see Laughto and Jacoby (1993).

5. The cash flows are modeled, for the sake of this valuation, to occur at annual intervals. Note that there is no inflation in these examples.

6. Operating leverage generally increases with the length of the project if costs are less risky than revenues. The higher unit costs for the short-term project

dominate this effect in this case.

7. As stated earlier, we presume that the time of project start does not affect the profile of production and sales or the project costs relative to that start time.

8. In these calculations, it is presumed that an option may be exercised only at times occurring at annual intervals. This corresponds to cumulating the cash flows to an annual figure in the calculation of the project value functions. If the possible exercise times were modeled to be continuously distributed, and with cash flows modeled to flow continuously, the qualitative results would not differ.

9. For study of the details of the optimal solution, and for representation of the results in a simulation context, the values may be recomputed conditional on $P^*$ (Laughton and Jacoby, 1991).

10. A more complete exploration of this example is presented in Laughton and Jacoby (1993).

11. The use of the short-term rate for discounting the long-term project would underestimate the effects on value of the increased discounting of the long-term revenues relative to the long-term costs.

12. If the operating duration is short enough (e.g., only one cash payment), then the bias is against the long term for American options (Laughton and Jacoby, 1993).

# Chapter 12

# Contingent Claims Evaluation of Mean-Reverting Cash Flows in Shipping

## Petter Bjerksund and Steinar Ekern

*This chapter applies contingent claims analysis to evaluation problems involving mean-reverting cash flows in shipping. The basic underlying premise is that the stochastic component of the instantaneous cash flow is characterized by an Ornstein-Uhlenbeck process. A number of generic valuation results are derived, including the present value of a European call option written on an asset whose value follows the Ornstein-Uhlenbeck process. The shipping applications focus on a time charter (T/C) contract with a mean-reverting spot freight rate. Analytical results are presented for the value of a T/C contract, the fixed forward rate applicable to a future T/C contract, and the value of a European option on a T/C contract.*

## 12.1 INTRODUCTION

Shipping activities are extremely risky. Uncertain freight rates are one major source of uncertainty. To alleviate the problems caused by highly volatile spot rates, for example, a number of additional contracts has been introduced. A time charter (T/C) contract locks in a fixed rate for a stated period from "now" onwards, say, for the immediate 13 weeks. A forward-rate agreement fixes the T/C rate for a period starting "later," say, for weeks 14 through 26. An option on a T/C contract gives the option holder the right, but not the obligation, at a future date to enter into the T/C contract at a rate agreed upon today.

As part of a proposed deal for, say, a 13-week T/C contract at a fixed rate, the charterer may ask for an option on another T/C rate for the subsequent 13 weeks. The shipowner may then be uncomfortable in suggesting an appropriate rate premium for including the option feature. More generally, casual contacts with people in the shipping industry suggest that the economic agents may lack adequate models and methods for evaluating the economic value of more complicated contracts under uncertainty.

This chapter is an attempt to show how recent advances in financial economics provide a useful tool bag to analysts and decision makers in shipping. By applying contingent claims analysis to their evaluation problems, agents may get improved estimates of "fair" economic values of contracts, consistent with "no arbitrage" and/or equilibrium considerations.

The chapter is intended to be largely self-contained and is structured as follows: The basic premise is that the stochastic component of the instantaneous cash flow from an operating ship is characterized by a mean-reverting Ornstein-Uhlenbeck process. Section 12.2 discusses this process and reviews its properties. Section 12.3 describes the evaluation rule for contingent claims by which risk-free discounting of the expected future value (under the so-called equivalent martingale probability measure) yields the current market value. Such analysis yields a number of useful generic evaluation results that later serve as building blocks for valuing various shipping contracts. Section 12.4 focuses on the T/C contract. We derive analytical results for the value of a T/C contract and for the fixed forward rate applicable to a future T/C contract. The major contribution of the chapter is in section 12.5, which presents a closed-form solution for the value of a European call option on a T/C contract. Section 12.6 concludes the chapter.

## 12.2   DESCRIPTION OF THE CASH-FLOW PROCESS

We first assume that the instantaneous cash flow generated by an operating ship, $D(t)dt$, may be described by the process:

$$D(t)dt = (aX(t) - b)\, dt. \tag{12.1}$$

In Equation (12.1), $a$ and $b$ are constants which depend on the characteristics of the particular ship and on the nature of the freight contract being under consideration. One natural interpretation is to let $X(t)$ represent the uncertain spot freight rate, $a$ the size of the cargo, and $b$ the operating cost-flow rate. Whenever the freight rate is quoted for the ship as a whole, $a$ would equal one.

Our basic premise is that $X(t)$ can be characterized by an Ornstein-Uhlenbeck stochastic process of the form:[1]

$$dX(t) = k(\alpha - X(t))dt + \sigma dZ(t). \tag{12.2}$$

The sign of the first term (drift term) is determined by the difference between the current value of the stochastic process, $X(t)$, and its long-range mean, $\alpha$. If $X(t) > \alpha$, the drift term is negative, and vice versa. The drift term thus tends to push the process $X(t)$ back to its long-range mean, $\alpha$. The constant $k > 0$ in Equation (12.2) represents the "speed of adjustment." With a higher $k$, the stochastic process $X(t)$ will have a stronger tendency to move back toward its long-range mean, $\alpha$, increasing the degree of mean reversion. The second term characterizes the volatility, with $dZ(t)$ being an increment of a standard Brownian motion (with zero mean and variance $dt$). To justify the Ornstein-Uhlenbeck assumption, one could argue that competitive pressures have a tendency to pull the state variable (e.g., the freight rate) back to its long-range mean.[2]

The value of the stochastic process in Equation (12.2) at a future date $T$, $X(T)$, conditional on the initial value $X(0)$, may be written as the stochastic integral:

$$X(T) = e^{-kT} X(0) + \left(1 - e^{-kT}\right) \alpha + \sigma e^{-kT} \int_0^T e^{kt} dZ(t). \qquad (12.3)$$

$X(T)$ is normally distributed, and its expected value,

$$E_0[X(T)] = e^{-kT} X(0) + \left(1 - e^{-kT}\right) \alpha, \qquad (12.4)$$

can be interpreted as an adaptive forecast based on (or a weighted average of) the current process value, $X(0)$, and the long-range mean, $\alpha$, with weights obtained from discounting at the "speed of adjustment" rate, $k$. To interpret $k$, note that $T = (\ln 2)/k$ gives the "half-time" at which the expected value $E_0[X(T)]$ is halfway between the long-range mean, $\alpha$, and the current value, $X(0)$. The variance of $X(T)$ is given by:

$$\text{Var}_0[X(T)] = \frac{\sigma^2}{2k} \left(1 - e^{-2kT}\right), \qquad (12.5)$$

which is increasing in $T$ and bounded from above by $\sigma^2/(2k)$.

Assumptions (12.1) and (12.2) specify the future cash flow at date $T$, $D(T)$, conditional on $D(0)$:

$$D(T) = e^{-kT} D(0) + \left(1 - e^{-kT}\right) (a\alpha - b) + a\sigma e^{-kT} \int_0^T e^{kt} dZ(t). \qquad (12.6)$$

$D(T)$, being a linear function of the normal variable $X(T)$, is itself normally distributed. Its expected value,

$$E_0[D(T)] = e^{-kT} D(0) + \left(1 - e^{-kT}\right) (a\alpha - b), \qquad (12.7)$$

is a weighted average of the current cash-flow value, $D(0)$, and the long-range mean value of the instantaneous cash flow, $a\alpha - b$. The weights are again based on discounting at the adjustment rate, $k$. Its variance is similarly given by:

$$\text{Var}_0[D(T)] = \frac{(a\sigma)^2}{2k}\left(1 - e^{-2kT}\right).\tag{12.8}$$

## 12.3   CONTINGENT CLAIMS EVALUATION

We assume that the risk-free rate of interest, $r$, remains constant during the period. This assumption corresponds to the existence of a traded risk-free asset with price dynamics,

$$dW(t) = rW(t)dt,\tag{12.9}$$

or alternatively,

$$W(t) = W(0)e^{rt}.\tag{12.10}$$

$W(t)$ represents the market value at time $t$ of a default-free zero-coupon bond.

Furthermore, assume that the market price per unit of diffusion risk $Z(t)$ is a constant, $\lambda$. This would be the case if there existed a traded *twin asset* in the economy with price dynamics:

$$dS(t) = (r + \sigma\lambda)S(t)dt + \sigma S(t)dZ(t),\tag{12.11}$$

or equivalently,

$$S(t) = S(0)\exp\left\{(r + \sigma\lambda - \tfrac{1}{2}\sigma^2)t + \sigma Z(t)\right\}.\tag{12.12}$$

The twin asset is assumed to pay no dividends.[3] We additionally invoke the usual "perfect market" assumptions, including continuous trading, no taxes, and no transaction costs.

An important implication from recent advances in financial economics is that the current value of a contingent claim having a future payoff $U(T)$ may be written as:[4]

$$V_0[U(T)] = E_0^*\left[e^{-rT}U(T)\right],\tag{12.13}$$

where the (risk-neutral) expectation is taken under the (certainty) equivalent martingale measure, allowing discounting at the risk-free rate, $r$.[5]

With the stated assumptions on the economy, the appropriate transformation from the actual probability measure to the equivalent martingale measure is:

$$dZ(t) = dZ^*(t) - \lambda dt, \tag{12.14}$$

where $dZ^*(t)$ has zero mean and variance $dt$ under the *-probability measure. Equivalently,[6]

$$Z(t) = Z^*(t) - \lambda t. \tag{12.15}$$

Using the transformation defined by Equations (12.14) or (12.15), the dynamics of the Ornstein-Uhlenbeck process under the *-probability measure can be rewritten as:[7]

$$dX(t) = k(\alpha^* - X(t))dt + \sigma dZ^*(t), \tag{12.16}$$

where:

$$\alpha^* \equiv \alpha - \frac{\sigma\lambda}{k}, \tag{12.17}$$

with $\alpha^*$ representing the long-range risk-adjusted mean.

Corresponding expressions for the cash flow process, $X(t)$, follow immediately when switching to the equivalent martingale measure. The future value of the stochastic process $X(T)$ can be written as:

$$X(T) = e^{-kT}X(0) + \left(1 - e^{-kT}\right)\alpha^* + \sigma e^{-kT}\int_0^T e^{kt}dZ^*(t). \tag{12.18}$$

If we let $\mu^* \equiv E_0^*[X(T)]$ be the expected value, and $(\sigma^*)^2 \equiv \text{Var}_0^*[X(T)]$ be the variance of $X(T)$ under the *-probability measure, then from Equation (12.4):

$$\mu^* = e^{-kT}X(0) + \left(1 - e^{-kT}\right)\alpha^*, \tag{12.19}$$

while the variance in Equation (12.5) remains unchanged:

$$(\sigma^*)^2 = \frac{\sigma^2}{2k}\left(1 - e^{-2kT}\right). \tag{12.20}$$

Having established the evaluation rule, the transformation to the *-probability measure, and the properties of the Ornstein-Uhlenbeck process under the *-probability measure, we now proceed to present some useful building blocks for evaluating some interesting shipping-related contracts.

With the adjusted Ornstein-Uhlenbeck process $X(t)$ under the equivalent martingale measure given in Equation (12.16), the net present value of a continuous, risk-free cash-flow stream, an uncertain future cash-flow amount, and an uncertain cash-flow stream, are given below:[8]

*Result 1*: The present value (at time 0) of receiving a continuous, risk-free dividend flow ($1 \cdot dt$) from date 0 through a future date $T$ is:

$$V_0 \left[ \int_0^T 1 \cdot dt \right] = A(T, r), \tag{12.21}$$

where the annuity factor, $A(T, r)$, is given by:

$$A(T, r) \equiv \frac{1 - e^{-rT}}{r}. \tag{12.22}$$

*Proof:*

$$V_0 \left[ \int_0^T 1 \cdot dt \right] = \int_0^T e^{-rt} dt = \frac{1 - e^{-rT}}{r} = A(T, r).$$

*Result 2*: The present value (at time 0) of receiving an uncertain payoff, $X(T)$, at some future date $T$ is:

$$V_0[X(T)] = (X(0) - \alpha^*) e^{-(r+k)T} + \alpha^* e^{-rT}. \tag{12.23}$$

*Proof:*

$$\begin{aligned} V_0[X(T)] &= E_0^* \left[ e^{-rT} X(T) \right] \\ &= e^{-rT} E_0^* [X(T)] \\ &= e^{-rT} \mu^*, \end{aligned}$$

where $\mu^*$ is given by Equation (12.19). Simple multiplication and rearrangement yield the desired result.

*Result 3*: The present value (at time 0) of receiving the continuous dividend flow $X(t)dt$ from date 0 through the future date $T$ is:

$$V_0 \left[ \int_0^T X(t)dt \right] = (X(0) - \alpha^*) A(T, r+k) + \alpha^* A(T, r). \tag{12.24}$$

*Proof:* From integrating Equation (12.23) over $t$ and using the definition of the annuity factor in Equation (12.22).

In interpreting Results 2 and 3, note that the last term on the right-hand side is a present value with risk-free discounting, provided that the process is at its long-range risk-adjusted mean, $\alpha^*$. The first term is the present value correction caused by the process currently being away from $\alpha^*$ at $X(0)$, with the discount rate equal to the sum of the risk-free rate, $r$, and the "speed of adjustment" rate, $k$.

Suppose now the process $X(t)$ is away from its long-range risk-adjusted mean of $\alpha^*$. Then, an economic agent would not be indifferent between receiving a variable flow corresponding to $X(t)$ or a constant flow corresponding to $\alpha^*$ for any arbitrary period of time. Results 4 and 5 relate the constant certainty equivalent level $\hat{\alpha}$ to $\alpha^*$ and the current value $X(0)$.

*Result 4*: The constant certainty equivalent dividend flow level, $\hat{\alpha}$, which is equivalent to receiving the continuous dividend flow $X(t)dt$ from 0 through $T$, is given by:

$$\hat{\alpha} = \alpha^* + (X(0) - \alpha^*) \frac{A(T, r+k)}{A(T, r)}. \tag{12.25}$$

*Proof:* $\hat{\alpha}$ is defined by:

$$V_0 \left[ \int_0^T \hat{\alpha} dt \right] = V_0 \left[ \int_0^T X(t) dt \right].$$

Apply Results 1 and 3 to obtain:

$$\hat{\alpha} A(T, r) = (X(0) - \alpha^*) A(T, r+k) + \alpha^* A(T, r).$$

Dividing through by $A(T, r)$ leads to Result 4.

*Result 5*: When $T \to \infty$, the constant certainty equivalent level, $\hat{\alpha}$, reduces to:

$$\hat{\alpha} = \alpha^* + (X(0) - \alpha^*) \frac{r}{r+k}. \tag{12.26}$$

*Proof:* Immediate, from $\lim_{T \to \infty} A(T, r) = 1/r$ when $r > 0$.

## 12.4 A TIME CHARTER CONTRACT

A time charter contract (or T/C contract) is an arrangement where the shipowner sells to the charterer the right and obligation to operate the ship for a fixed period of time. The terms of the contract specify what costs are to be paid by each party and the fixed compensation profile over time. The spot freight rate, $X(t)$, is stated as a T/C equivalent (with respect to who pays for what) and assumed to be payable continuously. In a freight market equilibrium, the net value of a T/C contract for the period from 0 through time $T$ equals the net value of the cash flow forgone from operating in the spot market for the same period. The latter may be written as:

$$V_0 \left[ \int_0^T D(t) dt \right] = a V_0 \left[ \int_0^T X(t) dt \right] - b V_0 \left[ \int_0^T 1 \cdot dt \right]. \tag{12.27}$$

*Result 6*: With the spot rate $X(t)$ stated as a T/C equivalent, the value of a T/C contract running from date 0 through some future date $T$ is:

$$V_0 \left[ \int_0^T D(t)dt \right] = aX(0)A(T, r + k) - B(T), \qquad (12.28)$$

where

$$B(T) \equiv a\alpha^* A(T, r + k) - (a\alpha^* - b) A(T, r), \qquad (12.29)$$

with the annuity factor $A$ as defined in Equation (12.22) above.

*Proof:* Apply Results 1 and 3 to the right-hand side of Equation (12.27), and rearrange, to get:

$$V_0 \left[ \int_0^T D(t)dt \right] = a\left[X(0) - \alpha^*\right] A(T, r + k) + (a\alpha - b) A(T, r). \quad (12.30)$$

The result follows from applying Equation (12.29).

Observe that $(a\alpha^* - b)$ is the risk-adjusted long-range mean of the instantaneous cash flow $D(t)$. Thus, on the right-hand side of Equation (12.30), the last term is the present value of being at the long-range mean cash flow and the first term is a present value correction for the $X$-process being at $X(0)$ rather than at $\alpha^*$.

Next, consider a forward contract written on a T/C contract, where the holder of the contract at date 0 undertakes the right and obligation to operate the ship from date $t$ through date $T$. The holder will thus receive the instantaneous cash flow $D(s)ds$ at all dates $t \leq s \leq T$. The current value of this cash flow is:

$$V_0 \left[ \int_t^T D(s)ds \right] = V_0 \left[ \int_0^T D(s)ds \right] - V_0 \left[ \int_0^t D(s)ds \right]. \qquad (12.31)$$

Using Result 6 and rearranging, we obtain:

$$V_0 \left[ \int_t^T D(s)ds \right] = a\left(A(T, r + k) - A(t, r + k)\right) X(0) - (B(T) - B(t)),$$
$$(12.32)$$

where $A$ and $B$ are defined by Equations (12.22) and (12.29), respectively.

On the other hand, from date $t$ through date $T$, the holder of the forward T/C contract will pay continuously at the fixed forward rate, $F$, agreed to at time 0. Its current value is:

$$V_0 \left[ \int_t^T F dt \right] = F\left[A(T, r) - A(t, r)\right]. \qquad (12.33)$$

*Result 7:* The forward rate $F$ agreed to at time 0 (which makes the value of entering the forward contract equal to zero) is given by:

$$F = [A(T,r) - A(t,r)]^{-1} V_0 \left[ \int_t^T D(s)ds \right], \qquad (12.34)$$

where $V_0[\int_t^T D(s)ds]$ is given by Equation (12.32).

*Proof:* Straightforward, from Equations (12.32) and (12.33).

## 12.5 EUROPEAN OPTION ON A T/C CONTRACT

Now consider an opportunity, but no obligation, at date $t$ to buy a T/C contract running from date $t$ through date $T$, by paying a lump sum amount $C$. At date $t$, the value of this option is:

$$Y(t) = max \left\{ V_t \left[ \int_t^T D(s)ds \right] - C, 0 \right\}. \qquad (12.35)$$

Applying Result 6, we obtain:

$$Y(t) = aA(T - t, r + k) \, max \left\{ X(t) - \frac{B(T - t) + C}{aA(T - t, r + k)}, 0 \right\}. \qquad (12.36)$$

$Y(t)$ may be interpreted as the terminal payoff from $aA(T - t, r + k)$ European call options written on $X(t)$, each with exercise price,

$$K \equiv \frac{B(T - t) + C}{aA(T - t, r + k)}. \qquad (12.37)$$

In order to find $V_0[Y(t)]$, we need the following result:

*Result 8:* The present value (at time 0) of a European call option written on $X(t)$, with arbitrary exercise price $K$ and maturity date $T$, is:

$$V_0[(X(T) - K)^+] = e^{-rT} \{(\mu^* - K)N[d] + \sigma^* n[d]\}, \qquad (12.38)$$

where $N[\cdot]$ and $n[\cdot]$ are the standard normal cumulative distribution and density functions, respectively, with,

$$d \equiv \frac{\mu^* - K}{\sigma^*}, \qquad (12.39)$$

and $\mu^*$ and $\sigma^*$ as defined in Equations (12.19) and (12.20).

*Proof:* See Appendix.

By the interpretation of $Y(t)$ in Equation (12.36), we arrive at the time 0 value of the option on the T/C contract:

*Result 9:* The present value (at time 0) of a European call option written on a T/C contract with a lump sum exercise price $C$ is:

$$V_0 [Y(t)] = aA(T - t, r + k)e^{-rt} \{(\mu^* - K)N[d] + \sigma^* n[d]\}, \qquad (12.40)$$

with $K$, $d$, $\mu^*$, and $\sigma^*$ as defined in Equations (12.37), (12.39), (12.19), and (12.20), respectively.

*Proof:* Immediate, from Equation (12.36) and Result 8.

## 12.6  CONCLUSIONS

This chapter implements contingent claims analysis to evaluation problems involving mean-reverting cash flows. It shows how recent advances in financial economics provide a useful tool bag to analysts and decision makers, in shipping as well as in other industries. Technically, the chapter is an exercise in risk-neutral evaluation, where estimates of the current market value are derived by risk-free discounting of the expected future value under the equivalent martingale probability measure.

The analysis is based on the premise that the stochastic component of the instantaneous cash flow is characterized by a mean-reverting Ornstein-Uhlenbeck stochastic process. As building blocks for later shipping contract evaluations, Results 1, 2, and 3 exhibit the current value of a risk-free cash-flow stream, a risky future lump sum amount, and a risky cash-flow stream, respectively. Results 4 and 5 relate the constant certainty equivalent cash-flow level to the long-range risk-adjusted mean cash-flow rate and to the current process value. Result 8 establishes the present value of a European call option written on an asset whose value follows the Ornstein-Uhlenbeck process. All these generic results hold quite generally, without restriction to a shipping context, under the assumed mean-reversion dynamics of the cash-flow stream.

Turning to more specific shipping applications, the instantaneous cash flow generated by an operating ship is assumed to be a linear function of the Ornstein-Uhlenbeck random variable. One natural cash flow interpretation is the random spot freight rate multiplied by the cargo size, less the operating costs. The spot freight rates are highly volatile. In a T/C contract the freight rate is fixed for a specified time period at contract inception. More complicated freight contracts include forward rate agreements and options on a T/C contract. Analogous to a term structure of interest rates, there is a similar term structure of freight rates. Valuable insight may be obtained by drawing on the literature on interest-rate derivative assets.

This analysis supplies appropriate decision support tools for assessing the "fair" economic value of freight contracts under uncertainty. In particular, Result 6 yields an analytical expression for the value of a T/C contract. Result 7 shows the forward rate agreed to at time zero. Finally, Result 9 provides a closed-form solution for the value of a European call option on a T/C contract with mean-reverting spot freight rates.

Compared with traditional informal methods for assessing various freight contracts in shipping, formal analytical models as those exemplified in this chapter should yield valuable decision support. Such analytical models are particularly useful as more objective guidelines for a mutually acceptable option premium, where intuition may easily fail. Tentative application of these models to selected shipping segments indicate that our suggested approach does, in fact, yield reasonable results of considerable interest to the shipping industry. By suitable reinterpretation, the results may carry over to other industries as well, in particular, extraction and processing of natural resources.

# APPENDIX

This Appendix derives Result 8 above using the equivalent martingale approach. Applying the evaluation rule, Equation (12.13), to the future payoff from the option, we obtain:

$$V_0[(X(T) - K)^+] = E_0^* \left[ e^{-rT} \left( X(T) - K \right) I \left( X(T) - K \geq 0 \right) \right]. \quad (12.A1)$$

In this equation, $I(\cdot)$ is an indicator function, taking the value 1 if its argument is true and 0 otherwise. It follows from Equations (12.18)–(12.20) that:

$$X(T) = \mu^* + \sigma^* w^*, \quad (12.A2)$$

where $w^*$ is a standard normal random variable with respect to the $*$-probability measure. Inserting Equation (12.A2) into Equation (12.A1) and rearranging, we obtain:

$$
\begin{aligned}
V_0[(X(T) - K)^+] &= e^{-rT}(\mu^* - K)N\left[ \frac{\mu^* - K}{\sigma^*} \right] \\
&\quad + e^{-rT}\sigma^* E_0^* \left[ w^* I \left( w^* \geq -\frac{\mu^* - K}{\sigma^*} \right) \right].
\end{aligned}
$$

Result 8 follows directly from the fact that:[9]

$$E_0^* \left[ w^* I \left( w^* \geq -\frac{\mu^* - K}{\sigma^*} \right) \right] = n \left[ \frac{\mu^* - K}{\sigma^*} \right].$$

## ACKNOWLEDGMENTS

The authors acknowledge comments by Bjørn Flesaker, David C. Mauer, and Lenos Trigeorgis (the editor). This research has been financially supported in part by the SIS Program of the Centre for Research in Economics and Business Administration at the Norwegian School of Economics and Business Administration.

## NOTES

1. For discussions and applications of the Ornstein-Uhlenbeck process, see, for example, Aase (1988), Breiman (1968), Merton (1971), and Vasicek (1977). See Brennan (1991), Equation (17), for the exact discrete time model corresponding to Equation (2).

2. It is an unfortunate feature of the Ornstein-Uhlenbeck process that it may take on negative values, which are inappropriate for most asset prices. In a different setting, Bhattacharya (1978) uses the alternative diffusion process:

$$dX(t) = k(\alpha - X(t))dt + \sigma X(t)dZ(t),$$

which cannot become negative.

3. In the case where the twin asset actually pays dividends, $S(T)$ would correspond to the market value of a self-financing portfolio consisting of the twin asset (i.e., where dividends are reinvested).

4. See, for example, Aase (1988), Cox and Huang (1989), Cox and Ross (1976), Harrison and Kreps (1979), and Harrison and Pliska (1981).

5. It is a necessary condition that the future payoff from the contingent claim, $U(T)$, is measurable with respect to the $\sigma$-algebra generated by the Brownian motion, $Z(T)$. In this chapter, we consider contingent claims whose future payoffs are functions of $Z(T)$ or $X(T)$, and the condition is thus satisfied.

6. It can be easily confirmed that the evaluation rule (12.13) and the transformation (12.15) yield consistent "no arbitrage" valuation of the two underlying assets (i.e., the default-free bond and the traded twin asset), as $V_0[W(T)] = W(0)$ and $V_0[S(T)] = S(0)$.

7. Note that when switching from the true probability measure to the equivalent martingale measure, $X(t)$ no longer represents the actual process but the process where drift rates have been risk-adjusted to allow evaluation using risk-free discounting (in a risk-neutral economy).

8. Brennan (1991) presented in his Equation (14), an expression corresponding to our Result 2.

9. It is easy to verify that:

$$\int_{-d}^{\infty} w \frac{1}{\sqrt{2\pi}} \exp\left\{-\tfrac{1}{2}w^2\right\} dw = \frac{1}{\sqrt{2\pi}} \exp\left\{-\tfrac{1}{2}d^2\right\} = n[d] = n[-d].$$

# Chapter 13

# Valuing Start-up Venture Growth Options

## Ram Willner

*Many new business ventures have the characteristics of growth options, allowing use of option theory. However, traditional option methodology assumes a continuous cash-flow generation process which is difficult to apply to the pricing of start-up companies. This chapter presents an alternative jump formulation for growth option valuation which may better capture the discovery (jump) nature of start-up companies. The required parameters include the average frequency of new discoveries and the expected value of the company at the time it undertakes full-scale operations. Actual applications with venture capitalists suggest that the model should be applied in several stages, each one contingent on earlier stages, thereby valuing a new business venture as a compound option.*

## 13.1 INTRODUCTION

Over the past decade, financial researchers and practitioners of capital budgeting have recognized that an investment project often has increased value due to associated options. The study of such options has been stimulated by Myer's (1977) recognition that projects provide real options, by harsh criticism of traditional discounted cash flow techniques for missing project-associated options (see Hayes and Garvin, 1982), and by the concurrent development of financial option-pricing theory. Project-associated options have typically been categorized as either operating options or strategic/growth options.

Operating options are associated with managerial flexibility in how a project is managed. For instance, Majd and Pindyck (1987) studied the option to delay irreversible sequential investment outlays, which can proceed at a maximum rate due to construction lags between outlays. Lee

(1988) considered unrestricted optimal investment timing resulting from the option to defer investment. Brennan and Schwartz (1985a) studied the option to temporarily shut down production in a gold mine when such production is uneconomical. Another example is the option to abandon a project with some mitigated loss, as studied by Myers and Majd (1990). Since the holder of an abandonment option has restrited loss, the option to abandon can be regarded as a put option. Mason and Merton (1985) and Trigeorgis and Mason (1987) have provided a review of such operating real options.

Growth or strategic options are opportunities that are made available in the future by undertaking a project but are not part of the initial project. For instance, launching a product into a new market may have a negative net present value (NPV) itself, but the project may provide exposure for the firm in the new market, opening up the way for future opportunities. Moreover, while high uncertainty in the new market may diminish the present value of the initial project's cash flows, it may mean access to a market with higher potential allowing the firm to make a *discretionary* follow-up investment. Such an investment option may be amenable to explicit valuation, as in McDonald and Seigel (1986), who considered undertaking a project whose value is stochastic while the firm must decide if and when to invest—all the while forgoing the possibility of current income from the project. Trigeorgis and Mason (1987) reviewed additional strategic options. For instance, they valued the option to expand a project later on by using binomial option-pricing approaches. Kester (1984) discussed the importance of establishing a brand name by providing the option to have market shelf space for future products. Both Myers (1987) and Kester (1984) considered R and D investments as strategic options. They asserted that an R and D investment is like buying a growth option in that R and D is a process for generating asset value on which the R and D investor has a contingent claim. This is essentially the option we consider in this chapter.

In pricing operating or growth options, most researchers assume that the value of a completed project follows a continuous-time stochastic process, and apply the Black-Scholes option pricing model (with appropriate extensions) to derive the stochastic partial differential equations which govern the option value. In particular, it is assumed—as in the Black-Scholes case—that a hedge can be created between the option and a "twin" security whose return is perfectly correlated with the option payoff. Finding such a security is regarded as no more difficult than finding a security with a beta similar to that of the project, as required in applying the CAPM to capital budgeting. It is not always clear that this is so.

According to CAPM, beta is a one-dimensional description of a security's market risk, which should determine the market return of the security. However, option pricing theory requires a twin security with a perfectly correlated return distribution so that a hedge can be formed, which, when arbitrage is avoided, establishes an option price. If, as is customarily assumed, the twin security price follows a continuous lognormal distribution, then identifying it presumes knowledge of its instantaneous mean return and variance. The instantaneous variance is a crucial input to pricing the option. We thus face the difficult task of finding a twin security's mean return and variance while requiring that the security be perfectly correlated with the project. It might further be argued that using the variance of a traded asset to represent that of a nontraded project may be inappropriate. An asset that is subject to the fluctuations of an active market may display more volatility than an otherwise identical asset that is not traded. However, such "comparabilities" are unavoidable so long as the dynamic assumptions for project values are the same as those for traded assets.

This chapter applies different assumptions for the generating process that governs the stochastic value of a project in the case of start-up ventures. It presents an alternative jump formulation that may better capture the essence of the discovery (jump) component of new ventures. The proposed methodology relies more on technological rather than market-based parameters. While this methodology also suffers from the difficulty of real-life parameter estimation, it is more natural and convenient for this type of application.

The rest of the chapter is organized as follows. Section 13.2 motivates the use of an options approach, rather than a discounted cash flow approach, for valuing start-up ventures. Section 13.3 develops a jump model for valuing start-up venture growth options. Section 13.4 relates some observations from actual use of the model by venture capitalists in valuing start-up ventures. The last section concludes.

## 13.2  MOTIVATING A GROWTH-OPTIONS VALUATION OF START-UP VENTURES

Several researchers, motivated by the current option-based approach to capital budgeting, have noted that R and D projects are essentially real growth options. For instance, Myers (1987) stated: "Discounted Cash Flow [technique] is no help at all for pure research and development. The value of R&D is almost all option value. Intangible assets' value is usually option value" (p. 12). This view regards an R and D project as undertaken not so much for its own cash-flow results, but rather for the market opportunity that a new development or discovery may offer. We believe that most start-up ventures are of this nature. Investment in a start-up company is usually not undertaken so as to initiate immediate selling of a product or service, but to start a multistage process that may eventually reach that point.

Even if a product or service has already been developed, often its market has not. As such, investment in a start-up venture can be seen to be similar to an investment in a compound real option. The typical start-up venture proceeds in several contingent stages, as portrayed in Figure 13.1.[1]

**Figure 13.1**
**Typical New Product Investment Time Line**

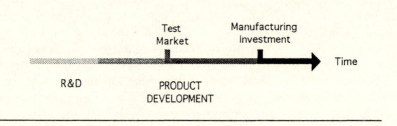

The real option-pricing approach as an alternative to the NPV rule is superior for valuing start-up firms in three regards:

1. Cash flow estimation;

2. Contingent cash-flow pattern treatment; and

3. Risk treatment.

*Cash Flow Estimation.* The NPV approach requires an estimation of the cash flows to be received after the manufacturing investment takes place. At the initial stages of start-up, this is often a very difficult or even impossible task. The options approach starts from a parameterized characterization of the cash flow–generating process. The advantage is that the parameters that characterize the process of cash-flow generation, rather than the cash flows themselves, are generally easier to estimate and can embody technological as well as economic/market factors. Specifically, the proposed option model will require estimating:

1. The expected frequency of discovery;

2. The expected percentage of value increase per discovery; and

3. The expected value of the company at the time it expects to undertake full-scale operations.

*Contingent Cash-Flow Pattern Treatment.* The NPV methodology does not explicitly account for the nonsymmetric cash-flow outcomes generated by the discretion managers exercise at the time of the manufacturing investment stage to halt or continue the project (i.e., the contingent nature of the underlying cash flows associated with real options). Although the resulting skewed cash-flow distribution can be accounted for by applying decision tree analysis (DTA), such analysis is tedious and is mostly ignored in practice. Contingent cash flows can be quite complex and can lead to an unwieldy number of branches for a decision tree. By starting with a cash flow–generating process and continuous probability distributions, rather than discrete DTA, many complex outcomes can be considered at once in a more compact option analysis.

*Risk Treatment.* Another problem associated with traditional NPV analysis in connection with the evaluation of contingent outcomes is that the discount rate typically applied in NPV analysis is based on symmetric outcome distributions and is generally too high for contingent cash-flow discounting. A theoretical assessment of the correct discount rate for asymmetric outcome distributions is not trivial. Trigeorgis and Mason (1987) gave a thorough exposition of these issues and demonstrated with examples that a regular risk-adjusted discount rate is generally not appropriate.

The proposed model in this chapter values a start-up venture as a real option. The underlying asset is the value potentially generated from a completed manufacturing investment. The exercise price is the cost of making that investment. Until the equity of a start-up firm is available to the market, our model regards its value as steadily increasing while research efforts progress. Occasionally, the equity value jumps up or down with new discoveries or due to competitive factors. Such jumps can be assumed to be uncorrelated with systematic market movements. The lack of active trading in company securities and the nature of the discovery process argue against a characterization of this process as a continuous diffusion process. More appropriately, the cash-flow generation process can be thought of as a jump process with an upward drift. The proposed jump model is formulated as a (market-diversified) risk-neutral semi-moment, which regards the jumps in the cash-flow generation process as uncorrelated with the market portfolio held by the start-up investor.[2]

More generally, the proposed model applies the option framework to capture the discretionary investment quality of start-up ventures. New ventures produce the opportunity to invest in a full or expanded scale manufacturing of a product developed by the entrepreneurial venture.[3] In this respect, value derives not only from the cash-flow potential of the venture, but also from the ability to decide at some future time if an economic scale manufacturing facility (ESMF) is a worthwhile investment.

## 13.3   A JUMP MODEL FOR VALUING START-UP VENTURE GROWTH OPTIONS

### 13.3.1   Analytic Formulation

We now proceed to formally develop a model which better captures the discovery nature of many start-up firms as options on the economic scale manufacturing facility (ESMF) cash flows. For illustrative purposes, consider the case of a biogenetic engineering firm searching for a bacterial mutation useful for commercial application. Embarking on this start-up venture leads to an investment decision that must be made by some later time $T$ (perhaps when funding runs out).[4] If at time $T$ the firm decides to incur the cost of the ESMF, $K$, then it will realize a series of ESMF generated cash flows having present value (at time $T$) of $P(T)$. If at time $T$, $P(T) < K$, then the ESMF will not be built and the loss will be limited to the initial investment. The potential gain if $P(T) > K$ will be $P(T) - K$, which is unlimited. Earlier, we noted that the potential value of $P(T)$ results not only from the initially envisioned product but also from additional products, markets and opportunities. This potential is captured by the variance of $P(T)$. The greater the variance the better because the loss is limited since we need not undertake the ESMF if $P(T) < K$, while the potential gain is greater.

Investment in the start-up venture thus yields an option on the value of the ESMF cash flows (the underlying asset) with exercise price the cost of the ESMF, $K$, expiration time, $T$, and price the initial cost of the start-up venture. At time $T$, the venture (option) holder gets $max(P(T) - K, 0)$. The option valuation thus recognizes, *ex ante*, that the optimal decision (ESMF go/no go) will be followed at time $T$.

Assume there are sufficient funds to maintain research activity until the known time $T$.[5] At that time, if the present value of ESMF cash flows accruing to the start-up venture, $P(T)$ [or at any time $t$, $P(t)$], is greater than the (assumed known) cost of building the ESMF, $K$, then the ESMF will be built. In addition, we make the following assumptions:

- $P(t)$ grows at an anticipated exponential rate corresponding to steady on-going research, except for occasional unanticipated jumps in $P(t)$ due to new discoveries.

- The benefit of discoveries may not be fully realized due to the potential entrance of competitors upon (coincident with) a new discovery.

- The long-run diminishing effect of new discoveries, both in terms of added value and of attracting new competitors, is recognized.

These assumptions are incorporated and formalized by assuming that the dynamics of $P(t)$ are given by the following jump process:

$$\frac{dP}{P} = \mu dt + (\gamma - \delta)d\Pi(Q), \qquad (13.1)$$

where $\mu$ denotes the anticipated rate of growth in $P(t)$, disregarding potential jumps; $\gamma$ is the percent change in $P$ if there is a discovery at time $t$; $\delta$ is the percent reduction in $P$ due to a concurrent entrance of competitors; and $\Pi(Q)$ denotes a Poisson process governing the occurrence of jumps with intensity $Q$, given by:

$$d\Pi = \begin{cases} 1 & \text{with prob. } Qdt \\ 0 & \text{with prob. } 1 - Qdt. \end{cases}$$

Since $d\Pi$ is a point process, $\gamma$ and $\delta$ can be denoted $\gamma_i$ and $\delta_i$, corresponding to the ith jump at time $t_i$. Conditional on jump $i$, the net percent change of $P(i)$, $\gamma_i - \delta_i$, is denoted as $a_i'$, and $P(i)$ is changed by a factor $(1 + a_i')$, denoted as $a_i$.

In the Appendix we show that, if we assume that the $a_i$ are i.i.d. and $a_i \sim \lambda a_i^{-(\lambda+1)}$, then $E(a_i) = \lambda/(\lambda-1)$ for $\lambda > 1$, and $\log(a_i) \equiv \Theta \sim \lambda e^{-\lambda\Theta}$ (i.e., $\Theta$ is exponentionally distributed).[6]

If there are no jumps by time $t$ (i.e., $t_1 > t$), then $P(t) = P(0)e^{\mu t}$, as depicted below in Figure 13.2. That is, prior to the decision on the ESMF investment anticipated at time $T$, we assume an exponential growth in $P(t)$, in the absence of jumps, due to ongoing research progress. In practice, as Figure 13.2 shows, there is typically an eventual decay in the growth of $P(t)$, but this generally occurs after the ESMF is constructed. This is not a binding concern for our model, which focuses exclusively on the ESMF investment option and growth in $P(t)$ up to time $T$. The eventual decay in ESMF cash flows is accounted for in our assessment of $P(T)$.

According to our earlier assumptions, there may also be random jumps in $P(t)$. We allow for positive increases due to new discoveries, but those increases are mitigated due to new competitive entrants (creating "net" positive jumps). Between jumps, the path of $P(t)$ is presumed to be smooth and exponential. Since there is no active trading of $P(t)$ and no dramatic change in information regarding its value, it is reasonable to assume that $P(t)$ grows in a smooth fashion as research progresses. Further assumptions below impose a decline in the average net jump size of $P(t)$ over time, allowing for diminishing returns of discovery. Given these assumptions, a typical path for $P(t)$ in the presence of net positive jumps is shown in Figure 13.3.

Figure 13.3 also indicates the terminal payoff generated by an investment at time $T$ as $\text{NPV}(T) \equiv P(T) - K$, contingent on the given path

**Figure 13.2**
**Assumed Growth in the Present Value of Economic Scale**
**Manufacturing Facility (ESMF) Cash Flows**

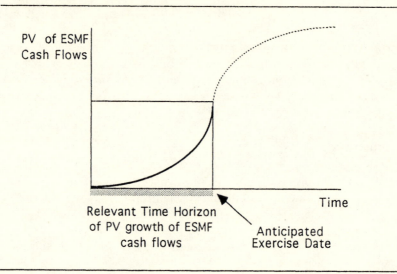

where $P(T) > K$. The initial value of the start-up venture is, in fact, an assessment of the expected present value of $\text{NPV}(T)$ under uncertainty, with negative values truncated at zero. We proceed next to find the terminal distribution of $P(T)$, which is tantamount to finding the terminal distribution of $\text{NPV}(T)$, since $K$ is constant.

## 13.3.2 The Terminal Distribution of ESMF Cash-Flow Value

To derive the terminal distribution of ESMF cash-flow value, $P(T)$, first consider $P(1)$, the value of $P(t)$ at the time of the first jump, $t_1$. In what follows, we use a superscript "$-$" after a given jump time, for instance "1" (i.e., "$1^-$"), to denote the value of $P(t)$ immediately prior to the occurence of jump $t$ (here, jump 1).

$$
\begin{aligned}
P(1) &= P(1^-) + dP(1) \\
&= P(0)e^{\mu t_1} + P(1^-)\alpha_1' \\
&= P(0)e^{\mu t_1} + P(0)e^{\mu t_1}\alpha_1' \\
&= P(0)e^{\mu t_1}(1 + \alpha_1') \\
&= P(0)e^{\mu t_1}\alpha_1.
\end{aligned}
$$

Similarly,

**Figure 13.3**
**A Typical Path of the Present Value of ESMF Cash Flows**
**with Net Positive Jumps**

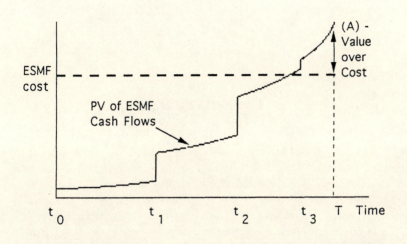

$$
\begin{aligned}
P(2) &= P(2^-) + dP(2) \\
&= P(1)e^{\mu(t_2-t_1)} + P(2^-)\alpha'_2 \\
&= P(1)e^{\mu(t_2-t_1)} + P(1)e^{\mu(t_2-t_1)}\alpha'_2 \\
&= P(1)e^{\mu(t_2-t_1)}\alpha_2 \\
&= [P(0)e^{\mu t_1}\alpha_1]e^{\mu(t_2-t_1)}\alpha_2 \\
&= P(0)e^{\mu t_2}\alpha_1\alpha_2.
\end{aligned}
$$

For the general case $(n)$:

$$
P(n) = P(0)e^{\mu t_n}\ \Pi_{j=0}^{n}a_j, \text{ with } \alpha_0 \equiv 1.
$$

For time $t$, $t_n < t < t_{n+1}$, then,

$$
P(t) = P(n)e^{\mu(t-t_n)} = P(0)e^{\mu t_n}\ \Pi_{j=0}^{n}\alpha_j e^{\mu(t-t_n)} \ , \text{ or}
$$

$$
P(t) = P(0)e^{\mu t}\ \Pi_{j=0}^{n}\alpha_j. \tag{13.2}
$$

Taking the expectation of Equation (13.2), using the independence assumptions and the results of the Appendix, we get:

$$
E[P(t)] = P(0)e^{\mu t}\ \Pi_{j=0}^{E(n)}E[\alpha_j]
$$

$$= P(0)e^{\mu t}\left[\frac{\lambda}{\lambda - 1}\right]^{Qt}, \tag{13.3}$$

where $Qt$ is the expected number of jumps for the Poisson process $\Pi$ in $(0, t)$. For convenience, denote $\left[\dfrac{\lambda}{\lambda - 1}\right]^{Qt}$ by $C(t)$. Then, by Equation (13.3):

$$P(0)e^{\mu T} = E[P(T)]/C(T), \tag{13.4}$$

and substituting into Equation (13.2) yields:

$$P(T) = \{E[P(T)]/C(T)\} \; \Pi_{j=0}^{n}\alpha_j . \tag{13.5}$$

Equations (13.2) (with $t = T$) and (13.5) provide equivalent descriptions of $P(T)$, but may be of differing usefulness. As shown in Figure 13.3, the distribution of $P(T)$ will determine the value of the start-up venture as a growth option. We need either Equation (13.2) or (13.5) to assess this distribution, and therefore we will need to estimate the parameters in these equations. Equation (13.2) requires its user to know the present value of the assets in place and be able to estimate their anticipated growth rate. Equation (13.5) requires estimating the expected value of $P(T)$. Both equations require estimating the average number of jumps in the value of $P(t)$ per unit time and the average net jump level (due to new discoveries, net of competitive entry).

Since $C \equiv E[P(T)]/C(T)$ is deterministic, we have from Equation (13.5) that:

$$P(T)/C = \Pi_{j=0}^{n}\alpha_j, \qquad \text{or}$$

$$\log\{P(T)/C\} = \sum_{j=0}^{n}\log\{\alpha_j\} = \sum_{j=0}^{n}\Theta_j, \text{ where } \Theta_j \equiv \log\{\alpha_j\}. \tag{13.6}$$

We now refine the model further by introducing the notion of a diminishing impact of new discoveries. We extend Expression (13.6) by including a deterministic jump-dampening factor, $\beta$, as follows:

$$\log\{P(T)/C\} = \sum_{j=0}^{n}\Theta_j e^{-\beta(t - t_j)}, \tag{13.7}$$

where $t_j$ is the time of the $j$th jump and $n$ is the number of jumps by time $t$. This means that the time of a jump is critical in assessing the value of $P(T)$.

Given the final expression of $P(T)$ in the form of Equation (13.7), it can be demonstrated that as $T$ gets large, $\log\{P(T)/C\} \sim \Gamma(Q/\beta, \lambda)$, where

$\Gamma(a, b)$ is the Gamma distribution with parameters $a$ and $b$.[7] By the chain rule of calculus, the distribution of $P(T)$, denoted $f_{P(T)}$, is finally given by:

$$P(T) \sim \frac{\Gamma(Q/\beta, \lambda)}{P(T)}.$$

### 13.3.3 A Jump Valuation Formula for Start-up Venture Growth Options

If we additionally assume that new discoveries, which are the only risk factors assumed to determine $P(t)$, are not correlated with the market and that investors in the start-up venture are well diversified, then the new venture will be priced without a premium charged for the discovery risk involved. Therefore, the growth option will be priced as if the expected growth rate for $P(0)$ is the risk-free rate, $r$. This means that whatever implicit discount rate is used to arrive at $P(0)$, the growth factor over time $t$ of $P(0)$ must be $e^{rt}$. Thus, to value the start-up venture as an option, we need only know the terminal distribution of $P(T)$ for each value over $K$, compute the expected value given this terminal distribution, and discount the expected value at the risk-free rate as shown below. The NPV of economically productive activities already in place should also be included in this valuation.[8] That is,

Value of start-up venture = Growth option value + NPV of assets in place

$$
\begin{aligned}
&= e^{-rt} \int_0^\infty max(0, P - K) f_{P(T)} dP + NPV \\
&= e^{-rt} \int_K^\infty (P - K) f_{P(T)} dP + NPV \\
&= e^{-rt} \int_K^\infty (1 - K/P) \, \Gamma(Q/\beta, \lambda) dP + NPV. \quad (13.8)
\end{aligned}
$$

The integral in Equation (13.8) is easily calculated by numerical integration.

## 13.4 MODEL APPLICATION

The pricing formula developed above in Equation (13.8) has been implemented by computer using numerical integration.[9] Initial application of the formula both in real as well as in simulated start-up venture valuations with several venture capital companies has resulted in the following observations, which will be explored further in the following sections.

1. Positive option premium assigned to start-up ventures: The venture capitalists were responsive to the possibility of investing in a firm, even though the net present value of cash flows at the time of ESMF did not appear to be positive, because of the potential for future growth with limited investment commitment.

2. The impact of model parameters: The venture capitalists reacted favorably to the model's technological parameters. They were of the opinion that the quality of discovery (jump size), rather than its frequency, was of primary importance.

3. The application of the model to consecutive contingent stages (compound option): Most venture capitalists anticipated multiple-stage financing and reinvestment points during the start-up venture process.

## 13.4.1  Positive Option Worth

The option premium is analogous to that for stock options (i.e., the option value is generally above current exercise value) and most evident for out-of-the-money options. In applying Equation (13.5), the possibility exists that the expected present value of cash flows at time $T$, $P(T)$, is less than or equal to the ESMF cost, $K$.[10] Nonetheless, the new venture opportunity still has positive value because of the limited downside loss and unlimited upside potential gain. In other words, the option still has value due to the asymmetric expected present value of the payoff (at time $T$), given the discretionary decision of committing $K$ to receive $P(T)$, $max(P(T) - K, 0)$.

This notion is depicted in Figure 13.4, which shows a positive option value despite zero expected net cash-flow value, $P(T) - K$. Venture capitalists found this concept appealing. Perhaps their experience with the difficulties of assessing the expected present value of cash flows at the time of the ESMF investment has led them to accept the notion of positive investment worth even though the anticipated cash flows currently do not warrant investing. The difficulty of cash-flow assessment was not necessarily regarded negatively, as it was also seen as related to unknown future opportunities.

Table 13.1 provides numerical examples illustrating how the start-up venture option value calculated from model Equation (13.8) varies with changes in the expected cash-flow value, $P(T)$, relative to the ESMF cost, with the other parameters held constant. The table shows that even when $E[P(T)]$ is \$1m below the cost of the ESMF (case 1), there is still a positive value, \$.1m, to the start-up venture. When at-the-money (i.e., zero-NPV), the start-up venture is worth \$1.13m (case 2). For an expected cash-flow present value of \$1m above $K$ (case 3), the start-up is worth \$2.86m. Note

**Figure 13.4**
**Positive Option Payout versus Zero Expected Net Cash-Flow Value**

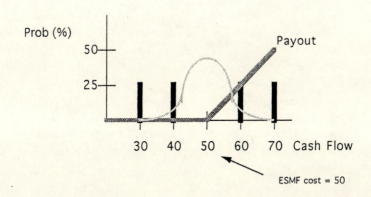

*Note*: Bars denote discrete probability distribution. Smooth curve denotes continuous probability distribution.

that this increase in start-up value with increasing $E[P(T)]$ is nonlinear. This is primarily due to the discretionary right, with no obligation, to invest at $T$ only if market developments are favorable. It is also partly due to the skewed modified Gamma distribution for $P(T)$ which forms a weighting scheme for the payoff values, $P(T) - K$, as calculated using Equation (13.8).

## 13.4.2 The Impact of Changes in Model Parameters

The varying impact of changes in the model parameters is also an interesting issue that arises in the application of the model. Table 13.2 below relies on case 2 of Table 13.1 as the base case, and illustrates the impact of a 10 percent change, *ceteris paribus*, in each variable. The impact of the changes presented in Table 13.2 is useful for assessing the relative importance of alternative actions, for example regarding net jump level (impact of a discovery) versus the number of jumps (frequency of discoveries). These two variables are most likely to be influenced by decisions on hiring and R and D facility investment. The table shows that a 10 percent increase in either variable has a similar effect on the value of the start-up venture. One

**Table 13.1**

**Examples of Start-up Venture Option Value for Varying Expected Cash-Flow Value**

|                                          | CASE 1 | CASE 2 | CASE 3 |
|------------------------------------------|--------|--------|--------|
| Expected cash flow value at $T$ $[P(T)]$ | 2.0    | 3.0    | 4.0    |
| ESMF cost $(K)$                          | 3.0    | 3.0    | 3.0    |
| $NPV$ at time $T$                        | -1.0   | 0      | 1.0    |
| New venture option value                 | .10    | 1.13   | 2.86   |
| Increase in option value                 | -      | 1.03   | 1.73   |

(Assumptions: expected net jump level= $1.05^*$, expected number of jumps = $3.0^{**}$, rate of jump level decline, $\beta = 0.3^{***}$, risk-free rate (T-bill Rate for $(0, T) = 8$ percent.)

*Notes:*

$\star$ The value $\alpha$ $(= 1 + \alpha')$ is presented in the tables rather than $\alpha'$, although the net jump is actually described by $\alpha'$. This value allows us to calculate the $\lambda$ parameter needed for the assumed exponential distribution of $\Theta = \log(\alpha_i)$.

$\star\star$ The expected number of jumps during the period $(0, T)$ establishes the Poisson parameter $Q$.

$\star\star\star$ Beta $(\beta)$ governs the rate at which the average jump level is diminished over time, $0 < t < 1$ ($T$ is normalized so that $T = 1$). The average jump level, in this example 5 percent, is multiplied by $e^{-\beta t}$ with $\beta = .3$, and so is diminished by 26 percent to 3.7 percent by $T = 1$.

might associate the net jump level representing the impact of a discovery with the quality of scientists, while the number of jumps might represent the frequency of discoveries associated with the number of scientists. To find the best start-up value improvement alternative, an assessment must also be made of the relative costs of hiring and R and D facilities needed to affect a given percentage change. The model can then suggest the relative net benefit of each investment alternative.

Most venture capitalists thought the cost of increasing the expected net jump level (e.g., by hiring better scientists) is generally lower than the cost of increasing the expected number of jumps (e.g., by hiring more scientists). Furthermore, since improvements in the net jump level (or size of jumps) was generally perceived as much more controllable than increasing the number or frequency of jumps, this was by far the control variable of choice.

**Table 13.2**
**Impact of a 10 Percent Change in Each Parameter on Start-up Option Value vis-à-vis Case 2 (of Table 13.1)**

|  | ORIGINAL VALUE | NEW VALUE | START-UP VALUE | Δ |
|---|---|---|---|---|
| *BASE CASE* |  |  | *1.13* |  |
| Expect Cash Flow at Time T [P(T)] | 3.0 | 3.3 | **1.52** | .39 |
| K (ESMF Cost) | 3.0 | 3.3 | **0.86** | -.27 |
| Expected Net Jump Level[4] | 1.05 | 1.055 | **1.26** | .13 |
| Expected Number of Jumps | 3.0 | 3.3 | **1.28** | .15 |
| Beta Value | 0.3 | 0.33 | **0.96** | -.17 |
| Period T-Bill Rate for (0,T)[5] | 0.08 | 0.088 | **1.12** | -.01 |

[4] For consistency with other parts of the text, the value $\alpha$ is presented in the table rather than $\alpha'$ [$\alpha'+1 = \alpha$] although the net jump is actually described by $\alpha'$.
[5] This value is questionable since an increase in the period Treasury Bill rate would probably also impact the estimate of E[P(T)] -- an adjustment not included in start-up value figure.

### 13.4.3   A Compound Option Application with Multiple Contingent Stages

Finally, for most new ventures, venture capitalists anticipate several rounds of financing to support and generally parallel the various "ramp ups" or stages of development and marketing. Although the process from product development to release in the market generally fits the pattern of Figure 13.1, it is more accurately portrayed in Figure 13.5, which depicts a case with three investment decision stages (at $T_1, T_2$, and $T_3$) in the financing of a start-up project. The value of each stage is the entitlement to the next financing option. Therefore, if the last option is priced using the earlier model, the preceding option can be priced as a claim on it. Using a backward iterative valuation approach, the start-up company value can be calculated as of the present time.

In Figure 13.5, the ultimate investment in an ESMF takes place in period 5 at a cost of $K_5$ for anticipated cash flows of $P(T_5) = \$10m$. This results in an option value of $8.21m as of period 2. The cost of acquiring that option is the required financing amount, $K_2$. This second stage is itself an option resulting from the initial investment of $K_1$ in period 1. The value of the start-up venture at the outset, according to the model, is $17.6m. As discussed earlier, this higher investment opportunity value ($17.6m versus the $10m expected cash-flow value in year 5) is due to the option premium, which is enhanced in this case by the compound option situation.

Figure 13.5
Investment Decision Stages (Compound Option Valuation) in Start-up Project Financing

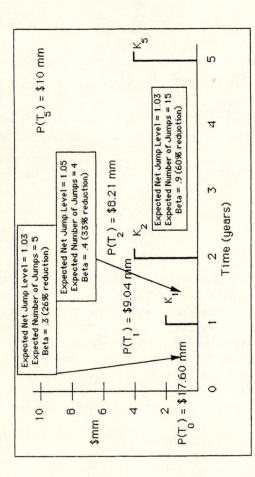

If this venture were valued instead as a single-option situation, the model would yield an initial start-up value of $12.32m (using the average values of the compound option situation parameters). This single-period value is also quite sensitive to the rate of decline in the impact of discoveries (the beta value). Since the "average" beta value is hard to define, however, it is hard to compare the multiple- and single-option situations directly. In fact, the sensitivity of the model to beta values is one of the practical difficulties encountered in applying the model to actual cases.[11]

## 13.5 CONCLUSION

Myers (1987) observed that "the standard discounted cash flow techniques will tend to understate the option value attached to growing, profitable lines of business" and that "the most promising line of research is to try to use option pricing theory to model the time-series interactions between investments" (p. 13). This chapter represents one attempt to do so by applying somewhat non-standard dynamics to the growth option-pricing problem. The result is an option-based valuation for start-up ventures that requires the estimation of a small number of parameters. These parameters are technical in nature and amenable to estimation by managers and their technical staff. The model can be applied to value a simplified growth opportunity (as depicted in Figure 13.1), or it can be extended to more realistic compound growth options (as depicted in Figure 13.5).

This chapter also advances the notion that entrepreneurs are primarily managers of growth options. Growth options can come about as a result of new business ventures, or as a result of a radically changing business environment. These options are attractive for their expansion potential and for their reduced risk exposure: if ESMF opportunities do not materialize, only the initial investment is lost. We suggest that if such investments are regarded as real options, they become amenable to option valuation. Option theory can, therefore, be useful in two ways: first, it can conceptually elucidate the value associated with start-up ventures and help managers make strategic decisions; and second, it can provide explicit quantitative models, such as the one proposed in this chapter, to allow for the concrete measurement of new venture value.

## APPENDIX

This Appendix shows that, if we assume the $\alpha_i$ are i.i.d. and $\alpha_i \sim \lambda\alpha_i^{-(\lambda+1)}$, then $E(\alpha_i) = \lambda/(\lambda - 1)$ for $\lambda > 1$ and $\Theta \equiv \log(\alpha_i) \sim \lambda e^{-\lambda\Theta}$ (i.e., $\Theta$ is exponentially distributed).

First, given $\alpha_i \sim \lambda \alpha_i^{-(\lambda+1)}$ with the $\alpha_i$ i.i.d., we show that:

$$E(\alpha_i) = \frac{\lambda}{\lambda - 1} \ , \ \text{for } \lambda > 1.$$

By the assumptions for $\gamma_i$ and $\delta_i$ (see main text), $\alpha_i > 1$. Then,

$$
\begin{aligned}
E(\alpha_i) &= \int_1^\infty \alpha_i \lambda \alpha_i^{-(\lambda+1)} d\alpha_i \\
&= \lambda \int_1^\infty \alpha_i^{-\lambda} d\alpha_i \\
&= \left. \frac{\lambda \alpha_i^{1-\lambda}}{1-\lambda} \right|_1^\infty
\end{aligned}
\tag{13.A1}
$$

The expression in (13.A1) converges if, and only if, $\lambda > 1$, and then it converges to $\frac{\lambda}{\lambda-1}$.

We next show that for $\Theta = \log(\alpha_i)$, if $\alpha_i \sim \lambda \alpha_i^{-(\lambda+1)}$ then $\Theta \sim \lambda e^{-\lambda \Theta}$. By the chain rule of calculus, given the probability density function (pdf) of $\Theta$, where $\Theta = \Theta(X)$, we have the identity:

$$\text{pdf of } X = \text{pdf } \Theta(X) \frac{d\Theta}{dX}.$$

Applying this identity (for $X = \alpha_i$):

$$\lambda \alpha_i^{-(\lambda+1)} = \text{pdf } \Theta(\alpha_i)(1/\alpha_i), \text{ or}$$

$$\text{pdf } \Theta(\alpha_i) = \lambda \alpha_i^{-\lambda} = \lambda e^{-\lambda \log(\alpha_i)} = \lambda e^{-\lambda \Theta}.$$

## ACKNOWLEDGMENTS

The author would like to thank Frank Schuller and the editor, Lenos Trigeorgis, for their help.

## NOTES

1. This figure is adapted from Butters et al. (1987).

2. This approach was first proposed by Cox and Ross (1976) for option processes which were shown to be independent of economy-specific risk preferences.

3. *Product* here refers either to a product or service.

4. If refinancing is feasible at times $T_1, T_2, ...T_n$, then a compound-option analysis must be applied, as discussed in the next section.

5. The approach can be extended to valuing an option with varying expiration time, but that is beyond the scope of this chapter.

6. The assumption for the distribution of $\log(\alpha_i)$ is somewhat restrictive since it implies that $\gamma_i - \delta_i$ is distributed on the interval $(0, \infty)$ and that the net movement in $P(t)$ cannot be negative. This mathematically attractive restriction is offset to some extent by allowing for jumps significantly less than expected on average.

7. The proof is available from the author.

8. Valuation by explicit addition of NPV and associated options has been called the Expanded-NPV or ENPV. See Trigeorgis and Mason (1987) and Bierman and Smidt (1988) on this point.

9. The program is available from the author.

10. Equation (13.5) is used rather than Equation (13.2) because the venture capitalists surveyed found this a more natural form for estimating model parameters.

11. One possibility for handling the beta value is to treat it as being fixed at a given level, essentially removing it as a model parameter.

# PART V

## OTHER APPLICATIONS: POLLUTION COMPLIANCE, LAND DEVELOPMENT, FLEXIBLE MANUFACTURING, AND FINANCIAL DEFAULT

# Chapter 14

# Investment in Pollution Compliance Options: The Case of Georgia Power

## Michael E. Edleson and Forest L. Reinhardt

*This chapter analyzes the actual investment decision of a utility faced with a complex capital budgeting problem involving real options. Georgia Power's coal-fired utility plants must comply with EPA-mandated sulfur dioxide pollution levels; it may buy or sell "pollution allowances" for any residual. To avoid heavy allowance purchases, it can install expensive "scrubbers" or switch to cheaper, low-sulfur coal. Standard DCF techniques compare the alternatives and a more complex analysis finds the least-cost compliance strategies. Both techniques, however, ignore the dynamic nature of the problem and the value of flexible managerial response. Real option techniques are then used to value and reassess the alternatives. Both the value of real options, and their impact on optimal investment decisions, are substantial.*

## 14.1   INTRODUCTION

In this chapter we examine the actual case of a utility facing a capital budgeting problem—how to best comply with the U.S. Clean Air Act. The 1990 Amendments to the Clean Air Act establish a system of tradeable permits for sulfur dioxide ($SO_2$) emissions, which are produced largely by coal-fired electric power plants and are held responsible for much of North America's acid precipitation. Under most earlier regulatory controls for air pollution, each source is allowed to emit up to a certain amount of a specified pollutant per year. The 1990 legislation departs from this traditional approach: a pollution source can sell part or all of its allocation of permits (also called allowances) to other sources, or can buy permits for additional emissions from others. It can also "bank" permits for future use or sale. A source's allowable emissions under the Clean Air Act Amendments thus depend not on its initial allocation of permits, but on the number of permits or allowances it holds after engaging in various trades. The total tonnage of permits allocated, however, is less than current $SO_2$ emissions, thereby guaranteeing reductions in total emissions.[1]

The advantages of such a system have been extensively discussed by economists.[2] Suppose that the acid rain damages caused by a ton of $SO_2$ emissions do not depend on the location of the source. Then, in any efficient solution, the marginal costs of pollution control must be equal across sources. However, because plants differ in their age, type of fuel consumed, and so on, the costs of achieving a particular reduction in emissions (say, 70 percent of current emissions) will ordinarily not be equal across sources. Thus, requiring each source to reduce its emissions by 70 percent (the traditional "command and control" approach) is generally inefficient. Suppose, instead, that the regulators create permits allowing a total of 30 percent of current emissions, allocate them among the various sources, and then allow the sources to trade these permits. This "market-based" approach would presumably equalize marginal compliance costs across sources, producing an efficient reduction in emissions.[3]

The flexibility inherent in the new legislation complicates coal-burning utilities' planning for compliance. Formerly, federal and state regulators determined the allowable level of emission; planning for compliance was essentially an engineering problem of choosing the least-cost way of reducing emissions to those levels. The degree of freedom provided by trading allowances under the new amendments, however, requires the simultaneous determination of how much to reduce emissions as well as how to best achieve the desired reduction.

The new law is scheduled to be implemented in two phases. During the five-year period from January 1995 to December 1999 (Phase One), each of about 100 large, coal-fired plants will receive allowances to emit 2.5 pounds of $SO_2$ per million British thermal units (Btu) of coal consumed. Most of the plants are currently emitting $SO_2$ at rates between one and two times the Phase One levels. When Phase Two begins in January 2000, the permit allocations will be reduced even further, down to 1.2 pounds per million Btu; the system will also be broadened to encompass an additional 900 sources.[4]

Several compliance options are available to utility managers. If they purchase additional allowances from other sources, they can leave their current operating procedures unaltered. Alternatively, they can switch to coal with a lower sulfur content: some coals contain less than 0.5 percent sulfur by weight, while others contain 3.0–4.0 percent. Finally, they can install flue-gas desulfurization (FGD) devices, commonly called scrubbers, which are capital-intensive pieces of equipment that reduce $SO_2$ emissions by up to 90 percent.

In the next section, we describe the particular problem of a single utility plant and the compliance decision it faces. Section 14.3 presents the standard capital budgeting analysis, while section 14.4 gives a real options solution. The final section discusses other considerations and concludes.

## 14.2 THE CASE OF GEORGIA POWER'S BOWEN PLANT

To appreciate a utility manager's problem at an applied level, we focus on Clean Air Act compliance at a particular coal-fired power plant: the Bowen plant, owned by the Southern Company's Georgia Power subsidiary.[5] Bowen is an enormous—but otherwise, not atypical—coal-fired utility plant regulated by the Clean Air Act Amendments of 1990. Bowen will receive 255,000 tons of allowances each year during Phase One, and 122,000 tons per year in Phase Two.

Built in 1975 for baseload generation, the Bowen plant annually converts some 8.4 million tons of Kentucky coal into about 21.5 billion kilowatt-hours of electricity, enough to satisfy the commercial, residential, and industrial demands of roughly a million Georgians. In the process, it produced about 267,000 tons of $SO_2$ in 1990, the year the amendments were passed; the coal it burns contains 1.6 percent sulfur by weight, a medium/low level, so that its current emissions are not far (only 5 percent) above the 2.5 pound/MBtu Phase One standard. Bowen has several alternative ways to comply with the amendments:

1. Bowen can continue to burn coal as at present and purchase needed allowances in Phases One and Two.

2. Bowen can "overcomply" by installing expensive scrubbers, and subsequently sell allowances in both phases. Scrubbers at Bowen would cost $800 million (including capitalized construction interest) and take three years to install.

3. Bowen can switch to different coal, with a 1 percent sulfur content, which would entail selling excess allowances in Phase One but buying them when Bowen's permit allocation drops in Phase Two. Coal with 1 percent sulfur costs more than Bowen's current fuel and is expected to become considerably more expensive in Phase Two.

Various permutations of these compliance strategies are possible. For example, Bowen could switch to low-sulfur coal during Phase One and then install scrubbers in time for Phase Two operation.

A phased diagram of the six major alternative compliance strategies and their corresponding allowance positions is shown in Table 14.1. The first three represent the "basic strategies" described above, here referred to as DO NOTHING, SCRUB, and SWITCH, respectively. The last three alternatives represent "hybrid strategies" over the two phases. For example, alternative A4 entails DO NOTHING in Phase One and SCRUB in Phase Two. Next to the action in each phase is the annual allowance position, in thousands of tons of $SO_2$ per year to buy or sell.

**Table 14.1**
**Alternative Compliance Strategies and Corresponding Allowance Positions in Each Phase (Thousands of $SO_2$ Tons/Year)**

| Alternative | Phase One: 1995-1999 | | Phase Two: 2000-on | |
|:---:|:---|:---:|:---|:---:|
| | Action | Allowances (000) | Action | Allowances (000) |
| A1 | DO NOTHING | buy 12 | DO NOTHING | buy 144 |
| A2 | SCRUB | sell 228 | SCRUB | sell 95 |
| A3 | SWITCH | sell 87 | SWITCH | buy 45 |
| A4 | DO NOTHING | buy 12 | SCRUB | sell 95 |
| A5 | DO NOTHING | buy 12 | SWITCH | buy 45 |
| A6 | SWITCH | sell 87 | SCRUB | sell 95 |

## 14.3  STANDARD CAPITAL BUDGETING (DCF) ANALYSIS

The standard approach to such a problem is simple discounted cash flow (DCF) analysis: determine a risk-adjusted discount rate, enumerate the magnitude and timing of the relevant cash flows for the various policies, and compute their net present values. To set up the capital budgeting problem, the determination of a proper discount rate is crucial. The company's own capital budgeting models use a discount rate of 10 percent, based on empirically derived costs of debt and equity and a target debt/capital ratio near the 50 percent level that prevailed in 1990. For simplicity, we will use this as the discount rate.[6]

The calculation of the relevant after-tax cash flows is relatively straightforward. The scrubber involves additional annual operating expenses ($28 million) and a 2 percent revenue reduction ($24 million) due to the electricity it consumes. The scrubber would require outlays of $143.85 million in 1992, $503.61 million in 1993, and $71.97 million in 1994, or a total $800 million capital cost (including capitalized interest at 10 percent during installation). Depreciation is 14 percent for 5 years and then 2 percent for 15 years, so that the resultant tax shield is worth about 23.6 percent of the investment in present value terms. A conversion to low-sulfur coal would require a $22 million investment and provides similar depreciation benefits. The conversion would also result in an increase in the price and quantity of coal fuel, and is thus expected to increase pretax costs by $6 million per year in Phase One and $44 million in Phase Two.

Since each alternative has an allowance position associated with it, the price and quantity of allowances to buy or sell will enter into the decision in each case. This decision is quite sensitive to the unknown future market price of the tradeable pollution allowances. We therefore need estimates of the price of tradeable allowances during the time frame of the analysis.

As a first cut, managers at Bowen's parent, noting that permits can be banked, deduce that the permits will rise in value at the cost of capital for comparable utility companies—about 10 percent. The reasoning is based on the theory of nonrenewable resources: since allowances, like a stock of oil or mineral ore in the ground, pay no dividends or interest while stored, their prices are expected to rise over time, so that the asset will deliver the required return.[7] This assumes that the convenience yield on allowances is zero.[8] Management further assumes that this price increase will end in the year 2010, as regulated plants are retired and new plants come on-line. These new plants must install scrubbers under the New Source Performance Standards of the 1977 amendments to the Clean Air Act.

These assumptions determine the expected *trend* of allowance prices over time, but not their initial *level*. Estimates of those levels, in the early 1990s, varied widely. The amendments themselves required the Environmental Protection Agency's administrator to sell limited numbers of permits for $1,500 per ton; this price was to be adjusted for inflation after 1990, but not for the real price increases expected by the Southern Company and other utilities.[9] Private trades in 1992 took place at considerably lower prices, in the range of $250 to $350 per ton. The Chicago Board of Trade held an auction of a small number of allowances (far less than Bowen's annual allocation) on March 30, 1993, with prices ranging from $122 to $450. The few announced off-exchange trades that took place during 1993 ranged from about $200 to $300. Management estimates a 1995 allowance price of $250.

Using these allowance price estimates, along with the quantity data from Table 14.1 and other case data, relevant cash flows are developed for the plant's life, until planned retirement in 2016. Table 14.2 summarizes the key cash flows, by phase, for the first three alternatives. Following standard DCF analysis, we determine that the net present cost of not investing is $266 million, the after tax expected cost of allowance purchases; the net present cost of the scrubber purchase alternative is $436 million. Thus, the incremental NPV of the scrubber project, relative to the base case (DO

Table 14.2
## Costs of Compliance for the Three Basic Alternative Strategies for the Bowen Plant (Cash Flows Shown in Millions of Dollars for Representative Years; Costs Shown as Positive Numbers)

| | 1992 | 1993 | 1994 | 1995 | 2000 | 2010-16 |
|---|---|---|---|---|---|---|
| **A1:    DO NOTHING** | | | | | | |
| Investment | 0 | 0 | 0 | | | |
| Allowance cost | | | | 3 | 58 | 151 |
| Lost revenue | | | | 0 | 0 | 0 |
| Added operating cost | | | | 0 | 0 | 0 |
| Total x (1 - tax rate) | | | | 2 | 36 | 93 |
| Less depreciation | | | | 0 | 0 | 0 |
| Net Present Cost = $266 | 0 | 0 | 0 | 2 | 36 | 93 |
| | | | | | | |
| **A2:    SCRUB** | | | | | | |
| Investment | 144 | 506 | 72 | | | |
| Allowance cost | | | | -57 | -38 | -100 |
| Lost revenue | | | | 24 | 24 | 24 |
| Added operating cost | | | | 28 | 28 | 28 |
| Total x (1 - tax rate) | | | | -3 | 9 | -30 |
| Less depreciation | | | | 42 | 6 | 6 |
| Net Present Cost = $436 | 144 | 504 | 72 | -45 | 3 | -36 |
| | | | | | | |
| **A3:    SWITCH TO LOW SULFUR** | | | | | | |
| Investment | 0 | 0 | 22 | | | |
| Allowance cost | | | | -24 | 18 | 48 |
| Lost revenue | | | | 0 | 0 | 0 |
| Added operating cost | | | | 6 | 44 | 44 |
| Total x (1 - tax rate) | | | | -11 | 38 | 57 |
| Less depreciation | | | | 0 | 0 | 0 |
| Net Present Cost = $168 | 0 | 0 | 22 | -11 | 38 | 57 |

NOTHING), is -$170 million, representing a value loss of over 20 percent of the investment cost.[10]

Given the different allowance positions shown in Table 14.1, the NPV estimates will vary if a different allowance price (other than $250) is used, and will vary in a different manner for each alternative. Figure 14.1 shows the NPV of each of the six compliance alternatives as the assumed 1995 allowance price varies. Negatively sloped lines in the figure represent strategies with a net short position in allowances, and positively sloped lines those with net long positions; lines whose slopes have higher absolute values represent strategies with greater degrees of exposure to uncertainty about allowance prices.

**Figure 14.1**
**Net Present Value (NPV) of Compliance Costs**
**(for the Six Alternatives A1–A6 described in Table 14.1)**

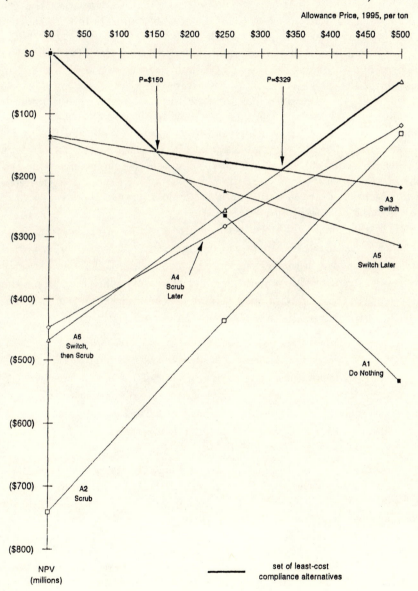

The first two strategies, A1: DO NOTHING and A2: SCRUB, are represented by the two lowest lines in Figure 14.1. The square boxes in the middle of the graph (at $250) correspond to the values calculated in Table 14.2. Note that as the expected initial allowance price increases above $250, doing nothing (the first alternative) becomes increasingly more expensive, while the scrubber alternative looks relatively more attractive. Above a "crossover" allowance price of $323, the scrubber appears to be a cheaper compliance alternative than doing nothing.

Figure 14.1 basically summarizes the results of a static NPV decision analysis in determining the least-cost compliance alternative, allowing comparison of the NPVs of all six alternatives. The "least-cost envelope" is shown by the broken dark line near the top of the graph. For 1995 allowance prices less than $150 per ton, Bowen's least-cost strategy is A1, namely, to continue to burn high-sulfur coal, unscrubbed, and to buy allowances. At 1995 allowance prices greater than $329, the optimal strategy in this context is A6, namely, to switch to low-sulfur coal in Phase One and then install a scrubber in time to operate using high-sulfur coal in Phase Two. At prices between $150 and $329, the least-cost strategy is to switch to low-sulfur coal for both phases (A3).

The traditional capital budgeting framework, however, because of its essentially static nature, cannot accommodate the value of flexibility or real options embedded in the various compliance strategies. This limitation is well understood by utility managers and regulatory officials, who for the time being generally rely on qualitative judgements concerning those option values. According to one recent policy study:

> The methods that optimize expected values or minimize variances already allow some of this desired flexibility to be incorporated. They, however, do not adequately capture the value of flexibility or provide a precise standard for comparing the flexibility of different compliance plans... A qualitative assessment of flexibility, based on the planner's experience and best judgement, may have to be used to evaluate compliance plans.[11]

Even the "pseudo-dynamic" nature of "phasing" the decision by allowing hybrid alternatives over the two phases (like A4, A5, and A6) does not fully address the dynamics of management's decision flexibility or its option value. The sets of NPVs shown in Figure 14.1 represent *commitment* to given strategies, regardless of any realized deviations in the future price of allowances. For example, the sixth alternative, "SWITCH, then SCRUB," is best if the starting allowance price is indeed $350. If the price then falls below $329, management would want to change to strategy 3 (just SWITCH), simply *not* scrubbing in the second phase. However, the values calculated up-front for each strategy do not allow for such managerial discretion. There is no consideration for the option value of being able to "move around the least-cost envelope" in an optimal manner. The quantification of this value is the subject of the next section.

## 14.4 A REAL OPTIONS ANALYSIS

Having examined the standard capital budgeting approach, we now turn to a real options analysis of the problem. Recently, various authors have integrated the value of important strategic flexibility and clearly defined options into the traditional capital budgeting decision.[12]

In this section, we attempt to simplify the complex investment decision, while applying option-based valuation techniques for dealing with the major uncertainty regarding the price of allowances. Using a financial option analogy here, the scrubber could be likened to the underlying share of stock, and the allowances it produces to dividends. The value of the scrubber depends directly on the present value of its "dividends"—and thus, on the allowance price. Bowen holds a call option to acquire the scrubber, with an exercise price of $800 million, the investment cost. This option "expires" in 2016 when the plant is abandoned.

The standard NPV rule is to invest when NPV > 0, which occurs here when the present cost of the scrubber matches the present cost of doing nothing (the "crossover" point at a $323 allowance price). However, investing in the scrubber constitutes early exercise of the option. In options terminology, rote application of the standard NPV approach would result in exercise as soon as the option was "in the money." In effect, however, the NPV must meet or exceed the option value in order to invest, since the opportunity cost of the option given up is not already considered as a relevant cost in the NPV analysis.

The option value derives substantially from the uncertainty in the price of the allowances.[13] Thus, one would begin by specifying the uncertainty of the price process, using a binomial tree as a rough approximation of the relatively continuous diffusion of allowance prices over time. The allowance price binomial tree is based on an initial price of $250, and annual price nodes reflecting a geometric price process with a 20 percent annual standard deviation and a 5 percent risk-free interest rate, with a risk-neutral equivalent probability of 0.5. The volatility parameter is the most important, but there is no real price data yet to generate an estimate. This will improve as the planned CBOT spot and futures markets for allowances develop. The assumed 20 percent standard deviation is too low a figure to explain the sporadic but volatile pricing during negotiated sales and auctions in the 1992–1993 period, but the uncertainty during this initial period is unusually high and is not likely to persist in the long term. At this level, allowances would be more volatile than equity markets, but less volatile than many individual stocks and commodities.

The allowance prices generated were used, at every node, in valuing the first two alternatives in Table 14.3. In Panel A1, the base case (DO NOTHING) is valued, with the binomial tree showing the present value of doing nothing for each future point in time and allowance price realization. Recall that the value of this alternative is simply the present value of the allowances required to be purchased. The valuation in this case is somewhat more complicated than in other option problems, since the uncertain asset does not have a market-traded spot or futures price. If no steps to reduce pollution are taken, the present cost of compliance will change over time in conjunction with the diffusion of the allowance price. The current value is estimated in the leftmost node of the tree to be -$266 million, confirming the value separately determined in Table 14.2.

A similar tree is shown for the scrubber alternative in Panel A2 of Table 14.3. Here, we calculate the present value of all future cash flows assuming the scrubber is installed *that year*.[14] Note that if allowance prices increase, the project value gets less negative, even turning positive for extremely high price levels. The incremental NPV of the scrubber at each node is found by subtracting the value in Panel A1 from that in Panel A2, and turns positive only in the top portion of the table. We also assumed that annual increases in the scrubber price are consistent with the drift of the price process of the allowances—failure to do this would be unrealistic and result in the "option to wait" looking unfairly attractive. Also, we arbitrarily allow no investment in the final year of the plant.

Before addressing the full complexity of management's decision by introducing the low-sulfur alternative, we first value the compliance costs given the option to either do nothing or to invest in the scrubber, at any time. Working backward recursively, at each node a comparison was made between doing nothing or investing in a scrubber. Such comparison takes into account the value of the scrubber investment (from Table 14.3), versus the option value of doing nothing, which incorporates both of the *next* period's possible values and any current cash flows. Except at extremely low allowance price nodes near plant termination, the option values of doing nothing now but keeping the option to invest open generally exceed the values of committing to doing nothing forever shown in Table 14.3, Panel A1. In 1992, the option value, or value of optimal compliance, is estimated at -$152 million.

This option-based cost of compliance ($152 million) compares favorably with committing to a fixed strategy of doing nothing ($266 million) or installing the scrubber immediately ($436 million). Even though the option to buy the scrubber is out of the money (at a $250 allowance price), the

## Table 14.3
## Binomial Present-Value Trees for Two Alternatives—
## Do Nothing (Panel A1) and Install Scrubbers (Panel A2)

A1:  Do Nothing (Scrubbers Never Installed)

| 1992 | 1993 | 1994 | 1995 | 1996 | 1997 | 1998 | 1999 | 2000 | ... | 2014 | 2015 |
|------|------|------|------|------|------|------|------|------|-----|------|------|
| -266 | -366 | -504 | -692 | -947 | -1295 | -1772 | -2423 | -3314 | ... | -34818 | -30374 |
|  | -249 | -342 | -471 | -644 | -881 | -1205 | -1648 | -2254 |  | -23676 | -20654 |
|  |  | -233 | -320 | -438 | -599 | -819 | -1120 | -1532 |  | -16100 | -14045 |
|  |  |  | -218 | -298 | -407 | -557 | -762 | -1042 |  | -10948 | -9550 |
|  |  |  |  | -203 | -277 | -379 | -518 | -709 |  | -7445 | -6494 |
|  |  |  |  |  | -188 | -258 | -352 | -482 |  | -5062 | -4416 |
|  |  |  |  |  |  | -175 | -240 | -328 |  | -3442 | -3003 |
|  |  |  |  |  |  |  | -163 | -223 |  | -2341 | -2042 |
|  |  |  |  |  |  |  |  | -152 |  |  |  |
|  |  |  |  |  |  |  |  |  |  | -11 | -9 |
|  |  |  |  |  |  |  |  |  |  | -7 | -6 |
|  |  |  |  |  |  |  |  |  |  |  | -4 |

A2:  Install Scrubbers (Scrubber Installed That Year)

| 1992 | 1993 | 1994 | 1995 | 1996 | 1997 | 1998 | 1999 | 2000 | ... | 2014 | 2015 |
|------|------|------|------|------|------|------|------|------|-----|------|------|
| -436 | -396 | -320 | -193 | -54 | 119 | 326 | 565 | 824 | ... | 18843 | 15517 |
|  | -530 | -504 | -447 | -372 | -277 | -160 | -25 | 122 |  | 11468 | 9084 |
|  |  | -630 | -619 | -589 | -546 | -491 | -426 | -356 |  | 6454 | 4709 |
|  |  |  | -737 | -736 | -729 | -716 | -698 | -680 |  | 3044 | 1734 |
|  |  |  |  | -836 | -854 | -869 | -884 | -901 |  | 725 | -288 |
|  |  |  |  |  | -938 | -973 | -1010 | -1051 |  | -852 | -1664 |
|  |  |  |  |  |  | -1044 | -1096 | -1153 |  | -1924 | -2599 |
|  |  |  |  |  |  |  | -1154 | -1222 |  | -2653 | -3235 |
|  |  |  |  |  |  |  |  | -1270 |  |  |  |
|  |  |  |  |  |  |  |  |  |  | -4195 | -4581 |
|  |  |  |  |  |  |  |  |  |  | -4198 | -4583 |
|  |  |  |  |  |  |  |  |  |  |  | -4584 |

option still has a net present value of $114 million ($152 versus $266). This option component is no second-order effect—it is significant in comparison to the magnitude of compliance costs being considered. Standard DCF approaches would have ignored this value but would have resulted in the correct decision in this case (if the allowance price is $250, do not buy the scrubber). From the binomial option value trees we estimated that the earliest possible "exercise" or scrubber purchase would be in 1996, and then only if the allowance price has had four years of positive surprises.

As noted, the option value is sensitive to the allowance price. The allowance price tree used here was initiated at an expected price of $250, yet even this current value is unknown. What if other values were used? We know that the option value (net of the do-nothing value, i.e., row 2 minus row 3 in Table 14.4) should increase with higher allowance prices. We also should surmise that the option will be bounded below by the values of the two static alternatives. A summary of the NPV for the DO NOTHING and SCRUB alternatives, along with the option value, is given in Table 14.4. The values we are already familiar with are listed below the allowance price of $250. At very low allowance prices, the option value is very close to the cost of doing nothing—the option itself is nearly worthless, being so far out of the money. Around the "crossover" or at-the-money point of $323, the option has considerable value, being about $200 million greater than either alternative alone.[15] As the allowance price gets very high, the option is in the money, and closes in on (but is still higher than) the value of the scrubber. This is illustrated in Figure 14.2.

The bottom line in Table 14.4 also shows the early exercise decision, indicating the impact of the allowance price and option value on the investment decision. For example, the entry under $250 reads "u96," meaning that the first optimal scrubber purchase does not occur until 1996, and then only in the very highest node. At an initial allowance price of $350, "u95uu96" indicates that a scrubber purchase will take place if the highest node is reached in 1995, or if the second-highest node is reached in 1996. Note that the standard DCF analysis would have indicated a scrubber purchase if the allowance price was above $323, whereas the option solution puts off the purchase, waiting for several further increases in the allowance price, even if the price already started well higher than $323.[16] Failure to account for the option value may result in investment in equipment at far too low a value, destroying considerable value in the process.

As the choice set is not limited to the DO NOTHING and SCRUB alternatives, we now expand the analysis to allow for a SWITCH to low-sulfur coal. This complicates the valuation somewhat, although we simplify by prohibiting a reverse-shift from SWITCH back to DO NOTHING (this eliminates path dependency, but underestimates the option value). As was done for the scrubber installation in Table 14.3, we calculate the present

**Table 14.4**

**Sensitivity Analysis of Option Value and Project NPV for the First Two Alternatives at Initial Allowance Prices Ranging from $100 to $600 (Present Values Are in Millions of Dollars)**

| Allowance Price | $100 | $150 | $200 | $250 | $300 | $350 | $400 | $450 | $500 | $550 | $600 |
|---|---|---|---|---|---|---|---|---|---|---|---|
| Option Value | -101 | -134 | -151 | -152 | -140 | -116 | -82 | -42 | 5 | 56 | 109 |
| A1: Do Nothing NPV | -107 | -160 | -213 | -266 | -320 | -373 | -426 | -479 | -533 | -586 | -639 |
| A2: Scrub NPV | -619 | -558 | -497 | -436 | -375 | -314 | -253 | -192 | -131 | -70 | -9 |
| Installation Timing | u00 | u98 | u97 | u96 | u96 | u95 uu96 | u95 uu96 | u95 uu96 | uu95 uu96 | uu95 uuu96 | uu95 uuu96 |

*Note*: The last row of the table provides the optimal investment timing schedule for installing the scrubber. For example, if the initial (1995) allowance price is $ 350, the entry "u95/uu96" indicates that the scrubber would not be purchased unless the one highest price node in 1995 is reached, or either of the two highest price nodes in 1996 is reached.

value of compliance at each node if the plant converts to low-sulfur coal and never installs a scrubber (the option to "upgrade" to a scrubber later will be investigated below). At an allowance price of $250, this alternative appears to be the best, giving an NPV of -$168 million, as already noted in Table 14.2.

With all three compliance modes analyzed, we apply the techniques discussed above to analyze the full option; the results of this option valuation are displayed in Table 14.5. At each node, a comparison is made as to the best course of action; in 2015, for example, this amounts to a simple selection of the least costly of the three alternatives.[17] The 5 **boldface** entries at the highest allowance prices (above the solid-line boundary) indicate scrubber purchases; the next 9 (only 4 shown) *italicized* entries reflect a switch to low-sulfur coal, and the bottom 10 entries (only 3 shown) show that nothing is done at the lowest allowance prices. Working backward through the tree, many of the values around the middle of the table exceed all the respective values of the individual alternatives, reflecting the option value inherent in the future opportunities emanating from those nodes. In 1992, the option value or value of the optimal compliance strategy is seen in the left-most node to be -$126 million.

This analysis was done based on an initial $250 allowance price. Table 14.6 provides a summary of all values across a range ($100-$600) of starting prices. The DO NOTHING (A1) and SCRUB (A2) values remain the same

Figure 14.2
NPV of the Project as a Function of the Initial (1995) Allowance Price for the First Two
Alternatives—Do Nothing (A1) and Install Scrubbers (A2)

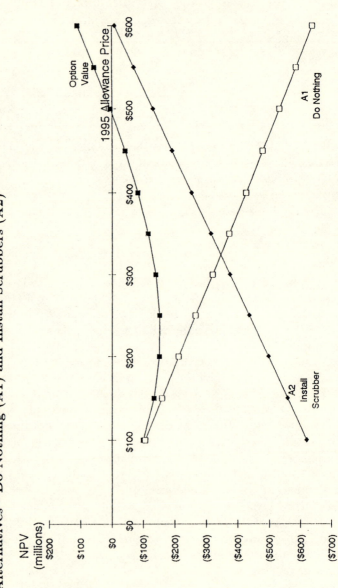

**Table 14.5**
**Option Valuation Binomial Tree with Exercise Schedule
(Allowing for Do Nothing, Scrub, and Switch Alternatives)**

| 1992 | 1993 | 1994 | 1995 | 1996 | 1997 | 1998 | 1999 | 2000 | 2001 | ... | 2014 | 2015 |
|------|------|------|------|------|------|------|------|------|------|-----|------|------|
| -126 | -143 | -148 | -128 | -53 | 119 | 326 | 565 | 824 | 1348 | ... | 18843 | 15517 |
|  | -147 | -181 | -214 | -236 | -229 | -160 | -25 | 122 | 446 |  | 11468 | 9084 |
|  |  | -159 | -204 | -254 | -308 | -357 | -385 | -356 | -167 |  | 6454 | 4709 |
|  |  |  | -164 | -213 | -274 | -346 | -430 | -519 | *-511* |  | 3044 | 1734 |
|  |  |  |  | -164 | -215 | -281 | -363 | -465 | -531 |  | 725 | -288 |
|  |  |  |  |  | -161 | -213 | -280 | -367 | -437 |  | -852 | *-1547* |
|  |  |  |  |  |  | -157 | -209 | -277 | -337 |  | *-1253* | *-1102* |
|  |  |  |  |  |  |  | -152 | -203 | -253 |  | *-907* | *-799* |
|  |  |  |  |  |  |  |  | -145 | -183 |  | . | . |
|  |  |  |  |  |  |  |  |  | -129 . |  | . | . |
|  |  |  |  |  |  |  |  |  |  | . | *-277* | *-250* |
|  |  |  |  |  |  |  |  |  |  | . | *-231* | *-202* |
|  |  |  |  |  |  |  |  |  |  |  | . | . |
|  |  |  |  |  |  |  |  |  |  |  | -7 | -6 |
|  |  |  |  |  |  |  |  |  |  |  |  | -4 |

*Note:* **Bold-face numbers** (above the solid line boundary) indicate nodes when installing scrubbers is optimal; *italicized numbers* (above the dotted line boundary) indicate optimal conversion to low-sulfur coal.

as in Table 14.4; a new row for SWITCH to Low-Sulfur (A3) has been added, and the option values have all increased due to the additional flexibility. These results are illustrated in Figure 14.3, with the option value representing the true value (cost) of the compliance opportunities available. Note that the SWITCH alternative (A3) "cuts across" the two extreme alternatives, appearing (as in Figure 14.1) to be the most reasonable and immediate alternative for an extremely broad range of allowance prices.[18] However, a look at optimal investment activity in Table 14.5 and the last line of Table 14.6 reveals that the low-sulfur conversion alternative is not as important as it seems. The binomial option "tree" shows that there is very little early conversion as the optimal decision (the first italicized entry is a single node in 2001). The "Installation Timing" row also shows that early conversion is not a serious consideration, except at the very highest initial allowance levels, and then only in the highest-price node in the third year. While simple DCF analysis points to immediate conversion as the optimal

Figure 14.3
NPV of the Project as a Function of the Initial (1995) Allowance Price for All Three
Basic Alternatives

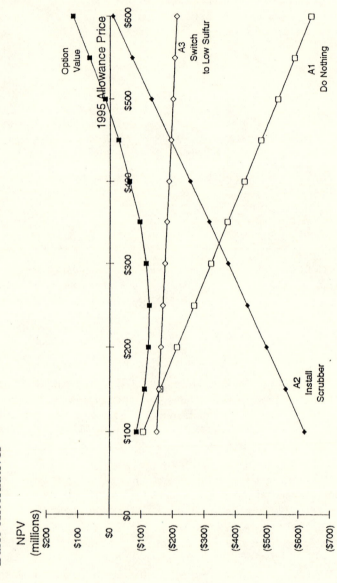

## Table 14.6
### Sensitivity Analysis of Option Value and Project NPV for All Three Basic Alternatives at Initial Allowance Prices Ranging from $100 to $600 (Present Values are in Millions of Dollars)

| Allowance Price | $100 | $150 | $200 | $250 | $300 | $350 | $400 | $450 | $500 | $550 | $600 |
|---|---|---|---|---|---|---|---|---|---|---|---|
| Option Value | -85 | -110 | -123 | -126 | -114 | -95 | -62 | -27 | 15 | 64 | 117 |
| A1: Do Nothing NPV | -107 | -160 | -213 | -266 | -320 | -373 | -426 | -479 | -533 | -586 | -639 |
| A2: Scrub NPV | -619 | -558 | -497 | -436 | -375 | -314 | -253 | -192 | -131 | -70 | -9 |
| A3: Switch NPV | -150 | -156 | -162 | -168 | -174 | -181 | -187 | -193 | -199 | -205 | -211 |
| Installation Timing | | u99 | u98 | u97 | u96 | u95 u96 | u95 uu96 | u95 uu96 | *94 uu95 uu96 | *94 uu95 uuu96 | *94 uu95 uuu96 |

Note: The last row of the table provides the optimal timing for the invest-ment alternatives. For example, if the initial allowance price is $500, the entry "*94/uu95/uu96" indicates that switching to low-sulfur coal would not occur un-til the one highest price node in 1994 is reached; a scrubber will not be purchased until either of the two highest price nodes in 1995 or 1996 is reached.

solution for any allowance price above $150, consideration of management flexibility pushes the need for conversion off to levels of beginning prices well above $500.

Intuitively, when faced with commitment to one of two extreme alter-natives (DO NOTHING or SCRUB), an intermediate choice looks very attractive. However, this is clearly an artificial construct, since the choice of extremes is not really a lifelong commitment but a long-lasting series of opportunities. Thus, the role of the SWITCH alternative, which was to provide a compromise, has already been effectively captured by the oppor-tunity (OPTION) to wait and decide later as uncertainty is resolved over time.

Another way to view the reduced importance of the low-sulfur conver-sion alternative is to look at the impact of its introduction on the cost of compliance. In the typical DCF analysis, the low-sulfur conversion provides present value benefits of about $100 million over the next best alternative (compare -168 to -266 at a price of $250 in Table 14.6). However, the actual increase in project value due to adding a SWITCH alternative is only $26 million (compare the Table 14.4 option value of -152 to the new option value of -126). The option of waiting has already provided much of the benefit to be gained by conversion, the other intermediate solution.[19] Thus, consideration of real option value not only seriously impacts both the valuation and operating decisions in a capital budgeting problem, it also sheds a different light on how we think about particular alternatives and their role in the process.

## 14.5   OTHER CONSIDERATIONS/CONCLUSIONS

We have so far addressed only the impact of allowance price uncertainty, through the options paradigm, on the capital budgeting and pollution compliance decision process. In this final section, we consider some additional regulatory and political complexities inherent in Clean Air Act compliance for utilities.

Several other complexities arising from the regulatory and political arenas also impinge on utilities' strategic decisions and can be analyzed within the real options framework. These can be grouped into three broad categories: (1) federal regulatory policy relating to allowance trading; (2) local regulatory policy (in public service or public utility commissions) affecting the allocation of cost and risk between utilities' shareholders and ratepayers; and (3) strategic behavior by utilities or states.

Rules governing allowance trading, and hence the value of allowances, are uncertain. The effect of regulatory uncertainty on the expected value of allowance prices is ambiguous. For example, if the probability rises that the U.S. Environmental Protection Agency (EPA) will issue rules that reduce incentives for nonutility sources to enter the market as allowance sellers, the expected price of allowances would presumably rise; if the probability rises that EPA will issue rules that make it easier for sources to obtain exemptions, this might lower the expected price. An increase in either probability, however, will increase the uncertainty about the allowance price. This price uncertainty, in turn, creates increased real option value from wait-and-see strategies. If spot and futures markets (planned tentatively for 1994) exist in these storable allowances, rational expectations concerning these uncertainties should already be reflected in market prices.

On the other hand, this sort of uncertainty may enhance risk-averse managers' tendencies not to rely on external allowance markets at all. Many companies (including Georgia Power and its parent) own multiple regulated plants, raising the possibility of intrafirm trading in allowances. The economic cost considerations of such trading are identical to arm's-length market trades but may appear quite different to risk-averse managers. Risk aversion may account for management's desire to be slightly long in the permit market at the firm level (i.e., to participate minimally in external allowance markets, and then only as a seller). A possible agency tension therefore exists between the implications of the real option approach and the traditional managerial viewpoint.

Rate-making procedures at the local level also affect utility decision making, even more profoundly than federal rules (and in ways that may not be incorporated into equilibrium allowance prices). Within the capital budgeting framework, if a utility knows for certain that it can include investments in pollution control equipment in its rate base, this will increase its incentives to comply by installing scrubbers; if fuel adjustment clauses are available, this will increase utility incentives to switch fuels. We have for simplicity assumed that utility *revenue* is invariant to the choice of compliance methods, and that is clearly not the case in most jurisdictions.

Finally, strategic behavior by utilities or government can affect the real option values in Clean Air Act compliance. We have not applied any equilibrium models to incorporate the feedback mechanism of firms', suppliers', or other actors' behavior into the process. There are also political concerns that may lead firms to pursue a seemingly suboptimal strategy in one dimension in order to "grease the skids" in another area; these effects are generally difficult to disentangle. Regardless of the difficulty of incorporating various complexities, however, we still feel it is valuable to know the costs and benefits of the basic quantifiable choices facing management.

We find that the application of real option valuation to pollution compliance is a current and real managerial problem of significant magnitude, and one where more traditional techniques may miss the boat, both in concept and in magnitude. If real option value is ignored, decisions under uncertainty will be based excessively on static considerations, and will not properly reflect the measurable dynamic advantages of strategic flexibility. As seen in the case of the Bowen plant, this may actually change the optimal investment decision. Short-sighted or poorly timed investments may result in mildly positive NPVs when a full dynamic consideration could better capture the full value. Indeed, a reasonable-looking "intermediate" solution may look far less impressive when viewed in the light of management's full discretion.

## ACKNOWLEDGMENTS

We wish to thank Carliss Baldwin and Lenos Trigeorgis, along with participants at several seminars, for their helpful comments. The support of the Harvard Business School Division of Research is gratefully acknowledged.

## NOTES

1. See the U.S. Clean Air Act Amendments of 1990, Public Law number 101-549, 104 Stat 2399 (1990).

2. For an overview, see Tietenberg (1992).

3. The argument is, of course, more complicated if the marginal benefits of pollution control are unequal across sources. For example, suppose some sources of a given pollutant were directly upwind from a residential community, and others downwind; suppose, also, that the local effects of the pollution on the health of nearby residents were important. Then, the allocation of the permits across sources would matter a great deal. This kind of problem, however, is held to be less serious for acid rain than for many other air pollution issues. Sulfur dioxide emissions can travel hundreds of miles before contributing to acid precipitation, so the precise location of sources matters less than, say, for acute airborne toxins or carcinogens.

4. The total annual sulfur dioxide emissions from U.S. electric utility plants in the mid-1980s amounted to about 16 million tons. This figure is supposed to fall to roughly 12 million tons during Phase One, and to 9 million tons in Phase Two. See Reinhardt (1992, p. 10).

5. The background for this case is in Reinhardt (1992).

6. There are several deeper issues concerning the development of this discount rate, but they are beyond the focus of this chapter.

7. For his theory of nonrenewable resources, see Solow (1974).

8. In considering the problem from an options standpoint, convenience yield may become significant, but it should be zero if, as the traditional capital budgeting methodology essentially assumes, only expected values matter.

9. See the U.S. Clean Air Act Amendments of 1990, section 416(c), 104 Stat 2627.

10. The net present cost of the third alternative, switching fuels, is $168 million.

11. See Rose et al. (1992, p. 84).

12. See the reference section for some of this work.

13. It derives, to a certain extent, from other uncertainties as well, such as changes in the relative prices of coal, and in interest rates and scrubber prices. These complicating factors are not directly addressed in this chapter.

14. Here we ignore the important problem of time-to-build.

15. Recall from the discussion of Figure 14.1 that the NPVs of the two alternatives are equal, or "crossover," at an allowance price of $323.

16. This result is partly driven by the lack of time-to-build, since there is re-

ally no benefit to building the scrubber early (compliance begins in 1995). An approximation would be to examine where the option analysis would have the scrubber in place by 1995 at the "midpoint" node. This occurs around an initial allowance price of $550, where the scrubber would be installed in 2 of 4 nodes in 1995, and 3 of 5 nodes in 1996. This is still *substantially* above the "at the money" or DCF investment point of $323.

17. Once a scrubber is installed, there are no further decisions; in that sense some of the numbers in the upper right of Table 14.5 are meaningless, in that a scrubber would never actually be installed at such later time, already having been installed earlier.

18. Note that "hybrid" alternatives 4, 5, and 6 are subsumed in the dynamics of the option "tree." The "BURN then SCRUB in 2000" alternative is like the third node in the year 2000 in Table 14.5, except that unlike the commitment to buy the scrubber (implicit in that alternative), the option value *also* reflects the opportunity to invest in 1997–1999 if allowance prices are even higher, or to "cancel" the purchase in 2000 if the allowance price falls short.

19. Such option interactions whereby the incremental value of an option is reduced in the presence of other real options are discussed in Trigeorgis (1993a).

# Chapter 15

# Optimal Land Development

## Laura Quigg

*This paper presents a model that values land as a real option, incorporating the option to wait to develop the property. This option to wait has value in an uncertain economy because land is more than just a site for constructing a particular structure at a particular time. Effectively, a landowner holds an American-style option to develop the land at an optimally chosen time in the future. With much uncertainty, it may pay to hold the land vacant, even in the presence of thriving real estate markets. In addition to a valuation model, we develop rules for an optimal investment strategy and present useful comparative statics results.*

## 15.1 INTRODUCTION

The value of a parcel of land can be determined as the net present value (NPV) of the stream of returns generated by the project that constitutes the highest and best use of the land. According to traditional capital budgeting, the investor determines the current worth of these rents based on the information available at the decision date. While it is possible to compare the value of an investment made today with one made tomorrow, or with a different-size project, the standard decision rule ignores the value of the option to delay the investment decision itself until a later date.

The model presented in this chapter values land as a real option, incorporating the option to wait to develop the property. This option to wait has value in an uncertain economy because land is more than just a site for constructing a particular structure at a particular time. A landowner holds an American-style option to build at an optimally chosen time in the future. The underlying asset for this option is one of several buildings, with exercise price equal to their respective construction costs. We here assume that there is a single underlying structure, although it is straightforward to extend the model to include the option to develop the most profitable of two or several risky assets (i.e., the alternative buildings that could be constructed). The resulting valuation formula has the advantage, relative to traditional net present value methods, that it is independent of investor preferences or a risk-adjusted discount rate, and that it is dependent only on observable or estimable variables. In effect, the valuation formula calculates the present value of cash flows under the explicit assumption that the investor follows an optimal strategy.

This analysis permits the formulation of rules about the timing and location of development and the derivation of comparative statics results. In particular, one well-known option-pricing result is that an increase in volatility, as measured by the price variance of the underlying asset, *ceteris paribus*, increases the value of the option (land) and increases the critical price of the underlying asset (building) at which it is optimal to exercise the option to build. An implication of this result is that policy actions meant to encourage growth may have the opposite effect if they result in increased uncertainty. With increased uncertainty, the increased option value of the land may be partially offset by a reduced building value, since future rents are discounted at a higher risk-adjusted rate. However, if this uncertainty represents unpriced, unsystematic risk, it will have no effect on the building price, and the land value will be higher.

Building cycles are usually explained through changes in the expected value of investments. Development lags serve as the primary culprit for severe swings in such cycles. However, other explanations may arise from situations in which the developer exercises the option to build. The decision to build is precipitated in our analysis through increased costs of holding vacant land (such as property taxes) or a reduction in the variance of developed property values. Building cycles occur because properties in a given urban area usually have highly correlated price processes. Therefore, when new information shows that it is profitable to exercise the option to build on one plot of land, it may also make it worthwhile to develop other tracts, leading to a building boom. This model incorporates the optimal timing decision that gives rise to building cycles that previous models ignore. On the other hand, when it is optimal to abandon one property, others in the neighborhood often experience the same pressures, leading to urban decay.

The presence of vacant land in thriving real estate markets is considered an anomaly in a certain world, but not when such land is viewed as an option under uncertainty. In an uncertain world, it may pay to hold the land vacant until an optimally chosen future date, even if building a particular structure now appears to provide higher profits than waiting.

Several papers have addressed the problem of optimal land development under uncertainty. In independent work, Williams (1991b) valued land as an option with stochastic construction costs and calculated the optimal times at which to build or abandon the property. Williams also allowed the developer initially to choose the optimal building size.[1]

Capozza and Sick (1992) combined the monocentric city model with the options pricing methodology. They evaluated the option to convert agricultural land into urban land, expanding at the fringes of an urban area. Households maximize their indirect utility functions by choosing the optimal distance between their residence and the central business district, weighing transportation costs against land rent. Capozza and Sick related the property values to the stream of future rents, separating systematic and unsystematic risks and attributing an expected return premium only to the former.[2]

In a binomial model, Titman (1985) also priced land as an option on a building. Titman presented an example in which the developer has a choice between different-sized structures and examined some comparative statics. This chapter uses the same methodology as Titman's paper, except that the option has an infinite life and can be exercised continuously, with a number of extensions and with demonstrated locational implications.

The chapter draws primarily on the natural resources literature. Of particular interest are the results derived by Tourinho (1979), who determined the value of a reserve of a natural resource given that the resource price is stochastic. He valued the reserve as a perpetual option on the extracted resource, and determined rules whereby a changing exercise price (extraction costs) and holding costs permit optimal early exercise. Later research (Brennan and Schwartz, 1985a; McDonald and Siegel, 1986; and Paddock, Siegel, and Smith, 1988) has examined various extensions to incorporate the option to shut down or abandon a project.

The chapter will proceed as follows. Section 15.2 develops a simple valuation model and interprets comparative statics results in the urban land context. The model accounts for the fact that even though land may be viewed as a contingent claim on one or several buildings, the buildings themselves may not be traded. However, we assume we can trade some portfolio of securities, the price of which is perfectly correlated with the building price process. In section 15.3 we relax that assumption to allow for a less-than-perfect, but constant, correlation with the particular structure price. Section 15.4 further demonstrates that the model continues to be valid whether the developer builds to sell immediately, or to hold. Section 15.5 incorporates stochastic construction costs into the model, replacing the initial assumption that costs are constant or changing at a deterministic rate. In the last section we conclude.

## 15.2 THE MODEL

This section presents a model to value land as an option under our most restrictive assumptions. Land is viewed here as a perpetual American option with a price $C$. The underlying asset, $S$, is the value of a developed structure discounted for a development lag. The exercise price, $X$, is the construction cost. The standard evaluation of this option using arbitrage-based methods requires a set of standard assumptions.[3]

The value of the underlying asset (i.e., the building), $S$, is assumed to follow a geometric Brownian motion with constant drift, $\mu$, and known variance, $\sigma_S^2$:[4]

$$dS/S = \mu dt + \sigma_S dz_S, \tag{15.1}$$

where $dz_S$ is the increment of a standard Wiener process.

We further assume an environment conducive for continuous riskless hedging; in other words, we assume that there is a portfolio that is perfectly correlated with the value of the building (the underlying asset on the property site). We will refer to it as the traded (correlated) portfolio.[5] The traded portfolio has a price, $P$, which is also assumed to follow a geometric Brownian motion, as follows:

$$dP/P = \alpha dt + \sigma_S dz_S. \tag{15.2}$$

Both the underlying asset and the traded portfolio are driven by the same Brownian motion, $z$, because they are assumed to be perfectly correlated. Furthermore, the traded portfolio is leveraged to give the same variance, $\sigma_S^2$, as our potential building. For the two to have the same drift (so that $\alpha = \mu$), however, some additional assumptions are necessary.[6]

The assumption that there is a traded portfolio is employed to justify the use of arbitrage-based valuation in a market with obvious friction. We are not required to trade the building (or the traded portfolio) to hedge the options. It is only necessary that the prices observed are as if the market were complete. If the real estate investment of traded firms is chosen in a manner consistent with value maximization, then real estate prices will be determined in equilibrium as if markets were really complete. Leland (1985) developed an approach for dealing with transactions costs; consequently, the violation of this assumption does not necessarily invalidate the options pricing argument.

In this section, we assume that the landowner incurs constant holding costs, $H$, which might consist of property taxes, property maintenance costs, or impending restrictive regulations. These costs of holding the option are analogous to the forgone dividends from not exercising a stock option and are necessary to ensure exercise of a perpetual option with deterministic exercise price (Merton, 1973). Stochastic construction costs (exercise prices) are also sufficient to ensure development. This notion of holding costs could be expanded to include the forgone convenience yield. The convenience yield can be viewed as the value of being able to profit from temporary local shortages through ownership of the physical commodity. The officebuilding owner has the ability to capture the benefits of temporary price variations, but the land owner would not be able to respond and build quickly enough to do so. Tourinho (1979) solved this option valuation problem with holding costs. He shows that the necessary and sufficient condition for exercise eventually to occur is that $H/r > X$, where $H$ are the holding costs per unit time, $r$ is the constant interest rate, and $X$ is the exercise price.[7]

We begin our analysis with constant holding costs as follows. Since a perpetual call is a function only of the underlying asset value, $S$, we have, by Ito's Lemma:

$$dC = \frac{1}{2}\sigma_S^2 S^2 C_{SS}\,dt + C_S\,dS - H\,dt. \tag{15.3}$$

To value the call, we can form a hedge portfolio, $V$, in which we hold one call and short $C_S$ traded portfolios. We have, again by Ito's Lemma:

$$dV = (\frac{1}{2}\sigma_S^2 S^2 C_{SS} - H)dt. \tag{15.4}$$

As portfolio $V$ is nonstochastic, it must earn the riskless rate, namely,

$$dV = (-C_S S + C)rdt. \tag{15.5}$$

Equating (15.4) and (15.5), obtains:

$$\frac{1}{2}\sigma_S^2 S^2 C_{SS} + rSC_S - rC - H = 0. \tag{15.6}$$

This ordinary differential equation can be solved by imposing four boundary conditions.[8] First, an assumption of free disposal restricts the option value to be nonnegative. Therefore, there is a structure price, $Z \geq 0$, such that $C(S) = 0$ for any $S \leq Z$ and $C(Z) = 0$. The positive value of the option is more than countered by the negative effect of the holding costs, and it is optimal to abandon the land when its value declines to $Z$. In addition, smooth pasting can also be required at $Z$ since the holders of options can be assumed to choose $Z$ optimally, giving the second boundary condition, $C'(Z) = 0$. Third, for sufficiently large $S$, the owner will want to build. If $W$ is the price at which it is optimal to invest, then $C(W) = W - X$. Finally, we can assume that owners decide optimally on when to build, so that we can require high contact at $W$: $C'(W) = 1$. Solving, we obtain:

$$C(S) = \begin{cases} 0 & \text{if } S < Z \\ A_1 S + A_2 S^u - H/r & \text{if } Z \leq S \leq W \\ S - X & \text{if } S > W \end{cases} \tag{15.7}$$

where    $u = -2r/\sigma_S^2$, and
$$A_1 = [1 - (1 - Xr/H)^{(u-1)/u}]^{-1}$$
$$A_2 = -A_1/uZ^{u-1} = 1 - A_1/uW^{u-1}$$
$$W = u/(u-1)(X - H/r)(1 - A_1)^{-1}$$
$$Z = u/(u-1)(H/r)[1 - (1 - Xr/H)^{(u-1)/u}].$$

We can derive several comparative statics results from this equation. First, for $Z < S < W$, $C(S) > max(0, S-X)$, namely, the value of the land exceeds what the owner would realize if he or she developed immediately. Therefore, when the current price is in the interval between the optimal abandonment value, $Z$, and the optimal development value, $W$, the land is more valuable if left vacant. In our model, vacant land is an option that has a value in itself. Even though it appears that profits are maximized with immediate development, the uncertainty of those profits may imply that the optimal strategy is, in fact, to wait.

Second, the effect of an increase in uncertainty is to increase the value of the land, other variables held constant. Intuitively, uncertainty adds a premium to the economic rent generated by the eventual exercise of the option, $max(0, S - X)$. This premium is like insurance that protects the owner against a decrease in the price of the completed structure's value. It can be shown that an increase in variance causes $Z$ to decrease and $W$ to increase, so that the building price at which it is optimal to build is now higher and the price at which it is optimal to abandon the land is lower.

Since different lots have different optimal investment and abandonment schedules, $W$ and $Z$, as given in Equation (15.7), these equations can be used to determine where and when to build or abandon property. A parcel for which $W \leq S$ should be developed immediately, while one for which $S < W$ should be left undeveloped until the current structure's price increases to the threshold $W$. Our model introduces price variance as a factor determining these thresholds. Builders develop certain tracts because they have lower optimal investment thresholds, $W$. These differing thresholds, in turn, may explain why there is further investment in already developed areas, rather than new development on more remote and uncertain land with higher $W$s. We also see large-scale abandonment where properties with correlated price processes have concurrently reached the abandonment threshold, $Z$. This threshold is attained more quickly when it becomes more certain that the property will never yield a profit. Our model shows that price variance has spatial implications, both in terms of development and abandonment.

We would also expect that it may be optimal to exercise the option to build on different land parcels at the same time. If the determining variables lower the optimal development threshold, $W$, for one building, it would also be optimal to begin construction on projects with correlated price processes. The increase in construction leads to a building cycle upswing. When the option to wait is not included in the decision process, a decreased building price variance may increase the value of the property, but does not have a clear impact on the timing decision. In our model, with smaller variance, the value of waiting is lower, and the building threshold price is lower. Therefore, construction can be brought on by a reduction in uncertainty. For low building values, if the building price variance increases, the building value may decrease. If the option to wait to build is not valued, the developer is more apt to abandon the property. If this option is valued, however, greater uncertainty also implies that the developer has more opportunity to make positive profits, so that the developer would be more likely to hold onto the property.

The third result is that when holding costs ($H$) increase, the value of the land decreases because the optimal abandonment threshold, $Z$, is higher and the optimal development threshold, $W$, is lower. In our context, this result implies that impending restrictions on building height or higher property taxes may encourage developers to build sooner. Other actions that put future profits at risk serve the same function as holding costs. The developer often must weigh such costs against the possibility of obtaining greater entitlements, such as rezoning from residential to commercial use.

Further, an increase in the construction cost ($X$) causes $Z$ and $W$ to increase, having the net effect of decreasing the lot's value. Moreover, in the absence of uncertainty (i.e., when $\sigma_S^2 \to 0$), the solution reduces to its certainty counterpart, i.e., $C(S) = max(0, S - X)$.

Finally, note that the formulas for the land values and for the trigger prices for optimal development and abandonment ($C, W,$ and $Z$, respectively) are not functions of the expected rate of change of the price of the structure (the drift term, $\mu$).[9]

## 15.3  ALLOWING FOR AN IMPERFECT HEDGE

In this section, we revisit the land valuation problem by partially relaxing the assumption that there is a traded portfolio that is perfectly correlated with the value of the potential structure to be built on the property. We show that, if we allow this correlation to be constant but less than one, hedging is still possible if the hedge ratio is properly adjusted.

Since we no longer assume that the traded portfolio and building price are perfectly correlated, we use subscripts to differentiate their variance and Brownian motion parameters. We assume that the white noise component of the building price process can be broken down into the sum of systematic and unsystematic elements,

$$dz_S = \rho_{Sp} dz_p + \rho_{Se} dz_e, \tag{15.8}$$

such that $dz_p$ is orthogonal to $dz_e$ and $\rho_{Sp}$ is the correlation coefficient between $dz_p$ and $dz_S$. (Previously, $\rho_{Sp}$ was assumed to be one, and $\rho_{Se}$ was assumed to be zero.) Therefore, Equation (15.1) becomes,

$$dS/S = \mu dt + \sigma_S \rho_{Sp} dz_p + \sigma_S \rho_{Se} dz_e. \tag{15.9}$$

By Ito's Lemma, the price of land seen as a contingent claim, $C(S,t)$, would move according to the process,

$$
\begin{aligned}
dC(S,t) &= C_S dS + C_t dt + \frac{1}{2} C_{SS}(dS)^2 \qquad (15.10) \\
&= [C_t + \frac{1}{2}(\rho_{Sp}^2 + \rho_{Se}^2)\sigma_S^2 C_{SS} S^2 + C_S S \mu] dt \\
&+ C_S S \sigma_S (\rho_{Sp} dz_p + \rho_{Se} dz_e).
\end{aligned}
$$

As before, we can form a hedge portfolio, $V$, by going long one call and short $X$ (to be determined) traded portfolios, so that,

$$
\begin{aligned}
dV &= dC - X dP \qquad (15.11) \\
&= [C_t + \frac{1}{2}(\rho_{Sp}^2 + \rho_{Se}^2)\sigma_S^2 C_{SS} S^2 + C_S S \mu] dt \\
&+ C_S S \sigma_S (\rho_{Sp} dz_p + \rho_{Se} dz_e) - X P \alpha dt - X P \sigma_p dz_p.
\end{aligned}
$$

Setting $X = C_S S \sigma_S \rho_{Sp}/(s_p P)$, we have,

$$
\begin{aligned}
dV &= [C_t + \frac{1}{2}(\rho_{Sp}^2 + \rho_{Se}^2)\sigma_S^2 C_{SS} S^2 + C_S S \mu] dt \\
&+ C_S S \sigma_S \rho_{Se} dz_e - C_S S (\sigma_S/\sigma_p) \rho_{Sp} \alpha dt. \qquad (15.12)
\end{aligned}
$$

To solve this equation, we need to make two additional assumptions. First, we assume that the idiosyncratic risk $dz_e$ is not priced, and therefore that the hedge portfolio should have an expected return equal to the risk-free rate, namely,

$$E[dV] = r(C - X P) dt.$$

Second, we assume that the drifts in the price processes (15.1) and (15.2) are equal to the riskless rate plus a risk premium $\lambda$. It is assumed that the traded portfolio captures a sizable subset of the priced risk factors, so that the particular building has an expected return that depends only upon its correlation with this broad-based portfolio. That is,

$$\mu = r + (\rho_{Sp} \sigma_S/\sigma_p)\lambda = r + \beta_S(\alpha - r) \tag{15.13}$$

$$\alpha = r + \lambda. \tag{15.14}$$

We treat our tradeable portfolio as a fully diversified "market" portfolio of assets, so that risk is priced depending on its correlation with this portfolio, as in the CAPM.

Substituting Equations (15.13) and (15.14) into (15.11) and (15.12) and solving, yields,

$$C_t + \frac{1}{2}\sigma_S^2 C_{SS} S^2 (\rho_{Sp}^2 + \rho_{Se}^2) + rSC_S - rC = 0. \tag{15.15}$$

We can evaluate $(\rho_{Sp}^2 + \rho_{Se}^2)$ readily. From Equation (15.8), assuming that $z_p$ and $z_e$ are standard Brownian motions, we can take the variances of both sides to get,

$$dt = \rho_{Sp}^2 Var(dz_p) + \rho_{Se}^2 + Var(dz_e) + Cov(dz_p, dz_e)\rho_{Sp}\rho_{Se}. \tag{15.16}$$

Given the assumption of orthogonality, the covariance term is zero, giving

$$dt = (\rho_{Sp}^2 + \rho_{Se}^2)dt, \text{ or } (\rho_{Sp}^2 + \rho_{Se}^2) = 1. \tag{15.17}$$

Therefore,

$$C_t + \frac{1}{2}\sigma_S^2 C_{SS} S^2 + rSC_S - rC = 0. \tag{15.18}$$

This equation is the same as in our previous case (i.e., it is the standard Black-Scholes partial differential equation). We can readily adjust for perpetual life (setting $C_t = 0$), holding costs, or an increasing exercise price, to obtain an equation similar to (15.6). Therefore, we have shown that under fairly unrestrictive additional assumptions, the assumption that there is a perfectly-correlated traded portfolio can be relaxed to one involving a constant (but high) correlation with the actual underlying structure.

## 15.4  HOLDING THE ASSET FOLLOWING DEVELOPMENT

We now relax the assumption that the builder sells the completed structure immediately, and that there are no risky time delays. We thus account for both the portfolio developer who builds to hold, and the merchant developer who builds to sell. This distinction has no bearing as long as the returns on the tradeable portfolio that are not perfectly correlated with those on the building are unsystematic.

Consider first the case in which the building cannot be sold immediately, but there is a perfectly correlated tradeable asset. Essentially, with this tradeable portfolio, all of the risk can be hedged. Assume that the building must be held for at least one year. If $P_t$ is the value of the perfectly correlated portfolio, and $S_t$ is the value of the structure, at time $t \geq 1$ year,

$S_t = \delta P_t$, where $\delta$ is some scale factor. Therefore, $S_0 = \delta P_0$. To create a transaction equivalent to selling the building today at a price $S_0$, we short $\delta$ tradeable portfolios and receive $\delta P_0 = S_0$ today, and sell the building at time $t$ for $S_t = \delta P_t$, which we can use to buy back the tradeable portfolio.

However, when there is imperfect correlation, the problem becomes more complex because $S_0 = \delta P_0$ does not necessarily imply that $S_t = \delta P_t$. Therefore, we cannot synthetically sell the asset upon exercise without completely eliminating all residual risk. Still, if the investor can diversify away this risk so that the uncertainty after exercise is not priced, then the holding period is immaterial. The investor simply discounts the ultimate sales price at the time of exercise, at the risk-free interest rate. There is no effect on the exercise strategy, and the earlier results are unaffected. Since idiosyncratic risk is not priced in our model, the land is valued as before.

Nevertheless, it is appropriate to make some comments about the case when the risk is not diversifiable. If this uncertainty must be priced, it may have a significant bearing on the valuation and comparative statics results derived previously. For example, greater uncertainty can lower the value of the building, because the flow of rents would be discounted at a higher risk-adjusted rate. Therefore, even though more risk increases the value of the land viewed as an option, *ceteris paribus*, this result becomes ambiguous if the option is written on an underlying asset that itself has a lower value because of the increased risk.

## 15.5  STOCHASTIC CONSTRUCTION COSTS

We now turn to the case of stochastic construction costs. We show that such costs can have a significant impact on land values and the timing and location of development. The problem in which both the underlying structure price and the exercise price are stochastic has been previously worked out in various forms (e.g., see McDonald and Siegel, 1986). Our approach follows Fischer (1978), who solved for the value of a finite-lived European option with a stochastic exercise price. We adopt some of his basic assumptions in order to solve for the case of a perpetual American option with a stochastic exercise price.

We use the same assumptions as in section 15.2, but treat both the building price, $S$, and the construction costs, $X$, as stochastic, and eliminate holding costs. Here, the drifts on the building price process and the traded portfolio price process are assumed to be equal, i.e., $\mu = \alpha$. While both these variables are random, their ratio, $w$, should reach some threshold at which it is worthwhile to exercise.

We assume that $S, P$, and $X$ follow lognormal price processes of the form:

$$dS/S \;=\; \mu dt + \sigma_S dz_S \qquad\qquad (15.19)$$
$$dP/P \;=\; \alpha dt + \sigma_S dz_S \qquad\qquad (15.20)$$
$$dX/X \;=\; \alpha_X dt + \sigma_X dz_X, \qquad\qquad (15.21)$$

where $\rho_{SX}$ is the correlation coefficient between $dz_S$ and $dz_X$. The real land value, $C$, is a function of both the stochastic building price and construction costs. It also can be seen as a function of the cost of hedging against changes in construction costs. The cost of hedging in this case can be expressed as the expected rate of return, $r_h$, on a security whose stochastic percentage changes in value are perfectly correlated with the stochastic component of the percentage changes in construction costs. While such a security may exist, it is only necessary that the expected rate of return on such a security be inferred from an equilibrium pricing model, such as CAPM.

By Ito's Lemma, the value of land, which is a function of $S$ and $X$, would satisfy the following process:

$$dC(S,X) \;=\; \frac{1}{2}(\sigma_S^2 S^2 C_{SS} + \sigma_X^2 X^2 C_{XX} + \sigma_S\sigma_X\rho_{SX}SXC_{SX})dt$$
$$+ \;\; C_S dS + C_X dX. \qquad\qquad (15.22)$$

Forming our hedge portfolio,

$$dV = dC - C_S dS - C_X/HdX = rVdt = r(C - C_S S - C_X/HX)dt, \quad (15.23)$$

should yield the riskless return. Solving, we get:

$$\frac{1}{2}(\sigma_S^2 S^2 C_{SS} + \sigma_X^2 X^2 C_{XX} + \sigma_S\sigma_X\rho_{SX}SXC_{SX})$$
$$- \; rC + rC_S S + (\alpha_X - \rho_h + r)C_X X = 0. \qquad\qquad (15.24)$$

Finally, we change variables, defining $q = S/X$, $D(q) = C(S,X)/X$, $\gamma = \alpha_X - r_h$, and $\sigma^2 = (\sigma_S^2 + \sigma_X^2 - 2\sigma_S\sigma_X\rho_{SX})$, to obtain:

$$\gamma D - \gamma q D_q + \frac{1}{2}D_{qq}q^2\sigma^2 = 0. \qquad\qquad (15.25)$$

This equation can be solved with boundary conditions analogous to those used in section 15.2. We assume that there is a hurdle ratio, $q = w$, at which it is optimal to construct the building (exercise the option), and that investors choose this decision variable optimally. That is,

$$D(w) = w - 1 \qquad\qquad (15.26)$$

$$D(q) \geq Max(0, q - 1), \qquad q \leq w \qquad\qquad (15.27)$$

$$D'(w) = 1. \tag{15.28}$$

The boundary condition in Equation (15.28) is the "high-contact" condition, which ensures that investors choose $w$ optimally. Finally, we assume free disposal, so that the last boundary condition becomes:

$$D(0) = 0. \tag{15.29}$$

The general solution to Equation (15.25) has the form,

$$D(q) = A_1 q + A_2 q^v \qquad 0 \le q \le w, \tag{15.30}$$

where $v = 2\gamma/\sigma^2$.

Using Equation (15.30) in boundary conditions (15.26) and (15.28), gives:

$$A_1 w + A_2 w^v = w - 1 \tag{15.31}$$

$$A_1 + v A_2 w^v = 1 \tag{15.32}$$

$$A_1 = 0. \tag{15.33}$$

Solving for $D(q)$, we obtain:

$$D(q) = A_2 q^v \tag{15.34}$$

$$w = v/(v - 1) \tag{15.35}$$

$$A_2 = v^{v-1}/v^v. \tag{15.36}$$

Applying the inverse transformation of the change of variables, $D(q) = C(S, X)/X$ and $q = S/X$, we obtain,

$$C(S, X) = \begin{cases} \dfrac{(v-1)^{v-1} S^v}{v^v X^{v-1}} & \text{if } S/X \le w \\[2mm] S - X & \text{if } S/X > w. \end{cases} \tag{15.37}$$

In the Appendix we prove the following proposition:

*Proposition 1.* A necessary and sufficient condition for early exercise of the perpetual option is that $\gamma = \alpha_x - r_h > \sigma^2/2$.

Note that when $\gamma > \sigma^2/2$, then $\alpha_x > \sigma^2/2 + r_h$. Intuitively, for early exercise to be optimal, the drift on the exercise price must be strictly greater than the risk-adjusted drift on the instrument used to hedge changes in the exercise price.

This case of stochastic exercise costs results in similar conclusions as that with holding costs above. First, land for which $S/X > w$ should be developed immediately. Owners of other parcels should await further price increases and/or cost decreases, because $C(S, X) > max(0, S - X)$ for $S/X < w$ (i.e., their values exceed what the owners would get if they build immediately).

Second, as in the previous case, an increase in uncertainty increases the land's value. However, an increase in overall uncertainty can come about either from greater building price or cost uncertainty, or from a lower correlation between the two.

Third, an increase in the rate of growth of the development cost $(a_x)$, *ceteris paribus*, would cause the value of the land to decrease. As the ratio of the building price and construction costs at which it is optimal to develop, $w$, decreases, it may become optimal to exercise the option to build on some lots.

Finally, note that the difference between the drift term of the costs and that of the instrument which hedges against cost changes, $\gamma \equiv a_x - r_h$, enters in the solutions (15.34)–(15.36). This is the case here because we have not assumed that these terms are equal, which was the case for comparable terms relating $S$ and $P$ $(\alpha = \mu)$. In addition, we have not assumed that the development costs, $X$, and the hedge security for these costs are related in the same manner as are the building price, $S$, and the hedge security for building values, $P$, under the assumption of incomplete hedging (section 15.3). While the drift differential, $\gamma$, may be difficult to estimate in practice, we have nevertheless shown that the assumption of constant or deterministically changing construction costs is not necessary for this methodology, and that the model can be extended to one where $\alpha_S \neq \mu$.

## 15.6   CONCLUSIONS AND EXTENSIONS

Although the option to wait to invest is inherently present in most capital budgeting decisions, it is not typically incorporated in standard valuation models. In this chapter, we present analytical solutions for the value of this option as it applies to land development, and obtain rules that determine optimal exercise strategies that differ from those in standard models. We show that the option to wait to invest adds value to the land over and above the value of expected rents based on what is known at the decision date. This option value provides a rationale for the existence of vacant land in the midst of otherwise thriving real estate markets. Our model has different implications for the impact of a change in the level of uncertainty than when this option is not taken into account. Greater volatility increases the value of land viewed as an option. This favorable effect will not be offset by a lower building value if the additional risk is primarily unpriced, or nonsystematic. Uncertainty has an impact on the development and abandonment decisions, with clear implications for the timing and location of investment. When the option to invest is ignored, uncertainty affects the building decision only insofar as it has an impact on the value of the developed property. There is an ambiguous effect on the investment decision across time or among properties.

Future extensions of this research might incorporate uncertainty (perhaps under asymmetric information) about the value of the developed property that is only partially resolved through time. The model could also be extended to value land on which the underlying asset could be any of several buildings. This is equivalent to an option on the most valuable of several assets (see the related work of Stulz, 1982, or Johnson, 1987). In addition, because interest rates are considered to have a strong impact on real estate values, interest rates could be treated as an additional stochastic state variable. A mean-reverting process might be used for the underlying structure price to capture temporary price swings.

Further, we have implicitly assumed so far that the land to be valued is vacant. However, the option to build a new structure may also exist when there is an old one already in place. We have also assumed that once the land has been developed, there is no opportunity to raze the new building and start again. This assumption can be relaxed if the sequential option to build again and again is explicitly valued. Carr's (1988) model on valuing sequential exchange opportunities could be useful in this type of situation.

Finally, empirical evidence on option-based land valuation is important, since it represents a new approach for which the accepted methodology has been relatively unchallenged. Quigg (1993) tested a similar model and estimated the relevant parameters. The results indicate that these models can provide theoretical land values that are reasonably good approximations of market prices.

## APPENDIX

This Appendix proves Proposition 1. We first need to impose economic restrictions on the general solution (15.30) for premature exercise to be optimal. First, note that $A_2 \neq 0$. If $A_2 = 0$, then by Equation (15.32) $A_1 = 1$. But if $A_1 = 1$, Equation (15.31) holds only if $w \to \infty$, so that exercise will never occur. Second, we require that $\lim_{q \to 0} D(q) = 0$. Since $A_2 \neq 0$, it is implied that $v \geq 0$. Third, $0 \leq D_q(0) \leq 1$; the left inequality results from limited liability, while the right inequality results from the restriction that the land is at most as valuable as the developed project. Since $D_q(0) = A_1, 0 \leq A_1 \leq 1$. Further, from Equation (15.32),

$$A_2 = \frac{1 - A_1}{vw^v}. \tag{15.A1}$$

Since $v \geq 0$ and $A_2 \neq 0$, it must be the case that $A_2 > 0$.

Finally, recall that the call must be a convex function of the underlying asset price when the distribution of returns on the asset is independent of the level of the asset price (see Theorem 10 in Merton, 1973). Therefore, $A_2 v(v - 1)q^{v-2} = D''(q) \geq 0$. Since $A_2 > 0$, then $v \geq 1$. When $v = 1$, by Equation (15.32) $A_1 + A_2 = 1$, but this relationship holds in (15.31) only when $w$ is infinite, and infinite $w$ is not consistent with premature exercise. Therefore, $v > 1$, or $\gamma > \sigma^2/2$.

## ACKNOWLEDGMENTS

This paper was prepared as part of my doctoral dissertation at the University of California at Berkeley. I gratefully acknowledge valuable discussions with Nancy Wallace, Hayne Leland, Robert Edelstein, Jim Wilcox, Peter Berck, and Phelim Boyle.

## NOTES

1. Williams (1990b) assumes that the state variable is the building's rent, rather than the building value, and that this rent follows a geometric Brownian motion. It is necessary to assume this process in order to solve the option-pricing problem using standard methods, but Williams's approach implies that if rent becomes zero at any point in time, the rent, and thus the value of the building, will be zero from then on. We avoid this limitation by valuing land as a contingent claim on the building value itself.

2. Like William, Capozza and Sic assumed that the state variable is the future rent. However, unlike Williams, they assumed that rent follows an additive Brownian motion, which allows rents to become zero, or even negative, with no permanent effect on the building value. Their assumption is essentially equivalent to ours of a building price-process that follows a geometric Brownian motion.

Capozza and Sick posed an individual household maximization problem that takes advantage of arbitrage-based option-pricing methods. However, the household facing this problem is unlikely to be able to hedge and diversify its portfolio. In order for arbitrage-based option valuation to be used in this way, one must assume that the asset is priced as if the markets were dynamically complete. This assumption is more readily applied in cases where investors have access to the broader real estate and securities markets. They also assumed that investors can continuously hedge with urban (developed) land itself, rather than by using a traded portfolio as the hedge instrument, as in our model.

3. First, there is a known riskless instantaneous interest rate $(r)$, which is constant through time and is equal both for borrowers and lenders. Second, land owners are price takers. Third, the completed building is sold immediately. Otherwise, the holding period before the asset is sold is counted as part of the development stage, and the underlying asset value is discounted accordingly. As shown in section 15.4, relaxing this assumption is inconsequential in the context of the model.

4. The resulting price distribution specifies that $\log S_t$ has a normal distribution. Thus, negative prices are disallowed. In Equation (15.1) successive price ratios are independently and identically distributed. Implicit is the assumption that the many sources of uncertainty that affect building values are sufficiently small and independent.

5. This portfolio trades in a frictionless market, and exists as a proxy for the untraded potential structure itself. This portfolio might consist of real estate securities and instruments whose prices are closely related to the path of inflation, as is real estate. In the next section, we relax the assumption that this portfolio is perfectly correlated and allow for an imperfect, but constant, correlation.

6. It is assumed that the variance of the traded portfolio represents the market risk of the asset, and that the underlying asset receives a return in compensation for this market risk only. We expand this notion in the next section, where the two assets are not perfectly correlated. It can readily be seen that Equations (15.13) and (15.14) reduce to $\alpha = \mu$ when the correlation is one, as in this section. Since the building cannot be traded, such a result is not arbitrage based. If $\mu > \alpha$, so that there is a liquidity premium, the same results follow, except that the difference in the drift terms, $\mu - \alpha$, remains in the final valuation equation.

7. A changing exercise price may also provide an incentive for early development. We introduce stochastic construction costs in section 15.5, and show the circumstances under which early exercise will occur.

8. For a more complete description, see the Appendices in Tourinho (1979).

9. The intutive explanation of why the drift term does not appear relies on the fact that the land is a dependent asset in a continuous-time framework. The arbitrage argument shows that the returns to the underlying asset can be duplicated by holding land and lending. The price of the building already reflects this stream of returns, i.e., the price is a sufficient statistic for the drift term in the relative pricing formula.

# Chapter 16

# Multiproduct Manufacturing with Stochastic Input Prices and Output Yield Uncertainty

## Bardia Kamrad and Ricardo Ernst

*This chapter considers the problem of valuing multiproduct production agreements in an environment characterized by capacity constraints, stochastic input prices, and output yield uncertainty. Using an option-theoretic framework or contingent claims analysis, it derives optimal production policies independent of preferences. We illustrate the model through an example and provide numerical results based on a lattice representation of the stochastic evolution of both the output yield and input prices. The model is particularly useful in providing insight into flexibility issues typically encountered in manufacturing environments.*

## 16.1 INTRODUCTION

In most manufacturing environments, commonly encountered sources of uncertainty account for variations in delivery time, quantity, and price. The time component of uncertainty is primarily due to the variability of lead times in delivery. Traditionally, decision makers have maneuvered around this through early placement of orders or by stockpiling needed resources at the expense of higher inventory costs. However, recent literature has been instrumental in promoting the benefits of a just-in-time (JIT) purchasing/delivery system as a means of managing time uncertainty.[1] Quantity uncertainty can be either external or internal. The former is often due to forecast errors of future sales or demand variations. In the latter, production yields are subject to random variations. This is attributable to rapid changes in design, technology, complexities in the manufacturing process, or the productive machinery itself. Nonetheless, managers have attempted to protect themselves against either type of quantity uncertainty by producing more than required and by maintaining inventories from which their contractual obligations could be met. Of course, this also comes at the expense of increased overhead, as manifested by higher wages, production, inventory, and maintenance costs.

While demand uncertainty in the analysis of production and inventory problems has spawned a host of articles over the last four decades, the academic literature is only just beginning to recognize the importance of quantity or yield uncertainty in production scheduling. Initially, motivated by yield variations in agriculture, Karlin (1958) considered the inventory implications of uncertain outputs. Since then, only a few authors have addressed the yield variability problem in a general production and inventory setting. Klein (1966) and White (1967), for example, modeled a single-stage system by identifying the reject allowance that optimizes the trade-off between overages and shortages. More recently, Porteus (1986), Sepehri, Silver and New (1986), and Lee and Rosenblatt (1982) provide additional insight to modeling yield uncertainty and production control in a single-stage setting. In serial (multistage) production systems, Yano (1986a, 1986b) and Lee and Yano (1985) have also considered yield variability, while Gerchak, Parlar, and Vickson (1986), Gerchak, Vickson and Parlar (1988), and Ehrhardt and Taube (1987) analyzed the impact of random yields in a single-period setting.

In most models of yield randomness, the resulting output level increases with the input. This, however, requires precise specification of the manner in which the output level distribution depends on the input level, although optimal input levels have been obtained without such a requirement. In other applications, yield variability has been conceptualized as the product of input quantity and a random multiplier. For instance, Gerchak, Vickson, and Parlar (1988) defined yield variability as the product of the input level and a random independent factor and provided a general profit-maximizing, single-period model under uncertain demand conditions.[2]

As in the previous work, we assume that the random yield rate is stationary, invariant with respect to batch size, and independent of the input level or the product type.[3] While we assume that demand is contractually fixed, we account for multiple sources of price uncertainty in the raw materials (inputs) required for the production of various items. Specifically, we consider the problem of valuing a production agreement in a setting characterized by output yield and input price uncertainty, typified by production and inventory capacity constraints, and incarnated by production flexibility in volume and product variety. Our objective is to formulate a valuation model that maximizes the value of the agreement (to the producer) and provides optimal production and inventory guidelines for follow-up.

Uncertainty in prices for any input or output in competitive markets results from fluctuations in supply and demand. In some situations, input prices are known while output prices vary randomly, as in mining, timber, and oil production ventures. In other situations, as those treated here, input prices are random while the output prices are contractually fixed. Computer chip manufacturing, electronic components, and special metal alloys for use in the aerospace industry are but a few examples in which the raw material costs are subject to uncertainty over time. In memory chip manufacturing, for instance, either gold or silver bonding is used, depending on the required specifications, whereas wafer production requires copper. For these and other similar raw material inputs, such as platinum, annual price swings of 25 to 40 percent are not uncommon.[4]

In evaluating projects under these conditions, the practice of replacing distributions of future prices by their expected values discounted at a constant risk-adjusted rate (as in conventional capital budgeting methods) is likely to result in errors. Where price uncertainty and strategic reactions to it are of paramount importance, the conventional discounted cash flow approach to valuation is destined to result in suboptimal decisions.[5] In our analysis, we adopt a contingent claims approach to valuation (e.g., justified by presupposing the existence of futures markets in the raw material).

A contingent claims approach to valuation is attractive since it can both quantify the value of flexibility, and obviate the need for determining the risk-adjusted discount rate.[6] A contingent claims approach to the valuation of real assets (e.g., projects, ventures and contractual claims) is based on the principles of financial option pricing developed by Black and Scholes (1973) and Merton (1973). The advantages of this approach to the valuation problem have been well documented in recent literature. For example, Pindyck (1986) considered the optimal exploitation of an exhaustible resource under uncertainty. Myers and Majd (1990) considered the value derived from an abandonment option. Brennan and Schwartz (1985a) valued production flexibility in mining ventures, while McDonald and Siegel (1985, 1986) valued projects when the firm retains a shutdown option and the option to defer initial investment, respectively. Majd and Pindyck (1987) examined the flexibility value of delaying construction activities in projects where a series of outlays must be made sequentially and where no cash flows are produced until the project is completed (as in aircraft production). Paddock, Siegel, and Smith (1988) valued offshore development petroleum leases, while Morck, Schwartz, and Stangeland (1989) valued timber production when output prices and inventories are stochastic. Andreou (1990) valued flexible plant capacity when market demand conditions are uncertain. Trigeorgis and Mason (1987) and Kensinger (1987) valued managerial flexibility from an options perspective, and Kulatilaka (1988) valued the flexibility of a flexible manufacturing system. Kulatilaka and

Marks (1988) considered the strategic value of flexibility in a world with incomplete contracting, while Pindyck (1991) examined project irreversibility and the investment option. Trigeorgis (1993a) considered the nature of option interactions when investments involve multiple real options.

This chapter develops a methodology for valuing risky production agreements in a setting characterized by multiple sources of input price uncertainty and output yield randomness. We assume production flexibility both in terms of volume and product type, assuming the demand and delivery schedule for each product type is known. Since the resulting valuation model can not be solved analytically, efficient numerical methods are invoked to provide solutions.

The chapter is organized as follows. Our assumptions and notation are provided in section 16.2, where we formulate the general valuation model as a problem in stochastic optimal control. Since the model does not yield analytic solutions, stochastic dynamic programming is used to obtain results whose solution is shown to depend on probabilities, preferences, and an exogenously furnished discount rate. In section 16.3, we provide an alternative numerical solution procedure by adopting a contingent claims framework. Specifically, a multinomial lattice procedure is used to approximate the stochastic evolution of input prices. One feature of this approach is that the methodology requires fewer estimated data and exploits market information more fully. By superimposing the production control problem on the price lattice, we develop a recursive procedure in which the state variable corresponds to the level of finished good inventories. Output yield uncertainty is then related to the state variable through an inventory balance equation.[7] Section 16.4 illustrates the model via a numerical example and discusses other features and applications. Section 16.5 concludes.

## 16.2    ASSUMPTIONS, NOTATION, AND MODEL FORMULATION

Consider a flexible production system capable of producing $M$ types of product alternatives. Each product (mode) $m$, $m = 1, \ldots, M$, requires as input specified quantities of various raw material. Assume there are $N$ different raw material types, although not all types need be utilized in the production of a single product type. The inputs are assumed to be standard commodities on which futures contracts trade. We also assume single modal capacity in that during each period of operation only one product type can be produced. The level (volume) of production regardless of product type chosen is $\bar{Q}$. The required raw materials are not stocked, but rather are assumed to be made available under a just-in-time order/delivery arrangement. However, the firm maintains an inventory of its output from which a contractually pre-established demand and delivery schedule can be met over a prespecified horizon of length $T$.

The production system is completely characterized by a cash-flow stream received over the agreement's duration, $[0, T]$. To that end, let $f\{P, A, R, t; D(d)\}$ denote the cash-flow rate at time $t$, given that the input price vector is $P(t) \in \mathbb{R}^N$, the contractually known output price vector is $A(t) \in \mathbb{R}^M$, the state of the system is $R(t) \in \mathbb{R}^M$, and the mode/level of operations currently in place is $D(d)$. $D(d)$ is an $M$-dimensional array whose elements $Q(m)$ define the mode $m$, $m = 1, 2, \ldots, M$, and its corresponding level of production $Q$, $0 \leq Q < \bar{Q}$. Since we assume single modal capacity, at any time $t$, $D(d)$ contains at most one non-zero $Q$.[8]

For valuation purposes, the stochastic properties of the cash-flow process need to be specified. We assume that the input price vector, $P(t)$, evolves stochastically over time according to the geometric Wiener process:

$$dP_j(t) = \alpha_j P_j(t)\, dt + \sigma_j P_j(t)\, dZ_j(t) \qquad\qquad j = 1, 2, \ldots, N, \quad (16.1)$$

where

$$\rho_{jk} = \frac{dZ_j(t)\, dZ_k(t)}{dt} \qquad\qquad j \neq k, \qquad\qquad j = 1, 2, \ldots, N.$$

Here, $\alpha$, $\sigma$ and $\rho$ are the instantaneous drift, volatility, and pair-wise correlation coefficients, with $dZ(t)$ being an increment to the Wiener process $Z(t)$. The above process implies that, conditional on $P(0) \in \mathbb{R}^N$, the joint distribution of input prices over $[0, T]$ is lognormal. This is a plausible assumption for prices to follow, at least as a first-order approximation, since the possibility of negative price realizations is precluded. Moreover, the implied distributional skewness is, to some degree, supported by empirical evidence for commodity prices such as gold, silver, and copper.

Further, define $n$ as an equi-width partition of an agreement's life, $T$, so that $\tau \equiv T/n = t_{i+1} - t_i$ represents the length of one production period, $i = 0, 1, \ldots, n-1$. Switches in production may be mode, level, or both, and are assumed to occur at discrete time intervals. As such, let $D_i(d)$ denote the mode/level vector of operations selected for implementation during period $[t_i, t_{i+1}]$, $i = 0, 1, \ldots, n - 1$. This choice may be restricted by the current mode and level of operations, $D_{i-1}(d)$, and the time $t_i$ state of the system $R_i$, with $R_i \equiv g(\delta_i, R_{i-1}, D_{i-1}(d), G(\tilde{y}))$, where $\delta_i \in \mathbb{R}^M$ is the time $t_i$ demand vector with components $\delta_{i,m}$; $i = 1, 2, \ldots, m$, $m = 1, 2, \ldots, M$; and $\tilde{y}$ is the random yield variable with distribution $G(\tilde{y})$. In our analysis, the state of the system, $R_i \in \mathbb{R}^M$, represents the (random) finished good inventory vector whose components have finite capacity $\mathcal{L}$, i.e., $0 \leq R_{i,m} \leq \mathcal{L}$, $i = 0, 1, \ldots, n$, $m = 1, 2, \ldots, M$.

Finally, let $\phi_i\{P, A, R; D_{i-1}(d), G(\tilde{y})\}$ represent the set of all feasible selections for $D_i(d)$. An admissible control, $\pi$, is defined as a sequence of feasible modes and corresponding levels of operation for use in successive periods. That is, $\pi \in \mathbb{R}^{M*(n+1)}$ with $\pi = \{D_0(d), D_1(d), D_2(d), \ldots, D_n(d)\}$, where for $i = 0, 1, \ldots n$, $D_i(d) \in \phi_i\{P, A, R; D_{i-1}(d), G(\tilde{y})\}$, with $D_0(d)$ being the initial active setting. To account for all feasible actions, let $\Phi_0$ denote the set of admissible controls with initial setting $D_0(d)$, namely,

$$\Phi_0 = \left\{\pi : \pi = \{D_0(d), \ldots, D_n(d)\}, D_i(d) \in \phi_i(\cdot), i = 0, 1, \ldots, n\right\}.$$

Whenever the mode and/or level of operations changes, a switching cost may be incurred. This cost at time $t_i$ is $\theta_i\{D_{i-1}(d), D_i(d)\}$. The cost of production during period $[t_i, t_{i+1}]$ is observed at time $t_i$ and is denoted by $C(D_i(d))$, which may be a monotonically increasing concave function over the production interval. An inventory holding cost, $H(R_i)$, is also incurred at time $t_i$, $i = 1, \ldots, n$. Given this setting, and conditional on a predetermined admissible control $\pi \in \Phi_0$, the value of the production agreement, $J_0^\pi(\cdot)$, is obtained via the set of stochastic control equations:

$$J_0^\pi\{P, A, R; D_0(d)\} = E\left\{\sum_{i=1}^{n}\left\{\int_{t_{i-1}}^{t_i} e^{-u(t-t_i)}f\{P, A, R, t; D(d)\}dt \right.\right.$$
$$\left.\left. -e^{-ut_i}\theta_i\{D_{i-1}(d), D_i(d)\}\right\} + e^{-ut_n}f\{P, A, R, T; D_n(d)\}\right\} (16.2)$$

In the above valuation Equation (16.2), preferences and aversion toward risk could be implicitly accounted for if the intertemporal utility for the decision maker(s) were known. Moreover, if variations in the output rate affect risk, then the exogenously furnished discount rate, $u$, may in fact be a function of the mode or level of production, namely, $u = u(D(d))$. Let $V_0(\cdot)$ be the value associated with the optimal admissible control, namely,

$$V_0\{P, A, R; D_0(d)\} = \sup_{\pi \in \Phi_0} \left\{J_0^\pi\{P, A, R; D_0(d)\}\right\}. \qquad (16.3)$$

To obtain $V_0(\cdot)$, we need to use dynamic programming. Toward this goal, let $V_i\{P, A, R; Q_{i-1}(m)\}$ define the maximum total expected value at time $t_i$, given that the input price is $P(t_i)$, the output price is $A(t_i)$, the state of the system is $R(t_i)$, and that $Q$ units of product $m$ ($m = 1, 2, \ldots, M$) were produced during the earlier period $[t_{i-1}, t_i]$, with optimal actions selected thereafter. Therefore, for $i = 0, 1, \ldots, n-1$, and for all potential realizations of $R_i \in g(\cdot)$ with $0 \leq R_{i,m} \leq \mathcal{L}$, $m = 1, 2, \ldots, M$, the recursion equation for computing $V_i(\cdot)$ is:

$$V_i(P, A, R; Q_{i-1}(m))$$

$$= \max_{m} \left\{ \max_{Q_i(m)} \left\{ E\left\{ \int_{t_i}^{t_{i+1}} e^{-u(t-t_i)} f(P, A, R, t; Q_i(m)) \, dt \right. \right. \right.$$

$$\left. \left. \left. + e^{-u\tau} V_{i+1}(P, A, R; Q_i(m)) - \theta_i(Q_{i-1}(m), Q_i(m)) \right\} \right\} \right\}, \quad (16.4)$$

s.t.

$$R_{i+1} = g(\delta_{i+1}, R_i, Q_i(m), G(\tilde{y})) \qquad (16.4a)$$

$$Q_i(m) \in \phi_i\{P, A, R; Q_{i-1}(m), G(\tilde{y})\} \qquad (16.4b)$$

$$P(t_{i+1}) = G(P(t_i)) \qquad (16.4c)$$

$$0 \leq Q_i(m) \leq \bar{Q} \qquad (16.4d)$$

$$0 \leq R_{i,m} \leq \mathcal{L}. \qquad (16.4e)$$

The first constraint depicts the dependency of the state variable at time $t_{i+1}$ on the demand, mode, and level of production, as well as the actual production yield during the period ending at time $t_{i+1}$. Constraint (16.4b) ensures the feasibility of the policy selected for implementation in period $[t_i, t_{i+1}]$, while the Markovian characteristic of the price process is captured in (16.4c). In completing the above dynamic program, appropriate boundary conditions also need to be specified. These conditions, for $i = n$ and for all potential realizations of $R_n$, $0 \leq R_{n,m} \leq \mathcal{L}$, $m = 1, 2, \ldots, M$, are given by:

$$V_n(P, A, R; Q_{n-1}(m)) = A(t_n)\delta_n - \theta_n\{Q_{n-1}(m), 0\} - H(R_n), \quad (16.5)$$

with $0 \leq Q_{n-1}(m) \leq \bar{Q}$, where $\theta_n(Q_{n-1}(m), 0)$ may be viewed as a close-down cost. Equations (16.4) and (16.5) allow the value of the venture to be computed numerically. This stochastic dynamic program can be viewed as a traditional valuation model in that the results rely on exogenously furnished estimates of the drift components, $\alpha_j$, $j = 1, \ldots, N$, and the risk-adjusted discount rate, $u$. The drift components, however, are typically non-stationary, preference dependent, and difficult to estimate.

To overcome these traditional limitations, in the following section we consider an alternative numerical approach for solving the valuation problem. In particular, by specifying the probability distribution of $\tilde{y}$, and by superimposing the control problem on an approximating lattice representing the stochastic evolution of $P(t) \in \mathbb{R}^N$, a new and more practical recursion is developed. The advantage of the transformed problem is that the drift terms need not be estimated. Moreover, the appropriate discount rate and probability assignments over the (price) lattice need not be exogenously specified. Instead, these values can be implicitly established within the framework of the model.

## 16.3   THE VALUATION MODEL

In this section, we develop a valuation model defined on a discrete-time lattice representing the stochastic evolution of input prices. We assume that the raw materials are standard commodities on which futures contracts trade.[9] This assumption allows the valuation process to proceed in an arbitrage-free framework, which in turn obviates the need for drift parameter estimates.[10] Specifically, risk diversification through an appropriate hedging policy in the futures market provides the opportunity to replace the actual drift parameters $\alpha_j$ in Equation (16.1), $j = 1, \ldots, N$, with their equivalent risk-neutral expectations $(r - c_j)$, where $r$ is the riskless rate of return and $c_j$ the convenience yield.[11] The convenience yield is assumed to be a constant proportion of the spot price, and represents the value of being able to benefit from the physical ownership of the raw material inputs through its availability at the required times.

In developing the lattice valuation model, we use the framework developed by Kamrad and Ritchken (1991) to approximate the joint lognormal distribution of the input prices with a $(2^N + 1)$ lattice jump process. For example, in considering the manufacturing process for production of memory chips requiring copper, gold, or silver as inputs, we limit the number of raw material types to three (i.e., $N = 3$). While copper is used in the production of the wafers, a common component to each product type, the products differ in their requirements for bonding, that is, either silver or gold. Gold bonding may be used for military purposes while silver bonding has regular commercial applications. Therefore, in our analysis, $M = 2$.

To approximate $P(t) \in \mathbb{R}^3$, let $P(t_0) = (P_1(t_0), P_2(t_0), P_3(t_0))$ represent the current input price vector such that after an elapsed time of length $\tau$ any one of the following potential price values could be realized:

$$(P_1(t_0), P_2(t_0), P_3(t_0)) \Rightarrow \begin{cases} (P_1(t_0)u_1, P_2(t_0)u_2, P_3(t_0)u_3) & w.p. \quad p_1 \\ (P_1(t_0)u_1, P_2(t_0)u_2, P_3(t_0)d_3) & w.p. \quad p_2 \\ (P_1(t_0)u_1, P_2(t_0)d_2, P_3(t_0)u_3) & w.p. \quad p_3 \\ (P_1(t_0)u_1, P_2(t_0)d_2, P_3(t_0)d_3) & w.p. \quad p_4 \\ (P_1(t_0), P_2(t_0), P_3(t_0)) & w.p. \quad p_9 \\ (P_1(t_0)d_1, P_2(t_0)u_2, P_3(t_0)u_3) & w.p. \quad p_5 \\ (P_1(t_0)d_1, P_2(t_0)u_2, P_3(t_0)d_3) & w.p. \quad p_6 \\ (P_1(t_0)d_1, P_2(t_0)d_2, P_3(t_0)u_3) & w.p. \quad p_7 \\ (P_1(t_0)d_1, P_2(t_0)d_2, P_3(t_0)d_3) & w.p. \quad p_8, \end{cases}$$
$$(16.6)$$

with $\sum_{i=1}^{9} p_i = 1.0$. Here, $u_j$ and $d_j$ represent the up and down jump magnitudes respectively, where for computational convenience the symmetry constraints $u_j = d_j^{-1}$ are imposed, for $j = 1, 2, 3$. To ensure that this approximating process converges in distribution to that of the continuous risk-neutral diffusion process, it is required that $u_j = e^{\lambda \sigma_j \sqrt{\tau}}$. The stretch parameter, $\lambda > 1$, guarantees a horizontal jump event during each period of length $\tau$, that is the event in which the price vector remains unchanged with probability $p_9$. For valuation purposes, the remaining eight probability terms are defined by:

$$p_q = \frac{1}{8} \left\{ \frac{1}{\lambda^2} \left\{ 1 + \sum_{i=1}^{2} \sum_{j=i+1}^{3} \Psi_{ij}^q \rho_{ij} \right\} + \frac{\sqrt{\tau}}{\lambda} \sum_{i=1}^{3} \Psi_{iq} \frac{\mu_i}{\sigma_i} \right\}, \qquad q = 1, 2, \ldots, 8,$$

$$(16.7)$$

where

$$\Psi_{ij}^q = \begin{cases} 1 & \text{if raw materials } i \text{ and } j \text{ have jumps in the same directi-} \\ & \text{on in state } q \\ -1 & \text{if jumps are in the opposite direction in state } q \end{cases}$$

$$\Psi_{iq} = \begin{cases} 1 & \text{if raw material } i \text{ has an up jump in state } q \\ -1 & \text{if raw material } i \text{ has a down jump in state } q, \end{cases}$$

with

$$\mu_i = r - \frac{\sigma_i^2}{2} - c_i \qquad \text{for } i = 1, 2, 3.$$

Here, $q$ represents a potential jump state. For instance, $q = 4$ represents the state in which the price of the first raw material increases, while those of the second and third decrease, as seen in Expression (16.6). Equation (16.7) implies that the horizontal jump probability $p_9 = 1 - \frac{1}{\lambda^2}$. Figure 16.1 provides a geometric representation of the lattice process in three time periods. To develop a valuation recursion procedure, let

$$P(i, j, k, l) = \left\{ P_1(t_i), P_2(t_i), P_3(t_i) \right\} = \left\{ P_1(t_0) u_1^j, P_2(t_0) u_2^k, P_3(t_0) u_3^l \right\}$$

$$(16.8)$$

represent the time $t_i$ value of the input prices given that the first input price is in state $j$, the second in state $k$, and the third input price is in state $l$, where for every $t_i$, $(j, k, l) \in \{\Im(i), \Im'(i)\}$, $i = 0, 1, 2, \ldots, n$. $\{\Im(i), \Im'(i)\}$ represents the set of feasible realizations for $(j, k, l)$, with

$$\Im(i) = \left\{ -i, -i+2, \ldots, i-2, i \right\}$$
$$\Im'(i) = \left\{ -i+1, -i+3, \ldots, i-3, i-1 \right\}.$$

Having defined the lattice price dynamics, we use a simple Bernoulli distribution to account for yield variability, primarily for ease of exposition.

**Figure 16.1**
**Multinomial Price Lattice with Three Sources of Uncertainty**

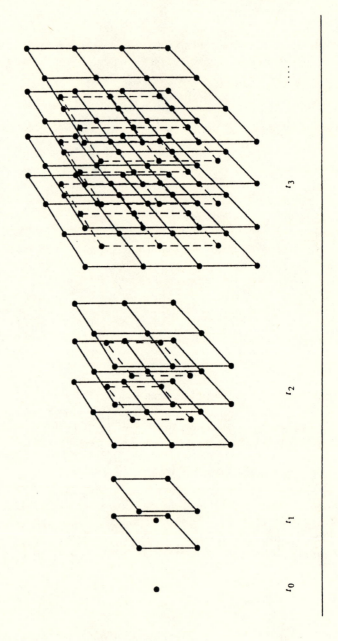

$t_0$  $t_1$  $t_2$  $t_3$

Specifically, the production yield factor for each product type at the end of each period is given by,

$$\tilde{y} = \begin{cases} \beta_1 & \text{w.p.} & a_1 \\ \beta_2 & \text{w.p.} & a_2, \end{cases} \quad (16.9)$$

with $0 < \beta_1 < \beta_2 < 1$, and $a_1 + a_2 = 1.0$. Though the distribution of $\tilde{y}$ may be somewhat uncompounding for most real world applications, it nevertheless provides the needed intuition for modeling purposes. Of course, at the expense of increased computational complexity, additional potential realizations for $\tilde{y}$ can be accounted for. Note also that, by definition, the probability distribution of the yield variable, $G(\tilde{y})$, affects the state of the system, $R(t)$, defined as the level of finished goods inventories for each product.

By precluding the opportunity for shortages or backlogging, and in light of output variability, the lower bound on the production quantities has to be modified in order to meet the demand. Using a conservative approach, as in Bassok and Yano (1992), the production quantity for each product during each period must satisfy the constraint:

$$max \left\{ \frac{1}{\beta_1} (\delta_{i+1,m} - R_{i,m}), 0 \right\} \le Q_i(m) \le \bar{Q} \quad i = 0, 1, \ldots, n - 1; \quad m = 1, 2,$$
$$(16.10)$$

where the initial inventory levels are assumed to be zero, i.e., $R_{0,m} = 0$.

Given $G(\tilde{y})$, the level of inventory at any time $t_i$ is then characterized by the state of the inventory, i.e., the state representing the dependency of the inventory level on the realization of $\tilde{y}$. Expressions (16.9) and (16.10) can be used to show that at time $t_i$ the potential number of inventory states is $(i + 1)$, $i = 0, 1, \ldots, n$. Accordingly, let $R_{i,m}^S$ represent the net inventory level at time $t_i$ for product $m$, given that state $S \in \{0, 1, \ldots, i\}$ of inventory has been realized. Subsequently, $Q_i^S(m)$ defines the quantity of product $m$ to be produced during period $[t_i, t_{i+1}]$ given the time $t_i$ level of inventory is $R_{i,m}^S$, $i = 0, 1, \ldots, n$, $m = 1, 2$. Realization of $S \in \{0, 1, \ldots, i\}$, however, depends on the dynamics of $G(\tilde{y})$, the condition that only one product type can be produced per period, and the corresponding state of inventory for each product type during the previous period, $S' \in \{0, 1, \ldots, i - 1\}$. The level of inventory at $t_i$, conditional on $S \in \{0, 1, \ldots, i\}$, can be easily obtained using an inventory balance equation. That is, for $m = 1, 2$,

1. if $S = 0$, then for every $S' \in \{0, 1, \ldots, j - 1\}$

$$R_{i,m}^0 = R_{i-1,m}^{S'} + Q_{i-1}^{S'}(m)\beta_1 - \delta_{i,m} \qquad \text{given } Q_{i-1}^{S'}(m) > 0 \quad (16.11a)$$
$$R_{i,m}^0 = R_{i-1,m}^0 - \delta_{i,m} \qquad \text{given } Q_{i-1}^{S'} = 0 \quad (16.11b)$$

2. if $S = 1, 2, \ldots, i$, then for every $S' = S - 1$

$$R_{i,m}^S = R_{i-1,m}^{S'} + Q_{i-1}^{S'}(m)\beta_2 - \delta_{i,m} \qquad \text{given } Q_{i-1}^{S'} > 0 \qquad (16.11c)$$

$$R_{i,m}^S = R_{i-1,m}^{S'} - \delta_{i,m} \qquad\qquad \text{given } Q_{i-1}^{S'}(m) = 0. \ (16.11d)$$

The above partitioning of the inventory states allows for consistency and tractability. Figure 16.2 provides a schematic representation of the inventory state convention. This defines the inventory dynamics resulting from yield randomness.

For valuation purposes, we use a stochastic dynamic program defined on the combined multinomial lattices of price and inventory. To that end, let $V_i((j, k, l), R_{i,m}^S; Q_{i-1}^{S'}(m))$ be the maximum total expected value of the project at time $t_i$, given that the price is $P(i, j, k, l)$, $Q_{i-1}^{S'}(m)$ units are produced in period $[t_{i-1}, t_i]$, $m = 1, 2$, $S' \in \{0, \ldots, i - 1\}$, and that the state of the system at time $t_i$ is $R_{i,m}^S$, $S \in \{0, \ldots, i\}$, $i = 0, 1, \ldots, n - 1$.

The valuation recursion equation for obtaining $V_i((j, k, l), \cdot)$, $i = 0, 1, \ldots, n - 1$, contingent on the expected realization of every feasible node $(j, k, l)$ and every inventory state $S \in \{0, 1, \ldots, i\}$, for $m = 1, 2$, is then given by:

$$V_i((j, k, l), R_{i,m}^S; Q_{i-1}^{S'}(m))$$

$$= \max_m \left\{ \max_{Q_i^S(m)} \left\{ E\left\{ f_i((j, k, l), Q_i^S(m), R_{i,m}^S; Q_{i-1}^{S'}(m)) \right. \right. \right.$$

$$\left. \left. \left. + e^{-r\tau} V_{i+1}^*(Q_i^S(m)) \right\} \right\} \right\} \qquad (16.12)$$

s.t.

$$\max\left\{ \frac{1}{\beta_1}(\delta_{i+1,m} - R_{i,m}^S), 0 \right\} \le Q_i^S(m) \le \bar{Q} \qquad (16.12a)$$

$$0 \le R_{i,m}^0 \le \mathcal{L} \qquad (16.12b)$$

$$0 \le R_{i,m}^S \le \mathcal{L} \qquad (16.12c)$$

$$(j, k, l) \in \{\Im(i), \Im'(i)\}. \qquad (16.12d)$$

In the above expression, $f_i((j, k, l), \cdot)$ represents the net total value from node $(j, k, l)$ at time $t_i$ from producing $Q_{i-1}^{S'}(m)$ units during period $[t_{i-1}, t_i]$, resulting in an inventory level $R_{i,m}^S$, while choosing to produce $Q_i^S(m)$ units during period $[t_i, t_{i+1}]$. Given node $(j, k, l)$ at time $t_i$, the production decision $Q_i^S(m)$, together with an optimal policy to be followed thereafter, results in an expected profit level over the remaining $(t_n - t_i)$ periods corresponding to the *argument* term of Expression (16.12),

Figure 16.2
Inventory State Progression

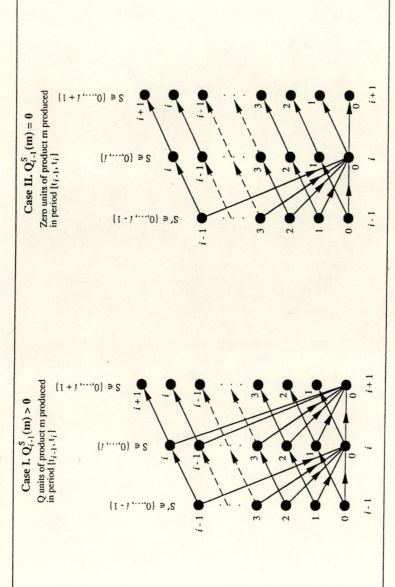

where for every $S \in \{0, \ldots, i\}$ and its corresponding feasible inventory $S' \in \{0, \ldots, i-1\}$:

$$
E\left\{ f_i\left\{ (j,k,l), Q_i^S(m), R_{i,m}^S; Q_{i-1}^{S'}(m) \right\} \right\} = \sum_{m=1}^{2} A_m(t_i)\delta_{i,m}
$$
$$
- \left\{ Q_i^S(m)\left\{ P_1 u_1^j \omega_1 + b_1(P_2 u_2^k \omega_2) + b_3(P_3 u_3^l \omega_3) \right\} \right.
$$
$$
+ C(Q_i^S(m)) + \theta_i(Q_{i-1}^{S'}(m), Q_i^S(m))
$$
$$
\left. + G^0\left\{ H(R_{i,m}^0) \right\} + G^1\left\{ H(R_{i,m}^S) \right\} \right\},
\qquad (16.13)
$$

where

$$
b_1 = \begin{cases} 1 & \text{if } m = 1 \\ 0 & \text{if } m \neq 1 \end{cases}
\qquad
b_2 = \begin{cases} 1 & \text{if } m = 2 \\ 0 & \text{if } m \neq 2 \end{cases}
$$
$$
G^0 = \begin{cases} 1 & \text{if } S = 0 \\ 0 & \text{if } S > 0 \end{cases}
\qquad
G^1 = \begin{cases} 1 & \text{if } S > 0 \\ 0 & \text{if } S = 0, \end{cases}
$$

with $\omega_h$ being the quantity of input material $h$ needed to produce one unit of finished product, $h = 1, 2, 3$ (i.e., material conversion factors). Moreover, the expected optimal value at time $t_{i+1}$ is denoted by $E\{V_{i+1}^*(Q_i^S(m))\}$. Given the realization of node $(j, k, l)$ at time $t_i$, the Appendix defines this expected value with respect to both price and yield probabilities.

We complete the solution process by identifying the time $t_n$ boundary conditions. Specifically, for every feasible node $(j, k, l)$ and state of inventory $S \in \{0, 1, \ldots, n\}$ with corresponding $S' \in \{0, 1, \ldots, n-1\}$ and $m = 1, 2$,

$$
V_n\left\{ (j,k,l), R_{n,m}^S; Q_{n-1}^{S'}(m) \right\}
$$
$$
= \sum_{m=1}^{2} A_m(t)\delta_{n,m} - \theta_n\left\{ Q_{n-1}^{S'}(m), Q_n^S(m) \right\} - H\left( R_{n,m}^S \right) \quad (16.14)
$$

s.t.

$$
Q_n^S(m) = 0 \qquad\qquad\qquad (16.14a)
$$
$$
0 \leq R_{n,m}^0 \leq \mathcal{L} \qquad\qquad\qquad (16.14b)
$$
$$
0 \leq R_{n,m}^S \leq \mathcal{L} \qquad\qquad\qquad (16.14c)
$$
$$
(j, k, l) \in \{\Im(n), \Im'(n)\}. \qquad\qquad (16.14d)
$$

The valuation recursion Equations, (16.12)–(16.14), define a stochastic dynamic program resulting in the value of the agreement together with the optimal production policy to be followed. This model can be viewed as a corrected version of the valuation approach given by Equations (16.4) and (16.5) of section 16.2. Note that in the latter model, the discount rate and probability values need not be exogenously specified, as they are obtained implicitly. The opportunity to properly hedge the risk of fluctuating prices allows an adjustment in the drift of the price process and subsequent discounting at the riskless rate. The new drift, $(r - c_j)$, is easily computed and is independent of preferences. While other valuation alternatives are available, the contingent claims methodology shown here has other advantages as well. First, the approach is dynamic, in that it can quantify the various flexibility options inherent in risky projects. Moreover, the valuation mechanism does not depend on the forecasts of input prices; the stochastic properties of these variables are instead fed directly into the analysis. The only assumption about future prices is that they follow certain "well-defined" stochastic processes. In the following section, we illustrate the model by analyzing a stylized example. In addition to the optimal solution and parametric analysis, questions regarding flexibility and its value are also addressed.

## 16.4 A NUMERICAL EXAMPLE

Consider a production agreement requiring the delivery of memory chips according to a predetermined demand and delivery schedule. The raw materials used in the production of the finished goods are copper (for wafer production), gold, and silver (for gold and silver bonding, respectively). There are two product types, for simplicity referred to as gold and silver chips, while the raw materials are referred to as input 1, 2, and 3, respectively. The duration of the project is assumed to be one year (i.e., $T = 1$), with the following demand/delivery schedule: $(\delta_{1,1}, \delta_{1,2}) = (0, 0)$; $(\delta_{2,1}, \delta_{2,2}) = (1, 2)$; $(\delta_{3,1}, \delta_{3,2}) = (0, 0)$; $(\delta_{4,1}, \delta_{4,2}) = (2, 1)$, implying $n = 4$ subperiods.

The production and finished good inventory capacities are assumed to be 5 units each, hence $\bar{Q} = \mathcal{L} = 5$ units. The production conversion factors are $\omega_1 = 2$, $\omega_2 = \omega_3 = 1$ units of raw materials. The sales prices are assumed to be time invariant with $A_1 = \$150$ and $A_2 = \$120$ per unit of gold and silver chips, respectively. The manufacturing and inventory holding costs are $3.00 and $2.00 per unit, respectively. The initial input price vector per unit of copper, gold, and silver is $[P_1(t_0), P_2(t_0), P_3(t_0)] = [\$14.00, \$20.00, \$15.00]$, with corresponding annual volatility and convenience yields of: $\sigma_1 = .30$, $\sigma_2 = .35$, $\sigma_3 = .25$; $c_1 = .05$, $c_2 = .03$, $c_3 = .03$. The risk-free rate of return $r = 10$ percent per annum, and the pairwise correlation coefficients are $\rho_{12} = \rho_{23} = \rho_{34} = .50$. The stretch parameter is $\lambda = 1.061$, resulting in a horizontal jump probability of $\frac{1}{9}$. In addition, the yield uncertainty variable is characterized by the following parameters: $\beta_1 = .60$; $a_1 = 0.6$; $\beta_2 = .95$; $a_2 = .40$. For the above choice of base-case parameters, the optimal solution is shown in Figure 16.3, where the net expected value of the agreement is \$500.50.

To gain some insight into these results, consider product 1 (gold chips) with a corresponding zero level of inventory at time $t_0$, with $Q_0^0(1) = 0$, $R_{1,1}^S = 0$, $S \in \{0,1\}$.[12] In period $[t_1, t_2]$, the optimal schedule calls for a production of $Q_1^1(1) = Q_1^0(1) = 3$ units, resulting in a net inventory of:[13]

$$
\begin{aligned}
R_{2,1}^2 &= R_{1,1}^1 + Q_1^1(1)\beta_2 - \delta_{2,1} = 0 + [(3)(.95)] - 2 = 1 \\
R_{2,1}^1 &= R_{1,1}^0 + Q_1^0(1)\beta_2 - \delta_{2,1} = 0 + [(3)(.95)] - 2 = 1 \\
R_{2,1}^0 &= R_{1,1}^0 + Q_1^0(1)\beta_1 - \delta_{2,1} = R_{1,1}^1 + Q_1^1(1)\beta_1 - \delta_{2,1} \\
&= 0 + [(3)(.60)] - 2 = 0.
\end{aligned}
$$

At time $t_2$, regardless of the inventory state, $S \in \{0,1,2\}$, $Q_2^S(1) = 0$ since $\delta_{3,1} = 0$. Accordingly, the time $t_3$ inventory levels are updated ("rolled over") to their new positions according to the convention set forth in section 16.3. In the last period of production, $[t_3, t_4]$, the optimal production quantity $Q_3^S(1)$ depends on $R_{3,1}^S$, $S \in \{0,1,2,3\}$. Here, $Q_3^3(1) = Q_3^2(1) = 0$, since sufficient quantities are available in their corresponding inventories to meet the demand. By contrast, since $R_{3,1}^1 = R_{3,1}^0 = 0$, the demand cannot be met unless production is resumed. Therefore, contingent on occurrence of $S = 0, 1$, we have $Q_3^1(1) = Q_3^0(1) = 2$.

The optimal production and inventory for product 2 (the silver chips) follows through in a similar manner. The flexibility to switch among various product types contingent on future market conditions (i.e., input prices) creates an additional value beyond that of a "dedicated" production system. This "flexibility value" is the difference between the value of the flexible system and the maximum of the dedicated systems. Using the same case parameters furnished earlier, the value of a dedicated system for gold or silver chips is \$321.70 and \$235.80, respectively. Therefore, the flexibility value associated with this flexible production agreement (worth \$500.50) is \$178.80, or 44.4 percent beyond the value of the most profitable "dedicated" production facility.

An interesting finding pertains to a change in the correlation coefficient values. In particular, when the correlation between the price of gold and silver increases (while others are held constant), their corresponding "dedicated" values tend to become more alike.[14] This observation can be useful in contract negotiation and substitute product agreements. To account for the yield component, sensitivity analysis with regard to the parameter $\beta_1$ was performed, while maintaining $\beta_2$ at .95. As the yield uncertainty decreases (i.e., $\beta_1$ increases), the value of the agreement increases. Figure 16.4 shows

Figure 16.3
Optimal Production and Inventory Control for the Numerical Example

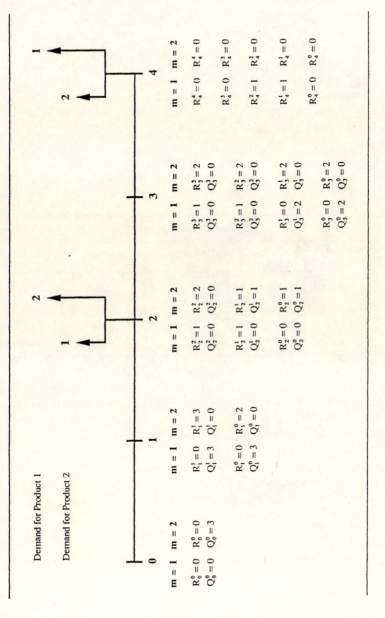

that the project's value is concave in $\beta_1$. Note that with $\beta_1 = 1.0$ (practically no yield uncertainty, since $\beta_2 = .95$), the project's value stabilizes at $561.40, a 31 percent increase in value over the case when $\beta_1 = .50$.

Another interesting feature is that of a corresponding change in the optimal production and inventory policy as a result of change in the yield variability. For example, corresponding to points $A$, $B$, $C$, and $D$ of Figure 16.4, there are different optimal policies. While enumeration of each optimal policy is omitted, Table 16.1 provides further interesting results. For instance, if yield was a controllable factor, then management should be willing to spend up to $58.80 (i.e., $559.30 - $500.50) to improve yield variability from $\beta_1 = .60$ to $\beta_1 = .80$.

**Table 16.1**

**Impact of Yield Variability on the Optimal Value of a Production System**

| Yield Variability Parameter ($\beta_1$) | Expected Value of System ($) | | | Flexibility Value ($) |
|---|---|---|---|---|
| | Flexible (Both products) | Dedicated (Product 1) | Dedicated (Product 2) | |
| .50 | 428.30 | 290.70 | 201.50 | 137.60 |
| .60 | 500.50 | 321.70 | 235.80 | 178.80 |
| .80 | 559.30 | 322.70 | 237.90 | 236.60 |
| 1.0 | 561.40 | 322.70 | 238.50 | 238.70 |

The valuation model illustrated here can also be used as an aid in establishing renegotiation prices in the event of unexpected input price increases. This can be done by following the lattice price nodes for which the project's value is negative. Alternatively, the same approach can be used in identifying "penalty" costs if contract abandonment were considered as an option. The model can also be employed to obtain the value both of production and inventory capacities. Specifically, the additional project value obtained by increasing capacity (in accordance with increased demand) should reflect the maximum cost of increased capacity (i.e., the capacity shadow price).

## 16.5 CONCLUSION

This chapter has examined an important decision problem concerning manufacturing firms, namely that of valuing production projects and agreements where input prices and output yields fluctuate randomly over time. The chapter has addressed the various problems involved in valuing produc-

**Figure 16.4**
**Project Value versus Output Yield Variability**

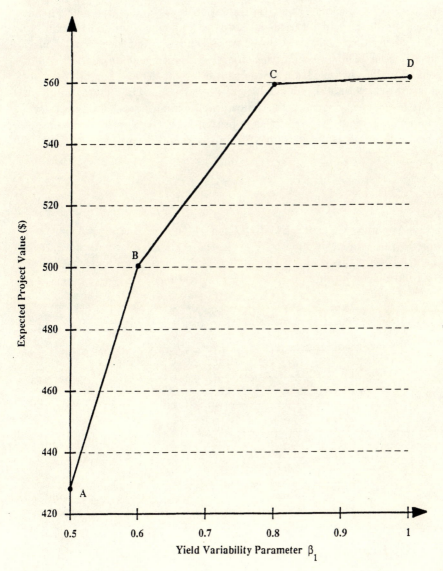

tion ventures characterized by such sources of uncertainty and significant operating flexibility. In particular, a lattice-based contingent claims valuation model was presented to derive the optimal value and policy to be followed.

While other valuation approaches are available, the advantages of this approach are threefold. First, the valuation technique is dynamic in that the methodology can be used in assessing and quantifying the flexibility value inherent in most risky projects. Second, the approach can identify optimal policies for reaching the objectives, contingent on market conditions. Finally, the valuation mechanism does not depend on the forecasts of future prices and is independent of preferences. The only assumption about future prices is that they follow "well-defined" stochastic processes. Another important feature of this approach is that the optimal exercise of operating options is not decoupled from the valuation process.

## APPENDIX

In this Appendix we define $E\{V^*_{i+1}(Q^S_i(m))\}$, the maximum total expected value of the project at time $t_{i+1}$, given the realization of node $(j,k,l)$ at time $t_i$. Toward this goal consider node $(j,k,l)$ where, after an elapsed time $\tau$, we have the following potential price realizations:

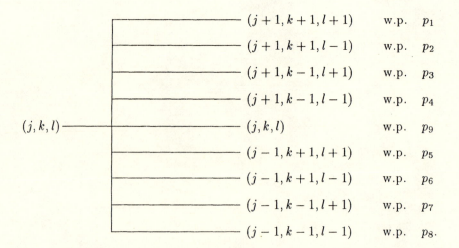

| | |
|---|---|
| $(j+1, k+1, l+1)$ | w.p. $p_1$ |
| $(j+1, k+1, l-1)$ | w.p. $p_2$ |
| $(j+1, k-1, l+1)$ | w.p. $p_3$ |
| $(j+1, k-1, l-1)$ | w.p. $p_4$ |
| $(j,k,l)$ | w.p. $p_9$ |
| $(j-1, k+1, l+1)$ | w.p. $p_5$ |
| $(j-1, k+1, l-1)$ | w.p. $p_6$ |
| $(j-1, k-1, l+1)$ | w.p. $p_7$ |
| $(j-1, k-1, l-1)$ | w.p. $p_8$. |

Furthermore, by definition, state $S \in \{0, 1, \ldots, i\}$ of inventory at time $t_i$ can reach either state zero with probability $a_1$ or state $S+1$ with probability

$a_2$ at time $t_{i+1}$. Accordingly, we can write:

$$
\begin{aligned}
E\left\{V_{i+1}^*(Q_i^S(m))\right\} = \; & a_1\Big\{p_1 V_{i+1}\big\{(j+1,k+1,l+1), R_{i+1,m}^0; Q_i^S(m)\big\} \\
& + \; p_2 V_{i+1}\big\{(j+1,k+1,l-1), R_{i+1,m}^0; Q_i^S(m)\big\} \\
& + \; p_3 V_{i+1}\big\{(j+1,k-1,l+1), R_{i+1,m}^0; Q_i^S(m)\big\} \\
& + \; p_4 V_{i+1}\big\{(j+1,k-1,l-1), R_{i+1,m}^0; Q_i^S(m)\big\} \\
& + \; p_5 V_{i+1}\big\{(j-1,k+1,l+1), R_{i+1,m}^0; Q_i^S(m)\big\} \\
& + \; p_6 V_{i+1}\big\{(j-1,k+1,l-1), R_{i+1,m}^0; Q_i^S(m)\big\} \\
& + \; p_7 V_{i+1}\big\{(j-1,k-1,l+1), R_{i+1,m}^0; Q_i^S(m)\big\} \\
& + \; p_8 V_{i+1}\big\{(j-1,k-1,l-1), R_{i+1,m}^0; Q_i^S(m)\big\} \\
& + \; p_9 V_{i+1}\big\{(j,k,l), R_{i+1,m}^0; Q_i^S(m)\big\}\Big\} \\
& + \; a_2\Big\{p_1 V_{i+1}\big\{(j+1,k+1,l+1), R_{i+1,m}^{S+1}; Q_i^S(m)\big\} \\
& + \; p_2 V_{i+1}\big\{(j+1,k+1,l-1), R_{i+1,m}^{S+1}; Q_i^S(m)\big\} \\
& + \; p_3 V_{i+1}\big\{(j+1,k-1,l+1), R_{i+1,m}^{S+1}; Q_i^S(m)\big\} \\
& + \; p_4 V_{i+1}\big\{(j+1,k-1,l-1), R_{i+1,m}^{S+1}; Q_i^S(m)\big\} \\
& + \; p_5 V_{i+1}\big\{(j-1,k+1,l+1), R_{i+1,m}^{S+1}; Q_i^S(m)\big\} \\
& + \; p_6 V_{i+1}\big\{(j-1,k+1,l-1), R_{i+1,m}^{S+1}; Q_i^S(m)\big\} \\
& + \; p_7 V_{i+1}\big\{(j-1,k-1,l+1), R_{i+1,m}^{S+1}; Q_i^S(m)\big\} \\
& + \; p_8 V_{i+1}\big\{(j-1,k-1,l-1), R_{i+1,m}^{S+1}; Q_i^S(m)\big\} \\
& + \; p_9 V_{i+1}\big\{(j,k,l), R_{i+1,m}^{S+1}; Q_i^S(m)\big\}\Big\}.
\end{aligned}
$$

# NOTES

1. See Ansari and Modaress (1990).
2. See also Tano (1986), Shih (1980), and Ehrhardt and Taube (1987).
3. Yield is assumed to be machine specific.
4. See Bodie and Rasansky (1980).
5. See Mason and Merton (1985) or Sick (1989).

6. The operating flexibility or managerial options within a project often result in an additional value component that conventional valuation techniques (such as NPV) do not capture.

7. This valuation recursion model can be viewed as a corrected version of the traditional valuation model presented in section 16.2 where the appropriate discount rate and probability for computing expectations need not be exogenously specified. These values are established internally within the model. An additional feature of this approach is that the model provides not only values but also optimal guidelines for selecting actions in response to future contingencies with regard to price and yield variations.

8. We have defined $m$ as the mode or product type, while $Q$ refers to the quantity to be produced under mode $m$, hence, $Q(m)$.

9. It is also possible to assume that prices are not directly linked to prices of commodities for which futures markets exist. However, for valuation purposes partial correlation of prices with a portfolio of other traded securities is required in an intertemporal CAPM setting. See McDonald and Siegel (1985) and Constantinides (1978) for an equivalent discount rate computation in project valuation.

10. An alternative valuation approach would be that of a market equilibrium. A general limitation of this approach is the difficulty of determining the stochastic properties of the cash-flow streams that depend on the stochastic input prices. Moreover, estimation of the expected rate of change in the input prices is extremely difficult.

11. Using Ito's Lemma and techniques of continuous-time arbitrage, it can be shown that $(r - c_j)$ is an equivalent martingale.

12. Note that the production quantity in the first period is zero. Whenever the production quantity during any given period is zero, we use the convention described in Equation (16.12) for tractability reasons.

13. In our computations, we rounded upward. A downward rounding would be more conservative.

14. The two will not be identical unless there exist perfect correlation and identical demand patterns.

# Chapter 17

# Default Risk in the Contingent Claims Model of Debt

## Anne Fremault Vila and Martha A. Schary

*This chapter presents a framework for risky debt valuation that draws from both the bankruptcy and the contingent claims valuation literatures. The opportunity to liquidate by either equityholders or debtholders can be modeled as a put option, and increases the value of the respective claims. We also show how the conflicting incentives of debt- and equityholders will affect the outcome of a default. Finally, we present a simple binomial example of involuntary bankruptcy to illustrate how the model can incorporate more realistic features of the bankruptcy law to value default risk. The chapter extends previous applications of option-pricing techniques to the abandonment decision and the valuation of corporate liabilities.*

## 17.1  INTRODUCTION

The 1980s witnessed an explosion in the amount of debt issued by U.S. corporations and a marked decline in the quality of debt issued. These developments have led to a dramatic increase in the likelihood of default. As a result, default risk has become a substantial factor in the pricing of a bond, both at the time of issue and as it trades in the secondary market.

Traditionally, financial ratio analysis has been used to predict the probability of bankruptcy, to establish credit ratings that rank corporate bonds based on their default risk, and to evaluate the default premium such bonds should contain.[1] However, as many bond investors have recently discovered, these techniques do not adequately assess default risk. Default risk reflects both the probability of default and the payout at default.[2]

Though largely ignored in the bankruptcy prediction literature, Merton's (1974) work represents a breakthrough in corporate bond analysis.

Merton recognized that the firm's bonds could be viewed as contingent claims since their value is contingent on the value of the firm and, therefore, they look very much like financial options. Using the options analogy, Merton showed that a firm's default risk could be directly incorporated into the prices of its securities. Hence, the pricing of corporate bonds is a natural extension of the option-pricing model which had been developed earlier by Black and Scholes (1973) and Merton (1973).[3]

As we will explain in more detail below, the traditional contingent claims model (CCM) includes stringent assumptions about the timing and outcome of bankruptcy. As the true default premium grows larger, these assumptions will lead to larger mispricing of the bond. In this chapter, we relax some of these assumptions and present an example that incorporates more realistic features of the bankruptcy law.[4] In particular, this extension focuses on the timing and outcome of bankruptcy based on the net worth criterion. We also suggest how our work could be extended to include the cash flow criterion for bankruptcy.

The present chapter develops a framework for thinking about the factors affecting the default premium and their effect on bond valuation, instead of setting up a large number of complex equations to capture our modifications to the CCM. Jones, Mason, and Rosenfeld (1985) illustrated the limited contribution of the latter line of inquiry. They incorporated several features of standard bond covenants into the CCM by adding several state variables and modifying the boundary conditions. After a considerable programming and computational effort, they obtained results that differ from the market value of the bonds by an average of 7 percent. As Fisher Black noted in his comments to their paper, this difference is surprisingly large, given the magnitude of the authors' efforts. We conclude from the experience of Jones, Mason, and Rosenfeld that it might be more fruitful to treat the CCM as a way of thinking about valuation issues in order to sharpen our knowledge of the factors affecting bond pricing and their relative strengths.

Our main findings can be summarized as follows. First, we argue that the claims on the firm's assets, stocks and bonds, contain a put option that will be exercised by the respective holders whenever the liquidation value exceeds the value of their claim in the surviving firm. Hence, equity and debtholders make separate decisions. This leads to interactions that will affect the value of debt and to the many different bankruptcy scenarios that we observe in practice. Second, by examining the optimal strategies for each securityholder, our model predicts when bankruptcies will lead to liquidation and when reorganizations or workouts will be used instead. Third, including the put option in a simple binomial valuation model leads to higher values for debt than those obtained in the standard CCM. This is because the legal system gives bondholders a valuable protection through their right to file for bankruptcy.

In previous work, Myers and Majd (1990) and Schary (1987) modeled the option to abandon as an American put option. In this chapter, we use this framework by illustrating how the degree of leverage can affect the abandonment decision and how the institutional features of bankruptcy can prevent optimal exit. Schary (1987) examined the interaction of leverage and the abandonment option through numerical analysis and found that: (a) the abandonment option has a positive value even when it seems unlikely that the firm will exercise it; and (b) leverage can radically change the optimal time to exercise the abandonment option. The present chapter extends previous applications of option-pricing techniques to the abandonment decision and the valuation of corporate liabilities.

The chapter is organized as follows. The next section outlines how actual bankruptcy law differs from the standard assumptions made in the CCM. In section 17.3 we develop a simple analytical framework to study the bankruptcy decisions of debtholders and equityholders and to illustrate how the conflicting incentives of these claimants can affect the outcome of a default. In section 17.4, some simple binomial examples of involuntary bankruptcy are developed. Section 17.5 concludes the chapter.

## 17.2   THE CONTINGENT CLAIMS MODEL AND BANKRUPTCY LAW

The original contingent claims model (CCM) makes four assumptions that are at odds with U.S. bankruptcy law and practice. First, the model makes no distinction between default, bankruptcy, and liquidation, but rather assumes that the three events are synonymous. A firm defaulting on a single payment—be it an interest or a principal payment—is considered to be bankrupt. Anyone familiar with actual defaults, liquidations, workouts, or bankruptcies will immediately recognize, however, the practical limitations of this assumption. In fact, cases abound of firms that have missed coupon payments or defaulted on short-term debt, but were nevertheless able to continue operations.[5] On the other hand, a bankruptcy petition can be accepted by the courts without any actual default on debt obligations.[6] A firm may liquidate in a bankruptcy proceeding (Chapter 7), reorganize in a bankruptcy proceeding (Chapter 11), or liquidate outside the bankruptcy process (voluntary liquidation).[7] Lane and Schary (1991) showed that in the United States there are 20 times more voluntary liquidations than there are bankruptcies each year.[8]

Second, CCM assumes that bankruptcy occurs when the value of a firm becomes less than the debt. Actual bankruptcy law, however, specifies that a firm must satisfy one of two criteria in order for its bankruptcy case to be accepted by the courts. The first specifies that net worth (assets minus liabilities) must be less than or equal to zero. While the CCM definition of default (when the firm value hits some lower bound) is independent of the capital structure of the firm, the net worth criterion is not. The higher the firm's leverage, the more likely it is that the value of its assets will fall below its liabilities. The second, alternate, criterion for bankruptcy is based on the firm's liquidity. This cash flow criterion defines a firm as bankrupt if it is unable to meet its current obligations. A firm might have bright prospects and a positive net worth but no liquid assets to meet current debt due, and so could be forced into bankruptcy by its creditors.

Third, CCM does not recognize that bankruptcy petitions are the result of a strategic decision by management, in the case of voluntary bankruptcy, or by creditors, in the case of involuntary bankruptcy. Bankruptcy is not the result of an exogenous event, but the outcome of a forward-looking, rational decision process. We discuss this dynamic aspect of bankruptcy in the next section.

Fourth, the CCM does not distinguish between the liquidation value and the ongoing value of the firm. Many firms have breakup values that differ markedly from their going-concern values. The model developed here includes a separate liquidation value to reflect this possibility.

Together, these features of actual bankruptcy practice make the evaluation of default risk much more complicated than in the CCM. The inclusion of all these features of the bankruptcy process, however, would lead to an extremely complex and cumbersome model and is beyond the scope of this chapter. Instead, we focus here on one of the bankruptcy criteria, the net worth criterion, and show how a rich set of results can be obtained from a simple extension of the CCM. We suggest further extensions in the concluding section of the chapter.

## 17.3   MODELING DEFAULT, BANKRUPTCY, AND LIQUIDATION

In this section, we analyze the incentives of equityholders and debtholders to liquidate the firm. In our discussion, we distinguish between liquidation through bankruptcy proceedings initiated by debtholders and voluntary liquidation initiated by equityholders. The basic intuition is that a bankruptcy filing is not an exogenously determined event, but a rational decision that preserves value for either debt- or equityholders. Each securityholder weighs the gain from continued operations against the gain from liquidation. If the gain from liquidation is greater, a bankruptcy petition will be filed or a voluntary liquidation procedure initiated.[9] No class of securityholders considers the entire value of the firm under either bankruptcy or continued operations, only their *own* piece.

## 17.3.1 The Equityholders' Bankruptcy Decision

In the standard CCM, equity is viewed as a call option on the value of the firm's assets. Because the call option has some value even when the value of the firm's assets is low, it is generally thought that equityholders will never want to file for bankruptcy or voluntarily liquidate the firm. In addition, equityholders' claims are typically severely diluted in a bankruptcy reorganization. For these reasons, it is safe to assume that equityholders will not file for bankruptcy in order to reorganize the firm unless they are threatened by debtholders who are themselves about to file.[10]

It is not safe to assume, however, that equityholders will never want to file in order to liquidate. On the contrary, at each point in time, equityholders can weigh the value of their call option on the firm against their payoff from immediate liquidation. When the firm's assets have a higher value in an alternate use, liquidation will be preferred. Before deciding to liquidate immediately, however, equityholders must consider whether it would be better to wait and possibly liquidate later: the immediate liquidation decision must take into account the optimal liquidation strategy in the future. Essentially, in addition to holding a call option on the firm's assets, equityholders also hold a put option on the current value of equity under continued operations, with an exercise price equal to the equity value in liquidation.[11] The put option analogy allows for the valuation of the right held by equityholders to liquidate the firm.

Consider a firm that has issued debt $(D)$ with a single payment $(B)$ due at maturity $(T)$, and equity $(S)$. Let $V^G$ be the going-concern value of the firm, and $V^L$ be the firm's immediate liquidation value.[12] We assume that $V^L$ is exogenously determined. As the residual claimants, equityholders receive $V^G - D(V^G)$ when the firm is able to meet its debt obligation, and $V^L - D(V^L)$ otherwise: we will specify $D(V^G)$ and $D(V^L)$ in section 17.3.2. In addition, equityholders hold an American put option, $A_\tau$, on equity value under continued operations, $V^G - D(V^G)$, with an exercise price equal to the equity value under liquidation, $V^L - D(V^L)$.[13] This put option is an increasing function of $V^L - D(V^L)$, the time to maturity $(\tau)$, and the standard deviation of the rate of change of $V^G - D(V^G)$. It is a decreasing function of $V^G - D(V^G)$ and the risk-free interest rate, r. Equityholders will choose to liquidate when:

$$S(V^G, \tau) \leq S(V^L, \tau), \quad \text{or}$$

$$V^G_\tau - D_\tau(V^G) + A_\tau \leq V^L_\tau - D_\tau(V^L), \qquad (17.1)$$

where $\tau \equiv T - t$ is the time to maturity $(T)$. Equation (17.1) shows that inclusion of the put option affects the value of equity, and hence, the value of the whole firm.

By rearranging the terms of Equation (17.1), we can graph the line of indifference for equityholders. Define $y = (V^G - V^L) - [D(V^G) - D(V^L)] + A_\tau$ as the equityholders' premium from continuing rather than liquidating.[14] Equityholders are indifferent to bankruptcy if $y = 0$. Thus, the equityholders' decision to (voluntarily) liquidate the firm can be graphically represented by $y \leq 0$, as shown in Figure 17.1. In the figure, the right-leaning $45°$ line through the origin represents the line of indifference for equityholders, *without* the put option. Above $y$ (to the northwest), the equityholders would liquidate; below $y$ (to the southeast), they would continue. *With* the put option, $y$ shifts to the left by an amount equal to the difference between the exercise price and the critical price, both measured in units of $V^G$.[15] [16]

**Figure 17.1**
**The Equityholders' Bankruptcy Decision**

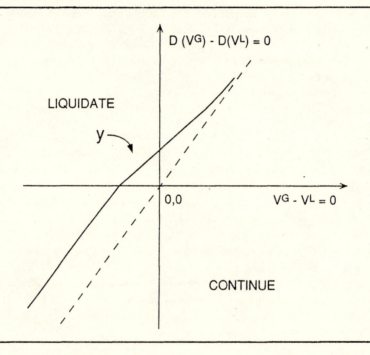

Despite its relative simplicity, Figure 17.1 captures how the timing of bankruptcy depends on the capital structure. The fact that $y$ crosses the horizontal axis to the left of the origin suggests that equityholders in a levered firm will wait for lower values of the ongoing firm before liquidating than will equityholders in an all-equity firm. Furthermore, the figure shows that it is not the degree of leverage, but the relative values of

$D(V^G) - D(V^L)$ that determine the equityholders' decision. For example, imagine two otherwise identical firms with debt-to-equity ratios of 0.5 and 1.2, respectively. Figure 17.1 implies that if the difference between $D(V^G)$ and $D(V^L)$ is the same for both firms, they have an equal chance of going bankrupt. If instead, the highly leveraged firm is expected to pay out in liquidation the same fraction of the going concern value of the debt, namely, $D(V^G)/D(V^L)$, then equityholders would be less likely to take the highly leveraged firm into bankruptcy. Because $V^G - V^L$ and the degree of leverage are not monotonically related, there can be scenarios with perverse outcomes in which equityholders in a highly leveraged firm take the firm into bankruptcy.

## 17.3.2 The Debtholders' Bankruptcy Decision

On occasion, debtholders will want to initiate bankruptcy proceedings in order to preserve the value of their claim. Analogous to the decision of equityholders, debtholders must also choose when to initiate bankruptcy.[17] However, bondholders cannot file an involuntary petition at any time, but only when the firm has met the net worth criterion for bankruptcy. (We defer discussion of the cash flow criterion to the next section.) This means that they hold a European put, in contrast to the American put held by equityholders. The two put options differ in other respects as well. The time to maturity of the debtholders' put is uncertain and depends on how frequently the value of the firm's assets falls below its debt obligations.

Recall that $D_\tau(V^G)$ is the value of debt if the firm continues operations without bankruptcy before $T$, and $D_\tau(V^L)$ is the value of debt with an immediate bankruptcy filing.[18] When debtholders choose bankruptcy, they receive $V^L$, which is less than $B$. If the net worth covenant is not violated ($V^G \geq B$), then the firm continues operations and debtholders receive $B + Q$, where $Q$ is their European put option. If the net worth covenant is violated ($V^G < B$), then the debtholders receive $V^G + Q$. The put option, $Q$, is written on their claim in the ongoing firm, with an exercise price equal to their claim in bankruptcy.[19] Hence, $D_\tau(V^G) = min(B, V^G) + Q$. Debtholders will file for bankruptcy when the net worth covenant is violated, $V^G < B$, and if:

$$D_\tau(V^G) = min(B, V^G) + Q < V^L = D_\tau(V^L). \qquad (17.2)$$

Rearranging terms allows the debtholders' premium for continuation over bankruptcy to be defined as $x = D(V^G) - D(V^L) + Q$.[20] The debtholders' bankruptcy decision can be shown graphically, as in Figure 17.2.

Above the $x$ line in the figure, debtholders want the firm to continue operations, below $x$ they would liquidate the firm if they could. Because

**Figure 17.2**
**The Debtholders' Bankruptcy Decision**

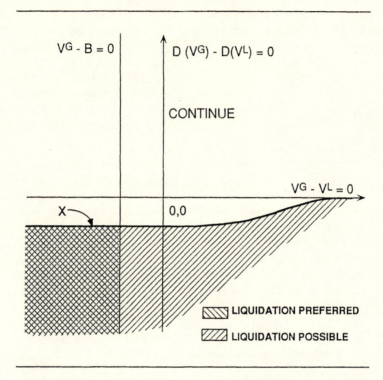

debtholders must wait until the net worth covenant is violated, the region below $x$ in which they can actually file for bankruptcy is the one to the left of the vertical line, $V^G - B$. For debtholders there is a monotonic relationship between the degree of leverage and the possibility of filing for bankruptcy. For highly leveraged firms, the vertical line, $V^G - B$, might be far to the right of the origin, making the probability of a bankruptcy filing quite high.

We have argued so far that both debtholders and equityholders hold put options. When equityholders have the right to liquidate the firm, as they do under U.S. law, the value of equityholders is increased by the value of their put option. This provides a protection (in addition to limited liability) against downside risk. The debtholders' put option is also established by U.S. law: the value of the opportunity to file an involuntary bankruptcy petition contributes to the value of the debtholders' put. While the specific institutional features of the bankruptcy law will affect the value of the put, it is clear that in a legal system in which debtholders can choose to file for bankruptcy, the value of the debt will be higher than that predicted by the

CCM.[21]

It is interesting to contrast this insight to the results of Franks and Torous (1989), who modeled the opportunity of Chapter 11 reorganization as an option to delay payments. This call option is held by management, which acts "in the best interest of shareholders." Bondholders are generally hurt by this option since Chapter 11 reorganization often leads to violations of absolute priority rights. As a result, the authors argued that bondholders have to be compensated in the form of a higher risk premium. Our work complements this approach. Priority is a postfiling issue, and the expected deviations are incorporated into the prefiling debt values. We have assumed no deviations from absolute priority and show that even before filing, some features of bankruptcy law give bondholders additional protection against management (or equityholders) running the firm into the ground. This additional protection, which we identify as a put option, results in a lower risk premium. Deciding which feature is stronger, the prefiling protection (our put) or the prefiling expectation of deviations from absolute priority (Franks and Torous's call), is an open empirical question.

### 17.3.3    When Do Firms Go Bankrupt?

The realization of bankruptcy is, therefore, the outcome of separate, and sometimes conflicting, desires of debtholders and equityholders. Figure 17.3 gives a composite picture of when a firm will go bankrupt by combining Figures 17.1 and 17.2. The features of this graph will be described in a counterclockwise order, beginning with region 1.

In region 1, both debtholders and equityholders want the firm to continue operations. Inside region 1 and to the left of the line $V^G - B = 0$, the firm is in violation of its net worth covenant but neither party wants to force it into bankruptcy. In region 2, there is a conflict between the two claimants. Because equityholders can liquidate the firm at any time, if they can pay the debtholders off in full, voluntary liquidation will occur.[22] Region 3 has the same conflict between debtholders and equityholders as region 2, but here, the net worth covenant is violated, so debtholders cannot be paid off in full and equityholders cannot force liquidation. The firm will continue operations.

Both debtholders and equityholders are in agreement to liquidate the firm in region 4. Conflict reappears in region 5, with debtholders wanting to liquidate while equityholders want to continue. Here, the net worth covenant is violated and debtholders can force bankruptcy. It is in region 5 that the put option, $Q$, acquires its value because it provides the opportunity for debtholders to act on their own interests. Moreover, region 5 illustrates the typical corporate finance case: debtholders have to drag the equityholders into the bankruptcy court, even though the firm is in a bad

**Figure 17.3**
**The Bankruptcy Outcome**

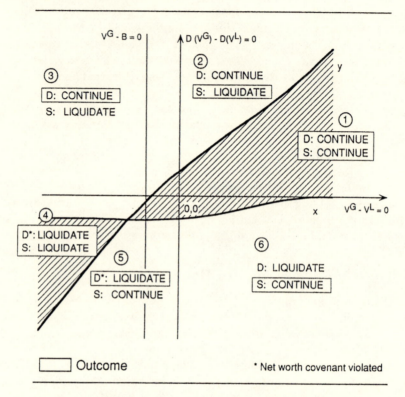

Outcome                                   * Net worth covenant violated

state. This is especially likely to happen in a highly leveraged firm, because
the small chance that the firm will improve is worth something only to the
equityholders. In region 6, debtholders would again like to force bankruptcy
on equityholders but cannot because the firm is solvent in the net worth
sense. Debtholders want to liquidate because their payment in liquidation
is higher than if the firm continued. This situation may arise if interest rate
movements lower the value of the existing debt's coupon payments.

   In sum, Figure 17.3 shows how the bankruptcy law resolves the conflict
between the two claimants. In regions 4 and 5, the firm is likely to liquidate because debtholders will be able to force bankruptcy on the firm. In
regions 2 and 6, workouts or a restructuring of the firm's liabilities outside
bankruptcy are likely. Defaults are likely to lead to liquidation in regions
1 (to the left of the line $V^G - B = 0$), 2, 4 and 5, but not in the other
regions. The figure shows that Chapter 11 bankruptcies are not likely to
arise when bankruptcy is defined only by the net worth criterion, because

there is no case in which the firm can file for bankruptcy yet equityholders would want to continue with a reasonable firm value. Equityholders are left only with their call option on future value and the value of postfiling control, as discussed by Franks and Torous (1989).

Figure 17.3 also illustrates how the features of the bankruptcy law interact with the firm's capital structure to affect the final bankruptcy outcome. For example, compare the outcomes for the leveraged firm shown in Figure 17.3 with the bankruptcy decision of an all-equity firm. An all-equity firm would liquidate whenever $V^G - V^L$ was less than zero. In contrast, the region in which a leveraged firm is likely to liquidate is considerably smaller.

## 17.4  DEFAULT AND BANKRUPTCY IN THE CCM: SOME ILLUSTRATIVE EXAMPLES

The figures presented in the previous section highlight the potential conflicts between the various claimants, categorize the outcomes of the bankruptcy decisions, and link the value of debt to the different types of outcomes. This conceptual framework is generally useful, but further insights into risky bond valuation can be derived by examining some simple binomial examples of involuntary bankruptcy.[23]

### 17.4.1  The Value of Debt in the CCM

To cast the original CCM in the binomial framework, consider a firm with a current value of $100 that has a probability of 0.59 of increasing in value by 16 percent each year and a probability of 0.41 of decreasing in value by 8 percent each year.[24] Figure 17.4 shows the value of such a firm, $V^G$, for two years. An 11.80 percent volatility of firm value is consistent with these numbers.[25]

Suppose the firm has promised to pay $101.12 to its debtholders at maturity of the debt contract in two years, with no intermediate coupon payments. Assuming risk neutrality and a risk-free interest rate of 6 percent, the present value of safe debt is $90. The debt, however, is not safe. In the standard CCM, bankruptcy will occur if at maturity $V^G < \$101.12$. As shown in Figure 17.5, this implies that the value of debt at the bottom-right node equals the lower value of the firm in two years. Taking expected values and discounting, gives today's value of the risky debt as $87.54. Today's equity is worth $12.45.

**Figure 17.4**
**Value of the Firm with Continued Operations**

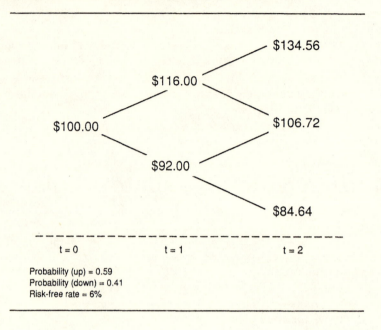

Probability (up) = 0.59
Probability (down) = 0.41
Risk-free rate = 6%

## 17.4.2   The Valuation of Risky Debt with Involuntary Bankruptcy

Now suppose that, at any time, the firm has the opportunity to liquidate at $V^L = \$93$. (This liquidation value may reflect the salvage value of the firm's assets.) Again assume a capital structure of \$90 of debt and \$10 of equity. The debtholders' decision is analyzed first. Remember that debtholders can only file for bankruptcy if the net worth condition is violated, namely, if $V^L$ is less than $B$. Figure 17.4 shows that this condition is violated at the lower-center node as well as at the lower-right node of the binomial tree. Thus, at these two nodes, debtholders can file an involuntary bankruptcy petition if it proves optimal.

Figure 17.6 shows the value of continued operations for debtholders. At the boxed lower nodes, debtholders hold a European put option, reflecting their opportunity to file for bankruptcy. At the remaining nodes, the net worth condition is not violated, so debtholders do not actually have the option to file for bankruptcy. The hypothetical value of the put is shown for comparison purposes.[26] Outside the boxed nodes, the value of the put option is shown in parenthesis because it is not being exercised. Inside the boxed note, the value of the put is added to the value of the debt.

**Figure 17.5**
**Value of Debt in the Original Contingent Claims Model**

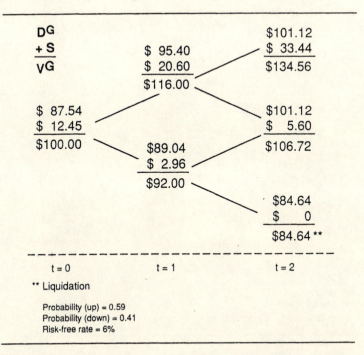

** Liquidation

Probability (up) = 0.59
Probability (down) = 0.41
Risk-free rate = 6%

Note that the value of the debt under continued operations differs from the original CCM model at three nodes in this example of involuntary bankruptcy. At the lowest node at $t = 2$, the value of the option is $3.78, so the value of the debt under continued operations is higher than in the original CCM by this amount. At $t = 1$, the lowest node has an option value of $2.36. At $t = 0$, there is no option value because the net worth condition is met. However, the debt value is again higher than in the original CCM because debtholders expect that if the firm value falls they will be able to use their option to file for bankruptcy. The value of debt at $t = 0$, $88.46, is the expected value of $95.40 and $91.40, where the latter includes the option value. Note that the expected value of the option raises the value of debt under continued operations by 92 cents, or about 1 percent. Hence, the CCM (yielding a debt value of $87.54 in Figure 17.5) would underprice the debt.

While Figure 17.6 shows the differences in the value of debt under continued operations, Figure 17.7 further illustrates the differences between the two models arising from the liquidation opportunity that bankruptcy presents. Beginning at $t = 2$ in Figure 17.7, the only possible bankruptcy decision is in the lowest node. At the other nodes the value of debt is

**Figure 17.6**
**Value of Debt under Continued Operations**

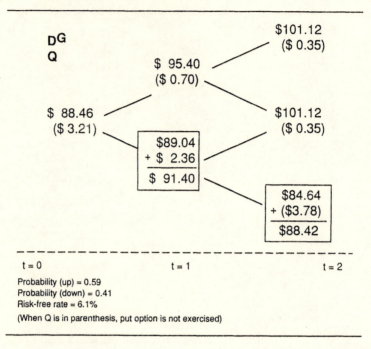

Probability (up) = 0.59
Probability (down) = 0.41
Risk-free rate = 6.1%
(When Q is in parenthesis, put option is not exercised)

worth more if the firm continues, corresponding to the situation in region 1 of Figure 17.3. At the lowest node, $D(V^G)$ is equal to \$88.42, but $D(V^L)$ is equal to \$93 because debtholders would obtain all proceeds of the liquidation. As Figure 17.7 illustrates, debtholders would clearly want to file an involuntary bankruptcy petition. This situation corresponds to region 5 in Figure 17.3 because equityholders get nothing in liquidation and so would always prefer to continue based on the small chance that the value of the firm might increase above $D(V^L)$.

Stepping back in time, the debtholders have a decision opportunity at the lower node at $t = 1$. As shown in Figure 17.6, $D(V^G)$ is equal to \$91.40 at this node. As Figure 17.7 shows, debtholders are owed \$95.40, the current value of $D(V^L)$, but if they file for liquidation through bankruptcy they will only receive \$93.[27] Debtholders will prefer this partial payment on what they are owed over keeping the firm alive. Again, this node corresponds to region 5 in Figure 17.3.

Figure 17.7 shows the value of debt at $t = 0$, under the assumption that debtholders make an involuntary bankruptcy filing at $t = 1$. The value of debt is higher than under the standard CCM because (a) there is a liquidation opportunity present and (b) debtholders will be able to use

**Figure 17.7**
**The Bankruptcy Decision by Debtholders**

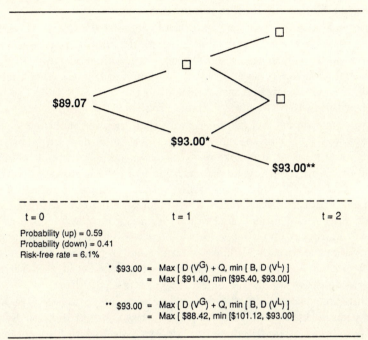

Probability (up) = 0.59
Probability (down) = 0.41
Risk-free rate = 6.1%

* $93.00 = Max [ D (V$^G$) + Q, min [ B, D (V$^L$) ]
       = Max [ $91.40, min [$95.40, $93.00]

** $93.00 = Max [ D (V$^G$) + Q, min [ B, D (V$^L$) ]
        = Max [ $88.42, min [$101.12, $93.00]

their option one period in the future. The combination of these features raises the value of debt by $1.53 or 1.7 percent over the standard CCM value. This value of debt should be the one observed in the market.

In sum, this binomial example has shown that inclusion of realistic features of the bankruptcy code will affect the value of debt in the CCM before bankruptcy. While this example illustrates the value of the legal protection debtholders have, it is also possible to construct examples in which the net worth criterion is never violated and so debtholders cannot file an involuntary bankruptcy petition when they would like. In this case, the bankruptcy law does not offer much protection and the value of the debt will be the same as in the standard CCM.[28]

## 17.5   CONCLUSIONS AND EXTENSIONS

This chapter has considered several features of U.S. bankruptcy law and the problems they pose to risky debt valuation. We have built a very simple analytical framework that shows how the conflicting incentives of debtholders and equityholders will affect the outcome of a default. We also discussed the occurrence of workouts, bankruptcies, and voluntary liquidations. In addition, the binomial examples of involuntary bankruptcy show how the original CCM may undervalue debt because it neglects the legal protection given to bondholders by the bankruptcy law.

To include all the important features of the bankruptcy law, three further extensions of the CCM model are needed. The first is a more accurate treatment of the bankruptcy criteria. First, one should model the net worth criterion for bankruptcy as a book-value–based constraint, rather than as the market-value constraint used here and in the original CCM. This distinction will lead to a two-state variable problem.

Second, one should include the cash flow criterion for bankruptcy. This extension would help to capture short-run considerations, surprises, and unanticipated losses to debtholders. This extension again would require a two-state variable model of the firm. The value of the firm would continue to be a state variable and would represent the long-run viability of the enterprise. The second state variable would be the amount of cash available to meet current obligations and would permit more careful distinctions between bankruptcy filings made for strategic reasons and those made as a result of financial distress. While the former may represent unanticipated losses for debtholders, the latter can be better anticipated because they arise from deterioration in the long-run prospects of the firm.

A third extension could allow interest rates to be stochastic. We have noted earlier in this chapter that interest-rate risk can contribute to default risk. The interaction of default risk and interest-rate risk needs to be more fully explored and will depend on the costs of recontracting outstanding debt.

Finally, any of these extensions will require improvements in the computational method. While all would add important features to the model and may improve the accuracy of the estimates of bond values, considerable effort must be expended to make them computationally tractable. These methods hold the promise to better capture the default options of leveraged firms.

## ACKNOWLEDGMENTS

We would like to thank Zvi Bodie for many helpful discussions and Daniel Raff and Timothy Bresnahan for suggesting some of the figures. We have received helpful comments from participants at the 1992 American Law and Economics Conference, and especially from three anonymous referees and from the editor, Lenos Trigeorgis.

# NOTES

1. See Altman, Haldemna, and Narayaman (1977), and Fabozzi (1991, ch. 17, 19).

2. Throughout this chapter, we focus on the effect of default risk on bonds. However, the arguments and results also apply to bank loans. Our model could be used, for example, to improve the credit analysis of lending officers.

3. For a review of the contingent claims model of debt, see Fremault and Schary (1992).

4. For a survey of previous extensions of the CCM, such as incorporating coupon payments, sinking funds, and safety covenants, see Fremault and Schary (1992).

5. Donald Trump's operations is one example.

6. For example, Eastern Airlines declared bankruptcy while holding substantial cash and without having defaulted on any debt payments. The filing was made in an attempt to preserve the ongoing value of the firm in light of the machinists' strike (*Wall Street Journal*, March 10, 1989, p. 1).

7. While liquidation is usually associated with small companies, it can also be used by large concerns. The liquidation of Drexel, Burnham and Lambert, and of Fruehaf (a top 200 manufacturing company) are illustrative examples (*Wall Street Journal*, February 13, 1990, p. C1; February 14, 1990, p. 1).

8. Involuntary bankruptcies account for 5 percent of all U.S. business bankruptcies. During the 1980s, 90 percent of all business bankruptcy filings were Chapter 7 filings (U.S. Department of Commerce, 1990).

9. A voluntary bankruptcy petition can be filed by management (acting on behalf of shareholders), while an involuntary petition is filed by debtholders. The treatment of voluntary and involuntary petitions is the same under U.S. law (see Jackson, 1986; Newton, 1985).

10. See Franks and Torous (1989), Gilson, John, and Lang (1990), and Weiss (1990) on the payout to equityholders in a reorganization.

11. In the original CCM model, equityholders hold a call option written on the value of the firm, with an exercise price equal to the next coupon payment. By put-call parity, this call option is related to a put option written on the assets of the firm. We argue that equityholders own an additional option, a put option with a different exercise price. To make the liquidation decision, equityholders evaluate their payout in liquidation, not the value of the next coupon payment. By put-call parity, the put we introduce is related to a call option on the value of the firm minus the value of the debt with an exercise price equal to the liquidation value of the firm.

12. $V^G$ corresponds to $V$ in the standard CCM model. Our extension requires a distinction between $V^G$ and $V^L$. This distinction arises from both direct bankruptcy costs (e.g., legal fees) and indirect bankruptcy costs (loss of customers, creditors demanding immediate payment). The model of Bulow and Shoven (1978) also made a distinction between the two values.

13. Geske (1977) also valued the equityholders' right to liquidate as a put option on the stock. He modeled the risk of default on a coupon-paying bond as a series of put options held by equityholders. Our use of the put option differs from his in two ways. First, we allow the liquidation decision to be made at any time (an American option), not just when the coupon must be paid (a European option). Second, while Geske sets $V^L$ to be the coupon payment on the bond, our value of $V^L$ is the entire value of the firm in liquidation.

14. We drop the time subscript for notational simplicity.

15. For an option written on a stock, the critical price is the stock price at which exercise of the option first becomes optimal. The critical price is less than the stock price for a put option.

16. While Figure 17.1 is centered at the origin for expositional purposes, it is not meant to suggest equal probabilities of the firm landing in each quadrant. In fact, there is a much lower possibility of the upper left quadrant than any of the others. Also, while the axes are orthogonal in this graph, they are actually correlated in some ranges. For extremely high values of $V^G - V^L$, the debt is safe and the axes are uncorrelated. However, when $V^G - V^L$ is at lower levels, debt is risky and $D(V^G) - D(V^L)$ will be positively correlated with $V^G - V^L$. At extremely low levels of $V^G - V^L$, both the firm and the debt are virtually valueless. Notice also that because the option declines in value with higher values of $V^G$, $y$ curves back to the 45° line to the right of the intersection of $y$ and $V^G - V^L$. Below the horizontal line, $y$ is parallel to the 45° line because equityholders should immediately exercise the option and liquidate the firm.

17. Van Horne (1976) modeled the initiation of bankruptcy proceedings by debtholders as a dynamic programming problem.

18. Note that here the value of debt is a function of either the value of the firm under continued operations or its value in bankruptcy. As mentioned before, in the standard CCM model there is no need to distinguish among these debt values because there is only one value of the firm, $V$, equal to $V^G$.

19. If we introduce different debt classes, then this put option will differ across classes.

20. Again, we drop the time subscript.

21. Because the net worth criterion limits when debtholders may file for bankruptcy, the values of debt in our model may not always exceed those in the CCM.

However, once the cash flow criterion is also incorporated, debt values will rise further and will certainly exceed those generated by the CCM.

22. The problem bondholders face here, namely the early redemption of their claims, is similar to the call feature in bonds and has been valued by Blume and Keim (1989), among others.

23. We present binomial examples rather than an analytical solution for two reasons. First, the binomial model can incorporate several, although not all features of the bankruptcy code. It is easy to reach the point of diminishing marginal returns to more sophisticated modeling. The binomial model provides a simple way of thinking about the problem, and is sufficiently flexible to incorporate many details of the bankruptcy process. Second, as the previous section has shown, the outcome of default is situationally dependent. The binomial model can be used, for example, to value debt of already bankrupt firms where more detailed knowledge of the payouts in each state is available. It can be used to value the strategy of equityholders as well. The binomial model also indicates to what extent the traditional CCM leads to mispricing in the various states.

24. These are risk-neutral probabilities consistent with the CCM. See Hull (1991) for details.

25. See Hull (1991) for an instructive discussion of the binomial presentation of option models.

26. The put option values were calculated using the Black-Scholes formula with an exercise price of \$93, $r = 6$ percent, $T = 1$ year, and $\sigma = 11.8$ percent.

27. This treatment of $D(V^L)$ corresponds to the treatment of zero-coupon debt in the bankruptcy law (see Jackson, 1986).

28. We have constructed examples of voluntary bankruptcy as well. The latter possibility, modeled as a put option held by equityholders, raises the value of equity, but leaves debt unaffected. This follows from the fact that equityholders can only hope to increase the value of their claim if all senior claimants have been paid in full. Including violation of these rights will presumably lower the value of debt, as in Franks and Torous (1989).

# Bibliography

Aase, K.K. (1988). "Contingent Claims Valuation When the Security Price is a Combination of an Ito Process and a Random Point Process," *Stochastic Processes and Their Applications* 28, pp. 185-220.

Ackerman, R.W. (1970). "Influence of Integration and Diversity on the Investment Process," *Administrative Science Quarterly* 15 (September), pp. 341-351.

Aggarwal, R. (1980). "Corporate Use of Sophisticated Capital Budgeting Techniques: A Strategic Perspective and a Critique of Survey Results," *Interfaces* 10, 2 (April), pp. 31-34.

Aggarwal, R. (1991). "Justifying Investments in Flexible Manufacturing Technology," *Managerial Finance* 17, 2/3 (May), pp. 77-88.

Agmon, T. (1991). "Capital Budgeting and the Utilization of Full Information: Performance Evaluation and the Exercise of Real Options," *Managerial Finance* 17, 2/3 (May), pp. 42-50.

Alberts, W.A., and J.M. McTaggart (1984). "Value-Based Strategic Investment Planning," *Interfaces* 14, 1 (January-February), pp. 138-151.

Altman, E., R. Haldemna, and P. Narayaman (1977). "ZETA Analysis: A New Model to Identify Bankruptcy Risk of Corporations," *Journal of Banking and Finance* 1, 1 (June), pp. 29-54.

Amihud, Y., B. Lev, and N.G. Travlos (1990). "Corporate Control and the Choice of Investment Financing: The Case of Corporate Acquisitions," *Journal of Finance* 45 (June), pp. 603-616.

Andreou, S.A. (1990). "A Capital Budgeting Model for Product-Mix Flexibility," *Journal of Manufacturing Operations Management* 3, pp. 5-23.

Ang, J.S., and S. Dukas (1991). "Capital Budgeting in a Competitive Environment," *Managerial Finance* 17, 2/3 (May), pp. 6-15.

Ansari, A., and B. Modaress (1990). *Just in Time Purchasing* (New York, NY: Freeman Press).

Ansoff, H.I. (1965). *Corporate Strategy* (New York, NY: McGraw-Hill).

Anthony, R.N. (1965). *Planning and Control Systems: A Framework for Analysis* (Boston, MA: Division of Research, Harvard Business School).

Anthony, R.N., and J. Dearden (1976). *Management Control Systems: Text and Cases* (Homewood, IL: Richard D. Irwin).

Aoki, M. (1992a). "Ex Post Monitoring of Team Production by the Main Bank," CEPR Discussion paper, Stanford University.

Aoki, M. (1992b). "The Japanese Firm as a System Attributes" (in Japanese). *Economic Studies Quarterly* 43 (December), pp. 401-418.

Aoki, M. (1992c). "Will the Corporate Governance Structure in Japan and the U.S. Converge?"(in Japanese). Luncheon speech presented at the IUJ-NYU International Conference, May 11-13, Tokyo, Japan.

Arrow, K. (1951). *Social Choice and Individual Values* (New York, NY: John Wiley and Sons).

Baldwin, C. (1982). "Optimal Sequential Investment When Capital Is Not Readily Reversible," *Journal of Finance* 37, 3 (June), pp. 763-782.

Baldwin, C. (1987). "Competing for Capital in a Global Environment," *Midland Corporate Finance Journal* 5 (Spring), pp. 43-64.

Baldwin, C., and K. Clark (1992). "Capabilities and Capital Investment: New Perspectives on Capital Budgeting," *Journal of Applied Corporate Finance* 5, 2 (Summer), pp. 67-87.

Baldwin, C., and K. Clark (1993). "Modularity and Real Options," Working paper, Harvard Business School.

Baldwin, C., and R. Ruback (1986). "Inflation, Uncertainty, and Investment," *Journal of Finance* 41 (July), pp. 657-669.

Baldwin, C., and L. Trigeorgis (1993). "Toward Remedying the Underinvestment Problem: Competitiveness, Real Options, Capabilities, and TQM," Working paper, Harvard Business School.

Baldwin, R. (1988). "Hysteresis in Import Prices: The Beachhead Effect," *American Economic Review* 78, 4 (September), pp. 773-785.

Baldwin, R., and P.R. Krugman (1989). "Persistent Trade Effects of Large Exchange Rate Shocks," *Quarterly Journal of Economics* 104, 4 (November), pp. 635-654.

Banz, R.W., and M.H. Miller (1978). "Prices for State-Contingent Claims: Some Estimates and Applications," *Journal of Business* 51, 4, pp. 653-672.

Barone-Adesi, G., and R. Whaley (1987). "Efficient Analytic Approximation of American Option Values," *Journal of Finance* 42 (June), pp. 301-320.

Bassok, Y., and C. Yano (1992). "Simple Optimal Policies for Finite and Infinite Horizon Problems for Single Stage Production Systems with Random Yields," Working paper, Northwestern University.

Bhattacharya, S. (1978). "Project Valuation with Mean-Reverting Cash Flow Streams," *Journal of Finance* 33 (December), pp. 1317-1331.

Bierman, H.J. (1988). *Implementing Capital Budgeting Techniques.* Financial Management Association Survey and Synthesis Series (Hagerstown, MD: Harper and Row).

Bierman, H., and S. Smidt (1988). *The Capital Budgeting Decision* (New York, NY: Macmillan), pp. 448-470.

Bjerksund, P., and S. Ekern (1990). "Managing Investment Opportunities under Price Uncertainty: From "Last Chance" to "Wait and See" Strategies," *Financial Management* 19 (Autumn), pp. 65-83.

Black, F., and M. Scholes (1973). "The Pricing of Options and Corporate Liabilities," *Journal of Political Economy* 81 (May/June), pp. 637-659.

Blume, M.E., and D.B. Keim (1989). "The Valuation of Callable Bonds," Working paper, Rodney White Center for Financial Research, Wharton School, University of Pennsylvania.

Bodie, A., and V.I. Rosansky (1986). "Risk and Return in Commodity Futures," *Financial Analysts Journal* 36, pp. 27-40.

Bower, J.L. (1970). *Managing the Resource Allocation Process: A Study of Corporate Planning and Investment* (Boston, MA: Division of Research, Harvard Business School).

Boyle, P. (1977). "Options: A Monte Carlo Approach," *Journal of Financial Economics* 4 (May), pp. 323-338.

Boyle, P. (1988). "A Lattice Framework for Option Pricing with Two State Variables," *Journal of Financial and Quantitative Analysis* 23 (March), pp. 1-12.

Brealey, R., and S.C. Myers (1991). *Principles of Corporate Finance* (New York, NY: McGraw-Hill).

Breeden, D.T., and R.H. Litzenberger (1978). "Prices of State Contingent Claims: Implications for Option Prices," *Journal of Business* 51, 4, pp. 621-651.

Breiman, L. (1968). *Probability* (Reading, MA: Addison-Wesley), pp. 347-350.

Brennan, M. (1979). "The Pricing of Contingent Claims in Discrete Time Models," *Journal of Finance* 34 (March), pp. 53-68.

Brennan, M. (1990). "Latent Assets," *Journal of Finance* 45, 3 (July), pp. 709-730.

Brennan, M. (1991). "The Price of Convenience and the Valuation of Commodity Contingent Claims," in D. Lund and B. Oksendal (eds.); *Stochastic Models and Option Values: With Applications to Resources, Environment, and Investment Problems* (Amsterdam: North-Holland), pp. 33-77.

Brennan, M., and E. Schwartz (1978). "Finite Difference Methods and Jump Processes Arising in the Pricing of Contingent Claims: A Synthesis," *Journal of Financial and Quantitative Analysis* 13, 3 (September), pp. 461-474.

Brennan, M., and E. Schwartz (1985a). "Evaluating Natural Resource Investments," *Journal of Business* 58, 2 (April), pp. 135-157.

Brennan, M., and E. Schwartz (1985b). "A New Approach to Evaluating Natural Resource Investments," *Midland Corporate Finance Journal* 3, 1 (Spring), pp. 37-47.

Brennan, M., and E. Schwartz (1978). "Finite Difference Methods and Jump Processes Arising in the Pricing of Contingent Claims: A Synthesis," *Journal of Financial and Quantitative Analysis* 13, 3 (September), pp. 461-474.

Brown, D.P., and M.R. Gibbons (1985). "A Simple Econometric Approach for Utility-Based Asset Pricing Models," *Journal of Finance* 40, 2 (June), pp. 359-381.

Broyles, J.E., and I.A. Cooper (1981). "Growth Opportunities and Real Investment Decisions," in F.G.J. Derkinderen and R.L. Crum (eds.), *Risk, Capital Costs and Project Financing Decisions* (Boston, MA: Martinus Nijholff Publishing), pp. 107-118.

Bulow, J.I., and J.B. Shoven (1978). "The Bankruptcy Decision," *Bell Journal of Economics and Management Science* 9, pp. 437-456.

Butters, J.K., W.E. Fruhan, D.W. Mullins, and T.R. Piper, (1987). *Instructor's Manual to Accompany Case Problems in Finance* (Cambridge, MA: Richard D. Irwin), p. 298.

Buzzell, R., B. Gale, and R. Sultan (1975). "Market Share: A Key to Profitability," *Harvard Business Review* 53, 1 (January-February), pp. 97-107.

Caballero, R.J. (1991). "On the Sign of the Investment-Uncertainty Relationship," *American Economic Review* 81, 1 (March), pp. 279-288.

Camillus, J.C. (1984). "Designing a Capital Budgeting System That Works," *Long Range Planning* 17, 2, pp. 103-110.

Campa, J.M. (1991). "Entry by Foreign Firms in the United States under Exchange Rate Uncertainty," *Review of Economics and Statistics.*

Capozza, D., and G. Sick (1992). "Risk and Return in Land Markets," Working paper, University of British Columbia.

Carr, P. (1988). "The Valuation of Sequential Exchange Opportunities," *Journal of Finance* 43, 5 (December), pp. 1235-1256.

Carter, E.E. (1971). "The Behavioural Theory of the Firm and Top Level Corporate Decisions," *Administrative Science Quarterly* 16 (December), pp. 413-428.

Cass, D., and J.E. Stiglitz (1970). "The Structure of Investor Preferences and Asset Returns, and Separability in Portfolio Allocation: A Contribution to the Pure Theory of Mutual Funds," *Journal of Economic Theory* (June), pp. 122-160.

Chung, K., and C. Charoenwong (1991). "Investment Options, Assets in Place, and the Risk of Stocks," *Financial Management* 20, 3 (Autumn), pp. 21-33.

Clark, J.J., T.J. Hindelang, and R.E. Pritchard (1984). *Capital Budgeting: Planning and Control of Capital Expenditures* (Englewoods Cliffs, NJ: Prentice Hall).

Constantinides, G.M. (1978). "Market Risk Adjustment in Project Valuation," *Journal of Finance* 33 (May), pp. 603-616.

Constantinides, G.M. (1982). "Intertemporal Asset Pricing with Heterogeneous Consumers and without Demand Aggregation," *Journal of Business* 55, 2 (April), pp. 253-267.

Constantinides, G.M. (1989). "Theory of Valuation: Overview and Recent Developments," in S. Bhattacharya and G.M. Constantinides (eds.), *Theory of Valuation: Frontiers of Modern Financial Theory, Vol. 1* (Totowa, NJ: Rowman and Littlefield).

Cooke, S., and N. Slack (1984). *Making Management Decisions* (Englewood Cliffs, NJ: Prentice-Hall International).

Copeland, T.E., and J.F. Weston (1982). "A Note on the Evaluation of Cancellable Operating Leases," *Financial Management* 11, 2 (Summer), pp. 60-67.

Copeland, T.E., and J.F. Weston (1988). *Financial Theory and Corporate Policy* (Reading, MA: Addison-Wesley).

Cox, J., and C.F. Huang (1989). "Option Pricing Theory and Its Applications," in S. Bhattacharya and G.M. Constantinides (eds.), *Theory of Valuation: Frontiers of Modern Finance, Vol. 1* (Totowa, NJ: Rowman and Littlefield), pp. 272-288.

Cox, J., J. Ingersoll, and S. Ross (1985). "An Intertemporal General Equilibrium Model of Asset Prices," *Econometrica* 53 (March), pp. 363-384.

Cox, J., and S. Ross (1976). "The Valuation of Options for Alternative Stochastic Processes," *Journal of Financial Economics* 3 (January), pp. 145-166.

Cox, J., S. Ross, and M. Rubinstein (1979). "Option Pricing: A Simplified Approach," *Journal of Financial Economics* 7, 3 (September), pp. 229-264.

Cox, J., and M. Rubinstein (1985). *Options Markets* (Englewood Cliffs, NJ: Prentice-Hall).

Crum, R., and F.D.J. Derkinderen (eds.) (1980). *Readings in Strategies for Corporate Investment* (New York, NY: Pitman).

Cyert, R.M., and J.G. March (1963). *A Behavioural Theory of the Firm* (Englewood Cliffs, NJ: Prentice-Hall).

Day, G.S. (1977). "Diagnosing the Product Portfolio," *Journal of Marketing* 41, 1 (April), pp. 29-38.

Dean, J. (1951). *Capital Budgeting* (New York, NY: Columbia University Press).

Derkinderen, F.G.J., and R.L. Crum (1979). *Project Set Strategies* (Boston, MA: Martinus Nijholff Publishing).

Derkinderen, F.G.J., and R.L. Crum (1984). "Pitfalls in Using Portfolio Techniques: Assessing Risk and Potential," *Long Range Planning* 17, 2, pp. 129-138.

Dixit, A.K. (1989a). "Entry and Exit Decisions under Uncertainty," *Journal of Political Economy* 97 (June), pp. 620-638.

Dixit, A.K. (1989b). "Hysteresis, Import Penetration, and Exchange Rate Pass-Through," *Quarterly Journal of Economics* 104, 2 (May), pp. 205-228.

Dixit, A.K. (1992). "Investment and Hysteresis," *Journal of Economic Perspectives* 6, 1 (Winter), pp. 107-132.

Donaldson, G. (1972). "Strategic Hurdle Rates for Capital Investment," *Harvard Business Review* 50, 2 (March-April), pp. 50-58.

Donaldson, G. (1984). *Managing Corporate Wealth* (New York, NY: Praeger Publishers).

Donaldson, G. (1985). "Financial Goals and Strategic Consequences," *Harvard Business Review* 63, 3 (May-June), pp. 56-66.

Donaldson, G. and J.W. Lorsch (1983). *Decision Making at the Top: The Shaping of Strategic Direction* (New York, NY: Basic Books).

Dothan, U., and J. Williams (1980). "Term-Risk Structure and the Valuation of Projects," *Journal of Financial and Quantitative Analysis* 15, 4, pp. 875-905.

Dybvig, P. (1988). "Inefficient Dynamic Portfolio Strategies or How to Throw Away a Million Dollars in the Stock Market," *Review of Financial Studies* 1, 1 (Spring), pp. 67-88.

Dybvig, P., and J. Ingersoll (1982). "Mean-Variance Theory in Complete Markets," *Journal of Business* 55, 2 (April), pp. 233-251.

Ehrhardt, R., and L. Taube (1987). "An Inventory Model with Random Replenishment Quantities," *International Journal of Production Research* 25, pp. 1795-1803.

Electric Power Research Institute (EPRI) (1987). "Evaluating the Effects of Time and Risk on Investment Choices: A Comparison of Finance Theory and Decision Analysis." Project report 2379-4 (January).

Ellsworth, R.R. (1983). "Subordinate Financial Policy to Corporate Strategy," *Harvard Business Review* 61, 6 (November-December), pp. 170-182.

Emery, D.R., P.C. Parr, P.B. Mokkelbost, D. Gandhi, and A. Saunders (1978). "An Investigation of Real Investment Decision Making With the Options Pricing Model," *Journal of Business Finance and Accounting* 5, 4 (Winter), pp. 363-369.

Fabozzi, F.J. (ed.) (1991). *Handbook of Fixed Income Securities* (Homewood, IL: Business One Irwin).

Fahey, L. (1981). "On the Strategic Management Decision Processes," *Strategic Management Journal* 2, 1 (January), pp. 43-60.

Fischer, S. (1978). "Call Option Pricing When the Exercise Price Is Uncertain, and the Valuation of Index Bonds," *Journal of Finance* 33 (March), pp. 169-176.

Fisher, A.C. and W.M. Hanemann (1987). "Quasi-Option Value: Some Misconceptions Dispelled," *Journal of Environmental Economics and Management* 14 (July), pp. 183-190.

Frankel, J., and R. Meese (1987). "Are Exchange Rates Excessively Variable?" in S. Fischer (ed.), *NBER Macroeconomics Annual* 2 (Cambridge, MA: MIT Press), pp. 117-162.

Franks, J., and W. Torous (1989). "An Empirical Investigation of U.S. Firms in Reorganization," *Journal of Finance* 44, 3 (July), pp. 747-769.

Fremault, A., and M.A. Schary (1992). "Default Risk and the Pricing of Corporate Bonds," in *Financial Engineering and Risk Management* (Osaka, Japan: Osaka Foundation for International Exchange).

Fremgen, J.M. (May 1973). "Capital Budgeting Practices: A Survey," *Management Accounting* 54 (May), pp. 15-25.

Friend, I., and M. Blume (1975). "The Demand for Risky Assets," *American Economic Review* 65, 5 (December), pp. 900-922.

Garman, M.B. (1985). "The Duration of Option Portfolios," *Journal of Financial Economics* 14 (June), pp. 309-315.

Gerchak, Y., M. Parlar, and R. G. Vickson (1986). "A Single Period Production Model with Uncertain Output and Demand," Proceedings of the 25th IEEE Conference on Decision and Control, pp. 1733- 1736.

Gerchak, Y., R.G. Vickson, and M. Parlar (1988). "Periodic Review Production Models with Variable Yield and Uncertain Demand," *IIE Transactions* 20, pp. 144-150.

Geske, R. (1977). "The Valuation of Corporate Liabilities as Compound Options," *Journal of Financial and Quantitative Analysis* 12, 4 (November), pp. 541-552.

Geske, R. (1979). "The Valuation of Compound Options," *Journal of Financial Economics* 7 (March), pp. 63-81.

Geske, R., and H. Johnson (1984). "The American Put Option Valued Analytically," *Journal of Finance 39* (December), pp. 1511-1524.

Geske, R., and K. Shastri (1985). "Valuation by Approximation: A Comparison of Alternative Option Valuation Techniques," *Journal of Financial and Quantitative Analysis* 20 (March), pp. 45-71.

Gibbons, M., and W. Ferson (1985). "Testing Asset Pricing Models with Changing Expectations and an Unobservable Market Portfolio," *Journal of Financial Economics* 14, 2 (June), pp. 217-236.

Gibson, R., and E.S. Schwartz (1990). "Stochastic Convenience Yield and the Pricing of Oil Contingent Claims," *Journal of Finance* 45 (July), pp. 959-976.

Gilson, S., K. John, and L. Lang (1990). "Troubled Debt Restructurings," *Journal of Financial Economics* 27, 2, pp. 315-354.

Gold, B. (1976). "The Shaky Foundations of Capital Budgeting," *California Management Review* 19 (Winter), pp. 51-59.

Gordon, L.A., D.F. Larker, and F.D. Tuggle (1978). "Strategic Decision Processes and the Design of Accounting Information Systems: Conceptual Linkages," *Accounting, Organizations and Society* 3, 4, pp. 203-213.

Gordon, L.A., and G.E. Pinches (1984). *Improving Capital Budgeting: A Decision Support System Approach* (Reading, MA: Addison-Wesley).

Gorry, G.A., and S. Morton (1971). "A Framework for Management Information Systems," *Sloan Management Review* 13 (Fall), pp. 55-70.

Hakansson, N. (1970). "Optimal Investment and Consumption under Risk for a Class of Utility Functions," *Econometrica* 38 (September), pp. 587-607.

Hall, W.K. (1979). "Changing Perspective on the Capital Investment Process," *Long Range Planning* 12 (February), pp. 37-40.

Hanemann, W.M. (1989). "Information and the Concept of Option Value," *Journal of Environmental Economic Management* 16 (January), pp. 23-37.

Hansen, L.P., and K.J. Singleton (1983). "Stochastic Consumption, Risk Aversion, and the Temporal Behavior of Asset Returns," *Journal of Political Economy* 91, 2 (April), pp. 249-265.

Harrison, J.M., and D.M. Kreps (1979). "Martingales and Arbitrage in Multiperiod Securities Markets," *Journal of Economic Theory* 20 (June), pp. 381-408.

Harrison, J.M., and S.R. Pliska (1981). "Martingales and Stochastic Integrals in the Theory of Continuous Trading," *Stochastic Processes and Their Applications* 11, pp. 313-316.

Hastie, K.L. (1974). "One Businessman's View of Capital Budgeting," *Financial Management* 3, 4 (Winter), pp. 36-44.

Hayes, R., and W. Abernathy (1980). "Managing Our Way to Economic Decline," *Harvard Business Review* 58, 4 (July-August), pp. 66-77.

Hayes, R., and D. Garvin (1982). "Managing as if Tomorrow Mattered," *Harvard Business Review* 60, 3 (May-June), pp. 71-79.

Hendricks, D. (1991). "Optimal Policy Responses to an Uncertain Threat: The Case of Global Warming," Working paper, Kennedy School of Government, Harvard University.

Hertz, D. (1964). "Risk Analysis in Capital Investment," *Harvard Business Review* 42 (January-February), pp. 95-106.

Higgins, J.M. (1978). "Strategic Decision Making: An Organization Behavioral Perspective," *Managerial Planning* 26 (March/April), pp. 9-13.

Hodder, J. (1986). "Evaluation of Manufacturing Investments: A Comparison of U.S. and Japanese Practices," *Financial Management* 15, 1 (Spring), pp. 17-24.

Hodder, J., and H. Riggs (1985). "Pitfalls in Evaluating Risky Projects," *Harvard Business Review* 63, 1 (January-February), pp. 128-135.

Hodder, J., and A.J. Triantis (1990). "Valuing Flexibility as a Complex Option," *Journal of Finance* 45 (June), pp. 549-566.

Hofer, C.W., and D. Schendel (1978). *Strategy Formulation: Analytical Concepts* (St. Paul, Minn.: West Publishing).

Hoshi, T., A. Kashyap, and D. Scharfstein (1990). "The Role of Banks in Reducing the Costs of Financial Distress in Japan," *Journal of Financial Economics* 27 (September), pp. 67-88.

Howard, R.A. (1968). "The Foundations of Decision Analysis," *IEEE Transactions on Systems Science and Cybernetics* 4, 3 (September) pp. 1-9.

Howard, R.A., J.E. Matheson, and K.L. Miller (eds.) (1977). *Readings in Decision Analysis* (Menlo Park, CA: SRI International).

Huang, C.F., and R. Litzenberger (1988). *Foundations for Financial Economics* (Amsterdam: North-Holland).

Hull, J. (1989). *Options, Futures, and Other Derivative Securities* (Englewood Cliffs, NJ: Prentice-Hall).

Hull, J. (1991). *Introduction to Futures and Options Markets* (Englewood Cliffs, NJ: Prentice-Hall).

Hull, J., and A. White (1988). "The Use of the Control Variate Technique in Option Pricing," *Journal of Financial and Quantitative Analysis* 17 (September), pp. 697-705.

Ingersoll, J., Jr. (1987). *Theory of Financial Decision Making* (Totowa, NJ: Rowman and Littlefield).

Ingersoll, J., and S. Ross (1992). "Waiting to Invest: Investment and Uncertainty," *Journal of Business* 65, 1 (January), pp. 1-29.

Jackson, T. (1986). *The Logic and Limits of Bankruptcy Law* (Cambridge, MA: Harvard University Press).

Jacoby, H.D., and D.G. Laughton (1992). "Project Evaluation: A Practical Asset Pricing Method," *The Energy Journal* 13, 2, pp. 19-47.

Jaikumar, R. (1989). "Japanese Flexible Manufacturing Systems: Impact on the United States," *Japan and the World Economy* 1, pp. 113-143.

Jensen, M.C. (1986). "Agency Costs of Free Cash Flow, Corporate Finance, and Takeovers," *American Economic Review* 76 (May), pp. 323-329.

Johnson, G., and K. Scholes (1984). *Exploring Corporate Strategy* (Englewood Cliffs, NJ: Prentice-Hall International).

Johnson, H. (1983). "An Analytic Approximation for the American Put Price," *Journal of Financial and Quantitative Analysis* 18, 1 (March), pp. 141-148.

Johnson, H. (1987). "Options on the Maximum or the Minimum of Several Assets," *Journal of Financial and Quantitative Analysis* 22 (September), pp. 277-284.

Jones, E.P., S.P. Mason, and E. Rosenfeld (1985). "Contingent Claims Valuation of Corporate Liabilities: Theory and Empirical Tests," in B. Friedman (ed.), *Corporate Capital Structures in the United States* (Chicago, IL: University of Chicago Press).

Kamrad, B., and P. Ritchken (1991). "Multinomial Approximating Models for Options with k State Variables," *Management Science* 37, 12, pp. 1640-1653.

Karlin, S. (1958). "One Stage Inventory Models with Uncertainty," in K.J. Arrow, S. Karlin and H. Scarf (eds.), *Studies in the Mathematical Theory of Inventory and Production* (Stanford, CA: Stanford University Press).

Kasanen, E. (1993). "Creating Value by Spawning Investment Opportunities," *Financial Management* 22, 3 (Autumn), pp. 251-258.

Kasanen, E., and L. Trigeorgis (1994). "A Market Utility Approach to Investment Valuation," *European Journal of Operational Research* (Special Issue on Financial Modeling) 74, 2 (April), pp. 294-309.

Kemna, A. (1993). "Case Studies on Real Options," *Financial Management* 22, 3 (Autumn), pp. 259-270.

Kensinger, J. (1987). "Adding the Value of Active Management into the Capital Budgeting Equation," *Midland Corporate Finance Journal* 5, 1 (Spring), pp. 31-42.

Kester, W.C. (1984). "Today's Options for Tomorrow's Growth," *Harvard Business Review* 62, 2 (March-April), pp. 153-160.

Kester, W.C. (1992a). "Governance, Contracting, and Investment Horizons: A Look at Japan and Germany," *Journal of Applied Corporate Finance* 5 (Summer), pp. 83-98.

Kester, W.C. (1992b). "Japanese Corporate Governance: A Source of Efficiency or Restraint of Trade?" in I. Walter and T. Hiraki (eds.), *Restructuring Japan's Financial Markets* (Homewood, IL: Richard D. Irwin).

Kester, W.C. (1993). "Turning Growth Options into Real Assets," in R. Aggarwal (ed.), *Capital Budgeting under Uncertainty* (Englewood Cliffs, NJ: Prentice-Hall), pp. 187-207.

Kim, S.H., and E.J. Farragher (1981). "Current Capital Budgeting Practices," *Management Accounting* 59 (June), pp. 26-30.

King, P. (1974). "Strategic Control of Capital Investment," *Journal of General Management* 2, 1 (Autumn), pp. 17-28.

Klammer, T.P., and M.C. Walker (1984). "The Continuing Increase in the Use of Sophisticated Capital Budgeting Techniques," *California Management Review* 27, 1 (Fall), pp. 137-148.

Klein, M. (1966). "Markovian Decision Models for Reject Allowance Problems," *Management Science* 12, pp. 349-358.

Kogut, B., and N. Kulatilaka (1994). "Operating Flexibility, Global Manufacturing, and the Option Value of a Multinational Network," *Management Science* 40, 1 (January), pp. 123-139.

Kolbe, A.L., P.A. Morris, and E. Olmsted (1987). "Evaluating the Effects of Time and Risk on Investment Choices: A Comparison of Finance Theory and Decision Analysis," Electric Power Research Institute (EPRI) P-5028, Project 2379-4 (January).

Kolbe, A.L., P.A. Morris, and E.O. Teisberg (1991). "When Choosing R & D Projects, Go with Long Shots," *Research-Technology Management* (January-February).

Kraus, A., and R. Litzenberger (1975). "Market Equilibrium in a Multiperiod State-Preference Model with Logarithmic Utility," *Journal of Finance* 30 (December), pp. 1213-1227.

Krugman, P.R. (1988). "Deindustrialization, Reindustrialization, and the Real Exchange Rate," Working paper, National Bureau of Economic Research.

Krugman, P.R., and R. Baldwin (1987). "The Persistence of the U.S. Trade Deficit," *Brookings Papers on Economic Activity* 1, pp. 1-43.

Kulatilaka, N. (1988). "Valuing the Flexibility of Flexible Manufacturing Systems," *IEEE Transactions in Engineering Management* 35, 4, pp. 250-257.

Kulatilaka, N. (1993). "The Value of Flexibility: The Case of a Dual-Fuel Industrial Steam Boiler," *Financial Management* 22, 3 (Autumn), pp. 271-280.

Kulatilaka, N., and A. Marcus (1988). "A General Formulation of Corporate Real Options," *Research in Finance* 7, pp. 183-200.

Kulatilaka, N., and A. Marcus (1992). "Project Valuation under Uncertainty: When Does DCF Fail?" *Journal of Applied Corporate Finance* 5 (December), pp. 92-100.

Kulatilaka, N., and S. Marks (1988). "The Strategic Value of Flexibility: Reducing the Ability to Compromise," *American Economic Review* 78, 3 (June), pp. 574-580.

Kulatilaka, N., and E. Perotti (1992). "Strategic Investment Timing under Uncertainty," Working paper, Boston University.

Kulatilaka, N., and L. Trigeorgis (1994). "The General Flexibility to Switch: Real Options Revisited," *International Journal of Finance* 6, 2 (Spring).

Lane, S., and M. Schary (1991). "Understanding the Business Failure Rate," *Contemporary Policy Issues* 9, 4 (October), 1991, pp. 93-105.

Larcker, D.F. (1981). "The Perceived Importance of Selected Information Characteristics for Strategic Capital Budgeting Decisions," *Accounting Review* 56 (July), pp. 519-538.

Laughton, D.G., and H.D. Jacoby (1991). "A Two-Method Solution to the Investment Timing Problem," *Advances in Futures and Options Research* 5.

Laughton, D.G., and H.D. Jacoby (1993). "Reversion, Timing Options, and Long-term Decision-Making," *Financial Management* 22, 3 (Autumn), pp. 225-240.

Lee, C.J. (1988). "Capital Budgeting under Uncertainty: The Issue of Optimal Timing," Journal of *Business Finance and Accounting*, 15, 2 (Summer), pp. 155-168.

Lee, W., J. Martin, and A. Senchack (1982). "The Case for Using Options to Evaluate Salvage Values in Financial Leases," *Financial Management* 11, 3 (Autumn), pp. 33-41.

Lee, H.L., and M.J. Rosenblatt (1982). "Optimal Inspection and Ordering Policies for Products with Imperfect Quality," *IEE Transactions* 17, pp. 284-289.

Lee, H.L., and C.A. Yano (1985). "Production Control in Multi-Stage Systems with Variable Yield Losses," Technical report, University of Michigan–Ann Arbor.

Leland, H. (1985). "Option Pricing and Replication with Transaction Costs," *Journal of Finance* 40 (December), pp. 1283-1301.

Levy, H., and M. Sarnat (1970). "Diversification, Portfolio Analysis and the Uneasy Case for Conglomerate Mergers," *Journal of Finance* 25, 4, pp. 795-802.

Levy, H., and M. Sarnat (1990). *Capital Investment and Financial Decisions* (Englewoods Cliffs, NJ: Prentice-Hall).

Logue, D.E. (1980). "Some Thoughts on Corporate Investment Strategy and Pure Strategic Investments," in R. Crum and F.D.J. Derkinderen (eds.), *Readings in Strategies for Corporate Investment* (New York, NY: Pitman), pp. 87-97.

Lorange, P. (ed.) (1982). *Implementation of Strategic Planning* (Englewoods Cliffs, NJ: Prentice-Hall).

Lucas, R.E., Jr. (1978). "Asset Prices in an Exchange Economy," *Econometrica* 46 (November), pp. 1429-1445.

Lund, D., and B. Oksendal (eds.) (1990). Stochastic Models and *Option Values: With Applications to Resources, Environment, and Investment Problems* (Amsterdam: North Holland).

Lutz, R.P. (1978). "Reconciling the Engineering Economy Feasibility Studies with Corporate Goals," *Engineering Economist* 23, 4 (Summer), pp. 265-274.

MacCallum, J.S. (1987). "The Net Present Value Method: Part of Our Investment Problem," *Business Quarterly* (Fall), pp. 7-9.

Magee, J. (1964). "How to Use Decision Trees in Capital Investment," *Harvard Business Review* (September-October).

Majd, S., and R. Pindyck (1987). "Time to Build, Option Value, and Investment Decisions," *Journal of Financial Economics* 18 (March), pp. 7-27.

Majd, S., and R. Pindyck (1989). "The Learning Curve and Optimal Production under Certainty," *Rand Journal of Economics* 20, 3 (Autumn), pp. 331-343.

Malernee, J.K., and G. Jaffe (1982). "An Integrative Approach to Strategic and Financial Planning," *Managerial Planning* 30 (January-February), pp. 35-43.

Mao, C.T. (1970). "Survey of Capital Budgeting: Theory and Practice," *Journal of Finance* 25, 2 (May), pp. 349-360.

Margrabe, W. (1978). "The Value of an Option to Exchange One Asset for Another," *Journal of Finance* 33, 1 (March), pp. 177- 186.

Marshuetz, R.J. (1985). "How American Can Allocates Capital," *Harvard Business Review* 63, 1 (January-February), pp. 82-91.

Mason, S.P., and C. Baldwin (1988). "Evaluation of Government Subsidies to Large-scale Energy Projects: A Contingent Claims Approach," *Advances in Futures and Options Research* 3, pp. 169-181.

Mason, S.P., and R.C. Merton (1985). "The Role of Contingent Claims Analysis in Corporate Finance," in E.I. Altman and M. Subrahmanyam (eds.), *Recent Advances in Corporate Finance* (Homewood, IL: Richard D. Irwin), pp. 7-54.

Mauer, D., and A. Triantis (1992). "Interactions of Corporate Financing and Investment Decisions: A Dynamic Framework," Working paper, University of Wisconsin–Madison.

Mazzolini, R. (1981). "How Strategic Decisions are Made," Long *Range Planning* 14, 3, pp. 85-96.

McConnel, J., and J. Schallheim (1983). "Valuation of Asset Leasing Contracts," *Journal of Financial Economics* 12 (August), pp. 237-261.

McDonald, R., and D. Siegel (1984). "Option Pricing When the Underlying Asset Earns a Below-Equilibrium Rate of Return: A Note," *Journal of Finance* 39, 1 (March), pp. 261-265.

McDonald, R., and D. Siegel (1985). "Investment and the Valuation of Firms When There is an Option to Shut Down," *International Economic Review* 26, 2 (June), pp. 331-349.

McDonald, R., and D. Siegel (1986). "The Value of Waiting to Invest," *Quarterly Journal of Economics* 101, 4 (November), pp. 707-727.

McLaughlin, R., and R. Taggart (1992). "The Opportunity Cost of Using Excess Capacity," *Financial Management* 21, 2 (Summer), pp. 12-23.

Merton, R.C. (1971). "Optimum Consumption and Portfolio Rules in a Continuous-Time Model," *Journal of Economic Theory* 3 (December), pp. 373-413.

Merton, R.C. (1973). "Theory of Rational Option Pricing," *Bell Journal of Economics and Management Science* 4, pp. 141-183.

Merton, R.C. (1974). "On the Pricing of Corporate Debt: The Risk Structure of Interest Rates," *Journal of Finance* 29, 2 (May), pp. 449-470.

Merton, R.C. (1976). "Option Pricing when Underlying Stock Returns Are Discontinuous," *Journal of Financial Economics* 3, pp. 125-144.

Merton, R.C. (1982). "On the Mathematics and Economics Assumptions of Continuous-Time Models," in W.F. Sharpe and C.M. Cootner (eds.), *Financial Economics: Essays in Honor of Paul Cootner* (Englewood Cliffs, NJ: Prentice-Hall).

Mintzberg, H. (1973). "Strategy Making in Three Modes," *California Management Review* 16 (Winter), pp. 44-53.

Mintzberg, H., D. Raisinghani, and A. Theoret (1976). "The Structure of 'Unstructured' Decision Processes," *Administrative Science Quarterly* 21 (June), pp. 246-275.

Monden, Y. (1981a). "What Makes the Toyota Production System Really Tick?" *Industrial Engineering* (January), pp. 36-46.

Monden, Y. (1981b). "Adaptable Kanban System Helps Toyota Maintain Just-in-Time Production," *Industrial Engineering* (May), pp. 29-46.

Monden, Y. (1981c). "Toyota's Production Smoothing Methods: Part II," *Industrial Engineering* (September), pp. 22-30.

Morck, R., A. Schleifer, and R.W. Vishny (1990). "Do Managerial Objectives Drive Bad Acquisitions?" *Journal of Finance* 45 (March), pp. 31-48.

Morck, R., E. Schwartz, and D. Stangeland (1989). "The Valuation of Forestry Resources under Stochastic Prices and Inventories," *Journal of Financial and Quantitative Analysis* 24, 4 (December), pp. 473-487.

Mossin, J. (1973). *Theory of Financial Markets* (Englewood Cliffs, NJ: Prentice-Hall).

Myers, S.C. (1977). "Determinants of Corporate Borrowing," *Journal of Financial Economics* 5, 2 (November), pp. 147-175.

Myers, S.C. (1987). "Finance Theory and Financial Strategy," *Midland Corporate Finance Journal* 5, 1 (Spring), pp. 6-13.

Myers, S.C., and S. Majd (1990). "Abandonment Value and Project Life," *Advances in Futures and Options Research* 4, pp. 1-21.

Newton, G. (1985), *Bankruptcy and Insolvency Accounting* (New York, NY: John Wiley and Sons).

Paddock, J., D. Siegel, and J. Smith (1988). "Option Valuation of Claims on Physical Assets: The Case of Offshore Petroleum Leases," *Quarterly Journal of Economics* 103, 3 (August), pp. 479-508.

Peavy, J.W. (1984). "Modern Financial Theory, Corporate Strategy and Public Policy: Another Perspective," *Academy of Management Review* 9, pp. 152-157.

Petit, T., and T. Wingler (1983). "Key Factors in Capital Budgeting," *Managerial Planning* 31 (May-June), pp. 21-27.

Petty, W.J., D.F. Scott, and M.M. Bird (1975). "The Capital Expenditure Decision-Making Process of Large Corporations," *Engineering Economist* 20, 3, pp. 159-172.

Pickles, E., and J.L. Smith (1992). "Petroleum Property Valuation Using a Binomial Lattice Implementation of Option Pricing Theory," Working paper, University of Houston.

Pike, R.H. (1983). "A Review of Recent Trends in Formal Capital Budgeting Processes," *Accounting and Business Research* 14 (Summer), pp. 201-208.

Pinches, G.E. (1982). "Myopia, Capital Budgeting and Decision Making," *Financial Management* 11, 3 (Autumn), pp. 6-19.

Pindyck, R.S. (1988). "Irreversible Investment, Capacity Choice, and the Value of the Firm," *American Economic Review* 78, 5 (December), pp. 969-985.

Pindyck, R.S. (1991). "Irreversibility, Uncertainty, and Investment," *Journal of Economic Literature* 29, 3 (September), pp. 1110-1148.

Pindyck, R.S., and D. Rubinfeld (1991). *Econometric Models and Economic Forecasts* (New York, NY: McGraw-Hill).

Piper, J.A. (1980). "Classifying Capital Projects for Top Management Decision Making," *Long Range Planning* 13 (June), pp. 45-56.

Pohlman, R.A., E.S. Santiago, and F.L. Markel (1988). "Cash Flow Estimation Practices of Large Firms," *Financial Management* 17, 2 (Summer), pp. 71-79.

Pollard, A.B. (1969). *A Normative Model for Joint Time/Risk Preference Decision Problems*, Ph.D. dissertation, Stanford University.

Porter, M.E. (1987). "From Competitive Advantage to Corporate Strategy," *Harvard Business Review* 65, 3 (May-June), pp. 43-59.

Porter, M.E. (1992). "Capital Disadvantage: America's Failing Capital Investment System," *Harvard Business Review* 72 (September-October), pp. 65-83.

Porteus, E.L. (1986). "Optimal Lot Sizing, Process Quality Improvement and Setup Cost Reduction," *Operations Research* 34, pp. 137-144.

Pratt, J.W. (1964). "Risk Aversion in the Small and in the Large," *Econometrica* 32 (January), pp. 122-136.

Pratt, J.W., H. Raiffa, and R.O. Schlaifer (1965). *Introduction to Statistical Decision Theory* (New York, NY: McGraw-Hill).

Prowse, S.D. (1990). "Institutional Investment Patterns and Corporate Financial Behavior in the United States and Japan," *Journal of Financial Economics* 27 (September), pp. 43-66.

Quigg, L. (1993). "Empirical Testing of Real Option-Pricing Models," *Journal of Finance* 48, 2 (June), pp. 621-640.

Raiffa, H. (1970). *Decision Analysis: Introductory Lectures on Choices under Uncertainty* (Reading, MA: Addison-Wesley).

Rao, R.K.S., and J.D. Martin (1981). "Another Look at the Use of Option Pricing Theory to Evaluate Real Asset Investment Opportunities," *Journal of Business Finance and Accounting* 3, pp. 421-429.

Rappaport, A. (1979). "Strategic Analysis for More Profitable Acquisitions," *Harvard Business Review* 57, 4 (July-August), pp. 99-110.

Rappaport, A. (1987). *Creating Shareholder Value* (New York, NY: Free Press).

Ravenscraft, D.J., and F.M. Scherer (1987). *Mergers, Sell-offs and Economic Efficiency* (Washington, D.C.: Brookings Institution).

Reinhardt, F.L. (1992). *Acid Rain: The Southern Company (A) and (B)*, Harvard Business School case 792-060 and case 793-040 (with Teaching Note 794-042, 1993).

Ritchken, P. (1987). *Options Theory, Strategy and Applications* (Glenville, IL: Scott, Foresman and Company).

Roberts, K., and M. Weitzman (1981). "Funding Criteria for Research, Development, and Exploration Projects," *Econometrica* 49, 5 (September), pp. 1261-1288.

Roll, R., and S.A. Ross (1984). "The Arbitrage Pricing Theory Approach to Strategic Portfolio Planning," *Financial Analysts Journal* 40 (May-June), pp. 14-26.

Roller, L.H., and M.M. Tombak (1990). "Strategic Choice of Flexible Production Technologies and Welfare Implications," *Journal of Industrial Economics* 38, 4, pp. 417-430.

Rose, K., R. Burns, J. Coggins, M. Harunuzzaman, and T. Viezer (1992). "Public Utility Commission Implementation of the Clean Air Act's Allowance Trading Program," National Regulatory Research Institute report 92-6 (May).

Rosenblatt, M. (1980). "A Survey and Analysis of Capital Budgeting Process in Multi-Division Firms," *Engineering Economist* 25, 4 (Summer), pp. 259-273.

Ross, M. (1986). "Capital Budgeting Practices of Twelve Large Manufacturers," *Financial Management* 15, 4 (Winter), pp. 15-22.

Ross, S.M. (1983). *Stochastic Processes* (New York, NY: John Wiley and Sons).

Rubinstein, M. (1974). "An Aggregation Theorem for Securities Markets," *Journal of Financial Economics* 1, 3 (September), pp. 225-244.

Rubinstein, M. (1976a). "The Strong Case for the Generalized Logarithmic Utility Model as the Premier Model of Financial Markets," *Journal of Finance* 31, 2 (May), pp. 551-572.

Rubinstein, M. (1976b). "The Valuation of Uncertain Income Streams and the Pricing of Options," *Bell Journal of Economics* 7 (Autumn), pp. 407-425.

Sahlman, W. (1988). "Aspects of Financial Contracting in Venture Capital," *Journal of Applied Corporate Finance* 1, pp. 23-36.

Sale, T.J. (1981). "Performance Measurement and Formal Capital Expenditure Controls in Divisionalized Companies," *Journal of Business Finance and Accounting* 8 (Autumn), pp. 389-420.

Samuelson, P., and R.C. Merton (1969). "A Complete Model of Warrant Pricing that Maximizes Utility," *Industrial Management Review* 10 (Winter), pp. 17-46.

Scapens, R.W., and T.J. Sale (1981). "Performance Measurement and Formal Capital Expenditures Controls to Divisionalized Companies," *Journal of Business Finance and Accounting* 8, 3 (Autumn), pp. 389-420.

Schary, M. (1987). *Exit, Investment and Technology Diffusion in a Declining Industry: An Empirical Study*, Ph.D. dissertation, MIT.

Schuller, F.C. (1988). *Venturing Abroad: Innovation by U.S. Multinationals* (Boston, MA: Quorum Books).

Sepehri, M., E.A. Silver, and C. New (1986). "A Heuristic for Multiple Lot Sizing for an Order under Yield Variability," *IIE Transactions* 18, pp. 63-69.

Shapiro, A.C. (1985). "Corporate Strategy and the Capital Budgeting Decision," *Midland Corporate Finance Journal* 3, 1 (Spring), pp. 37-51.

Shih, W (1980). "Optimal Inventory Policies When Stock-outs Result from Defective Products," *International Journal of Production Research* 18, pp. 677-686.

Shrivastava, P., and J.H. Grant (1985). "Empirically Derived Models of the Strategic Decision Making Process," *Strategic Management Journal* 6 (April-June), pp. 97-113.

Sick, G. (1989). *Capital Budgeting With Real Options*, Monograph, Salomon Brothers Center for the Study of Financial Institutions, New York University.

Siegel, D., J. Smith, and J. Paddock (1987). "Valuing Offshore Oil Properties with Option Pricing Models," *Midland Corporate Finance Journal* 5 (Spring), pp. 22-30.

Silver, E.A. (1976). "Establishing the Order Quantity When the Amount Received is Uncertain," *INFOR* 14, pp. 32-39.

Simon, H.A. (1960). *The New Science of Management Decision* (New York, NY: Harper and Row).

Smit, H.T.J., and L.A. Ankum (1993). "A Real Options and Game-theoretic Approach to Corporate Investment Strategy under Competition," *Financial Management* 22, 3 (Autumn), pp. 241-250.

Smit, H.T.J., and L. Trigeorgis (1993). "Flexibility and Commitment in Strategic Investment," Working paper, Boston University.

Smith, C.W., Jr. (1979). "Applications of Option Pricing Analysis," in J.L. Bicksler (ed.), *Handbook of Financial Economics* (Amsterdam: North-Holland), pp. 289-330.

Solow, R. (1974). "The Economics of Resources or the Resources of Economics," *American Economic Review* 61 (March), pp. 1-14.

Stapleton, R.C., and M.G. Subrahmanyam (1984). "The Valuation of Options When Asset Returns are Generated by a Binomial Process," *Journal of Finance* 39, 5 (December), pp. 1525-1539.

Stensland, G., and D. Tjostheim (1990). "Some Applications of Dynamic Programming to Natural Resource Exploration," in D. Lund and B. Oksendal (eds.), *Stochastic Models and Option Values* (Amsterdam: North-Holland).

Stulz, R. (1982). "Options on the Minimum or the Maximum of Two Risky Assets: Analysis and Applications," *Journal of Financial Economics* 10 (July), pp. 161-185.

Taggart, R.A. (1987). "Allocating Capital Among a Firm's Divisions: Hurdle Rate vs. Budgets," *Journal of Financial Research* 10, 3 (Fall), pp. 177-189.

Teisberg, E. Olmsted (1988). *Capital Investment Strategies under Regulation: A Binomial Option Pricing Approach*, Ph.D. dissertation, Stanford University.

Teisberg, E. Olmsted (1993). "Capital Investment Strategies under Uncertain Regulation," *The Rand Journal of Economics* 24, 4 (Winter), pp. 591-604.

Teisberg, E. Olmsted (1994). "An Option Valuation Analysis of Investment Choices by a Regulated Firm," *Management Science* 40, 4 (April), pp. 535-548.

Teisberg, E. Olmsted, and T.J. Teisberg (1991). "The Value of Commodity Purchase Contracts with Limited Price Risk," *Energy Journal* 12, 3, pp. 109-135.

Teisberg Associates and Applied Decision Analyses, Inc. (1990). "Risk and Managerial Flexibility in Power Plant Construction," Project report, Electric Power Research Institute (October).

Tietenberg, T. (1992). *Environmental and Natural Resource Economics* (New York, NY: Harper-Collins).

Titman, S. (1985). "Urban Land Prices under Uncertainty," *American Economic Review* 75, 3 (June), pp. 505-514.

Tourinho, O. (1979). "The Option Value of Reserves of Natural Resources," Working paper, University of California–Berkeley.

Treynor, J.L., and F. Black (1976). "Corporate Investment Decisions," in S.C. Myers (ed.), *Modern Developments in Financial Management* (New York, NY: Praeger).

Triantis A., and J. Hodder (1990). "Valuing Flexibility as a Complex Option," *Journal of Finance* 45, 2 (June), pp. 549-565.

Trigeorgis, L. (1986). *Valuing Real Investment Opportunities: An Options Approach to Strategic Capital Budgeting*, Doctoral dissertation, Harvard University.

Trigeorgis, L. (1988). "A Conceptual Options Framework for Capital Budgeting," *Advances in Futures and Options Research* 3, pp. 145-167.

Trigeorgis, L. (1990a). "A Real Options Application in Natural Resource Investments," *Advances in Futures and Options Research* 4, pp. 153-164.

Trigeorgis, L. (1990b). "Valuing the Impact of Uncertain Competitive Arrivals on Deferrable Real Investment Opportunities," Working paper, Boston University.

Trigeorgis, L. (1991a). "Anticipated Competitive Entry and Early Preemptive Investment in Deferrable Projects," *Journal of Economics and Business* 43, 2 (May), pp. 143-156.

Trigeorgis, L. (1991b). "A Log-Transformed Binomial Numerical Analysis Method for Valuing Complex Multi-Option Investments," *Journal of Financial and Quantitative Analysis* 26, 3 (September), pp. 309-326.

Trigeorgis, L. (1992). "Evaluating Leases with a Variety of Operating Options," Working paper, Boston University.

Trigeorgis, L. (1993a). "The Nature of Option Interactions and the Valuation of Investments with Multiple Real Options," *Journal of Financial and Quantitative Analysis* 28, 1 (March), pp. 1-20.

Trigeorgis, L. (1993b). "Real Options and Interactions with Financial Flexibility," *Financial Management* 22, 3 (Autumn), pp. 202-224.

Trigeorgis, L. (1994). *Options in Capital Budgeting: Managerial Flexibility and Strategy in Resource Allocation* (Cambridge, MA: MIT Press).

Trigeorgis, L., and E. Kasanen (1991). "An Integrated Options-based Strategic Planning and Control Model, "*Managerial Finance* 17, 2/3 (May), pp. 16-28.

Trigeorgis, L., and S.P. Mason (1987). "Valuing Managerial Flexibility," *Midland Corporate Finance Journal* 5, 1 (Spring), pp. 14-21.

Truitt, J.F. (1984). "Synergism: The Forgotten Capital Budgeting Dimension," *Managerial Planning* 32 (March/April), p. 47.

Turnbull, S.M., and F. Milne (1991). "A Simple Approach to Interest-Rate Option-Pricing," *The Review of Financial Studies* 4, 1, pp. 87-120.

U.S. Department of Commerce, Bureau of the Census (1990). *Statistical Abstract of the United States* (Washington, D.C.: U.S. Government Printing Office).

Van Horne, J. (1976). "Optimal Initiation of Bankruptcy Proceedings by Debtholders," *Journal of Finance* 31, 3 (June), pp. 897-910.

Vancil, R.F., and P. Lorange (1975). "Strategic Planning in Diversified Companies," *Harvard Business Review* 53, 1 (January-February), pp. 81-91.

Vasicek, O. (1977). "An Equilibrium Characterization of the Term Structure," *Journal of Financial Economics* 5 (November), pp. 177-188.

Von Bauer, E. (1981). "Meaningful Risk and Return Criteria for Strategic Investment Decisions," *Mergers and Acquisitions* 15 (Winter), pp. 5-17.

Von Neuman, J., and O. Morgenstern (1947). *Theory of Games and Economic Behavior* (Princeton, NJ: Princeton University Press).

Weaver, J.B. (1974). "Organizing and Maintaining a Capital Expenditure Program," *Engineering Economist* (Spring), pp. 1-35.

Weiss, L. (1990). "Bankruptcy Resolution: Direct Costs and Violation of Priority of Claims," *Journal of Financial Economics* 27, 2, pp. 285-314.

White, L.S. (1967). "Bayes Markovian Decision Models for a Multi-Period Reject Allowance Problem," *Operations Research* 15, pp. 857-865.

Williams, J.T. (1991a). "Equilibrium and Options on Real Assets," Working paper, University of British Columbia.

Williams, J.T. (1991b). "Real Estate Development as an Option," *Journal of Real Estate Finance and Economics* 4, 2 (June), pp. 191- 208.

Willner, R. (1987). *The Effect of Leverage Changes on Call Option Prices: Theoretical, Empirical and Capital Structure Implications*, Doctoral dissertation, Harvard University.

Wilson, B.K., and J.G. Kallberg (1991). "A Stochastic Valuation Model of Federal Oil and Gas Leases: The Post-Exploration Stage," Working paper, Georgetown University.

Wissema, J.G. (1984). "How to Assess the Strategic Value of a Capital Investment," *Long Range Planning* 17, 6, pp. 25-33.

Yano, C.A. (1986a). "Controlling Production in Serial Systems with Uncertain Demand and Variable Yields," Technical report, University of Michigan–Ann Arbor.

Yano, C.A. (1986b). "Optimal Policies for a Serial Production System with Setup Costs and Variable Yields," Technical report, University of Michigan–Ann Arbor.

Yeoman, J.C., Jr., and J.E. Hilliard (1992). "Contingent Claim Valuation of Timber Assets," Working paper, University of Georgia.

Zinkham, F.C. (1991). "Option Pricing and Timberland's Land-Use Conversion Option," *Land Economics* 67 (August), pp. 317-325.

# Author Index

# Subject Index

# *About the Editor and Contributors*

**GREGORY K. BELL** is currently a Senior Associate at Charles River Associates, an economics and management consulting firm in Boston, Massachusetts. He received his Ph.D. in Economics from Harvard University. Dr. Bell's work concerns international investment policy and pricing strategy, especially in the global pharmaceuticals industry. He is currently interested in using real options to model the research and development program of a major pharmaceutical firm.

**PETTER BJERKSUND** is an Associate Professor of Business at the Norwegian School of Economics and Business Administration in Bergen where he holds a Ph.D from as well. He is also associated with its Center for Applied Research in Economics and Business Administration. His research interests focus primarily on methods and applications of contingent claims analysis. He has published in such journals as *Financial Management, Journal of Business Finance and Accounting*, and the *Scandinavian Journal of Management*.

**PETER CARR** is an Assistant Professor of Finance at Cornell University's Johnson Graduate School of Management. He received his Ph.D. in Finance from UCLA's Anderson Graduate School of Management. His current area of research is in the valuation and hedging of derivative securities. He has published in the *Review of Financial Studies*, the *Journal of Finance*, and other journals and books.

**MICHAEL E. EDLESON** is an Assistant Professor of Business Administration in the Finance Area at Harvard Business School. He is also an Associate Professor of Financial Economics at West Point (Reserves). He reveived his Ph.D. in Economics from MIT. He is author of three books on investing and financial planning, and is currently researching in several areas of contingent claims analysis.

**STEINAR EKERN** is a Professor of Business at the Norwegian School of Economics and Business in Bergen, and is also a Scientific Advisor at its Centre for Applied Research. He holds a Ph.D. from Stanford University. He made early contributions to the "unanimity approach" to economies with incomplete markets. His current research includes contingent claims analysis, with applications to the petroleum and shipping industries. He published in leading journals, including the *Journal of Finance, Financial Management, Bell Journal of Economics, Economica, Energy Economics*, and *Decision Sciences*.

**RICARDO ERNST** is Associate Professor of Operations Management at Georgetown University. He holds an M.A. and a Ph.D. in Decision Sciences from the University of Pennsylvania. His research interests include strategic analysis of production and distribution systems, models and methods for inventory control, marketing and manufacturing relationships, and material management system development. His publications include *IIE Transactions, Naval Research Logistics, Journal of Operations Management, Journal of the Operational Research Society*, and *International Journal of Operations & Production Management*.

**TAKATO HIRAKI** is an Associate Professor of Finance at the International University of Japan. He received his Ph.D. from the University of Arizona. Dr. Hiraki has published numerous academic papers on the Japanese securities markets in such journals as the *Journal of Financial Research, Journal of Economics and Business, Financial Review*, and *Journal of Banking and Finance*. He is the co-editor of *Restructuring Japan's Financial Markets* (1993) with Ingo Walter, and has served as an editorial board member for the *Global Finance Journal*, and the *Journal of International Finance*.

**HENRY D. JACOBY** is the William F. Pounds Professor of Management in the Sloan School of Management, MIT. He holds a Ph.D. in Economics from Harvard University. He has served as Director of the Harvard Water Program and Director of the MIT Center for Energy and Environmental Policy Research. Currently he is co-director of the MIT Joint Program on the Science and Policy of Global Change. He is author, co-author or editor of five books and numerous articles on issues of policy analysis and investment planning in the areas of natural resources and the environment.

**BARDIA KAMRAD** is an Assistant Professor of Decision Sciences at the School of Business, Georgetown University. He holds a Ph.D. in Operations Research from Case Western Reserve University and M.S. degrees in Operations Research and Industrial Management from Case Western

Reserve and the University of Wisconsin. His current research interests include applied stochastic processes, contingent claims analysis, and capital budgeting. Professor Kamrad's publications have appeared in the *European Journal of Operational Research*, and *Management Science*.

**EERO KASANEN** is a Professor in Finance and Accounting at the Helsinki School of Economics and Business Administration, in charge of the finance program. He received his Ph.D. (DBA) from the Harvard Business School, and has consulted on strategic capital budgeting models and other issues. He has over 50 published articles and books, including *Financial Management, Journal of Economic Dynamics and Control, European Journal of Operational Research*, and *International Review of Financial Analysis*.

**NALIN KULATILAKA** is Professor of Finance and Economics at Boston University. He received his S.M. in Decision Science and Control Engineering from Harvard University, and his Ph.D. in Economics/Finance from the Sloan School of Management at MIT. He has consulted for several corporations and governments, and has taught in executive programs. His current research interests are in the valuation and use of real options. He has published numerous articles in professional journals, including the *American Economic Review, Journal of Finance, Management Science, Review of Economics and Statistics*, and *Journal of Econometrics*.

**VAN SON LAI** is an Assistant Professor of Finance at the Faculty of Administrative Sciences at Laval University in Canada. He received an M.Eng. in Water Resources Engineering from the University of British Columbia and a Ph.D. in Finance from the University of Georgia. He has worked as a consultant engineer for several water resources development projects, both in North America and elsewhere. His research interests are in contingent claims analysis applied to finance and financial institutions. He has published in the *Journal of Financial Services Research*, and *Research in Finance*.

**DAVID G. LAUGHTON** has been an Assistant Professor of Finance at the University of Alberta, where he has established a program to develop modern financial analysis methods. After earning a Ph.D. from Princeton and a career as a physicist, he received his Ph.D. in Finance from MIT. He has developed a modern evaluation system for the Canadian government, and has consulted with several corporations. His current focus is on applications in the petroleum and mining industries, including the evaluation of environmental requirements.

**LAURA QUIGG** has been an Assistant Professor of Finance at the University of Illinois, Urbana-Champaign, specializing in real estate finance. She received her Ph.D. in Finance from the University of California at Berkeley. Dr. Quigg developed a real option valuation model that focused on urban land, and tested the empirical implications of the theoretical model. The empirical research was published in the *Journal of Finance*. Her other research interests include real estate valuation and secondary mortgage markets.

**FOREST L. REINHARDT** is an Assistant Professor of Business Administration in the Business, Government, and Competition Area at Harvard Business School. He reveived his Ph.D. in Business Economics from Harvard University. He teaches courses on environmental management, examining pollution and natural resource issues and their implications for firms. He has written papers and numerous cases covering such industries as electric utilities, forest products, and pulp and paper.

**MARTHA A. SCHARY** is an Assistant Professor of Finance and Economics in the School of Management at Boston University. She received her Ph.D. from MIT. Her recent work on bankruptcy prediction and the cost of capital has been published by *The Rand Journal of Economics* and by The Brookings Institution. She is the author of *Cases in Financial Management* (1992). Her current research focuses on the integration of corporate strategy into the capital budgeting process through the use of contingent claims analysis.

**KENNETH W. SMITH** is a Principal with Mercer Management Consulting. He holds a Ph.D. in Mathematics and an M.B.A. from the University of Toronto. He has worked for the past seven years with leading corporations in Canada and the United States, advising principally in the area of industrial marketing and corporate strategy, including mergers, acquisitions and portfolio restructuring.

**ELIZABETH OLMSTED TEISBERG** is an Associate Professor at the Harvard Business School. She holds a Ph.D. from Stanford University. She has developed a course module on strategic response to uncertainty in Harvard's MBA program. Earlier she worked in management consulting for six years, and as an economist for an international oil company. Her publications include articles in *The Rand Journal of Economics, Management Science, The Energy Journal, Research-Technology Management,* and *Public Utilities Fortnightly*.

**ALEXANDER J. TRIANTIS** is an Assistant Professor of Finance at the School of Business, University of Wisconsin at Madison. He received his Ph.D. from Stanford University and was subsequently a Visiting Scholar at the MIT Sloan School of Management. He has written several papers in the area of real options, published in the *Journal of Finance*, and *Annals of Operations Research*.

**LENOS TRIGEORGIS** is currently Professor of Finance at the University of Cyprus. After receiving his MBA (MSIA) from Purdue University and a Ph.D. (DBA) from Harvard University, where he has also been a Research Assistant, he taught at the University of Massachusetts, the International University of Japan, and at Boston University. He has been published widely in numerous journals, such as the *Journal of Financial and Quantitative Analysis, Journal of Conflict Resolution, European Journal of Operational Research, Advances in Futures and Options Research, Journal of Economics and Business, International Journal of Finance, Managerial Finance, Financial Review, Financial Management, Financial Accountability and Management, Journal of Business and Economic Studies, Journal of Applied Corporate Finance, Midland Corporate Finance Journal*, and elsewhere. He is currently preparing two other books.

**ANNE FREMAULT VILA** is an Assistant Professor of Finance and Economics at Boston University's School of Management. She received a Ph.D. in Economics from the University of Pennsylvania, and has been a Research Associate of the Columbia Center for the Study of Futures Markets. Her research interests lie in the fields of market micro structure and derivative markets. She has published in the *Journal of Business* and elsewhere.

**RAM WILLNER** has been an Assistant Professor at the Tuck School of Dartmouth College and a visiting professor of Finance at New York University. He holds a doctorate from the Harvard Business School in Managerial Economics/Finance. He has been a senior research analyst in Fixed Income–Mortgage Research at Sanford C. Bernstein, and has previously worked for Citibank. He has written on the application of option pricing to credit valuation, real options, and agency theory.

ISBN 0-275-94616-9

HARDCOVER BAR CODE